T0313158

Praise for
The Asian Financial Crisis
1995–98

A combination of applied and highly practical economics that through reality bridges the gap between policy theory and actual implications and results, but more it is also a travelogue and a diary.

— **Richard Chenevix-Trench, Former CIO of Sloane Robinson**

Russell Napier's book offers an authoritative and highly erudite account of one of the most consequential events that reshaped the modern world. As a market participant and a keen observer, Russell offers a seat at the table for anyone who wishes to understand the challenges facing today's policymakers and how the Asia Pacific crisis birthed the age of debt. It is an indispensable guide.

— **Viktor Shvets, Global Strategist and Author of *The Great Rupture: Three Empires, Four Turning Points and the Future of Humanity***

A detailed retrospective on the development and evolution of the Asia Crisis drawn from the contemporaneous notes of a keen observer of economic and financial history... interesting food for thought for investors and policymakers alike.

— **Terrence Checki, Former Executive Vice President and Head of Emerging Markets and International Affairs, Federal Reserve Bank of New York**

The Asian crisis was a remarkable learning experience for everyone in finance. This blow by blow account is an important reminder of what we learned and the hard way we learned it.

— Lord Davies of Abersoch, Ex Standard Chartered plc and previously Minister for Trade and Small Business

The Asian financial crises marked the dawn of a new strain of highly virulent crisis that would, in time, come to afflict every advanced economy in the world. This lucid book offers a forensic and compelling account of its source, contours and consequences.

— Andy Haldane, Chief Economist at the Bank of England

A remarkable record of the highs and lows of Asia's boom and bust in the late 1990s – you feel you are watching the Asian financial crisis unfold before your eyes. This is an invaluable compendium of what really happened, as seen by a participant in the drama.

— John Greenwood, Chief Economist Invesco Ltd.

THE
ASIAN
FINANCIAL
CRISIS
1995–98

Every owner of a physical copy of this edition of

THE

**ASIAN
FINANCIAL
CRISIS**

1995–98

can download the eBook for free direct from us at
Harriman House, in a DRM-free format that can be read
on any eReader, tablet or smartphone.

Simply head to:

ebooks.harriman-house.com/AsianFinancialCrisis

to get your copy now.

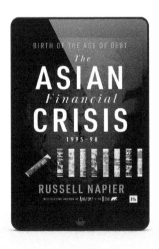

THE
ASIAN FINANCIAL CRISIS
1995–98

BIRTH OF THE AGE OF DEBT

RUSSELL NAPIER

HARRIMAN HOUSE LTD
3 Viceroy Court
Bedford Road
Petersfield
Hampshire
GU32 3LJ
GREAT BRITAIN
Tel: +44 (0)1730 233870

Email: enquiries@harriman-house.com
Website: harriman.house

First published in 2021.
Copyright © Russell Napier

The right of Russell Napier to be identified as the Author has been asserted in accordance with the Copyright, Design and Patents Act 1988.

Hardback ISBN: 978-0-85719-914-0
eBook ISBN: 978-0-85719-915-7

British Library Cataloguing in Publication Data
A CIP catalogue record for this book can be obtained from the British Library.

For my colleagues at CLSA from 1995 to 1998

"Forsan et haec olim meminisse iuvabit."
"A joy it will be one day, perhaps, to remember even this."
The Aeneid

CONTENTS

ABOUT THE AUTHOR

Professor Russell Napier has been an adviser on asset allocation to global investment institutions for over 25 years. He is author of *Anatomy of The Bear: Lessons From Wall Street's Four Great Bottoms* and Keeper of the Library of Mistakes, a business and financial history library based in Edinburgh. He has founded and runs a course called 'A Practical History of Financial Markets' and also an online marketplace (ERIC) for the sale of high-quality investment research to institutions. Russell is Chairman of the Mid Wynd International Investment Trust.

INTRODUCTION AND ACKNOWLEDGEMENTS

T his is another book about mistakes.

In my last book – *Anatomy of The Bear: Lessons From Wall Street's Four Great Bottoms* – I chronicled, by analysing opinions expressed in the pages of the *Wall Street Journal*, why intelligent investors were so keen to sell equities when they subsequently produced excellent long-term returns. While financial history in general and the history of investment in particular focuses on the individuals and institutions that get things right, the story of those who get things wrong is often ignored. While spectacular failure often makes it into a footnote, conventional failure is the background noise that barely reaches beyond a gentle hum in the pages of financial history. I hope that in *Anatomy of The Bear* I showed how common errors, when equities were cheap in 1921, 1932, 1949 and 1982, provided excellent signals that it was time to invest.

In this book I assess contemporaneous opinion both at the top of the bull markets in Asian equities from 1995 to 1996 and also, following a vicious bear market from 1996 to 1998, such opinion at the bottom of the bear markets in September 1998. On this occasion I rely not on the pages of the *Wall Street Journal* to assess such opinion, but on my own writing as an Asian equity strategist working in Hong Kong throughout that period. Many of the mistakes in this book are my own mistakes. You will find my own contemporaneous opinions from 1995 to 1998 throughout this book in boxed sections. What you will read in these sections is not the history of the Asian economic miracle nor the Asian financial crisis. You will read what financial market practitioners thought would happen in Asia, but didn't. That is a very different story from financial history, but it's the most important story for investors assessing why financial assets can become so misvalued. The opportunity for investors to profit was in determining the prevailing errors of

1

analysis in Asian financial markets in 1995 and 1996. They were very different errors that signalled the bottom of the equity bear markets in September 1998.

The end of the so-called Asian economic miracle and the events of the Asian financial crisis were about much more than money. They were about a conflict between very different societies fought on the battleground of capital markets. It was the first major battle in a war that continues to this day and will shape the rest of the 21st century. It is a war that was instigated by a Thatcher/Reagan revolution that launched a new form of capitalism that sought to change the world, armed with excessive amounts of debt, in pursuit of profit. While initially it looked like an old form of what might be called *laissez-faire* capitalism, it very quickly became a new form of capitalism probably best labelled financial capitalism. It was a form of capitalism that combined individualism with the aggressive use of balance sheet management for primarily personal profit. As early as 1983, Michael Milken was helping corporate America supercharge returns through the issuance of a record amount of speculative credit instruments known as junk bonds. The particular beneficiaries of this form of financial engineering were corporate management and incentives were soon put in place, primarily in the form of stock options, to incentivise such behaviour. The world has seen speculative corporate debt binges before, but this one was launched in a period when interest rates had just begun a decline that would last 40 years. The heady mix of ever cheaper debt combined with ever more stock options incentivised corporate management to export financial capitalism to the world. A simple narrative developed that it would sweep all before it.

The rise of financial capitalism occurred as the Berlin Wall fell and communism collapsed. It was widely assumed that the rest of the world would adapt to a capitalist system and the new financial capitalism found itself with a seeming myriad of opportunities for profit and, it was argued, only weak competition. The fact that many stock markets across the world, closed primarily by communist regimes, had reopened was one signal that the change to a more capitalist structure was underway. However, these were dangerous surface signals because in many societies the new form of capitalism spreading from the US was incompatible with local societal beliefs and structures. Each society in Asia was different in its own way, but in north Asia in particular there was a much more communal approach to societal organisation that could not and has not been reconciled with financial capitalism. This book charts the battle between the new financial capitalism and the various other forms of capitalism that existed then and still exist across Asia.

The Asian financial crisis was for many a victory for financial capitalism over the various forms of Asian capitalism. This book will explain why in fact there was no such victory. Asian capitalism adapted but fundamentally did not change. In north Asia in particular their form of social capitalism was strengthened by the confrontation in 1998 that left them with significantly undervalued exchange rates and benefiting from the new debt-charged consumption growth of the developed world. The Asian financial crisis set the scene for an age of debt in the developed world and this brought crises that have forced developed governments to confront financial capitalism in their own backyards. The result is that the age of financial capitalism is ending and something more akin to the social capitalism of Asia is being created. This book looks at that battle fought in the capital markets in Asia in 1998 and explains how a seemingly lost battle set the scene for the dangerous overextension of financial capitalism. In that overextension, financial capitalism reached extremes that led to financial collapse and societal repercussions that were ultimately unacceptable to both peoples and their political representatives. When the history of the 21st century is written, it will begin with the Asian financial crisis of 1998, which created global financial conditions that created the age of debt and triggered a structural shift to a new form of social capitalism in the developed world. The repercussions from events in Asia in 1998 have been and will be much wider than merely financial.

There are many people I need to thank for aiding in the creation of this book. This book would not exist without Abbie Perkins. In her original role as head of production at Credit Lyonnais Securities Asia (CLSA), she edited the original analysis that now appears in this book in the boxed sections. Despite having suffered through the editing process from 1995 to 1998, she volunteered to do it a second time and edited the first draft of this book. That the original work met with such approval was largely due to Abbie's ability to translate my rambling prose into English. I hope I have learned from her over the years and this book was somewhat less of an editing challenge. I would like to thank Abbie for her work, patience, perseverance, guidance and friendship over many years. Abbie and Peter Perkins were just two of the friends we met in Hong Kong who sustained us through a period of too much work, too much travel and too much chaos. In the maelstrom of 1995 to 1998 it was also the friendship of Ronnie and Julie Lim, Michelle Ring and Brendan Brady, Joan Kiernan and the formerly PJ King, Mark McFarland, Chris Lown, Sam Darwin, Jodie Gibbens and Emma Slade that brought us some much-needed sanity. It was also my good fortune to meet in Hong Kong a man from Paisley in Scotland called Donald Nimmo. Donny is a remarkable man who I am honoured still to call a friend. However bad things are they always seem lighter in his company and he distributes his wisdom in often blunt but always witty doses. I hope some of that wisdom and humour has rubbed off over the years and may even be reflected in this book.

I was fortunate enough to work with many colleagues at CLSA who were both excellent company and provided a rapid education of how things worked at the sharp end of capital markets. Mike McCoy's name will appear on various occasions in this book and I often today find myself looking at an investment situation and trying to find the 'McCoy' angle. The head of CLSA in London, Jonathan Compton, is the smartest investment maverick I have met. A trained barrister freed from the laws of evidence, he produced more unique investment ideas in an afternoon, usually after a glass or two of claret, than most of us can produce in a lifetime. Not all these turned out to be good investment ideas, but many were and being subjected to them is perhaps the greatest educational experience of my career. I also learned a lot from Dr Jim Walker, chief economist at CLSA, long before I had joined the firm. I learned even more in the journey through the boom and bust that was to come. CLSA lost its co-founder and inspiration, Gary Coull, at far too young an age. I keep on my desk a framed admonition from him which I refer to almost every day: "You have to read this and ask yourself: what's new, different, interesting? Where's the angle? If you can't tell me that, throw it away." Throw it away he often did and the authors always benefited from the disposal.

Part of my job during the crisis was to liaise with CLSA's numerous regional offices across Asia. This could be fraught with difficulties as in most organisations the centre is often accused, often correctly, of being 'out of touch' with the regions. Despite the tensions inherent in any such relationship I found great friendship and guidance from Amar Gill, then in Malaysia; from Mark Faulkner, Doug Clayton and Daniel Tabbush in Thailand; from Vincent Houghton, Jason Donville and Ian McCallum in Indonesia; Donald Skinner and Nel Friets in Singapore; and Brian Parker in Hong Kong. In those few mad years from 1995 to 1998 I travelled the world meeting institutional investors usually in the company of CLSA's institutional sales team. What should have been tedious and exhausting travels were made entertaining and invigorating when in the company of people like Nicolas Leouzon, Damian Dwerryhouse, Hideki Nozawa, George Hansom, Tim McKenna, Rob Eberley, Martin Cornett, Bill O'Rahilly, Sumio Kato, Nao Kamiya, Andrew Riddick, Evelyn Moore, Jay Plourde, Tara McNamra, Nick Hornby amongst many others. Throughout all of this CLSA had a head of research, Edmund Bradley, who forced the company to produce high quality research on time. This may sound simple but it was not easy or our competitors would also have managed it. It is even clearer today that the company added significant value to its clients during this tumultuous period and a significant portion of the credit for that must go to Edmund.

While this book covers the period from 1995 to 1998, much of the analysis of the period has benefited from what I have learned since about financial markets. In pursuit of greater understanding I founded 'A Practical History of Financial Markets' course in 2004 and it is still going strong. Over many years I have benefited from the wisdom of my fellow teachers – Herman Brodie, Edward Chancellor, Jamie Dannhauser, Jon Compton, John Greenwood, Gordon Pepper, Derry Pickford, Andrew Smithers, Peter Warburton and Stephen Wright. The search for greater understanding continued with the foundation of The Library of Mistakes in 2014 and I would like to thank everyone who has contributed to its foundation and its continued success.

I was delighted that Harriman House was supportive of a follow-up book to *Anatomy of The Bear*. I would like to thank Craig Pearce for his support and particularly Kay Hawkins, whose editing has made this book much more intelligible and I think much more readable.

I would like to conclude by thanking my family. The Napier family is now split between Scotland, Northern Ireland and New York but this does not take away from what it is. To my mother and two brothers, I owe everything for their love and support over many years. Though my Dad is not around anymore he is with us all every day in many different ways and his strong, simple but wise advice is always present. Writing books is an anti-social activity even if done in a period of social distancing. This means being away from family life for an extended period and thus any book is always the result of a burden shared. To Sheila, Rory and Dylan for all their help and support my thanks and love. Without family, what's the point anyway?

Russell Napier,
Scotland, 2021

PART ONE
Learning the hard way
- a beginner's guide

Tuesday, 9 September 1997

Harry – Hello. Hello. It's Harry here.

FM – Ah, Harry who?

Harry – Harry from PT XYZ, we met in Jakarta last year.

FM – Oh yes. Hi Harry.

Harry – We need some money.

FM – Sorry?

Harry – We need some money.

FM – Dollars or rupiah?

Harry – Any money, any money, we need some money.

FM – What maturity?

Harry – Any maturity, any maturity, we need some money.

FM – I'm sorry Harry we don't [line from Indonesia goes dead].

Phone conversation on Tuesday, 9 September 1997 between a fixed interest fund manager at HSBC Hong Kong and the chief financial officer of an Indonesian corporate

Harry and his company stood on the edge of bankruptcy less than two months after they had benefited from one of the biggest economic booms in history. Having spent years turning down cheap foreign finance, Harry was now begging for it, but not a penny was to be found.

Harry of course was not his real name and neither was PT XYZ a real company. This transcript I produced for institutional investors in September 1997 did not reveal those details for fear of heaping more problems upon Harry and risks upon the fund manager who received the call. By September

1997, Asia was full of Harrys and they didn't just operate out of the finance departments of Asian companies. On 8 October 1997, a very similar call was placed, but this time from the Ministry of Finance of the government of Indonesia and it was to the International Monetary Fund (IMF). This country of almost 200 million people had run out of money.

It was not the only country in Asia that was suddenly on the verge of bankruptcy. A financial feast had turned to famine in just a few months.

There's no money left

The consequences of running out of money transcended finance and economics. By May 1998 in Indonesia, over 1,000 people had been killed in riots and President Suharto's 31-year tenure was over.

It was no ordinary recession that brought such chaos to Asia. In the Asian financial crisis the decline in gross domestic product (GDP) per capita, measured in US dollar terms, was of a huge magnitude: Indonesia –56%, South Korea –34%, Malaysia –30% and Thailand –27%. Investors who sold billions of US dollars and other currencies to buy Indonesian equities lost 90% of the value of their investment, in US dollar terms, in little over a year. Losses in other regional stock markets may not have been as bad, but they were still eye-watering declines in the US dollar value of investments: Hong Kong –58%, Malaysia –87%, the Philippines –78%, Singapore –59%, South Korea –71%, Taiwan –36% and Thailand –89%.

Savers had invested to benefit from the famed Asian economic miracle. They got the notorious Asian financial crisis. This is the story of that crisis, but not a history of it. It is told primarily through the writings of someone who was there at the time and who was trying to assess the economic and financial outlook both before and then through the chaos. It is a story of what it is like, as an investor, to live through one of the largest ever financial crises without the benefit of knowing where and when it will end.

In learning the investment lessons from that crisis, the mistakes in forecasting the future you will find in this story are probably more important than the successes. They are my mistakes – your author.

The so-called Asian economic miracle turned crisis

I was enfranchised to make these mistakes as I was, at the age of 30, hired to advise global equity investors on where and where not to invest in Asia. As the Asian Equity Strategist for one of Asia's largest stockbroking companies, I lived through and chronicled this economic miracle that became a crisis.

I landed in Hong Kong in May 1995 to join the wild party in financial markets that was a key part of the so-called Asian economic miracle, but by the time I left in September 1998, much of the region was on financial life support provided by the IMF and the crisis looked like it could trigger a global depression. In just over two years, what was widely admired and praised as an economic miracle had turned into what is now widely known as the Asian financial crisis. Portfolio investors and commercial bankers lost hundreds of billions of US dollars in little more than a year.

The collapse threatened the solvency of the global financial system, bankrupted Russia and brought devaluation and economic chaos to Brazil. It also did something that was to prove even more destructive, as it created, in its aftermath, the conditions that were to fuel one of the biggest debt booms in global history – a debt boom that in 2021 continues on its destructive course.

It all began in the rear end of a koala. For three and a half years I chronicled the end of a boom and then the storm of the Asian financial crisis from the 33rd floor of what was then called the Lippo Centre in Admiralty, Hong Kong.

The two-towered building had been built by Australian entrepreneur Alan Bond. The Bond Centre, as it was originally called, was completed in 1988 when Alan Bond was at the zenith of his success. Bond was a proud Australian, though born in England, and he had the two towers designed in the shape of trees, each complete with a series of climbing koalas. My office was in the rear end of one of those koalas hanging out over Admiralty with a view across Hong Kong harbour to Tsim Sha Tsui. On a clear day, of which there were increasingly few, you could see the hills of the New Territories. China was not visible but, because of the pollution, you could often smell it.

The rear of this particular koala had its own warning about the perils of assuming that enterprise funded with excessive debt is an enterprise built upon firm foundations. Alan Bond went spectacularly bankrupt just a few years after the Bond Centre was completed. This was not the only casualty associated with the Bond Centre. After Bond's demise, the building became the Lippo Centre and the Lippo Group of Indonesia was almost mortally wounded in the Asian financial crisis.

Of the two towers of the building, one was named the Peregrine Tower after the stockbroking company that was to be one of the more high-profile casualties of the Asian financial crisis. Local Feng Shui experts suggested that it was the shape of the glass koala that brought such bad luck to those that were associated with this building. Perhaps they were right, but during the time I occupied the rear of the koala, there was little good luck to be had anywhere in Asia.

My job in Hong Kong was to write papers advising professional investors on which of the many Asian equity markets to invest in and which to avoid. *The View from the Rear of the Koala* would have been a striking title for these writings, but perhaps too outrageous even for my famously irreverent employer, CLSA.

Instead, I settled on something much more prosaic for these musings with two words from a song called 'Northern Muse' written by Van Morrison. The writings you will find reproduced here, mainly written in the low light of an early Hong Kong morning, are as they hit the press from 1995 to 1998, published under the banner of *The Solid Ground*. From the outset, I saw the irony in that title as there is no such thing as anything solid in forecasting the future – financial future or otherwise. That is both the curse of those who try to forecast and also the appeal of the pursuit to the enquiring mind.

Fortunately, the job of an investor or their adviser is not to accurately forecast the future, but to forecast it more accurately than the consensus. These writings attempted that task without of course knowing anything about the future.

Mistakes and misconceptions in the fog of war

Historians know what happened next and this informs, often wrongly, their interpretation of events and decisions at the time. Misconceptions and mistakes are analysed without any understanding of how reasonable they seemed to those wrapped in their own fog of war. What follows here is a story of those mistakes made in the fog of war and of the major, then prevalent, misconceptions and their role in creating one of the world's worst financial crises.

The content published here was written from 1995 to 1998 and cannot be described as history because it was written in an attempt to forecast the future. Now that we know that future, we can assess what advice, whether right or wrong, proved of value to those trying to secure positive real returns from their investments in the teeth of one of the world's greatest financial crises. Your author believes that it will be advice that will be helpful for investors still involved in the battle for investment survival.

It was perhaps John Kenneth Galbraith who best described why memories, even perhaps if they are someone else's, are "utilitarian" and can protect us all, at least somewhat, from the "luminous insanity" that sometimes pervades markets:

> The story of the boom and crash of 1929 is worth telling for its own sake. Great drama joined in those months with a luminous insanity. But there is the more sombre purpose. As protection against financial illusion or insanity, memory is far better than law. When memory of the 1929 disaster failed, law and regulation no longer sufficed. For protecting people from the cupidity of others and their own, history is highly utilitarian.
>
> **John Kenneth Galbraith, *The Great Crash 1929*, Preface to the 1975 edition**

No extrapolation allowed

As an over-confident 30-year-old arriving in Hong Kong in 1995, the first thing I did on entering my office was to print out and pin on a board behind my desk the phrase "No extrapolation allowed". This was aimed at reminding myself that I couldn't hope to get paid for mere extrapolation, something I discovered is actually only partly true, but it was also aimed at warning colleagues that I was not interested in any analysis that consisted of deploying a ruler and a pencil and drawing a line between two points.

There was an awful lot of such analysis about in 1995 in the middle of the Asian economic miracle and it is something that becomes incredibly prevalent in bull markets. One can indeed get paid for it and, if in the right place at the right time, can get paid very well for it too. That was a path I could have chosen and while it can be lucrative, it can lead to a short career for you and your clients.

Beside the exhortation against extrapolation, I pinned a Deuchars IPA beer mat – a fine Edinburgh beer – behind my desk to remind me that the worst that could happen was that I would end up back in Edinburgh drinking much better beer than was then available in Hong Kong. That didn't seem like such a big downside, and thus perfectly equipped with a determination to avoid extrapolation as a form of analysis, a beer mat and an attitude to career risk perhaps bordering on the reckless, I set out to analyse the Asian economic miracle. I even had a Chinese name, courtesy of my secretary, that meant 'precious stone of scholarly determination'. A name to live up to.

Understanding the fundamentals

To understand the perspective and analysis in this book, you will need to understand a little, just enough, about how credit and money are created and destroyed. It was a failure to understand this and instead a focus on what most investors call 'the fundamentals' that led so many people to lose so much money in the Asian financial crisis. These fundamentals are all derived from analysis of the operations, likely profitability and balance sheets of individual companies.

The reasoning goes that a company's share price will primarily reflect these fundamentals and that other factors for consideration, such as macro factors related to money and credit, just get in the way of forecasting what really drives equity prices over the long term. That focus predominantly on these fundamentals can be helpful and sometimes is indeed the best approach to estimating returns from equities.

The longer the holding period of your investments, the more important the fundamentals are. There are circumstances, however, usually when a money and credit boom are underway, where even for long-term investors there is a great danger in focusing too much on the fundamentals.

The stock market index that best measures the capital performance of Asian ex Japan equities peaked in January 1994 and did not sustainably exceed that level until the summer of 2010. At its low in March 2020 that capital index was just 12% above the level it first reached in January 1994.

In most of Asia by 1995, the fundamentals were the product of a money and credit boom and they were to deteriorate rapidly when that money and credit boom ended. When the true fundamentals were finally established investors were nursing huge losses. The seemingly positive fundamentals were driven by the excessive growth in money and credit that were the products of huge capital inflows impacting upon managed exchange rate regimes.

These factors were determining the fundamentals that investors were focused on. There was little realisation that cause and effect ran from money and credit to the fundamentals when the tide of capital flowed into Asia. That realisation came only on the ebb of the tide.

How the Asian central banks and then the commercial banks acted to transmute capital inflows into local currency money and credit was the key to understanding the fickle foundations of the Asian economic miracle. I had learned the basic mechanisms of money and credit creation analysing the US banking system as a fund manager in Edinburgh. Watching the 1990–91 US banking crisis unfold and how monetary policy settings impacted or failed to impact bank credit growth and thus money growth, was a great way to learn quickly. No form of analysis will always provide the right answer or even the better answers that we need to profit in purchasing financial assets the prices of which are always discounting the future.

In the conditions in Asia pertaining at that time, however, an understanding of money and credit was the key skill required to understand the investment outlook. In the Asian economic miracle, a hyper-charged credit cycle was underway and there was little in financial history to suggest that it could be sustained. That those credit cycles relied increasingly on short-term capital inflows to sustain them suggested that the time was near when the unsustainable would indeed be unsustained. How to assess when the unsustainable credit cycle is about to end, at least in managed exchange rate regimes, is what most of the contemporaneous writing you will find here is about.

A bit about financial history

An understanding of financial history is also a key tool in understanding how credit cycles peak and the consequences of that peak and then decline. With degrees in law and no formal qualifications in economics, business or finance, I had found that I could learn a lot about financial markets from reading financial history.

It struck me as curious then, and still does today, that so few professional investors know how financial markets have behaved in the past when faced with some of the stimuli they expect them to be impacted by in the future. I'm not sure that it is an approach to understanding cause and effect that would be tolerated in other professions, but it is a very pervasive approach in investment.

Many investors were at sea when, boom, the only thing most had known in Asia turned to bust. There was plenty of guidance as to what would probably happen, but it was all hidden in history books and not economic textbooks. Few thought those history books could be a guide to the 'modern' investor, but they were to prove to be one of the best guides we had.

As the years progressed, I came to rely more upon financial history as a guide to the financial future and in 2004 established a course in financial history for professional investors, 'A Practical History of Financial Markets', at the Edinburgh Business School in Scotland. Although this book covers the period from 1995 to 1998, you will find many references to periods in financial history before then that I believe proved useful in assessing the financial future. This book now serves as another guide on how to spot an over-exuberant credit cycle, how to work out when it is ending, and what to do when it does.

Investment is not a physical science, but a pursuit to establish price by human beings who bring key psychological biases to the endeavour. The importance of those biases waxes and wanes, but at some although not all times, they become overwhelmingly important. The history of those periods, when these psychological biases overwhelm the rational mind, are essential reading for any investor and the story of the boom and bust in Asia, from 1995 to 1998, is one of those periods.

The lessons from such periods remain largely untaught in the finance faculties of our leading universities. They are not periods in which the behaviour of investors fits readily into the academic models that have much greater validity in periods when more rational, if not irrational, behaviour pervades. As this book is composed of daily writings from the period when an illusion ended, it is also a guide as to what happens when illusions end and the search for a new certainty begins.

Much of this book, written between 1995 and 1998, is uncontaminated by hindsight bias. Along with these views from the investment trenches you will also find new commentary that I have now added written with the benefit of hindsight. That commentary seeks to distil the key lessons for investors from the crisis era from a long and hopefully somewhat detached distance. This is then not a history of the Asian financial crisis per se, but a story of what it was like to guess "what was at the other side of the hill", much as the Duke of Wellington explained to be "all the business of life":

> All the business of war, and indeed all the business of life, is to endeavour to find out what you don't know by what you do; that's what I called "guessing what was at the other side of the hill".

Historians, looking backwards as their profession dictates, always know what is "at the other side of the hill" and thus their analysis of the state of mind of participants at the time is often naturally ill informed. This benefit of hindsight is particularly dangerous when writing the history of financial markets. Markets are discounting mechanisms and are always pricing in the future. This is particularly so in financial markets where so much of the value of an investment is based upon an uncertain future. The purchaser of a chair, for instance, does not expect an uncertain return from that chair, and it is very likely to still be providing all the expected functions of a chair long after its purchaser has ceased to be. When the future for the chair is so predictable, most of its value and hence price can be established in assessing all the things we know about it before purchase and those features almost certainly will not change.

In financial markets where corporate earnings and dividends change, where interest coupons are paid or not paid, where inflation rises and falls, and where exchange rates oscillate, however, the opinions on all those ever-changing variables are encapsulated in prices sometimes changing by the second. The prices of financial assets are replete with opinions about the future, and historians looking from "the other side of the hill" often miss the key determinants of price for those guessing what they don't know based on what they do know.

For the financial market historian, there is thus great value in the study of the contemporaneous opinion of those pricing financial assets. Like the Iron Duke, they sought "to endeavour to find out what you don't know by what you do", and in that pursuit they regularly failed. The common failures in such pursuits are worthy of study and this book attempts to study such failure – in this case largely my own!

The benefit of hindsight

In my first book *Anatomy of the Bear: Lessons from Wall Street's Four Great Bottoms*, I plumbed the *Wall Street Journal* in an attempt to establish what the combatants in the battle for investment survival foresaw in real time. It was in their common errors, often paraded as wisdom in the *Wall Street Journal*, that *Anatomy of the Bear* sought answers to the question as to how one might invest at the bottom of a US equity bear market.

This book seeks to do something similar but this time relying upon my own contemporaneous opinion regarding the future. While hindsight bias must slip into any edited version of contemporaneous opinion, this book is an attempt to show forecasting 'warts and all' rather than being covered with the heavy makeup of hindsight.

As I think *Anatomy of the Bear* showed, it is in the mistakes commonly made that prices are diverted from their true value and thus opportunities created for long-term investors. This book thus lays out my own mistakes and, of course, I could not resist, includes some successes. The aim is to improve in the "endeavour to find out what you don't know by what you do" while acknowledging that investors will never know what is at the other side of the hill. Wellington seemed to get better at guessing what was at the other side of the hill the more he tried. Wellington's troops paid a high price when he got it wrong and investors pay with their pocketbooks or the pocketbooks of their clients for mistakes made in real time with real money. The aim of this book is to allow the reader to learn from mistakes made in the heat of investment battle without ever having to waste any of their financial ammunition.

Boom and bust

I had already wasted a bit of financial ammunition when I arrived in Hong Kong. In what had been a short career, less than five years when I landed at Kai Tak airport, I had already seen the incredible impact that a money and credit boom had had in lifting the price of shares to astronomical valuations in Japan and then dashing them.

In Japan, fundamental investing had been of limited use in calculating just how high equity prices could rise, when they might stop rising and how quickly they might then decline. Similarly, in Taiwan, a stock market then closed to direct foreign participation, equity valuations had risen to astronomical levels by 1989, only to then crash spectacularly. In both cases a boom in money and credit seemed to have played a key role, heavily influenced by an attempt to manipulate exchange rates.

Such booms and busts were considered infrequent and the exceptions to the norm that, even if they could be understood, were safely ignored by an investor seeking to select equities to own for the long run. We have now had what most people would consider the 'long run' and in 2020 the capital indices of both Taiwan and Japan were still below their 1989 highs. Even investors for the 'long run' need to pay attention to the scale of the credit boom underway when they decide to invest.

As the 25 years from 1995 were to show, levels of both credit and money growth played key roles in creating unstable systems that resulted in gross damage to the savings of those whose wealth was tied up in financial markets. While exceptional investors rode out all the stock market collapses invested in the shares of companies they had correctly identified as representing good value, most investors had neither the genius, nor the luck, nor the fortitude to benefit from such an approach. For these investors, the macro factors regularly whipsawed their investment returns and in that volatility they often sold low and bought high.

Macro factors and financial market pricing

For all but the exceptional investor, some consideration of macro factors proved to be essential in assessing the future returns from financial assets. In the Asian financial crisis one learned quickly which macro factors counted and which didn't. Too late for many, the focus shifted from the 'miracle' of high economic growth to the instability of how it had been financed.

Having witnessed the stock market bubbles inflate and burst in Japan and Taiwan, I was predisposed to believe that there was more to assessing the outlook for asset returns than the so-called fundamentals scrutinised by micro investors. One day in a bookshop in the City of London, I stumbled upon a book that purported to be able to explain, at least in part, the relationship between macro factors and financial market pricing. It was called *Money, Credit and Asset Prices*. It summed up the lifetime's work of Gordon Pepper and had just been published.

Gordon Pepper, whom I was subsequently lucky enough to persuade to become a teacher on 'A Practical History of Financial Markets' course, had been the 'guru of the gilt-edged' market through the 70s and 80s. As an analyst of gilts, British government debt, he had also developed an uncanny knack of forecasting the direction of the UK stock market. It turned out his research for the stockbroking firm W. Greenwell & Co. had been avidly read by Margaret Thatcher and she was to turn to him for policy advice in later years.

I remember very well the day I read *Money, Credit and Asset Prices*. What occurred to me instantly was that this analysis, all taken from the UK and the United States, would be particularly useful when applied to jurisdictions where exchange rate management policies were in place, as they then were across Asia.

Solving equations had never been my forte, but it was obvious, even to me, that such solutions were much easier to solve when one started with one known variable. Asia's managed exchange rates provided the known variable in the equation for anyone trying to solve the equation of money, credit and asset prices. This was an approach to analysing the investment outlook for Asia that was not widely used and certainly not given much credence by investors enamoured of the higher economic growth rates of Asia.

That such higher economic growth rates would produce high returns on equity investments was a mantra that was often repeated and rarely questioned. I had already witnessed just how in practice the operation of a managed exchange rate helped with forecasting future asset price levels.

Hong Kong and the currency board system

In Hong Kong, from 1990–91, inflation and interest rates had gone in different directions and that was a divergence that was not supposed to happen according to the limited number of economic textbooks I had read in studying for the Society of Investment Analysts exams. The decline in interest rates in Hong Kong, while inflation and economic growth had risen, led to a major rise in the price of local equities as people shifted away from the fixed-interest investments and deposits that offered such poor real returns.

Equity investors in Hong Kong were benefiting from the positives for corporate earnings and dividends resulting from higher economic growth while also benefiting from the lower interest rates used to discount future earnings. That combination of higher earnings and a lower discount rate led to higher net present value calculations for future earnings and thus higher share prices.

This surprising divergence in inflation and interest rates was the direct result of the currency board system, a particular form of exchange rate management system that operated in Hong Kong and effectively imported US interest rates to the British colony regardless of the local level of inflation. The colony was importing interest rates set according to levels of growth and inflation expected in the United States, but in an economic system experiencing growth and inflation at the higher levels being generated through its economic links to China.

The economic textbooks had been fairly silent on such divergences as they focused primarily on how money and credit flowed and influenced economic activity in flexible exchange rate regimes. That interest rates and inflation could diverge so markedly, with clear impacts for asset prices, was something I had thus already seen in action. That they would diverge in a more painful direction was not just likely, but inevitable – but when?

A 'miracle' in Asia or the mispricing of financial assets?

While Hong Kong had the strictest form of managed exchange rate in Asia – the currency board system – some form of currency management was in force across the whole region. Through their choice of managed exchange rates, the Asian authorities had put in place the one known variable that would significantly increase the chances of using the *Money, Credit and Asset Prices* form of analysis to produce better quality forecasts of financial market prices. The more interest rates were likely to be out of sync with underlying economic conditions, the greater the prospect of asset price volatility and, thus, investment opportunity.

This was not a form of analysis that was widely applied at the time in Asia as investors were convinced that what was driving Asia was literally a *miracle* that had something to do with what was in the air, in what was believed to be a unique brew of culture, entrepreneurship and policy settings that all but guaranteed higher economic growth and, it was argued, higher returns from investment in equities.

That there is no connection between levels of economic growth and returns from equities is a key conclusion from financial history, but it was the dominant belief among investors in Asia in the mid-1990s. Between that perception and the reality of how managed exchange rates could deliver but also end credit booms lay the mispricing that was to prove so destructive of the wealth and livelihoods of millions.

The mispricing of financial assets in Asia was also driven by a dominant cultural misconception. A key precept behind the Asian economic miracle was a belief that it was founded on something called Asian values. What the Asian financial crisis revealed was that the Asian values foreign investors believed underpinned the Asian economic miracle were very different from the Asian values perceived by Asians themselves. The foreigner looked to Asia as a region of hard working, hard saving peoples imbued with what the Westerner might call family values. In some ways the Western investor saw in Asians, particularly the Chinese diaspora that dominated business across much of the region, a form of the puritan spirit that they supposed had played such a key role in the success of capitalism, at least according to Max Weber's famous exposition in *The Protestant Ethic and the Spirit of Capitalism*. The combination of these same virtues identified by Weber were supposed to be the secret to high levels of savings and capital formation and a political backing for pro-growth economic policy settings all against the background of political stability.

That foreign investors had come to define Asian values so specifically in relation to the region's economic success proved dangerous. To many Asians, Asian values were about placing communal rights above the rights of the individual, and this was hardly in tune with the foundations of capitalism that foreign investors understood and ultimately represented. Much of the capital structure of the region and also economic policy settings reflected this very different set of Asian values and it was often manifested as links between business and politicians that were very far from what developed world investors were used to. The values that foreign investors saw in Asia might have been prevalent among the population of Chinese descent, but such people were often minorities within complex and fragile social structures held together by policies that conflicted with what Weber would have described as capitalism.

The foreign investor paid up for Asian values without actually understanding what those values were and how those values conflicted with their role as providers of capital. When the miracle became a crisis, they rapidly relabelled Asian values as *crony capitalism* and instead of an asset, they priced this form of Asian value as a liability. That the values foreign investors thought were aligned with capitalism were so opposed to it was to become very apparent when the IMF rode into Asia with its prescriptions for change. Those prescriptions were seen by many, most notably Mahathir Mohammad, the prime minister of Malaysia, as in direct conflict with Asian values. According to the non-Asian policy makers driving the IMF intervention in Asia, foreign investors needed the destruction of crony capitalism if capital outflows were to cease, exchange rates to stabilise and interest rates to decline. These were the same investors who only months before had very willingly poured capital into that same system. Just how that clash of two sets of values played out in the crisis and has played a key role in establishing the age of debt, is also the story of this book.

The investment crowd

When I arrived in Asia, a crowd had formed. A crowd is very different from a set of individuals:

> A crowd quite often seems to overflow from some well-guarded space into the squares and streets of a town where it can move about freely, exposed to everything and attracting everyone. But more important than this external event is the corresponding inner movement: the dissatisfaction with the limitation of the number of participants, the sudden will to attract, the passionate determination to reach all men.

> **Elias Canetti, *Crowds and Power,* 1960**

By 1995 the investment crowd in Asia had long ago burst into the squares and streets. In 1993, passing through screening at the airport in Kuala Lumpur, the security agent had seen that I was carrying a pile of investment research. He told me that he would make my progress through security particularly difficult unless I gave him a stock tip.

The crowd had the passionate determination to reach all men, and women, and by 1995, it seemed to have succeeded. In Malaysia, the crowd had embraced secondary market trading in burial plots as one of the roads to riches. It seemed that all men had been reached – dead or alive. To live among such a crowd but to avoid its "passionate determination to reach all men" is not easy, but it helps to arrive from outside and fairly late.

I was fortunate enough to arrive in Hong Kong as an outsider *after* having witnessed the "inner movement" of the crowd from the safer distance of Edinburgh and London. Crowds do not welcome outsiders who resist the inner movement, as I soon discovered. Like any young person seeking to learn quickly, I sought out the advice of the older 'Asian hands' who might really know what was going on. These insiders, whom I was sure knew more about what was going on in Asia than I did, were well informed, but they were also intoxicated with success and the mutual affirmations of others. They too were part of the crowd. It is a lesson that has remained with me that it is always essential to get the opinions of an outsider on any investment proposition.

Those whose job it is to follow a particular asset class can very easily form a crowd and crowds are full of feedback loops that create, for those in the crowd, a view of the future for asset prices that an outsider often finds divorced from fact or analysis. It is the easiest thing in the world to assume that it is the insiders who know more about the facts in any given situation. However, when a crowd has formed, the insiders are more likely to be caught up in the extrapolation from current conditions that is the easy and thus most acceptable form of analysis to those in the crowd. It really does not matter whether the insiders are corporate leaders, finance ministers or humble stockbroking analysts, they are likely to find their opinion contaminated once they are embraced by the "inner movement" of the crowd.

In my initial period in Hong Kong, I travelled widely across Asia to talk with the heads of research at the CLSA regional offices and often they were able to arrange meetings with senior central bankers and people in the finance ministry. The uniformity of opinion, regardless of the source, I found to be deeply concerning and often directly at odds with the data I was analysing in my office 33 floors up in the glass koala. While it was fun to scoot about Asia and spend time working and socialising with colleagues, it was also dangerous.

The crowd is an attractive place to be. There is company in the crowd, there is no dissonance and everyone agrees with you – what's not to like? I soon cut back on the travelling and tried to stick to the data in the belief that in the battle between appearance and reality it was safer, as a forecaster, to be closer to reality. That the reality was more evident in the data than on the ground was perhaps the best indicator that a crowd had formed.

The hidden reality

Perception can trump reality for a long time in financial markets, so the key question was when the worsening in the external accounts would come, bringing the tightening of money and credit that would very likely result in lower equity prices. The new reality of the Asian economic miracle seemed to me to already rest on some very shaky foundations and was thus unlikely to be sustainable for much longer.

The fundamental reason why it could not be sustained was because the region's current accounts were already in significant deficit and the ability to maintain stable exchange rates and produce high levels of economic growth thus relied upon ever larger capital inflows. While ever larger capital inflows were possible, the deterioration in the quality of those inflows, in the form of ever larger sums of short-term capital inflow and less long-term capital inflow, suggested that it was increasingly dangerous to bet on their continuation.

As the Asian economic miracle story took hold, a larger and larger proportion of the capital flowing to Asia was for the purchase of listed equities, the local currency bond markets being virtually non-existent in 1995. This inflow of capital for the purchase of liquid investments was very different from foreign direct investment (FDI) – investment that primarily ended up in bricks, mortar and machinery or in some other form of productive capacity. Money flowing in for the purchase of equities was, at least in theory, highly liquid and could leave as quickly as it arrived. FDI funds could flow in quickly, but as they then took the form of usually physical capital, their rapid exodus was highly unlikely.

The analysis in *Money, Credit and Asset Prices* suggested that should a country managing its exchange rate turn from external surplus to external deficit, then its monetary policy would tighten. What had been a flood of money and credit could turn to a drought and there would be very negative consequences for the price of the assets that had benefited from the flood. Indeed, the little financial history I knew at that stage, mainly focused on the consequences of the boom in petro-dollar lending through the 1970s, suggested that such a drought could be dire for the economy and bank solvency, and could easily escalate to trigger a vicious recession, or worse.

What I did not know at that stage, and I think nobody in the equity markets knew, was just how much of the capital inflow fuelling the asset price party was coming through US dollar borrowing by Asian corporations and investors. It was not to be until much later in the saga of the Asian financial crisis that I stumbled across the incredible data relating to the size of US dollar borrowing that would create such havoc when the Asian exchange rates finally devalued.

Not for the last time, equity investors were blissfully unaware of what was happening in the credit markets and the impact that was having, directly and indirectly, on the outlook for economic growth and financial stability. If I didn't know it already, the Asian financial crisis taught me that equity investors need to be very aware of what is happening in credit markets and particularly foreign currency borrowing by the local private and government sector.

To this day, professional investors still operate largely in asset-class silos and crucial information that relates to the financial future does not flow between those silos. Over and over again it is the end client who pays the price for this specialisation that confines their fund manager to such dangerous intellectual ghettos where the outlook for capital is for limited opportunity and low life expectancy.

China's new focus

There was in 1995 a very specific reason why I thought the time was near for an external account deterioration, a tightening of money and credit, and a decline in equity prices. Not long before I had arrived in Asia, an event had taken place that was to ultimately trigger the Asian economic crisis and also the birth of the age of debt.

On 1 January 1994, China unified its official and market exchange rate and effectively devalued the renminbi by 50% relative to the US dollar. By that stage about 80% of China's trade was already priced using the market rate, but the devaluation still had an important impact on both trade and capital flows. More importantly, this lower Chinese exchange rate arrived just as the country was shifting its huge resources in labour from agriculture to manufacturing.

Deng Xiaoping's so-called 'southern tour', from January to February 1992, had sent a very clear message to China's budding entrepreneurs that the mobilisation of capital and savings, even if mobilised in the pursuit of riches, was now legitimate. Millions of previously relatively unproductive farm workers poured into the cities to work in the new factories created by the ideologically enfranchised entrepreneurs.

For those competing with China in export markets, the devaluation of the renminbi really intensified the already growing competitive pressure from China. It was this 1994 renminbi devaluation combined with the mass mobilisation of resources in China that was to change the world, with the first very visible sign of that change appearing in Asia.

The structural shifts in China were accelerating just as the North American Free Trade Agreement (NAFTA) had come into effect in January 1994 and as Mexico had devalued its exchange rate in January 1995. For an analyst focused on the interplay between the external accounts and the managed exchange rate, this sudden surge in competitiveness in China and Mexico acted as a starting gun for a tightening of monetary conditions across Asia.

By May 1995, the deterioration in the current accounts of Asian countries was already underway and as China mobilised ever more resources for its export drive, the pressure was only likely to intensify. China's current account surplus of US$1.5bn in 1995 had, by 1997, become a surplus of US$37.0bn.

By December 1995 Mexican exports were growing by 20% year on year and the country's current account had returned almost to balance following a US$30bn deficit in 1994. The worse the other Asian countries' current accounts became, the more they were reliant upon accelerating capital inflows to ensure their exchange rates remained stable, while their economies continued to grow at the high rates that investors had come to accept as normal. A lot was now bet on an acceleration of those capital inflows, but those flows were increasingly short term in nature.

The consequences of the flood of capital into Asia

Capital was flooding in to take advantage of higher economic growth, but increasingly it was also the source of that growth. The flood of capital was so great that it not only funded the current account deficits but forced major intervention in the foreign exchange markets by the Asian authorities to prevent their exchange rates rising relative to the US dollar. This act of intervention led to an accumulation of more US dollar assets by the Asian central banks, but crucially in the process led to the creation of more domestic money to pay for those assets.

The money the central banks credited to the sellers of the foreign currency, in their exchange rate intervention, was in the form of newly created local currency commercial bank reserves. Asian commercial banks, flush with surging reserves, reacted by increasing the size of their loan books. In so expanding their loan books, the fractional reserve banking system created money in that act of alchemy that has been with us since the 17th century. The capital inflows to Asia, combined with the Asian central banks' intervention to prevent undue exchange rate appreciation, was thus feeding both a credit boom and a money boom.

In effect, the accumulated savings of generations of the developed world, now being assigned for investment in Asia, were being turned into money in Asia as this was the only way in which the local authorities could prevent their exchange rates from appreciating. A stock of money that had been accumulating for generations, known as savings, was being transformed into a flow of ever more Asian money. This enforced increase in the supply of credit and money led to lower interest rates and thus the capital inflow itself was creating the money and credit boom that created seemingly robust 'fundamentals'.

I had seen such booms play a key role in pushing the price of Japanese and Taiwanese equities to what were by 1995 agreed to have been bubble valuations. Through this alchemy the capital inflows to Asia were creating their own positive fundamentals, but investors were not focused on this symbiotic relationship between their own capital inflows and the economic and asset price booms they were witnessing.

While financial textbooks teach that capital flows react to reflect the fundamentals, it was not a new idea that, in certain conditions, they could actually change the fundamentals. In *The Alchemy of Finance*, published in 1987, George Soros put forward his theory of reflexivity in which capital flows themselves could create the better fundamentals that would in turn attract even more capital flows to that particular asset.

In my opinion, it was just such reflexivity that was underway in Asia. With growing Asian current account deficits, it was only the capital inflows, increasingly dominated by the inflows for the purchase of listed equities, that were creating the easy credit and easy money that sustained high economic growth and a rising stock market. While Soros had focused upon reflexivity in relation to certain corporate asset classes, such as real estate investment trusts (REITs) and conglomerates, the reflexivity in Asia had seen capital inflows change the fundamentals of entire economies.

Of course, reflexivity works in both directions. If the capital inflow should slow, exchange rates would be under pressure, and the authorities would have to sell their foreign exchange reserves and contract the supply of local currency bank reserves to support the exchange rate. Interest rates would likely rise and asset prices likely fall. The managed exchange rate regimes made such a reaction very probable should capital inflows slow and should they reverse, then an economic slowdown would turn into something much worse.

What had been a virtuous circle for investors pouring short-term portfolio capital into Asia could quickly turn into a vicious circle should they stop. Soros's theory of reflexivity was not part of the standard education of those pouring capital into Asia. They and their clients were to pay a high price for instead believing the standard economic models that did not admit to the observable fact that, in some circumstances, the capital flows determine the key fundamentals. Investors equipped with the conventional models were about to fail conventionally.

The change in capital flows

It was the structural changes in China and the launch of NAFTA, with its negative impact on Asian current accounts, that had made the forecast of a vicious liquidity cycle in Asia much more likely to be correct. Initially, the current account deterioration was mild and the capital inflows remained robust. Those who had focused on the negative impacts from the devaluation of the renminbi (RMB) and the Mexican peso were forced to backtrack on their opinions.

This was a mistake, but a mistake that was easy to make when you worked in a financial services industry keen to extol the virtues of the Asian economic miracle that could now in mid-1995, a year and a half after the event, endure even a Chinese exchange rate devaluation! The mechanism through which the RMB devaluation and the mass mobilisation of China's excess labour would eventually tighten credit and monetary conditions in Asia was working only slowly, and as a result most investors could not afford to recognise it and invest accordingly.

With the benefit of hindsight, the mechanism through which the RMB devaluation tightened monetary policy seems assured, but at the time, investors read the slow deterioration in Asian countries' external accounts as a sign that their competitiveness would not be unduly undermined. Even had Asia maintained its competitiveness relative to China, the fact was that current account deficits were already large; domestic growth was high, sustained by very easy money and credit; and any hiatus in capital inflows was very likely to lead to at least an economic slowdown.

So the argument for investors was somewhat circular. The positive fundamental of high economic growth was likely to remain if you thought China's devaluation would not eventually undermine Asian competitiveness, but for it to remain high, your capital had to keep flowing in at current or even greater levels. This is an uncomfortable reality to live with for an analyst or a fund manager. It is uncomfortable because nobody can know when those capital flows will abate.

The demolition of capital controls and the much higher liquidity in domestic equity markets meant that this short-term capital might not just stop coming but could even reverse! The liquidation of existing equity holdings and ensuing capital outflow could happen very quickly, but what would be the chimes at midnight that signalled the negative reflexivity associated with a change of capital flows had begun?

There was a major problem working for a stockbroking company and publishing analysis that suggested the flood of capital into Asia was creating a very vulnerable financial system. That capital inflow was the main source of the company's profits! The employees of all stockbrokers, including my employer, were all benefiting greatly from the flood of portfolio capital through the financial services industry to access the Asian growth story.

Stop buying? It's a bull market! No way!

Many people were getting rich through pay and bonuses, financed by commissions from the capital inflow, and also by investing in the booming stock markets themselves. This was a difficult environment to arrive into as a 30-year-old concerned that the party was fuelled by excessive credit and money growth and that that growth was likely to at least subside, if not end.

I was recommending that those foreign investors, who ultimately paid the salaries and bonuses and pushed the local stock markets ever higher, should stop. Whether that opinion was ultimately to be right or wrong, it was probably not going to be good for business, pay and bonuses in the short term. In a world where bonuses are large and awarded annually, the short term dominates the institutional dynamic. Most analysts whose remuneration is ultimately derived from brokerage commission thus tend to be positive most of the time.

Internally, it is much easier to be a bull; and while bulls in bull markets get paid, bears in bull markets get fired. If it's to be a bear market, then neither bulls nor bears get paid. The risk/reward of this model of remuneration strongly favours the adoption of bullish opinions. Bears get invited to fewer parties. It can be lonely and dangerous being a bear. In Asia in 1995 there were few bears.

In the crowd that forms in a bull market, myopia is increasingly evident. Part of my job as the Asian equity strategist was to attend the morning meeting every day at which the firm's best daily ideas would be singled out to then be 'broked' to professional investment managers across the world. In return for these best ideas, the clients of the firm were supposed to buy or sell Asian equities through CLSA and the firm would earn commission on those orders.

Of course, everyone in the room knew that foreign investors were much more likely to buy than sell Asian equities as the flood of capital intent on benefiting from Asian's high economic growth showed no signs of abating. There was much more money to be made by phoning institutional investors with buy ideas than sell ideas. To walk into a morning meeting every day, mainly comprised of salespeople, and suggest that they advise their clients to sell Asian equities was akin to telling individual salespeople and the company to turn away business. To say it was not favourably received would be a bit of an understatement.

Every salesperson could provide testimony from the smartest guys in the room, their clients, the professional fund management community, that this was in fact a great time to buy Asian equities. When the smartest guys in the room, many of them with decades more experience than the newly arrived strategist, were so positive, how could the firm be betting its future on an inexperienced analyst with such a pessimistic outlook?

People were quite literally throwing money at us, so why should we be telling them to stop? There is an institutional dynamic towards myopia in such situations still best summed up in the words of Sinclair Lewis: "It is difficult to get a man to understand something, when his salary depends upon his not understanding it!"

I found morning meetings to be a painful affair because I held a different opinion from most of the other participants. However, the main reason I found them painful was because I thought it was stupid to have to come up with our best ideas on a daily basis. As someone who had been a fund manager, it was ridiculous to believe that our clients wanted five or six new ideas every day to help them manage their portfolios. No professional fund manager in the world turned over their portfolio at the rates which such a plethora of daily advice was designed to accommodate, and CLSA was just one of the firms broking a flood of daily ideas to the fund management community.

I had many friends who were professional fund managers and there was universal agreement that the stockbroking community was churning out far too much opinion backed by far too little analysis. I did not think that it was a controversial opinion and as it came direct from the client base, the company was bound to listen. However, it was an opinion that held virtually no sway within the stockbroking community.

Stockbroking firms and investment banks are populated by, and often run by, very highly paid salespeople who know that the firm's success is based almost entirely upon their persuasive abilities on the telephone! To keep them in front of their clients every single day they needed something new to say every single day.

Much of the research selected each day to be highlighted to fund managers may have been of poor quality and likely to be wrong, but it did not matter that much. What was important was that the salesperson had a reason to phone their client at least once a day and perhaps more. It was even likely that the client would ignore all of this advice but still feel obliged to deal with the salesperson because of the 'service' being provided. Anyone who has never worked in a sales-driven organisation needs to watch *Glengarry*

Glen Ross, a Pulitzer-prize winning play by David Mamet, and also a film, that very accurately explains the psychology of selling and its consequences.

To say that such a culture was alien to me was very much an understatement, having gained my grounding in investment experience in a fund management partnership in Edinburgh that was very focused on the fiduciary relationship it had with its clients. However, every morning I had to go to the morning meeting where the expectation was that I would provide a new idea to be fed into the great sales machine that would generate commission. I could think of no greater oxymoron than 'daily strategy' and yet here I was expected to provide daily strategy. Creating daily opinions was bound to lead to failure, and indeed the company had already fired three Asian regional strategists in the previous year who had been forced to chase their tails pursuing such 'strategy'.

It took a while to realise that this time-honoured way of extracting broking commission was not going to change simply because, as an ex-fund manager, I was relaying the news that the clients did not want it. All of us face institutional imperatives and the institutional imperative for an organisation with a large sales team is to produce something for them to sell. Although that dynamic has mitigated somewhat over the past 25 years, it remains a dominant force in finance.

It is a topic I will return to throughout this book, but the excessive levels of turnover in holdings of financial assets is part of the industry-wide institutional dynamic that has done huge damage to the structure of the financial system and investment returns. In 1995 I found myself part of that institutional dynamic and struggling every day to focus my research, the CLSA sales teams and our clients on longer-term issues. The struggle to lengthen time horizons is largely futile in a bull market and the bull market was still raging when I arrived in Hong Kong in May 1995.

Hyper-liquidity and short termism

A belief that there is always ample liquidity to reverse investment mistakes leads to poorer research, less consideration and ultimately poorer allocation of the scarce savings over which professional investors have stewardship. Having seen that dynamic from both the investment management perspective and the stockbroking perspective, I am convinced that it cannot change proactively. It will change probably under the burden of legislation, but it is highly unlikely that it will change through the choices of those who operate the system.

There are significant financial incentives to reward activity, and as Charlie Munger is wont to say: "Show me incentives and I'll show you outcomes." The wrong incentives played a major role in creating the huge capital inflows to Asia that fuelled the money, credit and asset price boom. Despite ever more legislation to regulate the financial system, the same wrong incentives remain largely in place today.

There are of course some notable and honourable exceptions to this prevalent short termism, but on the whole, the investment industry is based upon a fallacy that one can dance in and out of liquid securities and through this process enhance investment returns. It was the creation of ever more liquidity in ever more financial assets that enabled this drift to an investment time frame that is in fact the enemy of good investment returns.

This hyper-liquidity in financial assets was the key factor that destroyed financial stability in Asia in the 1990s and led to economic misery for millions. The problem for an analyst who could see the instability of the financial foundations was how to survive long enough to watch them crumble from within an institution built to benefit from that very hyper-liquidity.

A bear in a bull market

That I survived as an analyst offering daily bearish opinion had much more to do with luck than anything else. It was my very good fortune to have accepted a job with a company that was run by people prepared to see the profit in holding a different opinion. The CLSA I joined was the Asian broking operation of a large French bank, but it was very much the creation of two former journalists, Gary Coull and Jim Walker.

The Canadian, Coull, and the Australian, Walker, very much saw themselves as outsiders in a world of insiders in British colonial Hong Kong and saw the opportunity for their firm partly based in the irreverence which they both enjoyed. As journalists, these wild colonial boys knew the value of a good story and knew that to compete with the establishment they would have to offer something very different from the consensus.

From its inception as Winfull Laing and Cruickshank in 1986, the two steered the company towards the iconoclastic analysis and opinion that would set the start-up apart in a world of old-school British stockbrokers and the increasingly dominant global financial behemoths. The head of sales in Hong Kong, Mike McCoy, was also a man who revelled in irreverence as another outsider, this time an American, in the British colony. Although he had to drive revenue through his team of highly paid salespeople, he also enjoyed being different and was more likely to tolerate something somewhat less commercial if it was cocking a snook at establishment views.

Finally, the company had a chief economist who had already made his name as having strong and non-consensus views on just about everything. Dr Jim Walker – no relation to Jim Walker, the firm's co-founder – had already proved that one could have strong opinions and stick to them and be rewarded for that insight and candour. It was more than helpful that he had also concluded that the exchange rate intervention policies of Asia could not be sustained indefinitely.

Another crucial advantage was that CLSA's business was largely confined to earning brokerage commission on secondary market turnover and its capital markets division at that stage was not a key source of profits. Thus, unlike other stockbroking companies, the company was not dependent upon selling new issues to investors to profit from the Asian economic miracle.

Demand for such new issues tends to be particularly strong in a bull market and thus the incentive for analysts to offer bullish opinions when their employers are very dependent upon revenues from this source is very strong. That CLSA had not then got a seat at the capital markets table proved to be a boon for an analyst increasingly convinced that the Asian economic miracle would end with a bang and not a whimper.

CLSA had already seen that strong opinions sold and that it could conceivably profit even in a bear market given its revenues came from trading commissions. This allowed me to hold strong non-consensus opinions for much longer than would have been possible in just about any other stockbroking firm. Any analyst who is a bear in a bull market needs a lot of luck to still have a job when the game of musical chairs finally stops.

It was my luck to work for a company and with colleagues who were prepared to live with the negative business consequences of such opinions for longer than others. I strongly suspect that had I been working for any other stockbroking company, I would have been out of a job long before the Asian economic miracle finally became the Asian financial crisis. Even at a company such as CLSA it was far from clear that I would survive long enough to see what I thought was largely an illusion end.

The greatest credit bubble the world has ever seen

This book seeks to show that there are important lessons for investors from the course of the Asian financial crisis. It also has a much larger aim, in that it seeks to show how that crisis led to the creation of a global financial architecture that produced the biggest debt boom in history.

It is a debt boom that has, by 2021, already led to spectacular economic busts, mass insolvency, crippling unemployment, the displacement of millions of people and radical political change. With world debt-to-GDP ratios at record highs even before the impact of the Covid-19 induced economic crisis, the negative direct economic, social and political consequences from this age of debt will likely plague the global outlook for at least another generation.

How the Asian financial crisis established the foundations for this new age of debt relates to the policy choices of the Asian authorities that were a direct consequence of the crisis. These policies had dramatic impacts on the developed world, leading to lower inflation and lower interest rates, and also to the clear lesson from the crisis that developed world monetary policy would, in certain circumstances, change to alleviate the distress of financial markets participants.

The result was that the price of borrowing declined and the availability of credit along with the appetite for risk rose. The ability of poorer quality credits to borrow increased. The ability to profit from using debt to buy assets increased. The r sks of using debt declined. It was the perfect storm for the financialisaton of the global economy that brought riches to the few and deep uncertainty to the many.

The Asian financial crisis taught many lessons to investors, peoples and policy makers who confused a credit bubble with an economic miracle. It is the greatest of ironies that it established the foundations for the greatest credit bubble the world has ever seen. What follows is the story of the crisis, told from the perspective of someone who tried to forecast its twists and turns, the lessons to be learned from it, but also the tragedy of its legacy.

PART TWO
The road to devaluation

What do we mean by 'Asia'?

The Asia I analysed from May 1995 to September 1998 was not the Asia you see on a map or visit as a tourist. As a stockbroker, the focus on what is important for business and what is important for portfolio investors and their clients, is the size of the Asian stock markets. Some countries in Asia did not have stock markets, so there was no need to analyse or visit them. There were other countries whose stock markets were so small that foreign investors were simply unable to buy or sell sufficient stock in them.

There were many stock markets that placed restrictions upon just how much of their stock market foreigners could buy and thus restricted the importance of those markets to foreigners. Some 48 countries make up what we regard as Asia today, so what I was left with after considering all of these factors was a very reduced number of countries to analyse; what was left was the Asia I worked in, and it was a very strange world indeed.

Investors had long before divided the region geographers might call Asia into three portions, with Japan and Australia seen as distinct asset classes. As recently as 1989, Japan was the largest stock market in the world, representing 42% of world stock market capitalisation, and foreign investors had been investing increasingly actively there since the 1960s. It was still a very large stock market in 1995, and one of the richest countries in the world. It was seen as being very different from the other stock markets of Asia, which were very small and where GDP per capita was much lower. Indeed, GDP per capita was so low that most countries in Asia were classified by investors as what are known as emerging markets.

Australia, like Japan, was very much a developed country and foreign portfolio investors had been investing in Australian securities for well over 100 years. As it happened, both Japan and Australia were recovering from huge speculative booms that had burst in the early 1990s. When investors said they were investing in Asia, they really meant they were investing in the so-called emerging markets in Asia that happened to have, often due mainly to an accident of history, the largest stock markets.

All of these countries' equity markets were lumped together in an index, basically a basket of equities, that tracked the rise and fall of all the equities in that index. The investors who said they were investing in Asia were usually paid to make sure that they secured a better return than the return anyone could have acquired by simply buying all the stocks in the index and never making another decision. This forced almost all these investors to pay huge attention to the composition of this index when they allocated their capital to what was called Asia, but was actually a small section of what any layperson would call Asia.

When I wrote about this in May 1996, I called it "the tyranny of benchmarks" and that is a phrase that seems to have stuck as a description of how it impacts investment decisions. What made it into this index and what weightings determined what investors called the Asian equity 'asset class'?

This asset class comprised equities of some of the world's poorest countries, but also some of the world's richest. It spread from Pakistan in the west to South Korea in the east, and from China in the north to Indonesia in the south. These countries, their peoples and their economies had very little in common, but they were not in Europe or the Middle East, or Africa or the Americas, so they were lumped together in an index of equities for Asia.

All of these very different societies were now open to capital inflow primarily from the savers of the developed world. How very different societies and financial systems coped with that inflow, and then its outflow, is the story of the Asian financial crisis.

When foreign investors allocated capital to Asian equity markets they did not do so based upon the best opportunities for returns; instead they had to stick close to the Asian Equity Index. They put their capital into Asia driven not by their assessment of future returns; but as to which countries they chose to invest in, this was largely determined by the composition of the index.

That one country could attract capital simply because it had a large stock market, and another, potentially with a much bigger economy and better investment potential, would attract little because it had a small stock market, was a result of this index benchmarking. That capital would flow based on the size of existing market capitalisation – and not necessarily because of expected returns and risks – was and is a key feature driving portfolio capital.

Some institutional investors invest their funds more closely aligned with the benchmark than others, but all pay some reference to it. In the 1990s, investors in Asia found themselves primarily measured against the MSCI Asia ex Japan Index, which comprised 11 different countries. All investors had to be very aware of the weightings of the index between those countries and those weightings, based only on the equity market capitalisation available to foreigners, bore no relationship to the size of the Asian economies, their populations or the scale of opportunities available to capital. Three of the smallest Asian countries (Hong Kong, Malaysia and Singapore) comprised over 50% of the investable universe for foreign investors.

Equity investors who told their clients they were investing to participate in the growth of Asia and who followed a benchmark weighting were committing almost 57% of their clients' capital to Hong Kong, Malaysia and Singapore (see Table 2.1). Yet these three countries represented just 1% of the population of the other countries included in the benchmark index and just 13% of GDP (see Table 2.2)!

Table 2.1: MSCI Asia ex Japan Index weightings 3Q 1996

Hong Kong	24.90%
Malaysia	18.70%
Singapore	13.10%
Taiwan	10.30%
India	7.70%
Thailand	7.50%
South Korea	6.70%
Indonesia	5.60%
Philippines	4.30%
Pakistan	0.60%
China	0.60%

Table 2.2: Asia by population and GDP 1996

	US$bn	Population (m)
China	522	1,208
South Korea	377	44
India	294	919
Taiwan	261	21
Indonesia	175	191
Thailand	143	59
Hong Kong	132	6
Malaysia	71	20
Singapore	69	3
Philippines	64	69
Pakistan	52	126

There were Asian countries with very large populations, such as Bangladesh, Vietnam and Myanmar, where foreign investors could not invest in listed markets at all. There were two large equity markets in Asia – Taiwan and South Korea – where foreign ownership was still restricted and this was reflected in lower weightings in the benchmark index. China and India, both with restricted foreign ownership of their stock markets, barely featured on the radar screen for investors despite their huge populations.

Investors who were influenced by country weightings within the benchmark indices were thus allocating capital to the Asian economic miracle through investment in just a few very small economies. As we shall see, the impact of such large capital inflows on the economies and markets of small countries, most of whom operated managed exchange rates, was to be profound. In the bizarre world of portfolio investment a few very small Asian countries had to adapt to and cope with massive foreign capital inflows seeking to benefit from the economic growth of something the developed world called 'Asia'.

As an Asian equity strategist, I was thus writing about a very strange asset class indeed. Not only was it entirely unrepresentative of the growth that investors said they had come to participate in, but two of the largest markets in the indices were Hong Kong and Singapore where GDP per capita was already among the highest in the world. These city-states had advanced service-orientated economies and their stock markets were dominated by bank and property companies, and not the Asian manufacturers or domestic consumption-orientated stocks that many investors thought of as the likely beneficiaries of the Asian growth story.

Stock markets, as a venue for raising capital, are suited to large companies and thus even in the less developed stock markets of Asia, it was only the largest companies that were listed. These large companies were also often banks and property companies. The stock markets of Asia, and particularly those that had large weightings in the benchmark index, were entirely unrepresentative of the economic activity in the local economies. Investors who had brought their portfolio capital to the region to invest in the Asian economic miracle found themselves investing in companies that did anything but represent the nature of that supposed miracle.

These distortions help to explain why so much of the contemporaneous commentary that follows in this book is focused on just a few Asian countries that represent such a small proportion of what we think of as that place called Asia. In particular, readers will find a particular focus on Thailand in this book that seems outsized compared to its modern place in the Asian investment firmament.

The canary in the coal mine

My focus on Thailand, particularly in 1996, was driven by a recognition that the Asian economic miracle story was very much being unveiled as false in Thailand before anywhere else. Writing for an audience of investors, the focus on Thailand was driven by my focus on why the miracle was more a function of too much capital driving too loose a monetary policy in countries running exchange rate management regimes.

These regimes were widespread across Asia, and if they had resulted in distortions and fragilities in Thailand, then those same distortions and fragilities would have been created elsewhere. Thailand seemed to be the canary in the coal mine and likely to suffer first if the tide of capital turned and the noxious air of tighter monetary policy began to impact the region.

While Thailand was not to devalue the baht exchange rate until 2 July 1997, signs that growth was slowing and that credit quality problems were mounting were evident from the middle of 1996. The focus on Thailand also revealed a story that was largely unknown to foreign institutional investors – that the corporate sector had huge dangerous foreign currency borrowings.

That such a time bomb lurked on the balance sheets of corporates across Asia is something we discovered as time progressed. The economic slowdown and growing credit problems led us to ask the right questions for all the economies in Asia. The answers we got to those questions revealed something that was not an Asian economic miracle but something that became known as the Asian financial crisis.

A whirlwind of reports, drinks and long days

I arrived in Hong Kong on 8 May 1995 and within the first month had attended my employer's one-week investment conference, written and published my first Asian equity strategy report, visited the company's research teams in Indonesia, the Philippines and Singapore, and presented to the company's clients in Hong Kong, Denmark, Glasgow, Edinburgh, London, Geneva, Paris, Kuwait, Bahrain and Abu Dhabi. Among all of the business, there was also the client entertainment and that usually included dinner and drinks afterwards. I mention this because it was not to be an untypical monthly schedule and it was to last for three-and-a-half years.

Many of the pieces you will read in this book were written between 6.30–8.30 am on a day that never ended before nine o'clock at night. Beyond the correction of grammatical errors and typos, they are unaltered from their original production, written as the sun rose on the behind of the koala.

The roles of exchange rates and central banks

Much of this analysis focuses on exchange rates as a guide to expected returns from equities. This was particularly important in Asia at this time when exchange rates were not market determined. When analysing any managed exchange rate, a key variable to assess is whether the exchange rate is overvalued or undervalued. This is probably more important than assessing whether equities are cheap or expensive.

When a country running such a policy runs an external surplus, its central bank intervenes to prevent an exchange rate appreciation. That intervention adds to their stock of foreign currency, known as foreign currency reserves. What is crucial to understand is that those purchases of foreign currency are financed not with existing domestic currency, but with money the central bank creates for the transaction. By choosing to manage its exchange rate, the central bank is allowing the supply of money in the country to adjust depending upon the condition of its external accounts.

An external surplus that puts upward pressure on the exchange rate forces the central bank to create money, but a deficit forces them to destroy money. The central bank does not assess what is the correct amount of money for domestic economic conditions, but adjusts the supply of money to whatever level is necessary to keep the exchange rate at the targeted rate. This can result in there being excessive amounts of money in the economy compared to its potential growth rate and it can also result in there being a contraction in the supply of money below the potential growth rate.

The story of how the Asian economic miracle became the Asian financial crisis is how the managed exchange rates forced many Asian countries from monetary and economic feast to famine.

The problem for most of Southeast Asia in particular in 1995, was that current account deficits were large and worsening; this indicated that exchange rates were overvalued but not necessarily so. If it was indicating that the exchange rates were overvalued, this meant the region had become much more reliant on net capital inflows to finance those deficits. If that capital did not arrive, then monetary policy would tighten and growth would slow.

It was important to try to establish whether Asia now had uncompetitive exchange rates and was vulnerable, should capital not arrive. The next few years would prove that many Asian countries did have uncompetitive exchange rates and were susceptible to an economic slowdown should capital inflows slow, cease or reverse. In the summer of 1995 capital was still flooding into Asia.

The story so far: booming economies and slumping currencies?

June 1995

In keeping their currencies suppressed, the central banks have added excess liquidity to the system and boosted the level of asset prices. The downside is that inflation has also occurred. There is general scepticism regarding reported levels of inflation across Asia. Despite reported low inflation figures, there are problems of lost competitiveness across the region. Hong Kong is the most obvious example, but Malaysia, Thailand and Singapore all have industries facing severe difficulties. So what happens next?

What if the US dollar rises? Asia will face a very difficult period. Marginally competitive industries will be severely squeezed – shipbuilding in Singapore, food producers in Thailand, shoe producers in Malaysia and everything in

Hong Kong. More importantly for investors, domestic liquidity will decline. Basically, to undervalue your currency against the rest of the world, you have to provide excess liquidity of a given degree. The nearer your currency then rises to its correct market value level, the fewer notes you will need to artificially depress the value…

In the short term, the game continues and liquidity conditions remain favourable for investors. The slump of the US dollar this year had produced a further surge in liquidity and the Asian central banks have injected funds to depress their currencies. This surge of liquidity is only beginning to impact the regions' equity markets … in Hong Kong the party is about to enter a new pitch of intensity. However, this will signal the end of the party and the arrival of a serious hangover. The hangover will be so awful that long-term investors should sell now.

Those of an adventurous nature should stay longer but remember to leave before midnight … most commentators are not focusing on the risk that Asia will have to adopt its own monetary policies. The current monetary policies are accepted as the status quo. The rules must change sometime and we expect that this will happen sooner rather than later. Continue to enjoy the party in Singapore, Malaysia and Thailand. However, be prepared to recognise that one day you will have to wake up and you will not be playing poker but mah jong.

Despite large and growing current account deficits, particularly in Southeast Asia, there was strong growth in foreign exchange reserves. This showed that net capital inflows far exceeded the size of the current account deficits. In intervening to prevent the exchange rate from rising, the authorities exchanged newly created local currency for foreign currency. The rise in foreign reserves was the counterpart for an increase in the size of the domestic central banks' balance sheets.

I was wrong to refer to this money as 'notes' earlier as it is created in the form of commercial bank reserves – an electronic transfer that can be transformed into banknotes at the commercial bank's request. Today we might call this action by the central banks quantitative easing with the central banks' balance sheets creating ever more commercial bank reserves as its holdings of government debt, in this case the debt primarily of the US government, expanded.

In Asia, the local commercial banking systems responded to this increase in their available reserves in the way that one would expect, and they accelerated their loan growth and their money creation. That commercial banks, and not central banks, create most of the money we spend every day is a fact that is still not fully understood properly by all investors. The most eloquent description of how they do so still comes from the pen of John Kenneth Galbraith:

> The process by which banks create money is so simple that the mind is repelled. Where something so important is involved, a deeper mystery seems only decent. The deposits of the Bank of Amsterdam (1609–1791) were, according to the instruction of the owner, subject to transfer to others in settlement of accounts. The coin on deposit served no less as money by being in a bank and being subject to transfer by the stroke of a primitive pen. Inevitably it was discovered … that another stroke of the pen would give a borrower from the bank, as distinct from a creditor for the original depositor, a loan from the original and idle deposit. It was not a detail that the bank would have the interest on the loan so made. The original depositor could be told that his deposit was subject to such use and perhaps be paid for it. The original deposit still stood to the credit of the original depositor. But there was now also a new deposit from the proceeds of the loan. Both deposits could be used to make payments, be used as money. Money had thus been created. The discovery that banks could so create money came very early in the development of banking. There was that interest to be earned. Where such reward is waiting, men have a natural instinct for innovation.

John Kenneth Galbraith, *Money Whence it Came, Where it Went,* 1975

The reserves commercial banks hold today with the central bank fulfil the role that gold once did. As long as they hold sufficient reserves with the central bank and meet other regulatory requirements, they are free to create money just as Galbraith describes. This commercial bank-created money does not usually circulate as bank notes, a privilege still retained by governments in most if not all jurisdictions, but it is created in the form of a transfer to the borrower that becomes their deposit. The borrower spends those new deposits on, say, their house purchase and the house seller then spends the deposits and thus new money has been created and circulates in the economy.

The central banks of Asia, in intervening to prevent the appreciation of their exchange rates, were creating ever more bank reserves and thus enfranchising the local commercial banks to lend aggressively and create ever more money. This flood of money kept interest rates lower than they would otherwise have been, assuring that the banks had few difficulties in finding customers who wanted to borrow.

Given the dynamic as to how money is created in a managed exchange rate regime, the direction of the US dollar exchange rate was to play a key role in the Asian financial crisis. The piece above refers to the already evident squeeze on the competitiveness of some industries in Southeast Asia by May 1995. With the local currencies linked to the US dollar, competitiveness was likely to fall further if the authorities were then forced to push their exchange rates higher in line with a strong US dollar. That would be bad for the listed companies whose business was export orientated and this was widely understood.

What was less well understood is how the rise in the US dollar would, all other things being equal, tighten liquidity in the managed exchange rate regimes. The more the local central banks had to intervene to assure the rise of their currencies in line with the US dollar, the more the money creation process outlined earlier would be reversed. In their intervention, the central banks would shrink bank reserves and thus constrain the ability of the local commercial banks to lend and create money.

In May 1995, few considered that such a dynamic would occur. It was argued that the flow of capital into Asia was so large that even if the US dollar was rising, there was still likely to be intervention to slow the appreciation of the local currency and thus the money creation dynamic would still be intact. As it turned out, the US dollar had reached a multi-year low in early 1995 and had begun a prolonged appreciation in value that played a key role both in forcing central banks to defend their exchange rates and in slowing capital flows into the region.

Writing above in June 1995, I argued that "Most commentators are not focusing on the risk that Asia will have to adopt its own monetary policies". It was the rise of the US dollar, the deterioration in Asian external accounts, and its impact on domestic Asian liquidity that was to bring, around 18 months later, the reality of such a huge change in the monetary system for which investors were entirely unprepared.

How the Asian economic miracle turned into the Asian financial crisis was primarily related to how those capital flows slowed and then stopped coming. Working for a stockbroking company in Asia from 1995 to 1998, I had a front-row seat to witness the impact of both the flow and ebb of this tide of capital. In May 1995, we were near high tide. The ebb began in the second half of 1996, but it was not until September 1998 that the tide was fully out. The reports that follow track in detail the process of the flow and ebb and what it was like when the old certainties ended and a miracle became a crisis.

Given just how inappropriate this monetary policy was in the summer of 1995, it was still possible that the local authorities might walk away from the exchange rate management policies by increasing interest rates and letting the exchange rates rise. They did not take the opportunity to do so even though such a move would clearly have ended the economic and asset price boom and would have been a very bold step. The opportunity was there in 1995 to take the punchbowl away from this particular party, but no Asian policy maker took that audacious path.

In choosing the exchange rate management target, central bank independence had been surrendered. The central banks were forced to adjust the size of their balance sheets according to the pressure on the exchange rate. To change the managed exchange rate policy was not within the remit of the central bank. The implications of such a move were so profound that they required the endorsement of the politicians.

In the middle of an Asian economic miracle there were few in government who would take such a decision, basking as they were in the praise heaped upon this new growth model underpinned by something called Asian values. It was market forces that brought the game of poker to an end and this is the story of how they did so. It is also the story of how investors had to learn to play a new game and were woefully ill-equipped when poker did indeed become mah jong.

A currency tempered in the fire that was Mexico

July 1995, Indonesia

Once upon a time, a broadsword was only a weapon of true quality if it had been tempered in fire. The tempering process added new strength to the blade. The strength of the blade was increased by this metallurgical process. The strength of a currency peg is based upon a psychological process. Norman Lamont can vouch for the fact that there is little which can add stability to a currency peg when the psychological strength dissolves. The strength of a currency peg is tempered in a psychological 'fire'.

The collapse of the Mexican peso created such a 'fire' and sent it raging through the world's currency markets. Having passed through the flames, the surviving currency pegs have been tempered and thus strengthened. The rupiah/

US dollar crawling peg, one of the world's weakest pegs, has been one of the biggest beneficiaries of the tempering process.

Bank Indonesia is likely to begin to tighten interest rates in the third quarter of this year. We expect there will be strong buying of the rupiah and Bank Indonesia will intervene to prevent undue currency appreciation. The bank will attempt to sterilise the intervention by increasing the outstanding issues of SBIs (treasury bills). History suggests full sterilisation is unlikely. Rising rupiah liquidity will significantly improve the outlook for the equity market.

Arriving in Asia in the summer of 1995, it was easy to see that moral hazard was a key force driving capital flows into the region. Recent events in Mexico had created what was understood at the time to be a change in risk dynamics. In December 1994, the Mexican government had devalued their exchange rate, threatening huge losses to the foreign institutional investors that had bought *tesobonos* – US dollar-denominated debt instruments issued by the government of Mexico.

These instruments paid coupons in US dollars and offered investors a much higher yield than they would have received in US Treasury securities. There was of course a risk that the government of Mexico would run out of US dollars and be unable to pay its foreign creditors as it had done as recently as 1982. The higher yield of the *tesobonos* was the reward for investors accepting such risk and now investors would have to accept losses for taking that risk. The lower Mexican peso exchange rate made it very difficult for the government to access sufficient US dollars to pay their creditors. The gamble on Mexico had not paid off, but then suddenly it did.

In January 1995, the United States, in conjunction with the IMF, put together a US$50bn package of public money for Mexico that allowed the country to remain current on interest and principal payments on the *tesobonos*. Those foreign investors, mainly US portfolio investors, speculating on the higher yields offered by the *tesobonos* were bailed out from massive losses.

That the United States and the IMF could mobilise so much public money to protect foreign investors from loss, as a side effect of supporting the government of Mexico, had a profound impact on the risk/reward outlook for investors in emerging markets. These investors, convinced that the emerging market exchange rates were likely to receive some form of public support should they be under downward pressure, could pick up this extra yield over US dollars with limited risk. In a world where a few basis points of extra yield could make the difference between underperformance and outperformance, this change in the risk profile of emerging market currencies had a big impact.

The extra yields on some Asian currencies, particularly the Indonesian rupiah, were so large that this gamble could boost yields high enough to create not just outperformance but a healthy bonus. It was very clear in 1995 that the Mexican intervention by the IMF, supported by the United States, had profoundly changed investors' risk profiles even if those who launched the intervention did not recognise its impact.

Writing in 2003, Robert Rubin, the US secretary of the Treasury who utilised the US Exchange Stabilization Fund for that intervention, had a very different assessment of its impact:

I had never heard anyone say that they had been more inclined to invest in emerging-market economies because of the Mexican support program.

Robert Rubin, *In an Uncertain World: Tough Choices from Wall Street to Washington*, 2003

As a front-line participant in emerging market investment in 1995, it was very clear that the intervention had indeed created a greater appetite for emerging market investment. The Asian currencies had come under downward pressure during the so-called tequila crisis, but the bailout programme had ended that pressure. The relative stability of the Asian currencies through the tequila crisis went a long way to convincing investors that the Asian currencies would not fall against the US dollar. Even if they did, investors had decided that the United States and the IMF were clearly on hand to make sure that foreign investors would not lose money in such a situation.

The perception was that the risk of loss from investing in Asian currencies had just been significantly reduced. The same message spread to bankers who began to significantly increase their US dollar lending to Asia. The more adventurous investor borrowed foreign currency to invest in the high-yielding Asian currencies – the so-called 'carry trade'. All of these capital inflows forced more exchange rate intervention by the Asian authorities, more domestic liquidity creation and, inevitably, higher equity prices.

When the piece above was written in July 1995, Indonesia's foreign reserves totalled just US$9bn. Within two years they had reached US$16bn as the central bank intervened to prevent the appreciation of the exchange rate even as the US dollar strengthened and the country's current account deficit worsened.

As I suggested in July 1995, there was to be a surge of capital inflows to Indonesia following the intervention by the IMF and the United States, which had the effect of bailing out portfolio investors from disastrous investments in Mexican *tesobonos*. The Indonesian equity market responded to such inflows and liquidity as expected, and from June 1995, when this piece was written, to its peak in February 1997, the MSCI Indonesia Index rose 36% in US dollar terms. The capital tide was still coming in.

Jakarta was a wonderful place to visit to assess just how this massive liquidity creation was being spent on the ground. Sitting by the swimming pool at the Grand Hyatt in the evening, you could hear the evening call to prayer from the mosques ringing around the city. On my first visit, I went for lunch in a local restaurant by myself and was immediately presented with a tray of food.

Wishing to be polite, I ate it all. Then another tray of food arrived, so I started on that. This was quite a lot of food, but I managed to eat it when a third tray of food arrived. I wondered how the Indonesian people were so thin given how much they ate for lunch. I then realised that the other diners were selecting only individual plates from each tray while the remainder was returned to the kitchen!

In other parts of Jakarta, investment bankers were responding to the demand for Indonesian securities by turning out trays full of tasty securities for the flood of incoming capital. There was a feast.

BOP surplus to boost asset prices: more fuel on the fire

August 1995, Thailand

The current account is only one element of the balance of payments. The current deterioration in the current account is being accompanied by a growing balance of payments surplus. In other words, the capital account is booming and in 2Q 1995, Thailand reported its biggest ever balance of payments surplus and current account deficit at the same time!

The 1994 capital account of Bt361bn acted to more than offset the Bt214bn current account deficit. The composition of the capital account has altered dramatically over the years. In 1990, net FDI represented 25% of net capital inflows. In 1994, net FDI was a negligible Bt853m and thus, capital inflows were dominated by debt. If capital inflows continue to more than offset the deterioration in the current account, then baht liquidity will continue to rise. Economic growth and inflation will accelerate and the current account will worsen further. This is the current dilemma facing the Bank of Thailand.

The surge in capital flows into Thailand in 2Q 1995 is not due to FDI. The inflows are due to international investors buying baht to secure a yield pick-up over the US dollar. Perhaps more importantly, the inflows are due to Thai corporates borrowing US dollars and then buying baht to invest in Thailand. The cause is the high level of domestic interest rates ... any actions to mop up liquidity will have the impact of raising interest rates. Raising interest rates exacerbates the problem of interest rate arbitrage and surging capital inflows.

Normally, a deteriorating current account would help raise Thai interest rates. However, on this occasion, the reverse is occurring as capital inflows are producing a balance of payments surplus despite the worsening current account. The Bank of Thailand has only very limited responses, without resorting to capital controls. Capital inflows will continue, while the interest rate differential remains high. Rising liquidity will boost economic growth and inflation. This will produce problems for the Thai economy towards the end of 1996. The rapidly rising liquidity significantly increases the rewards to be had in holding Thai equities.

The change in the composition of capital inflows was very important in the story of how an economic miracle became a financial crisis. Thailand and other countries in the region were replacing stable long-term capital funding for their current account deficits with short-term, primarily debt-focused, funding.

FDI inflows are not particularly interest rate sensitive. While they involved an initial purchase of the baht, that was soon exchanged for the physical capital, machinery and equipment that formed a particularly illiquid form of asset. That was a form of capital inflow that came in and tended to stay and, in its deployment, created economic growth, employment and often, in due course, exports.

The new money that was flooding in, particularly from portfolio investors, was interest rate sensitive and was focused on liquid assets such as short-term debt instruments and equities. Those who sought to play the interest rate differential with US dollar instruments could thus remove their funds at short notice on maturity. Investors who bought equities could see higher prices resulting from lower interest rates but were likely to change their minds should interest rates rise. The funding for Thailand's current account deficit had shifted away from long-term capital inflows to short-term inflows that could be quickly reversed.

As this analysis from August 1995 shows, it was evident that Thai corporations were indulging in a foreign currency borrowing binge. While some Asian corporates were borrowing their US dollars at long tenors, many were borrowing for very short periods. They exchanged their newly borrowed US dollars for baht that they then used for domestic investment. Should they ever have problems in rolling over their short-term US dollar debt, they would have to liquidate their baht investments to fund US dollar repayments.

Writing in August 1995, one could see that this shift from more stable long-term capital inflows to short-term debt capital was storing up problems for the future. This growing fragility, even more than the growing current account deficits or the rise in the US dollar, raised warning signs that the region was building its Asian economic miracle on increasingly fragile foundations.

As the piece above suggests, this could not continue forever and there could be problems for the Thai economy towards the end of 1996. What I could not have foreseen in June 1995 was that those problems would be big enough to create an Asian financial crisis and, through the political responses to that crisis, change the world of finance for a generation.

High quality and low valuations: everyday low prices

August 1995, Taiwan

A rapid deterioration in Taiwan's external accounts and the cross-straits disagreement has produced a 30% fall in the value of the Taiwanese equity market from its peak at the beginning of the year. The deterioration in the balance of payments is primarily due to the impact of a stronger yen that has produced a surge in the value of imports. The initial worsening of the external accounts will dissipate as the year progresses and the J curve effects spur export growth.

The recent weakness of the yen will provide more immediate relief. Traditional yield gap and yield ratio analysis had provided significant buy and sell signals in the past. Both the yield gap and yield ratio suggest that equities have rarely been this cheap. Relative to earnings, equities are also close to historically low valuations.

Predicting the future of cross-straits relations is fraught with difficulty. China's stance is clear and has been unchanged for many years. The ball is in the Taiwanese court and we believe there are various indications that they will adopt a pragmatic approach and accept their de facto independence, reducing destabilising claims for de jure independence. Current equity valuations discount serious economic disruptions in Taiwan. Such disruptions are very unlikely.

Investors have a rare opportunity to gain exposure to high-quality Taiwanese equities at PE ratios which are attractive on a regional and a global basis.

It is sometimes easy to forget the unresolved sovereignty dispute that remains right at the heart of Asia: the claim of the People's Republic of China (PRC) to sovereignty over the Republic of China, also known as Taiwan. In 1995 it was an issue basically ignored by institutional investors in the region. Although for all intents and purposes Taiwan is a fully independent and sovereign country, the PRC still reacts strongly when other countries treat it as such.

The more independent Taiwan actually became, and it was becoming significantly more democratic and independent during the 1990s, the greater the friction with China became. On 7 July 1995 the PRC announced it would be conducting missile tests in the seas near Taiwan. This was their response to a decision by the US administration to grant a visa to the president of Taiwan to provide an address at his alma mater, Cornell University. With that decision the US seemed to recognise the sovereignty of Taiwan that the PRC denied.

The missile tests duly took place from 21 to 26 July 1995 in the seas just north of Taiwanese territory. The PRC also mobilised land forces in Fujian province facing Taiwan. There was more missile testing in late October and publicly conducted amphibious assault training by the People's Liberation Army (PLA) in November. There were more missile tests in March 1996 as the PRC sought to discourage the Taiwanese from supporting President Lee in the upcoming elections – a move that backfired.

The US response to this was an announcement in March 1996 that it was sending two carrier groups to the seas off Taiwan, the US Navy's biggest deployment in Asia since the Vietnam war. I remember the alarm in Hong Kong at this news and equity markets tumbled, but the PRC ultimately backed down and the sabre rattling by both sides stopped; from the lows of February 1996, the Taiwan stock market then doubled by September 1997.

I had flown to Taipei during the crisis to consult with local political experts and gauge their assessment of the likelihood of war. This is not exactly what I expected to be doing as an Asian equity strategist and I was entirely unqualified to make such assessments.

Institutional investors were bringing the same skill sets to investment in Asia that they had long employed in the developed markets. These were not skills that allowed anyone to assess the geopolitics that proved so important in assessing the correct value for Taiwanese equities in 1995 and early 1996.

As it happened, the arrival of two US carrier groups was the end of the crisis and not the beginning of an even larger one. That did seem the most likely outcome, but the possibility that two nuclear powers would engage in some form of conflict over the sovereignty of Taiwan was not negligible in 1995 and 1996. Throughout the long period from the opening of China to foreign investment, there has been a need to assess geopolitical factors relating to how China's growing economic and military power will be accepted by the rest of the world.

In 1995, investors got an early taste of how relations between the US and China, in this case in terms of the issue of Taiwan sovereignty, would not always run smooth. It was also a reminder that the skill set needed to assess the correct value for investments is not always provided by a business school education.

It was peculiar to be in Taiwan knowing that the US carriers were on their way and not knowing what that might mean. I sat in my hotel room watching the news hoping to hear of any developments that might lead to them turning around. When I switched on CNN, the first thing I saw was the view across the sea from my house in Bangor, County Down. My next-door neighbour, an expert on the politics of Northern Ireland, was being interviewed in his living room and the view behind him was almost identical to the view from my house next door.

As the news focused on the outstanding sovereignty issues of my native Ulster, I sat in Taipei doing my best to understand the enormity of what a dispute over sovereignty meant for Asia.

Weak dollar, strong markets; strong dollar, strong markets

August 1995, Regional

I am led to believe that a bungee jumper experiences a 'rush' during both phases of their senseless journey – down and up. However, not all pastimes can provide pleasure in both phases of the journey, as fellow Guinness drinkers may agree.

Free-falling with the US dollar had indeed been very pleasurable for investors in Asia. Boosts to liquidity and corporate earnings have produced a 'rush' for Asian asset prizes. Investors may find the return journey rather less enjoyable but can expect its duration to be limited. However, it may be particularly alarming if you jumped believing you were attached to elastic; beware – it's a chain.

With the dollar staying at current levels and Greenspan cutting interest rates, the outlook for Asian equity markets is excellent. The Asian economies operating currency intervention policies will be forced to adopt a loose monetary policy when they need a tight monetary policy. Asset prices will benefit. However, when the US dollar begins its rally, investors should be on notice that liquidity is tightening and growth is slowing. There is pain at the end of the chain.

Investors buying into the Asian economic miracle did not want to consider that the high growth they were buying into was partially a reflection of the trend in the US dollar exchange rate. They told their clients and I think believed that they were buying cheap equities that would benefit from higher economic growth in Asia. That the valuation of these equities and also Asia's economic growth itself could be the product of a weak US dollar was something not to be considered.

It had been the decline in the US dollar, combined with strong capital inflows, which had forced the central banks to create the excess liquidity that was fuelling high economic growth and ever higher local asset prices. The Asian growth story was supposed to be about good fundamentals and those special 'Asian values' and not the direction of the reserve currency on the international exchanges.

Throughout this period of a rising dollar, which had begun in early 1995, institutional investors often referenced the declining valuations of Asian equities as reasons to invest. This insistence on basing investment decisions on such value considerations, as the rise of the US dollar negatively impacted domestic liquidity conditions, was perhaps the biggest mistake investors were to make in this period. They may not have liked the fact that the Asian growth story relied so much upon managed exchange rates and the direction of the US dollar exchange rate, but refusing to recognise that dynamic was dangerous and ultimately very costly.

Even for those of us who considered that a weak US dollar was very important in the recent history of the Asian growth story, there was also a problem: how does one predict the course of the US dollar on the international exchanges?

Forecasting the future is a difficult business, but forecasting the future direction of exchange rates is particularly so. The currency markets are the biggest and most liquid financial markets of all. In the currency markets there are probably millions of buyers and sellers on any given day ranging from large institutional investors to the family planning a foreign holiday.

It was to turn out that the US intervention in support of Mexico in January 1995 was to mark the low point for the US dollar and the peak for the yen. From its high of 80 yen to the US dollar in April 1995, the Japanese currency was to decline to 147 yen to the US dollar by August 1998. The rise of the US dollar and the decline of the yen were key triggers for the chaos to come in Asia.

Few had any idea of just how weak the financial structure of Japan had become and how the collapse of many of its largest financial institutions would play a role in pushing the yen ever lower and the US dollar ever higher. There were plenty of signs of the weakness of the Japanese financial system. Two Japanese financial institutions had failed in December 1994 and in the summer of 1995 Cosmo Credit had witnessed a deposit run and required government support. That summer both Kizu Credit Union and Hyogo Bank had avoided collapse and losses to depositors only through government intervention.

That Japan's banks had been weakened by the collapse of the stock market and property prices was well documented. It was so well documented that it was easy to believe that it was a problem that somehow the Japanese authorities were solving behind the scenes. It was becoming more evident in 1995 and on into 1996 that the problem had not been solved. In the investment 'silo' of Asian ex Japan equities, few considered just how important the weakness of the Japanese economy and its financial system would become in assessing the investment outlook.

None of us knew just how strong the US dollar was to become, but we had just seen that the 'sugar rush' for Asian investors from US monetary policy could continue. The US Federal Reserve cut interest rates from 6% to 5.75% in July 1995, making those high local currency Asian yields even more attractive and stimulating further capital inflow.

That US rates were to stay below 6% for the next 25 years, apart from a brief period from March 2000 to February 2001, is something that would have been shocking news to investors in 1995. That this prolonged structural collapse in US interest rates was a consequence of events in Asia over the next few years, and of the new international monetary system that was patched together in its wake, would have been more shocking still.

Sector allocation and stock selection: chaff or wheat?

September 1995, Regional

Investing in Asia has become much more complicated over the past five years. Before 1990, the markets were much smaller and reasonably illiquid. The corporate sector divided neatly into two categories. There were companies with good management in stable industries benefiting from the emergence of the Asian economies. Then there were the asset traders. They bought and flipped assets (companies, property and stocks), had low-quality management and low-quality earnings, and benefited from their acuity and contacts.

The poor fund manager who did not entrust their clients' capital to the asset traders has probably now been deserted by many of those clients due to his or her significant underperformance. Asian bankers, even more so than your average banker, were quick to see the security in rising asset prices and have placed a significant portion of their depositors' money with the asset traders. The assets traders and the bankers have seen their profits boom, far outstripping gains that could be made from general economic development.

The ascendancy of the asset traders and their financiers is a feature of liquidity-driven markets throughout history. History also teaches that successful asset traders need more than a ruler, a pencil and a grasp of extrapolation to gain acceptable returns on capital throughout the business cycle. In short, as liquidity dries up, those that were first shall be last.

The profits to be made in asset trading in Asia, much of it financed by debt, had become so attractive as to divert capital from productive activities. Arriving into this great liquidity-driven party, it was striking how this was all taken as normal. There was little questioning going on about how very high bank loan growth, often in excess of 20% year on year, could be consistent with good credit quality. Investors were playing the Asian economic miracle by investing in banks and property companies, seen at that time as an obvious geared strategy to benefit from general economic growth.

As time progressed, the debt-funded investments – mainly property projects – proposed as the best plays on this high economic growth became more grandiose and frankly outrageous. None of this seems abnormal when the world is awash with liquidity. Arriving into Asia in May 1995, it seemed that speculation was increasingly replacing economic activity. This was hardly a new phenomenon:

Speculators may do no harm as bubbles on a steady stream of enterprise. But the position is serious when enterprise becomes the bubble on a whirlpool of speculation. When the capital development of a country becomes a by-product of the activities of a casino, the job is likely to be ill-done. The measure of success attained by Wall Street, regarded as an institution of which the proper social purpose is to direct new investment into the most profitable channels in terms of future yield, cannot be claimed as one of the outstanding triumphs of laissez-faire capitalism.

John Maynard Keynes, *The General Theory of Employment, Interest and Money,* 1936

When the tide of capital turned it was indeed to be the asset traders and their financiers and their investors that lost most in this particular casino. That their collapse was to create a set of circumstances that would enfranchise the asset traders and their financiers to play this game on a global basis was something that I never considered. Rather than warn of the dangers of too much debt and financial engineering, the policy reactions to the Asian financial crisis set up the perfect environment for the asset traders and their financiers to ply their trade on an even grander scale. The "whirlpool of speculation" that was to follow dwarfed even the excesses of Asia and changed the world.

Underwriting Hong Kong

20 November 1995, Hong Kong

Last month, the heads of 30 Chinese state-owned firms in Hong Kong met in secret in Shenzhen, according to the latest *Far Eastern Economic Review*. The main topic of conversation was Hong Kong or, more precisely, what businesses and assets to buy in the run-up to June 1997. The CEOs were told to do their bit to boost confidence and help ensure a smooth transition.

From Hong Kong's point of view, the timing couldn't be better. The economy is in the doldrums and the forces of deflation are still evident. For some time the Hong Kong authorities have done their best to conceal the territory's economic plight and reported GDP growth and inflation have remained high. On the other hand, we have been convinced that the powers of deflation would inevitably assert themselves and reduce the level of asset prices in Hong Kong. However, the PRC authorities have now entered the fray to side with the Hong Kong government against the powers of deflation; the risk/reward ratio for holding over the next 12 months has changed significantly.

The economy may not bottom this quarter, but the fact that China has made it a three-line whip for state-owned firms to expand their Hong Kong operations aggressively can mean only one thing: China will underwrite Hong Kong's asset prices for at least the next 18 months. Moreover, it is doing it with the only thing that matters in Hong Kong – money.

The rise in US interest rates combined with slowing growth in China had taken its toll on Hong Kong. GDP growth was just 1.3% year on year in 3Q 1995 and was to be recorded at just 1.6% in 4Q 1995. These were very low levels of growth by Hong Kong standards, but the economy had in fact bottomed by 3Q 1995.

As the handover of Hong Kong to the PRC was approaching, there were legitimate fears of a drain on capital, but the news of this meeting in Shenzhen raised the prospect that this could be more than offset by capital inflow from China. The prospect of that capital inflow, targeted as it was on the purchase of Hong Kong's corporate assets, was enough I thought to tip the balance in favour of the rise in Hong Kong's foreign exchange reserves and money supply growth that would mean deflation was now unlikely.

The dip in Hong Kong's foreign reserves in 3Q 1995 was soon reversed and they were to grow by 7% over the next year. By the time the handover occurred at the end of June 1997, foreign reserves had grown by 31% from their November 1995 level. Just how much of the capital inflow into Hong Kong in the run-up to the handover came from the PRC is impossible to tell. Wherever it came from, it ensured that, as the Hong Kong Monetary Authority (HKMA) created more Hong Kong dollars as part of the currency board operation, Hong Kong had a year-on-year growth in money supply above 20% by 1997, and the economy and the stock market were booming when the PRC regained sovereignty over Hong Kong in July 1997.

By the end of 1995 faith among investors in the Asian economic miracle was undaunted. There were as yet no signs of the unwinding of some of the excesses I had highlighted, but despite that I was still employed and off to visit the firm's clients in the United States and Europe.

On the way back from a Christmas holiday in the UK, I stopped in India to visit my colleagues in the CLSA India office – my first visit to India. I knew that our office in Nariman Point Mumbai was by far the most expensive real estate in which the company operated. Indeed, at that time, I think office rental costs in Nariman Point were the most expensive in the world.

The growing financial community wanted to be adjacent to each other and the traffic in Mumbai was so bad that everyone fought for the limited amount of office space on the tip of this peninsula in the huge land mass of India. I didn't know what to expect but it was far from opulent. That night on leaving the office, I stood on the steps and watched a goat eat a cardboard box in front of the building. That seemed peculiar enough until a camel and then an elephant walked past.

My fiancée's grandmother had given me a very fine bottle of port for Christmas and I was loath to leave it where it might disappear, so I took it to the various meetings with government officials and businesspeople. They didn't blink an eye, treated this as entirely normal, and made sure that it was placed somewhere secure for the duration of the meetings. I surmised that it was probably one of the less eccentric things that Indians had seen from the British citizens who had previously spent time in their country.

The last fence

March 1996, Hong Kong

Investors drool when governments adopt the wrong monetary policy. When economic policy and monetary policy diverge, asset price volatility is almost guaranteed. There is no prospect of Hong Kong's economic cycle and monetary cycle converging in the foreseeable future. For the past two years, these cycles have diverged with negative impacts for Hong Kong's asset prices. Chinese economic growth collapsed while Alan Greenspan raised interest rates.

Even after the long-term interest rates peaked, the danger period was not over for the owners of assets in Hong Kong. Hong Kong's inflation rate began to come down and real interest rates rose. This was the period of greatest risk for investors. That period of risk had passed by last November and we upgraded our recommendation on Hong Kong from underweight to overweight. The probability of a dramatic divergence in the economic cycle and the monetary cycle has reduced due to stronger than expected US growth figures, but a divergence is still very much on the cards.

In the short term there are clouds on the horizon, but there are now major global forces acting to push the Hong Kong equity market higher … friction between two air masses causes thunder and lightning. The friction between the economic cycle of the world's largest emerging economy and the monetary cycle of its most mature, causes the financial equivalent of thunder and lightning.

Economic activity in Hong Kong had long been driven by the Chinese economic cycle, but its interest rates, a product of the currency board system, followed US interest rates. It was a monetary policy that worked by creating exchange rate stability, but it came at the price of economic volatility and in particular asset price volatility.

The basic principle of the currency board system was to allow the colony's money supply to expand and contract based upon the demand for Hong Kong dollars at the pegged exchange rate. This was the strictest form of the managed exchange rate and it could see major swings in the amount of money circulating in the economy. It could create high economic growth and inflation, but it could also create recession and deflation. With no ability for any policy maker to act to offset booms and busts via independent monetary policy, those booms and busts were likely to be of greater magnitude than those investors had experienced in developed markets.

In December 1994, Chinese inflation had reached 27%. Policy makers were alarmed by the rising inflation and had already launched an austerity drive in mid-1993. That austerity drive continued through 1995 and into 1996. By March 1996, Chinese inflation was below 10%. This was austerity with Chinese characteristics.

Real economic growth had fallen from its 2Q 1993 high of 15% year on year, but in 1Q 1996 the economy was still growing at 11%. Hong Kong's imported US dollar interest rates were set by a US central bank focused on its own GDP growth rate of 2.6% and its inflation rate of 2.7%. US interest rates had risen sharply from 3% in early 1994 to 6% by January 1995. Now US interest rates were falling. This was occurring as real GDP growth in China was still very high despite the austerity programme.

US nominal interest rates seemed increasingly inappropriate for economic conditions in Hong Kong. At the start of 1996, the Hang Seng Index was still 17% below the level it had reached in January 1994, before the rise in US interest rates had begun. From the start of 1996, the Hang Seng Index was then to rise almost 70% to its peak in August 1997, before the full force of the Asian financial crisis brought one of the greatest stock market crashes in Hong Kong's history.

As part of the bull market in Hong Kong equities, investors got particularly excited about a play on China's economic emergence that was known as the red chips. The Red Chip Index rose by 350% from January 1996 to August 1997. The index level was to be back below January 1996 levels before the crisis was over.

As the relationship between Hong Kong and China was so important, everyone was looking for an angle on how to express this through equity selection in Hong Kong. I was perhaps not looking in the right place, but in June 1996 I went along to a conference to hear former President George HW Bush speak.

As the former de facto US ambassador to China in 1975, he had seen huge changes in the country. I took notes but sat at the back of the room, ready to make a dash for the lunch buffet that would follow his address. Not wishing to find myself at the back of a long queue for lunch, I rushed straight to the venue while others shuffled their papers and chatted with colleagues. When I arrived at the buffet the only other person there was President George HW Bush. He explained that he liked to get to the buffet early otherwise he didn't get to eat. We discussed China and the handover of Hong Kong over vol-au-vents.

The arms race was on among the broking community to hire the mainland Chinese expert with real insight into what would happen in Hong Kong after the handover. Many doubted the credentials for such a role of those hired and at CLSA there was no exception. One day at the morning meeting, the debate turned to whether our particular mainland Chinese expert was all that he said he was. A Scottish colleague, a former officer in the Hong Kong police force, leaned across the table and assured me that he was indeed the real deal. He knew this because in his former profession he had been assigned as a surveillance officer to follow him.

Claret: shrinking supply, rising demand

8 May 1996, Regional

Mark Twain once famously remarked, "Buy Land – they're not making any more." Twain was wrong. Within a few years, the Flatiron building was completed on an 'unbuildable' site in New York and the Back Bay in Boston was reclaimed. Twain's attempt to identify an asset class offering fixed supply and rising demand was wide of the mark (although he has since been proved correct in remarking that golf ruins a good walk).

As the CLSA HQ overlooks the Tamar Basin site, we are constantly reminded that land, like gold, is not in fixed supply. However, unless there is a quantum leap in forging technology in China, there is a fixed supply of vintage wine in the world. Indeed, an unnatural desire to consume this investment actually produces a reduction in supply. There are cyclical and structural positives for wine demand emanating from Asia.

Over the past year, the Bank of Japan (BOJ) has stuffed the pockets of the owners of financial assets. The economic recovery in Japan may be about to bring this liquidity-driven period for financial assets to an end, but we are only just beginning to see the spillover into real assets. The Jackie O auction may be a unique event, but the auction fetched 7.5× estimates at the same time that Sotheby's and Christie's reported very good sales for Impressionist art. One of Monet's Haystack series was sold last week above its 1989 price (1989 was the peak year for art and classic car prices).

Another cyclical positive is Japan's economic recovery. Once upon a time, a bottle of scotch in the Ginza cost more than the flight to Scotland. Those days have gone, but wine consumption in Japan will recover.

There are major structural positives for wine demand due to the emergence of the Chinese consumer. In most countries in the world, junk mail is dominated by pizza purveyors, but in Hong Kong one gets shoved under one's door glossy 150-page brochures listing local retail outlets where one can purchase 'The world's most expensive watches'.

The power of the brand name in Asia is well documented and Chinese consumers account for more than 50% of the world's cognac consumption. Anecdotal evidence suggests that the Hong Kong consumer is discovering the cachet associated with fine wine. Asian demand produces a dual positive for wine prices. Unbelievably, many Asian purchasers buy for consumption, aggravating the supply shrinkage. Long-serving gold bugs curse the name Paul Volcker. Gold prices can go down as well as up. However, should wine prove an unsuccessful investment, there is solace to be found at the bottom of every bottle. CLSA's 1995 *en primeur* top tipples are Mouton Rothschild, Latour and Pichon-Lalande.

Investing in the Asian consumption story was difficult. Many of the listed companies in Asia were focused on banking, property development, property ownership or the provision of electricity, telecoms and other utility services. It was difficult to find listed companies that would benefit from the growth of the Asian consumer that just about everyone was sure would produce exceptional profits over the long term. It was particularly difficult to invest in the growth of consumption in China, as the Chinese stock markets were still small and dominated by the companies that the Chinese state had brought to market – few of these produced products that Chinese consumers wanted to buy.

The purchase of wine did indeed prove to be one way to benefit from the Asian consumption story. An investor buying a case of 1995 Mouton Rothschild or Latour has seen the value of their investment increase ten-fold.

The investor in 1995 Pichon-Lalande has had to be content with just an eight-fold increase on their investment. This insight into the attractiveness of wine as an investment I owe to Mike McCoy and it is something, as a beer drinker, that I was unlikely to have stumbled across without his guidance. The fact that claret has performed so well tells the story of how a portfolio investor should have invested in 1996 to benefit from the rise of the Asian consumer.

There were a select band of luxury-branded product manufacturers, listed primarily in Europe, who were the key beneficiaries of the Asian consumer boom. The institutional investor chasing the Asian growth story by investing in Asian equities missed the opportunity to benefit from that story by investing in companies listed on their own domestic markets.

That new land was being created in Hong Kong I could see from my office window. One day, a little pile of sand appeared in Hong Kong harbour just in front of Wanchai. This pile of sand was already the product of more than a year's work to create an island to host the extension to the Hong Kong Convention and Exhibition Centre. Each day I watched it grow from this pile of sand to the building that would host, on 30 June 1997, the handover of Hong Kong to Chinese sovereignty. Like some form of constitutional egg-timer, the pile of sand grew each day, signalling that the greatest change in Hong Kong's history was growing ever closer.

From last to first

4 July 1996, Thailand

Of all the major emerging markets, Thailand has been the worst-performing market in the first half, after South Africa. A tight monetary policy acted to reduce valuations. However, it is now clear that the political backlash against that policy is bearing fruit with the resignation of the central bank governor and a series of interest rate reductions in bank determined interest rates. So is this the clarion call for the Thai market? No.

Clearly the reduction in interest rates is good news for the market, likely to continue and should ensure that Thailand is not one of the worst-performing global markets over the next six months. However, that is not to say that it will beat the benchmark, or that holders of the foreign stock will benefit from any rally. There is a problem of timing and a problem of risk.

The market desperately needs local participation. When the MSCI changes take effect on 2 September, fund managers will have their largest positive benchmark bet in the Thai market. After investing cash balances in Taiwan, they will then have to follow up by trimming other weightings to continue the move towards a 10% weighting. This process will be taking place over the next few months.

It is very difficult to see a continued commitment of funds to the Thai market by foreigners. Thus the locals will have to play a major role in sustaining any rally. Local participation is likely to be postponed until nearer the year end.

Due to high levels of local ownership, the Thai market is not an efficient discounter and the 2Q 1996 results are still likely to come as a shock. With a 2.6% year-on-year devaluation of the baht against the dollar 2Q on 2Q, there may be a negative transmission impact from balance sheet currency mismatching onto the profit and loss statement (P&L). This may compound the problems caused by the falling currency. The Thai retail investors can still obtain 9.25–10.25% for Thai baht deposits and even higher yields on promissory notes. The analysis of switching rates from last September suggests that three-month deposit rates would have to be nearer 7% before there would be a move from deposits into equities. That level of interest rates may still be some months away.

The end clients of institutional investors had probably no idea just how important changes in the benchmark index were in terms of influencing where their funds were invested in the great geographical expanse we call Asia. In 1996, Taiwan significantly opened its equity market to foreign ownership. As the equity indices sought to reflect market capitalisation available to foreign investors, the weighting of Taiwanese equities was increased and all other country weightings declined.

For reasons entirely unconnected with the expected returns from any investment in the index, investors found themselves having to liquidate existing investments across the region and invest the proceeds in Taiwan. The capital outflow associated with such an adjustment, if large enough to offset other flows, could put downward pressure on the local exchange rates. To the extent that the local authorities would not permit a decline in the exchange rate, they were forced to sell their foreign exchange reserves to defend the exchange rate and in this process tighten domestic monetary policy.

A decision made by the government in Taipei to open its stock market to greater foreign ownership forced a change in equity index benchmarks that, at the margin, changed monetary policy in Asian countries operating managed exchange rate regimes. The impact was the greatest on those countries that had secured a very large proportion of the capital inflow driven by the peculiarly high weighting they had initially secured in the indices. That the monetary policy and the economic outcomes for millions of people were altered by the decision in Taipei to permit higher foreign ownership of equities was bizarre.

The more foreign ownership was permitted in other markets, particularly in the potentially very large markets of India and China, the more this dynamic of liquidation in other Asian markets would accelerate. It could, of course, be offset by ever larger flows of capital into Asian equities in total.

Foreign investors' reallocation of capital from Southeast Asia and Hong Kong to Taiwan in 1996 indicated how shifts in asset allocation in the region had potential impacts for monetary policy, economic growth and not just directly for the prices of domestic equities. The need for institutional investors to follow benchmark indices and adapt to changes in those indices had, and still has now, economic as well as investment implications, particularly for emerging markets operating managed exchange rate regimes.

Global deterioration: the markets finally look east

30 July 1996, Japan

What has changed to turn global equity markets bearish? The only surprise over the past few weeks has come from Japan. In the United States, the bond market has been well behaved, the shape of yield curve unchanged and Greenspan's comments supportive. Earnings growth in the United States has been ahead of expectations. However, in a three-day period, the yen rallied 3.1% against the US dollar on speculation that Japanese interest rates would rise. This currency movement would appear to be the catalyst for the sell-off.

The sudden strength of the yen is indicating that the flow of excess liquidity out of Japan into the United States is ending. This is bad news for global equities as Japan had been the source of the excess liquidity which had been driving the US equity and bond markets. The reason that the flows overseas are probably abating is that the economic recovery in Japan is requiring these funds. The period of history when an accommodative stance by the BOJ drove markets is over.

Changes in the value of the yen had become particularly important at this time because it was the main source of something called 'carry'. In the age of free capital flows, which had dawned through the 1980s, it was possible to borrow in one currency to invest in the assets of another. This form of investment is known as 'carry' and it manifests itself primarily through investors borrowing in currencies with low interest rates to invest in currencies with high interest rates.

The investor earns more income than they have to pay in interest, but of course is very vulnerable to loss should the exchange rate of the currency they borrow in appreciate relative to the currency they invest in. For many investors such a form of investment would be classified as too dangerous. However, where potentially large profits are involved there will always be someone tempted by the risk. In the mid-1990s, the cheap currency to borrow to fund such investment was the Japanese yen and this is the 'excess liquidity' I referred to in the piece from 30 July 1996.

Japan was dealing with the consequences from the bursting of an asset-price bubble and the unwinding of the financial engineering – in Japanese, *zaitech* – that created not just low economic growth but solvency problems for the local financial system. The consequence was a steady decline in inflation and the BOJ was reducing interest rates in an attempt to bolster economic growth and reverse a recent deflation.

For many investors the aggressive scale of this monetary response was likely to continue and as Japanese interest rates declined well below US interest rates, the yen was likely to fall relative to the US dollar. This created an opportunity to borrow yen at very low interest rates and invest them in US dollar-denominated assets and pick up the extra income as profit with limited prospects of currency losses.

As long as the yen declined relative to the US dollar, these investors would also secure capital gains from the currency adjustment. What surprised investors was that the yen could weaken while the carry trade also reversed. Japanese banks in particular became less aggressive in their lending for offshore activities as the yen weakened but also as the perilous condition of their balance sheets became more evident. Few investors in Asian equities were focused on the impact for the Asian economies and stock markets from the increasingly evident financial difficulties in Japan.

The increasing evidence of weakness in the Japanese banking system was making it more expensive for Japanese banks to borrow, particularly in the Eurodollar market, and this had important consequences for Asia. In September 1995 a trader at Daiwa Bank in New York had been arrested for covering up a trading loss of just over US$1bn.

That Japan's tenth largest commercial bank could have had hidden such losses, admitted by the bank to cover a period of 11 years, stunned markets. If a Japanese bank could hide such losses in its theoretically well-regulated US branch, what might they be hiding in their Japanese operations? The need for state intervention at Cosmo Credit Cooperative and Kizu Credit Cooperative in 1995 was followed by state intervention at Taiheiyou Bank in March 1996 and the state-ordered suspension of operations at Hanwa Bank in November 1996. In June 1996 the Japanese government had launched a huge intervention, in conjunction with private banks, to prevent the collapse of the housing loan corporations known as Jusen.

The caution regarding lending to Japanese banks increased with each revelation. This was important for Asia as Japanese banks loaned both US dollars and yen to Asian corporations. These banks had cheap access to yen in the form of the deposits at their extensive Japanese branch network bolstered by large corporate yen deposits. However, Japanese banks had to borrow most of the US dollars they loaned in Asia and elsewhere in the money markets. In these markets, increasing caution as to the liquidity and solvency of Japanese banks resulted in the growth in what was known as the 'Japan premium'.

At the margin it was costing Japanese banks more to borrow US dollars and this would impact the price at which they could lend US dollars in Asia. Indeed it could impact whether they would lend US dollars at all, given the fine margins they were already working on before the 'Japan premium' began to grow.

For many investors, the currencies of Asia were considered to be quasi US dollars, especially as they had weathered the storm of the devaluation of the Mexican peso in December 1994. The determination of the local authorities to hold their exchange rates steady relative to the US dollar meant that yen could safely be borrowed to invest in the higher-yielding currencies in Asia as long as one thought the yen would not appreciate markedly in relation to the US dollar.

This flow of money, borrowed in yen but then sold for the purchase of Asian local currencies, just added to the upward pressure on Asian exchange rates and forced the authorities to intervene, thus creating more domestic liquidity. It was not just particularly aggressive investors who saw the profits to be made from financing investments in Asia funded by yen. Japanese institutional investors, receiving ever lower yields on their yen portfolios, also decided to increase their holdings of US dollar and quasi US dollar investments.

These flows of capital from Japan were thus highly influenced by changes in the yen exchange rate. As long as the yen was falling relative to the US dollar, further capital flows into Asia seemed probable. However, should the yen begin to rise, some of the investors, particularly those who had borrowed yen to finance their investments in Asia, were likely to liquidate their Asian investments to purchase yen and reduce their yen borrowings.

On any given day, investors watched the yen/US dollar exchange rate in the knowledge that any strengthening of the yen might reverse the 'carry' trade in Asia with negative implications for monetary policy and asset prices. The role that balance sheet problems at Japanese banks might play in slowing or reversing the carry trade, even if the yen did continue to decline, was rarely if ever contemplated.

This flow of capital from Japan complicated analysis of the situation in Asia. In normal circumstances a strong US dollar would have been negative for the local liquidity conditions as the local central banks intervened to force their currencies higher in line with the US currency. However, the rise of the US dollar and the decline of the yen accelerated the 'carry' trade capital inflows into Asia and meant that, even in a rising US dollar environment, there were rapid rises in foreign exchange reserves and money creation.

These capital flows more than offset the negatives for the region associated with a rising US dollar. The problem was that they were reliant upon the Japanese banks being prepared to lend yen for such speculation, and also that the borrower was not making capital losses on their investments in Asia. If these factors changed, there would likely be capital outflow associated with the carry trade and the US dollar might well still be rising.

The long-term capital inflows, primarily in the form of FDI, had been replaced with short-term capital inflows, some of which were based upon the willingness of Japanese banks to lend and assumptions that Asian asset prices could not decline in yen terms. The hangover from the great Japanese asset bubble that peaked in 1989 was still casting its shadow over the Japanese banking system. Would things stabilise or deteriorate? And if they deteriorated, would the Japanese banks continue to finance the 'carry' trade that had become such a key source of capital inflows to Asia?

The rally in the yen at the end of July 1996 turned out to be very brief. However, the fact that this rally pushed interest rates higher in Thailand, as the local authorities intervened to prevent the capital exodus pushing the baht down relative to the US dollar, should have served as a warning to investors still seeking to profit from the Asian economic miracle.

If 'the miracle' relied upon low interest rates creating high economic growth, just a change in the direction of capital flows was evidently capable of pushing interest rates higher. The rise in the yen was not the only catalyst that could trigger a reverse of capital flows and tighter monetary policy in Asia. Capital losses on the investments that carry traders held in Asia could also quickly wipe out any profits from an investment that was largely funded by debt.

Investments funded with debt are investments weakly held, given the consequences for profits and ultimately solvency should their prices decline. The arrival of the yen-carry traders as investors in Asia had thus further increased the fragility in those Asian economies that were forced to loosen monetary policy when capital flowed in and tighten it when the tide of capital ebbed.

Buy rupiah

30 July 1996, Thailand/Indonesia

The Thai baht depreciation was less severe than that in Indonesia, but Reuters reported that this was only sustained by US$340m of net purchases of Thai baht by the Bank of Thailand. There is no obvious evidence that this is an orchestrated run on the currency by hedge funds, but rather a flight of the interest-rate sensitive funds which have been placed on Thai baht deposits.

There has been a significant flow of funds into the Thai baht for the yield pick-up and HSBC allowed their Power Vantage account holders to switch into and out of baht with one telephone call. With US$37bn there is no doubt that the Bank of Thailand can sustain the peg. However, it is clear that the cost of buying back baht is to send interest rates higher and the overnight rate rose from 11.5% to 15% today.

It was interesting that even as the US dollar weakened against the yen last week, baht interest rates headed higher, indicating that there was still downward pressure on the Thai currency. More importantly, the three-month interbank rate spiked from 9.5% to 11.5% as the BOT bought back the currency yesterday. Even the longer-term outlook is challenged as the scare stories concerning Thai banks and the economic recovery in Japan are likely to lead to an end to the major US dollar loans being made to Thai banks from the Japanese Life companies.

The sole bull case for Thailand has always been that interest rates will fall. However, should this downward pressure on the currency remain, then rates will have to remain around current levels and the bull case would quite quickly turn into a bear case – given the current condition of the economy, what will happen if interest rates rise? It is difficult to see why there would now be a flow of funds back into the Thai baht. We do not expect a strong upward run in the US dollar from these levels, but this would only exacerbate Thailand's problems should it occur.

The ringgit has been under marginal pressure and has thus been largely ignored in the current debate over currencies. However, to the extent that it has been ignored, it may be the most important currency movement of the past few weeks. There is general agreement that Malaysia is ignoring economic reality and will eventually have to see interest rates rise even further and economic growth slow.

High interest rates slowed the Thai economy quickly because loan-to-deposit rates were high at 115%, but in Malaysia tightening began when loan-to-deposit ratios were 80%. However, loan-to-deposit ratios in Malaysia have now risen to over 90% and we are much nearer to the period when rising interest rates will impact economic activity.

Selling of the currency could be the event which finally inflicts that slowdown. If Bank Negara intervenes to hold the currency at the current level, then they will be buying back currency. With loan-to-deposit ratios still rising, this would further act to quickly dry up the excess liquidity.

Whether the currency is fundamentally undervalued or not, Bank Negara was expending foreign exchange reserves for a two-year period in 1994 and 1995 to support the currency. However, a belief in the undervalued nature of the ringgit is the cornerstone to financing the current account deficit. Should there be any doubt about this, then the flow of funds across the causeway would only be sustained if interest rates moved higher. Should there be any steady downward pressure on the currency, then there could be a nasty unwinding of the Malaysian situation. Thus the ringgit should be watched very closely as a sell-off may provide the long-awaited catalyst needed to reduce liquidity and produce a dawning of reality in Malaysia.

When does a crisis begin? Many histories of the Asian financial crisis date its beginning to the decision on 2 July 1997 by the Thai authorities to devalue the Thai baht exchange rate. By then the devaluation was a *fait accompli*. What marked the beginning of the crisis was the high tide for capital inflows and the ebb of those flows that then followed with the consequences of tighter liquidity and lower asset prices.

This piece, written in July 1996, noted that there were some days on which that tide was now going out. Thai foreign exchange reserves, it turned out, had peaked in June 1996 and the share price of the country's biggest bank, Bangkok Bank, also peaked that June. While we could not know by just how much reserves would decline in defence of the baht exchange rate, the fact that they were declining at all, following years of expansion, indicated that it was time to be much more cautious.

We did not know it at the time but, with the benefit of hindsight, the beginning of the Asian financial crisis is best dated to the summer of 1996. Thai foreign exchange reserves had peaked, indicating that the wave of capital inflow into Asia was beginning to abate, and the share prices of Thai banks had peaked, indicating that the period of excessive liquidity was ending.

The analysis written in July 1996 focused on just how extended the Thai banking system had become. The commercial banks had loaned more money than they had on deposit and funded this by issuing debt instruments. It turned out that they had borrowed these funds at short maturities and most of the loans they financed were for long maturities.

Commercial banks are in the business of borrowing short and lending long, but this is usually financed by a deposit base which is unlikely, especially in the age of government guarantees of retail deposits, to become unavailable. There were no such government guarantees for investors who held the short-dated commercial paper issued by Thai commercial banks and, it turned out, this form of funding could disappear quickly. That short-term funding could dry up quickly, when it was used to fund loans that were long term and almost entirely illiquid, was to become a key problem for Thai banks, especially as the market already had its suspicions about the quality of the loans made by Thai banks.

In May 1996 Bangkok Bank of Commerce had been taken over by the state. In June there were arrests associated with its mismanagement and alleged fraud of US$2.2bn. In June 1996 US regulators had ordered Bangkok Metropolitan Bank to close its US operations due to regulatory deficiencies.

That the Thai banking system had large loans to a commercial property market in Thailand that was obviously in massive oversupply had been something investors had known for several years. The squeeze on domestic liquidity in Thailand, which began in the summer of 1996, was impacting an overextended banking system with already questionable asset quality. That Thai commercial bank share prices peaked in June 1996 indicated just how the market could focus on the short-term outlook in a liquidity-driven equity bull market. When the liquidity began to dry up, as this analysis suggested was beginning in the summer of 1996, the focus began to switch to the long-term issue of just how sound the loans were that were extended by Thai banks during the boom.

Capital inflows had become so important in determining local interest rates that one had to have a view on the direction of such flows to forecast the outlook for the local equity markets. This was not a form of analysis that sat well with most analysts equipped with degrees in finance and economics. They had learned that capital flows effectively reacted to changes in the fundamental data in the form of economic growth, inflation and corporate earnings. As long as these variables remained positive, the standard approach was to believe that more capital would be attracted to invest in the growing opportunities.

To argue, as I did, that the fundamentals were largely the product of the capital inflows, was to fly in the face of traditional analysis. Arguing that the capital flows determined the fundamentals was problematical, but there was a bigger problem with resting one's analysis on the direction of capital flows. How could one seek to forecast the direction of capital flows that were so important in determining the fundamentals of Asian growth? Who really knew how much capital could continue to pour into Asia? Who really knew when it might slow or stop?

For the stockbroking analyst seeking to make such forecasts, were they doing any more than trying to second-guess the decisions of their own clients? I was fully aware of how much more difficult such forecasting was and also the circular nature of the argument – forecasting that stock markets would fall if there was less foreign buying of them!

However, what was already evident in Thailand by the middle of 1996 was that countries that were particularly reliant upon portfolio flows to finance their current account deficits while managing their exchange rates could see their interest rates rise and fundamentals deteriorate as a result. It was also evident that US dollar borrowing by local corporates had played a key role in fuelling the capital inflow. That such credit could dry up rapidly is something that I was familiar with, having studied the drying up of US dollar credit flows that triggered the numerous emerging market defaults in the early 1980s.

There was ultimately a simple choice: I could pretend that the fundamentals would lead the capital flows or accept the growing evidence in the summer of 1996, which happened to fit with my existing opinions, that the fundamentals could be altered by the capital flows. Pretending did not appeal as a form of analysis. I stuck to the more dangerous task of trying to forecast capital flows and focus on how these could undermine the fundamentals of the Asian economic miracle.

As the piece above reveals, it was also becoming clearer throughout 1996 that other countries with clear and obvious mal-investment, such as Malaysia, could see a tightening of liquidity conditions that would unveil some, and perhaps many, of their obvious excesses. These observations were not popular in Thailand or Malaysia. In both countries, initially, the local CLSA analysts and sales teams were deeply opposed to the opinions of someone looking primarily at macro data who rarely visited their countries.

Local policy makers were also beginning to get wind of these contrary opinions that could perhaps play a role in deterring investment in their countries. With the local politicians increasingly complaining to the local offices, the pressure to be correct on what were becoming increasingly strident calls on Thailand and Malaysia increased significantly. As CLSA was to discover, as the economic conditions in Asia deteriorated, the authorities would get more active against those they deemed to be playing a role in the slowdown in capital inflows and the tighter monetary policy that followed.

One-way bets

1 August 1996, Regional

If one of the problems facing Thailand is a global liquidity deterioration, then these higher interest rates could persist for a prolonged period. To the extent that foreign portfolio investors continue to sell and repatriate funds, then this selling pressure on the baht will continue.

The important thing to remember is that you do not need to see capital outflows to see downward pressure on the baht. As time rolls on, the current account has to be financed by capital inflows. Thailand needs to attract fresh capital inflows on a weekly basis to finance the deficit and keep interest rates low.

At this point in time, FDI flows appear not to be forthcoming, foreign portfolio flows are negative and thus interest rate sensitive flows are all important. The current very high level of interest rates is caused by Thai corporates covering their US dollar liabilities. This selling is likely to ease as the stability of the baht is maintained, but at this stage the source of the necessary capital inflows would appear to be interest rate sensitive flows. This is not good news.

Already by July 1996, some Thai corporates were concerned about the wisdom of borrowing US dollars to make Thai baht investments. At this stage, their concerns were probably more about the capital losses they were making in the local equity and property markets than any genuine fear that the baht would be devalued relative to the US dollar. The greater the level of debt used to fund an investment, the smaller the decline in the price of that investment required to turn a profit into a loss.

By the summer of 1996, capital losses on the debt-funded investments were beginning to accrue. A previously virtuous circle of capital gains encouraging more US dollar borrowing, more capital inflows, more domestic liquidity creation and higher asset prices was increasingly close to turning into a vicious circle. The more domestic asset prices fell, the more those who had borrowed US dollars to finance their purchases might have to not just sell those assets but also sell baht to repay their US dollar liabilities. The piece above, written in August 1996, was picking up the beginning of that vicious cycle that was to wreak such havoc on the economy and people of Thailand.

The huge amounts of foreign currency debt issued by Asian banks and non-financial corporations was the greatest revelation for almost all investors during the Asian financial crisis. That it came as such a shock was remarkable. There was macro data available for foreign investors on the level of foreign currency debt outstanding, though it was not as comprehensive as it is today.

Even as an analyst paying more attention to the external accounts than most people, I had simply missed the data. Incredibly, the analysts who covered individual stocks seemed to be none the wiser, and in their defence, the disclosure by Asian companies of their true balance sheet position was poor. The balance sheet weakness resulting from such currency mismatches between assets and liabilities was simply never mentioned in analysis of Asia's listed companies in the great Asian equity bull market.

Most embarrassingly of all, the US dollar debt that was washing across Asia was, in many cases, provided by the same organisations we were working for! Many of the stockbroking operations in Asia, who published the economic analysis and stock analysis upon which foreign investors relied, were subsidiaries of developed world banks. However, it was possible to work in one of those subsidiaries without ever meeting someone from the banking part of that business or knowing anything about their operations in Asia.

I remember visiting the Credit Lyonnais banking operation in Manila and finding the local team had never had a visit from anybody in the broking subsidiary asking what they were up to. In the Asian financial crisis, lessons were learned the hard way that equity investors needed to be very aware of what was happening in the world of credit. That is a lesson that comes in useful again and again, as even now the silos created in the world of finance often lead to great build-ups in debt of which many equity investors are unaware. Such ignorance by many investors was to play a key role in the so-called great financial crisis that was to ravage the global economy in 2008 and 2009.

This time it's serious

2 August 1996, Regional

Having met so many bears in the past few weeks, it is an instinctive reaction to become more bullish. It's difficult. Sentiment swings are usually associated with falling markets, but this time it's different. For the first time that I can remember, investors in Asia are questioning the key assumption of Asian investment: high economic growth equals good returns from equities.

Sentiment swings usually question the short-term outlook, but there is a growing swell of pessimism concerning the long term. In particular, investors point to the export slowdown pan-Asia as indicative that Asia's export competitiveness is falling, and across the region return on equity is low. At this stage it is irrelevant whether their concerns are legitimate or not, the point is that their caution is unlikely to produce the usual 'buy on a dip' reaction which has characterised Asian markets for the past number of years.

The instinctive 'buy on a dip' school has learned a tough lesson in Thailand this year. The failure of Asia to follow through on the bullish moves in the United States, Eastern Europe and Latin America suggests that the current bearishness will prevent a major rebound in the MSCI Index from occurring.

The news from the United States over the next few weeks will clearly be crucial in determining the movements of the markets. However, if the news is not supportive, then there is unlikely to be a sustained bounce in Asia.

Investors in Asia had seen major deteriorations in the local current accounts in the 1990s, but much ink had been expended explaining how these were actually positive deteriorations. In particular, it was argued that the surge in import growth, which outstripped export growth, was driven by the importation of capital goods and equipment. These imports would turn into the increased capacity that, in due course, would result in much higher levels of export growth.

While it was possible that Asia's larger current account deficits indicated that they had become less competitive, perhaps as a result of the devaluation of the RMB in 1994, that argument was largely dismissed. However, by the second half of 1996 there was still little evidence of the export boom that the supposed importation of capital goods had portended. As 1996 progressed and the much-awaited export acceleration did not develop, investors wondered whether the massive devaluation of the RMB in 1994 and perhaps also the creation of NAFTA had indeed undermined Asia's competitiveness.

This raised the spectre that Asia's exchange rates were overvalued, a radical conclusion given that we had witnessed constant upward pressure on the exchange rates due to the abundance of capital inflows. If they were in fact overvalued, then Asia was not going to export its way to much smaller current account deficits while maintaining the current value of the exchange rates.

The inability of this key fundamental to improve as expected made it increasingly clear how reliant Asia was on ever more capital inflows to keep the currency stable and economic growth at expected rates.

Baht attack: 3% of reserves spent

2 August 1996, Thailand

Today the *Financial Times* (FT) reports that over the first four trading days of this week (Thai markets were closed on Tuesday but the baht continues to trade in Singapore and Hong Kong), the Bank of Thailand has spent US$1bn of their US$37bn in forex reserves defending the baht.

In the most recent edition of *The Solid Ground Quarterly*, it is pointed out that the baht has fallen 2.6% against the US dollar 2Q 1996 on 2Q 1995. It is suggested that this may act to depress corporate results as there will be a negative impact on the P&L due to unhedged debt exposure.

The Property Perfect results are the first set to show such a deterioration with an unrealised forex loss of 18m baht in the quarter. With Thai's revaluing liabilities on a quarterly basis, there should be more of this to come. This will not be good for sentiment. It is unlikely to deter Thai corporates who are hooked on cheap US dollar debt. If it ever resulted in a move out of US dollar debt into baht debt, then the downside for the market would be extreme as interest expense would rise and liquidity fall as baht selling ensued to retire US debt.

Today the overnight interest rates have come down, with Bangkok Bank's rate falling from 25% to 15%, but the three-month rate remains unchanged at 12%.

The reflexive nature of capital outflows impacting the fundamentals that drove investment into Asia was just beginning to appear. This was a small adjustment to profits driven by the movement in the exchange rate, but it showed how Thai corporate profits could be undermined by a reversal of capital flows.

Now there was evidence that the fundamentals could indeed be negatively impacted by a change in the direction of capital flows. It was to be less than a year before the Thai authorities devalued the baht, but the dynamics of tighter liquidity, foreign exchange translation losses and problems for property companies were already evident by the summer of 1996.

By this stage many of my colleagues were tired of the stream of bearishness from the Asian regional strategist who was, in their opinion, so bad for business. Now the macro musings from Hong Kong were showing up as higher interest rates and, at the margin, lower corporate profits. When the discount rate rises and the corporate earnings growth rate declines, a fall in equity prices is sure to follow. It was the change in trend, at this stage only in Thailand, in the summer of 1996 that provided the first evidence that the Asian economic miracle was in trouble.

Caution

5 August 1996, Regional

Over the weekend I caught up with two and a half weeks of back reading. The bearishness which I encountered on my trip seems to pervade the press also. In 18 July's *Far East Economic Review* (entitled *Bulls Run From Asia*), David Brennan (managing director, Baring International Asset Management) comments upon the change of mood among his clients.

For the first time they are questioning the long-term outlook for Asia with particular reference to economic growth and political risk. In today's *Wall Street Journal Asia*, Andrew Dalton (chairman, International Division, Mercury Asset Management) states that he has reduced his exposure in Asia from a double weighting against the MSCI to a neutral weighting.

The broking fraternity has struck a similar tone, with Warburg questioning the long-term returns to be had from equities which have low returns on equity and Peregrine Securities attributing the export slowdown to a loss of competitiveness. All the comments in the press and on television are of a similar vein – Asia does not look exciting but Hong Kong is OK-to-positive. It is always tempting to be bullish in the face of such bearishness.

However, a loss of faith in the long-term returns by the UK institutional investor would be a disaster for Asia. The Caps median weighting last September in Asia was 25% against a benchmark weighting of 6% in Asia. These investors have had a three-year bull bet in Asia without any absolute gains. Should the growing pessimism surrounding the long term spread from Asian specialists to global asset allocators, then there are good reasons to remain cautious on the Asian markets. The risks remain high particularly should the Asian markets underperform the United States again in 1996.

The scale of the overweight to Asian equities noted here in mid-1996 is truly staggering. UK pension fund investors had actually committed more capital to Asia ex Japan equities than they had to US equities! These were very large funds, and in an age when the mutual fund business was much smaller and exchange traded funds non-existent, they were the elephants in the Asian investment jungle.

I suspect the modern reader will simply not believe that these large sophisticated investors invested more in Asia ex Japan than the United States, given that US equities now comprise fully 60% of global stock market capitalisation. Well it was true and it was based primarily on a simple belief that the higher economic growth in Asia, compared to the United States, would lead to an outperformance for Asian equities.

That there is no relation between high economic growth and returns from equity investment is a key lesson from financial history. It was a lesson ignored in this period as investors bid up the price of Asian equities and shunned the equities of what they then considered to be the low-growth US economy.

In 1996, UK investors were particularly slow to see the potential in US equities in general and were unconvinced by the potential of the new technology that many already speculated would revolutionise business. Jeff Bezos sold his first book online in July 1995. Netscape, a web browser with a world market share thought to be in excess of 90%, listed in August 1995 and its share price rose from an initial public offering (IPO) price of US$28 per share to close that day at US$75.

A revolution had begun but UK investors were not convinced – and anyway, their holdings in Asia had underperformed the US equity market since the devaluation of the RMB in January 1994. This was not, it was reasoned, a good time to change your mind and lock in such underperformance to bet on a speculative economic revolution in the United States triggered by a new and still largely unknown technology.

The willingness to take such huge relative bets in Asia ex Japan equities relative to US equities was partially driven by a particularly bizarre form of benchmarking. UK pension fund manager performance was not measured relative to a benchmark index, but relative to the pension fund peer group. Thus a manager who wanted to be overweight any stock market had to make sure that they were overweight relative to the current weighting of the peer group.

Each quarter the data was released that let each manager know what the average UK pension fund had allocated to each global asset class. The manager who thought they could outperform their peers by having more money in Asian equities would have to increase their weighting in these equities if the average weighting had risen. This form of benchmarking created a particularly dangerous dynamic.

If the average weighting increased over the course of a quarter, many fund managers, keen to express their bullishness on the outlook for Asian equities, were virtually forced to invest more. The impact of such a movement was to push the Asian weighting for the next quarter to a higher level and trigger the same adjustment. And so it went on – until one day it didn't.

Once again this was a dangerous dynamic in which a virtuous circle, propelling more capital to Asia, could turn into a vicious circle. It was a dynamic so taken for granted that nobody really questioned that UK pension investors would always have more money invested in Asian equities than US equities. Sometimes in markets the most extreme things are taken to be normal and persistent because they have, for quite some time, been normal and persistent.

Economic textbooks do not admit to the sort of madness that had driven capital inflows into Asia. They are based on the assumption that the free movement of capital allows capital to track down the best global opportunities and invest accordingly. In that world, the flow of capital acts to increase the efficiency of scarce resource allocation.

While that may have been happening among the direct investing community, I saw almost none of that in the flows of portfolio capital I witnessed coming into Asia. Considerations far divorced from expected future returns, such as benchmark weightings, were the key drivers of capital flows. Institutional investors were also increasingly focusing on ever shorter time horizons. The number of mutual funds that invested in Asia grew rapidly as news of the Asian economic miracle spread to the retail investor.

An investment institution seeking to encourage inflows to these open-ended funds would do so by advertising that they had beaten the Asian Equity Index. The marketing team wanted outperformance and they wanted the annual, even quarterly, outperformance that they could display prominently in their advertising campaigns. For the managers of mutual funds, time horizons were particularly short and there were more and more mutual fund managers in the Asian markets.

Little has changed in terms of investment time horizons. That the business of international capital flows could be so divorced from the economic theory of what drives capital allocation leads to a dangerous misunderstanding of how global finance and the economy work. We learned those lessons the hard way in Asia in those years, but they were lessons constantly ignored in the decades that followed.

Powerful financial lobby groups campaigned for ever greater liquidity in capital markets as promoting the efficiency of capital allocation. However, that liquidity just facilitated ever shorter time horizons and ever larger destabilising swings in capital flows. Such rapid flows are actually inimical to the business of selecting investments based on the prospects for their long-term returns and focus investment on other characteristics. Had the Asian economies been recipients of only long-term capital inflows and not the short-term flows that were to exit so quickly, the region would not have had such a spectacular boom nor the bust that by the second half of 1998 threatened to bankrupt the global financial system.

Having your cake and eating it

6 August 1996, Malaysia

There are problems in strictly applying the decoupling analogy to Malaysia. The authorities do not have a stated currency policy and can permit a greater degree of currency flexibility. However, the volatility in their foreign exchange reserves does show that they actively intervene to prevent the currency trading at its market-determined level. Thus the deterioration in their current account will act to produce upward pressure on interest rates should they decide to prevent currency depreciation.

Mahathir made a statement yesterday in which he said that higher interest rates would not be used to tackle the current account deficit. Mahathir prefers import controls. Across Asia there is an increasing sign that governments will attempt to avoid the negatives associated with their currency policies by using administrative measures.

Malaysia proposes import controls and Thailand has imposed capital controls. If permitted, there is a commitment within the Association of South East Asian Nations (ASEAN) and the Asia-Pacific Economic Cooperation to reduce such controls; then they could allow these countries to have their cake and eat it. The pressures of decoupling are already forcing some governments to consider backtracking on their commitments to reducing the restrictions which surround their economies.

For foreign investors in Asia at this time, one of the greatest risks was that the Asian authorities would resort to draconian administrative measures in an attempt to stabilise their exchange rates while seeking to bolster economic growth. As someone who read financial history, I was very well aware that capital controls had been the rule rather than the exception through most of the post-war period. Indeed they had only been lifted relatively recently but still long enough ago that most investors in Asia were very unfamiliar with them as a policy tool.

Capital controls had been lifted partially in recognition of their failure as part of a grander economic policy that had refused to allow markets to determine prices. This orthodoxy in 1996 was that they were a failed policy and the implementation of policies that would reduce the role of markets in determining prices, through administrative measures, seemed highly unlikely to just about everyone.

As we shall see, investor opinions changed dramatically on the prospects of the replacement of market forces with administrative measures as the crisis progressed. Even when the IMF had arrived in Asia it was not clear that the conditions for the bailouts, more market pricing and fewer administrative measures, would be accepted. It was an important lesson that the investment game is not always played under the same rules.

Governments have the power to change the rules often – to the surprise of investors, who assume the rules are set in stone. That such a response, to suspend market forces, was flagged up by Mahathir Mohamad, then prime minister of Malaysia, even as the economic boom continued, indicated the tussle to come between two very different views as to how resources should be allocated.

As the piece above noted, by August 1996 the Thais had implemented policies that made it increasingly difficult for foreigners to borrow and short sell the Thai baht. That was a mild form of capital control compared to those widely employed across the world from 1945 to around 1980, but it was a non-market response that raised eyebrows at the time.

There were many countries in Asia where the operation of market forces, red in tooth and claw, seemed to me to be incompatible with the local socio-political goals. In the boom, investors assumed that so-called Asian values would be supportive of the growth of market forces at the expense of administrative measures. In my opinion, Malaysia was particularly unlikely to permit such forces to operate unfettered given the country's New Economic Policy that, by 1991, had morphed into a programme called the National Development Policy.

These innocuous-sounding policies of the Malaysian government were actually major government interventions in the economy to assure that the wealth generated would be more equally spread. This policy was seen as necessary following the race riots in Malaysia in 1969 and their aftermath. While there were many causes of tension between the different races in Malaysia, many believed that the greater level of wealth accrued by the Chinese population, relative to the Bumiputra population, was a key cause of the bloody chaos in a country that had only gained its independence from the UK in 1957.

The policies implemented initially as the New Economic Policy sought to level opportunity across the communities (Malaysia also has a large population of people of Indian descent) through positive discrimination. The lack of social unrest that followed can be seen as a major success of the policy, but it did increasingly lead to abuses.

By the 1990s, it had morphed into a policy where key Bumiputra individuals sought and obtained favours from the government that allowed them to become particularly wealthy. Wealth was indeed being created among the Bumiputra population, but it was far from equally spread within it. The prime minister of Malaysia believed these policies were necessary to reduce social tension, but others believed that such policies were best classified as crony capitalism.

As market forces had delivered easy monetary conditions, the Malaysian state found it easy to continue to be in the business of pushing wealth towards its favoured Bumiputra entrepreneurs. However, when market forces dictated tighter monetary policy and even the creative destruction supposed to accompany economic contractions, would the government stand by and watch its work towards wealth redistribution reversed?

As the then prime minister of Malaysia, Mahathir Mohammad, was a key architect of the New Economic Policy, he was, in my opinion, very unlikely to allow the market to reverse, partially or otherwise, what he saw as his life's work. In August 1996, I was highlighting that the prime minister's comments on interest rates could ultimately have very important consequences for investors. If he refused to allow the rise in interest rates dictated by the operation of the managed exchange rate, then the options were to allow the exchange rate to float or seek to prevent the capital outflows that were pushing interest rates higher. The socio-political need to fasten wealth to those to whom the government had allocated it suggested to me that it was Malaysia that would be particularly likely to revert to capital controls, to subvert market forces, when the going got tough.

Malaysia had long been my favourite country in Asia and its wonderful cultural diversity, the associated diversity of its cuisine and its friendly people were key reasons that made it such a great place to visit. The major market forces that were beginning to show their hand by mid-1996 would clearly be seen by some as likely to threaten what had been a long period of domestic harmony in Malaysia.

It was easy in the investment business to see everything as just a series of prices on a Bloomberg screen, but these were increasingly symbols of something that represented a profound change for Asia. Market forces brought expansion and they also brought contraction, and large economic contractions can bring socio-political turmoil. The social fabric, particularly of Southeast Asia, was fragile, a legacy of generations of mass immigration and colonial era use of indentured labour; and that fragility would be tested by what was to come. By 1998 there were riots and associated deaths in both Malaysia and Indonesia.

Badgers, skunks and killer whales

7 August 1996, Regional

The black and white consequences of mispricing for the shareholder depend upon whether they are involved with a badger, a killer whale or a skunk. A badger is a cautious, secretive creature which is not comfortable in daylight, but revels in the dark. During the economic upswing, the good banker is uncomfortable with the prevalent banking practices and is cautious knowing that night follows day. When the inevitable transfer of title to assets begins, the badger bank finds that most of the companies' assets are correctly described as such.

The killer whale is a large species protected by law and sometimes cosseted in an oceanarium. There are some banks which are so big and so important that their behaviour is carefree and their survival and protection ensured by government. The killer whale bank is inevitably underwritten by the public sector, as the public good demands. Then there are skunks. Skunks smell. As the inevitable transfer of title of assets progresses, there are always skunks.

In the second year of my investment career, my employer had set me to analyse US banks. This was in theory a big job for a novice, but in practice it was a non-job. This was October 1990 to October 1991, and everyone knew you had to be mad to buy shares in a US bank. There was a commercial property meltdown in key cities and a severe recession in New England that led to the collapse of the Bank of New England in 1991, at that time the biggest bank collapse in US history.

Indeed, just as I wrote a recommendation that the company should buy shares of Citibank, the company was removing clients' deposits from the same bank just in case the bank collapsed! However, my time was not wasted. Learning about how commercial banks work was the most valuable thing I have ever done in my career. There are many mysteries to commercial banking and many of them remain mysteries even to investors with decades of experience.

How banks create money and how their balance sheets impact their earnings are crucial mechanisms that anyone investing in any stock market needs to understand. It may be that that understanding is rarely useful; but when it is useful, it is incredibly useful. That there were skunks among the Asian banking system was not hard to determine if you had already lived through a credit boom and bust.

Having analysed some very good US banks in the early 1990s, it was very obvious that the banks of Southeast Asia were not very good banks. It was important to understand this fragility in assessing which macro-economic policies might be sustainable and which would do more damage than good, given how they would create further problems in an already weak banking system.

Banks really were black and white in Southeast Asia in this period, but it was something that most economists did not consider when they made their forecasts. Indeed when the IMF arrived, one of their greatest failures was to not understand just how weak the local banks were and how they could not withstand the standard IMF austerity prescription.

Lessons may have been learned by the IMF, but they were not learned by economists. Most of the forecasting errors associated with what became known as the great financial crisis of 2007–08 were associated with a failure to understand the fragility of the credit system in most developed world countries. It should be compulsory for any investment analyst, economist or institutional investor to spend a prolonged period analysing the credit system in general and commercial banks in particular. Whether it's a badger, a skunk or a killer whale remains a key assessment for an investor in any country. The smell of skunks in Southeast Asia was powerful in the summer of 1996, but it was a smell that most investors chose to ignore in pursuit of short-term profit.

The baht: will they or won't they?

12 August 1996, Thailand

On Friday, the government called fund managers to Bangkok to outline the way forward for the Thai economy. According to the deputy prime minister, Amunay Viravan, Thailand would seek to introduce a 'wider fluctuation' for the baht without altering the pegged basket. At the same meeting Rerngchai Marakond ruled out a widening of the band: "We therefore see no need to alter our exchange rate policy as a response to the current economic problems. I hope this is very clear." It seems clear that there is a longer-term plan to make the baht more flexible, but it is absolutely imperative at this stage to convince the markets that there is no risk of a change to the system.

The message should by now be getting through to corporate Thailand that US dollar-denominated debt is not as cheap as it appears. So even if the move to widen the bands is 18 months away, it should already be impacting the behaviour of corporate Thailand. Faced with rolling over a US dollar five-year loan, a corporate treasurer will have to add a new risk premium to the cost of that debt given that there is an increasing likelihood of greater volatility in the baht/US dollar exchange rate.

Should a trend begin in which corporates roll over US dollar funding into baht funding, then Thailand is likely to see a rapid fall-off in the balance of payments surplus which it has been reporting ever since it introduced the peg in 1984. This surplus has been the key driver keeping interest rates at reasonable levels and liquidity abundant. Going cold turkey on US dollar debt is a major long-term structural positive, but there will be pain involved.

The cat was out of the bag. Once the market comes to believe that there is a risk of an exchange rate devaluation, even if it is reasoned that it is many months in the future, capital starts moving. It was moving in Thailand long before the devaluation of the baht on 2 July 1997. It did not help that government ministers were even debating, or disagreeing, as to the scale or the timing of such a move.

The seemingly impossible, a devaluation of the baht, was now admitted to be possible. The capital that had bet on that impossibility had to react accordingly. The greater uncertainty led to a further acceleration in capital outflow. Any announcement of a 'gradual' devaluation is highly likely to result in an adjustment in the exchange rate that would be described as anything but 'gradual'.

Reasons to be careful: the end is not nigh

26 September 1996, Regional

For the third consecutive year capital returns from Asian equities have been poor. To state the obvious, this makes the markets closer to being a buy than they were in December 1993. However, does it make them a buy now? No.

Standard financial analysis does not admit to the operation of extrapolative expectations based upon historic price performance. In economics in particular, higher prices, in almost all cases, are supposed to lead to lower demand and the reverse is also true. The exception to this rule was established by a lawyer from Lanarkshire in Scotland who drifted into financial journalism.

Robert Giffen, latterly Sir Robert Giffen, established that demand for the price of some goods actually rose as their price rose and declined as their price fell. His analysis did not apply to asset markets and he would probably have been appalled to know that one day savings were to be partly allocated upon prices' impact on index weightings, rather than expected investment returns.

Capital was lured by higher prices and higher index weightings and the decline in the price of Asian equity assets, when it came, did not lead investors to invest more. It was to force many of them to sell.

With other global stock markets continuing to outperform Asian markets, the relative weighting of Asian equities in the benchmark index was declining. The value of investors' holdings of Asian equities also declined, but the decision to be so extremely overweight in markets now consistently underperforming was raising real risks for institutional investors. Table 2.3 shows the MSCI Far East ex Japan Free Index US dollar returns for 1994, 1995 and 1996.

Table 2.3: MSCI Far East ex Japan Free Index US$ returns

1994	1995	1996 YTD
−19.0%	+6.81%	+4.46%

These real risks related specifically to their own career risk at least as much as the risk to their clients' funds. A professional investor who is wrong is relatively safe in their job if they are wrong as part of a crowd. However, if the crowd begins to disperse and they are the only one with an extended position in the poorly performing asset class, then their career risk rises.

As the comment from September 1996 above shows, US investors were not being tempted into Asia by the relative underperformance of Asian equities. There was plenty of excitement and potential profit for them at home as it became clearer that new US technology IPOs could be a way to rapid riches.

Poor returns for Asian equities, despite reasonable earnings growth, was reducing valuations for Asian equities. While many expected lower valuations to trigger foreign purchases, time marched on and if anything the poor price performance of Asian equities was discouraging and not encouraging capital inflows.

Beware

1 October 1996, Indonesia

From May last year to the end of April this year, Indonesia was one of the CLSA's top market picks. This bullishness was driven by the outlook for a balance of payments surplus and ensuing abundant liquidity. However, with the first widening of the currency band such an outcome looked less likely (we downgraded the Indonesian market to Neutral). With the second widening of the band it became more unlikely still.

With the currency now at the weak end of the new range, it is time to become even more cautious on Indonesia. There is now ample flexibility, within the current exchange rate system, for Bank Indonesia to proceed with the monetary tightening necessary to induce the money growth slowdown which is very necessary. Not the time to buy the market.

As time progressed, it became more difficult to believe that the problems brewing in Thailand would not impact the rest of Asia. As someone speaking to professional investors every day, I heard how they were reconsidering investments, at least to the Southeast Asia region, because of what they were learning more generally about the foundations of the Asian economic miracle from the unveiling of the micro and macro instability in Thailand.

The Jakarta Composite Index had risen by 50% from May 1995 to April 1996, but with downward pressure on the exchange rate, the negative dynamics impacting Thailand seemed more likely to impact Indonesia and it seemed just too dangerous to continue to invest. The stock market was to go higher still and despite growing problems elsewhere in Asia, it did not peak until early July 1997. It was dangerous to stay to the end of this particular party. In the decline that followed from the July 1997 peak, investors lost 90% of their investment measured in US dollar terms.

I was now finding it difficult to be positive on the outlook for any of the Asian markets except Hong Kong. There is huge internal pressure on a stockbroking analyst to be positive on something. A buy recommendation is much more likely to find a receptive audience internally, but also with the end client.

While only a handful of clients can sell a stock as they have to own it first. A much larger percentage of clients are likely to be in a position to buy a stock as they won't already own it. With buy recommendations likely to fall upon more fertile ground than sell recommendations, the stockbroking business churns out a very high percentage of buy recommendations. The internal inertia to produce buy recommendations is not as powerful for strategists as it is for individual stock analysts and it's highly likely that the client has something in any given country that they could still sell in response to a sell recommendation from a strategist.

However, the internal pressure for a strategist to be recommending something to buy is still high. If the institutional investor sells Asian equities to buy European equities, the Asian broking community gets one set of commissions. If, however, the customer can be persuaded to switch within Asia, then there were two sets of broking commissions! Many institutional investors were managing specifically Asian equity mandates and thus they had to invest somewhere in Asia no matter how bad things got. A blanket sell recommendation on all Asian markets might lose at least half of the transaction! The brightest prospect still seemed to be in Hong Kong, which was still benefiting from the combination of high levels of economic growth in China, signs that the Chinese austerity programme was ending and lower US interest rates.

Bad medicine

2 October 1996, Thailand

Taking the Bangkok International Banking Facility (BIBF) moves to conclusion (i.e., all Thai companies fund locally) as a worst-case scenario, we estimate that for the CLSA Thailand basket (ex the banks), a move to wholly onshore borrowing would increase funding costs enough to pull net profits down by 20% on a full-year basis. While this is a material shock to profits (and we will over the next week be reviewing the impact of the BOT's moves on our forecasts), it is unlikely that the BOT will push Thai companies this hard immediately, particularly at a time of cyclically weak profitability.

Knock-on consequences for providers of funds are serious too. By funding locally, debt service payments must rise by up to 50% (BIBF dollar loans at 9.5% replaced by baht at 13.5%) and interest cover will fall. The credit risk of lending to corporates rises as a result and profit gearing to movements in interest rates along with it. Is that welcomed by Thai banks? We think not. In short, the BOT proposal would inflict some tough medicine on an already weak economy.

The Thai government had opened the BIBF in 1993. The aim was to promote Bangkok as a centre for regional finance where primarily foreign currency would be lent across Asia. In practice however the facility was used primarily by Thai corporates to borrow foreign currency to finance their investments in Thailand.

By October 1996 the authorities were waking up to the size of this massive currency mismatch on Thai corporate balance sheets enabled by the creation of the BIBF. Forcing corporates to repay their US dollar debt would force them to liquidate their Thai assets and sell Thai baht or borrow more in Thai baht. The most likely outcome from such a policy would be to tighten liquidity in Thailand. This was unlikely to produce positives for investors in Thai equities and corporate earnings would likely be negatively impacted.

Someone looking at the macro data is in no position to make high-quality calculations about the impact on corporate earnings from their forecasts. In many cases the direction may be all that is necessary, but without the assistance of equity analysts, the focus has to be on direction rather than magnitudes. If you cannot convince the analysts that your macro forecasts are correct, then they will simply not change their forecasts.

This is a constant problem as the equity analyst's bonus is often rewarded on how well they rank in annual polls – completed by institutional investors – that rank analysts as you might rank vegetables at the village fete. A high-ranking analyst can expect higher pay and bonus going forward. While you might think that this incentive structure might encourage objectivity, it actually encourages analysts to herd together in their forecasting. Particularly in a bull market, pay and bonus will be reasonable as long as you are not particularly wrong compared to your peers. To go out on a limb and have wildly different forecasts than the consensus, primarily based upon the opinion of some macro forecaster, is just too dangerous a thing for an equity analyst to do.

In enlisting the analysts to tell the story of what the bear case might mean for individual stocks, I had several strokes of luck. The first was that the CLSA Thai office was one of the first regional offices to see that the macro deterioration I had forecast was likely to continue. First at a sales level but then also at an analyst level, they began to adjust their opinions and then earnings forecasts in light of the likely economic deterioration.

Being on the ground in Thailand it was incredible just how quickly they began to see and report back on brewing problems that we could not pick up from Hong Kong. They were really quick to see things in a different light when they removed the rose-tinted spectacles of the Asian economic miracle.

Things were not so easy elsewhere, particularly as primary issuance was still underway with all the positive consequences for wages and bonuses that entailed for staff in local offices. However, I was able to persuade most offices that scenario analysis using more bearish macro variables should be included in research, just in case I was right. This approach allowed the analyst to stick with their own forecast while, usually reluctantly, including something somewhere in the report about what might happen if the company's strategist happened to be right on deteriorating macro variables.

I have always been surprised as to just how little scenario analysis there is in investment research. There was a certain machismo associated with an analyst making and defending a forecast and either being right or wrong. Wrongly, in my opinion, their bonuses are often directly linked to just such behaviour. However, it is the fund manager who ultimately pulls the trigger to invest or disinvest and has to live with the consequences of their decisions.

For most of them, scenario analysis only helps with their decision and the commitment of the analyst to their forecast often leads to distracting discussion about that key number rather than about how the company works and the sensitivity of corporate earnings to changes in key variables. Even among clients who expect high-conviction buy and sell calls on individual equities, there is a need for an understanding of the risks associated with those convictions.

By shifting the CLSA stock analysts to some degree of scenario analysis we began to add a greater element of education and less machismo to the business of forecasting. The use of the decimal point in forecasting creates a certainty, for the reader but also the author, that is dangerously misleading. In the Asian financial crisis it wasn't just the numbers to the right of the decimal point that were meaningless. Most of the forecasted numbers to the left of the decimal point were very wide of the mark. The faux certainty inherent in the forecasts of corporate earnings in 1996 led some investors to proclaim that Asian equities were particularly cheap just as their share prices were about to collapse.

The general reluctance to change earnings forecasts without ungentle persuasion was illustrated to me in the middle of 1997 when I bought a copy of *The Bold Riders* for each of our senior analysts in Asia. *The Bold Riders* is an excellent book by the wonderful Trevor Sykes that outlines the key corporate shenanigans of the financial boom in Australia in the late 1980s.

It shows how those excesses, all reported against a background of ever growing corporate earnings, brought their perpetrators to bankruptcy or near bankruptcy soon thereafter. *The Bold Riders* includes so many of the tricks of the trade, in terms of how to flatter a P&L account and a balance sheet, that I thought it would be incredibly beneficial reading for our analysts trying to work out where the bodies in corporate Asia were buried.

I remember buying and distributing over 20 copies to our analysts, but I later discovered that none of them had read it! Australia in the late 1980s was another time and another place and could not possibly contain lessons for analysts covering the Asian economic miracle. Despite the fact that the CLSA headquarters were in a building built by one of the greatest of *The Bold Riders*, Alan Bond, there was little acceptance that Asian business practice could have followed the dangerous course of the recent Australian boom.

There has to be a reason why we constantly forget the investment lessons of the past. One of those reasons is that we are always keen to believe that we are not as stupid as our ancestors. While it is true that the sum of human knowledge is always advancing, albeit with some detours into intellectual cul-de-sacs, the human psyche is strongly influenced by greed and fear.

When the wrong incentives are in place, the norm rather than the exception in the investment business, then those two forces will always be amplified; and financial history is full of examples of how bad incentives produce bad behaviour, how bad behaviour is successfully hidden and how it is eventually revealed. *The Bold Riders* is as good an exposition of all three phases of how greed and fear operate in an economic boom as has ever been written, but among our analysts it went unread.

Sayonara

4 October 1996, Japan

From the beginning of 1994 to the end of 1995, Japanese bankers increased their loans to Asia by 55%. Japanese bankers poured US$40bn of new capital into Asia over this two-year period. This US$40bn was sufficient to finance two-thirds of the combined current account deficits of the six MSCI constituent countries running current account deficits in 1994–95 (Singapore, Taiwan and China were running surpluses). One-third of total loans were to Thailand.

This flow of funds from Japan has played a crucial role in funding the current account deficits in Asia as portfolio flows subsided from the very high 1993 levels. As deficits have to be funded on an ongoing basis, the key question is whether the Japanese banks will continue to be such aggressive lenders to Asia. There are various indications that the rapid pace of loan growth is unlikely to continue.

There was enough data available to know that foreign currency lending, particularly from Japanese banks, had played a crucial role in funding Asia's current account deficits. The data however was largely ignored and, if considered at all, it was assumed that such credit flows must continue.

We should all have been paying much more attention to the role of foreign currency bank lending in general and lending from Japanese banks in particular. The focus of investors remained on the belief that high economic growth would produce high returns from investment in equities. That economic growth had been dangerously funded was something that investors were yet to focus upon.

TFB tells it like it is

7 October 1996. Thailand

The president of Thai Farmers Bank (TFB) has been cautious about the banking system in Thailand for the past couple of years. However, on Thursday his pessimism reached new levels. He told the *FT* that TFB would soon see 8% of its loans non-performing. Remember TFB is one of the highest-quality banks in Thailand and during the last crisis maintained a much higher-quality loan book than its competitors.

The president specifically stated that he believes TFB will continue to have one of the best loan books in Thailand. Thus, system-wide, we are looking at double-digit percentages of bad loans on the loan book. This is before the refinancing which will increase interest expense for some corporates by up to 70%. A tenth of bank loans are about to produce no yield. Provisions for bad debts will have to be accelerated. The last bastion of earnings growth for the market is rapidly seeing a worsening in the outlook. If this source of earnings growth disappears, interest expenses rise significantly and top-line growth slows. Wipeout!

By this stage, the bad news for Thailand just kept coming and coming. It was tempting to think that the market was moving to discount some of the now very publicly available information about a dire credit meltdown that was increasingly being revealed. In just over two years the value of the Thai Equity Index would decline by more than 80% in US dollar terms. The president of TFB may have rung the bell for the end of the Thai equity bull market, but still few were listening.

A foreign field which is forever Malaysian?

10 October 1996, Malaysia

While foreign portfolio investors commit capital to the emerging market of Malaysia, the recipients of that capital are investing in the emerging markets of Europe, Central Asia, Africa and Latin America. Over the past few months there has been a growing trend for Malaysian corporates to announce plans for investment outside Malaysia. Why now?

While the sums of money committed so far are not material, the trend may be indicative of a lack of investment opportunities at home. If returns on capital in Malaysia are acceptable, why does Land & General wish to invest in Azerbaijan, YTL in Zimbabwe and Malaysian Resources in Croatia? Is it that the lucrative privatisation deals purchased for low PEs by issuing high PE paper (remember the late 60s conglomerates boom?) are running out? Or is it that at the top of the economic cycle there is some caution about committing capital for marginal and perhaps falling returns? If so, there are macro as well as micro consequences.

The Malaysian authorities appear determined to maintain the value of the ringgit relative to the US dollar. The simple dynamics of this exercise involve the attraction of significant sums of foreign capital given that the current account deficit will be around 6.9% of GDP this year. If the well-connected Malaysian entrepreneurs are finding fewer rich pickings at home, is there a prospect that foreign direct investors will also find fewer reasons to invest in Malaysia?

In 1992, FDI inflows were 2.4× the current account deficit, but in 1995, that ratio had fallen to just 0.56×. Recently, there have been some high-profile foreign investor pullouts in Penang due to rising wage rates and staff turnover ratios as high as 60%.

Officially unemployment is 1.8%, but the authorities are willing to admit in private that it is in effect lower. In Malaysia, 20% of the workforce is imported. With FDI in 1995 24% off its 1992 peaks, labour problems may already be acting to deter investment. It is early days, but the growing trend for investment overseas could be a warning signal for domestic earnings. If this view on investment is shared by the foreign investor, then financing the Malaysian current account deficit could become increasingly difficult, with negative repercussions for domestic liquidity.

There is always a focus on flows of foreign capital into emerging markets in particular. Throughout this book there is reference as to how such flows can change the credit and monetary conditions of countries that operate managed exchange rates – a policy particularly prevalent in emerging markets.

Analysts get excited about the scale of foreign buying and selling. This is a product of availability bias as stockbroking analysts are very close to the source of such funds. They can see the selling and buying through their dealing desks and they can phone up and speak to the professional investors moving the capital about. There is often almost no focus on local capital outflows.

Despite the fact that data for such outflows is available, it is not as widely studied as the capital inflow numbers. Most analysts are not as close to the locals who are responsible for such capital outflows and thus they do not understand the motivations that drive them. Capital outflows still often made the headlines – particularly in the local press – but these stories were rarely commented upon as being important by stock market analysts.

Malaysians had a certain amount of pride that their corporate sector was so active on the acquisition trail outside Malaysia and that their construction companies were winning orders across the world. The keenness for corporate Malaysia to invest its capital outside the country did raise questions as to why foreign investors were so keen to invest in Malaysia.

The accelerating capital outflows from Malaysia suggested that these managers of corporate capital could find higher returns at lower risks on their money outside Malaysia. Investors need to pay attention to such outflows of capital from local investors. Locals are almost invariably better at assessing risk and rewards domestically than foreigners.

That 20% of the workforce of Malaysia, a country of 20 million people, were foreigners should have been telling investors something about the attractiveness of Malaysia as an investment destination. The excessive growth in money supply over many years had not created any major acceleration in inflation in general or in wages in particular. There were many factors contributing to this, but an important factor was the ability to import foreign workers – primarily labour from Indonesia.

This major flexibility in the workforce provided an illusion that the country was capable of high levels of non-inflationary growth – a wonderful combination for investors who benefit from both high earnings growth and the low interest rates that support equity valuations. However, there is a limit to just how many foreign workers can enter any country while social cohesion is maintained. Even with the incredible flexibility in the labour force exhibited by Malaysia in the early 1990s, there were limits as to how far this source of non-inflationary growth could go.

Of course, underlying the problems in Malaysia and elsewhere was the constant and rapid movement of Chinese agricultural labour into the Chinese manufacturing workforce. Malaysia's imported workforce extended its competitiveness, but the price of Chinese labour was even lower than the labour that Malaysia was able to import. The current account deficit was not improving and local capital was rushing for the exit. Should foreign capital form the same opinion as local capital, there would be severe downward pressure on the ringgit.

Risk premiums

14 October 1996, Indonesia

The story of 1996 for Indonesia has been rising risk premiums: the Megawati riots, Suharto's health problems, the Astra/Sampoerna debacle, the widening of the currency bands. Now comes another rise in the risk profile with the news that five people have been killed and Christian churches burned in East Java.

The Christian population is largely Chinese. So valuations for equities have been falling through the year in Indonesia as the market has made little progress while buoyant earnings growth has continued. However, the risk profile is rising and this is particularly important when combined with the widening of the currency bands.

The likelihood of Bank Indonesia being continually forced into a loose monetary policy by a surge of capital inflows is decreasing rapidly. Indeed with the wider currency bands and a deteriorating capital inflow outlook, the authorities now have the flexibility to tighten monetary policy. It is time to be underweight the Indonesian market.

On 27 July 1996 a mob, organised by the Indonesian military, stormed the headquarters of the Indonesian Democratic Party. The party's leader, Megawati Sukarnoputri, the daughter of former President Sukarno, was seen by the establishment as a threat to the continuation of the rule of President Suharto and there were elections due in early 1998.

The attack on the headquarters was part of a wider attempt to remove Megawati as head of the party. Five people died in the fighting that day and many were injured both then and in the riots that followed in Jakarta. It was not just such overt political problems that Indonesia faced in 1996. There were also deeper more dangerous divides in the country.

Indonesia, like Malaysia, had a wealth divide partially based along lines of religion and race. The Chinese diaspora had been deeply involved in business throughout Asia, often for centuries. They were citizens and often they were particularly successful in business. The wealth and power of the Chinese population, particularly in Southeast Asia, were often resented and many families that were ethnically Chinese had gone to great lengths to assimilate.

In Indonesia, the country with the world's largest Muslim population, the situation was further complicated by the fact that many of the powerful ethnically Chinese population were Christian. In an economic downturn in any country there is always a risk of tension between the haves and the have-nots, but in Indonesia there were added layers of ethnic and religious tension.

Investors in Indonesia and elsewhere in Southeast Asia were increasingly aware that social unrest could form part of the uncertainty that clouded the outlook. In an economic expansion, these were risks that were simply not considered; but in an economic contraction, these were risks that few investors, local or foreign, were well equipped to access.

Many foreign investors had invested in companies that were controlled by families that were ethnically Chinese and some were also Christian. Few investors ever considered that the ethnicity and religion of a company's controlling family were relevant in assessing the likely return from investing in its shares. However, if Indonesian society blamed such businesspeople for their economic woes, could they continue to control their lucrative local franchises? What would a change in control mean for minority shareholders?

The divides in Indonesian society raised some very difficult questions for foreign investors as the economic situation deteriorated. Some assessment of just how socially cohesive a society might be in an economic downturn is an essential consideration for any investor and one simply taken for granted in most developed world countries. Failure to understand societal reactions to extreme economic pressures cost investors dear in Asia in this period and regularly resulted in large losses in Latin America.

Portfolio investors in particular rely upon the continuation of a rule of law that allows them to enforce their property rights in a court before an independent judiciary. If an economic contraction threatens the continuation of the rule of law, then investors can, and have, lost everything. The Indonesian economy was still doing well in October 1996, but the murders in East Java and the burning of churches showed that dangerous social tension was not far below the surface.

More loan defaults

18 October 1996, Thailand

This market is still too risky. A few weeks ago Somprasong was rumoured to be defaulting on its loans. The company denied the story, pointing out that their assets were still valued at higher levels than their liabilities and thus the sale of some assets would restore the company to health.

Today, Juldis Development announced that they would be defaulting on some interest payments, but they would be selling some assets to meet capital repayments. According to an article in today's *Bangkok Post*, the following companies are also pursuing the same policy: First Pacific Land, Ban Chang, Univest Land and Rattana Real Estate.

In case these parties have failed to notice, there has been a complete deliquification of the property market in Thailand. This is a common trait in Asia where faith in the long-term capital appreciation of property deters sellers from cutting prices and thus a clearing price is not reached. If Somprasong and Juldis are liquidating property assets simultaneously, won't this push prices lower, particularly if other developers have decided that selling their assets is the only way to avoid debt defaults?

Finally, and most worryingly, both Juldis and Somprasong have outstanding convertible bonds. These provide the cheapest possible financing for any corporate in Thailand. Despite this, both corporates face the prospects of defaulting on their debts. If this is the plight of the companies with the cheap financing, then those companies without such financing must really be feeling the pinch.

Who carries the can on debt defaults? The banks and finance companies – but particularly the finance companies who have loans secured on property. This squeeze on their revenue is occurring at a time when the larger banks are less keen to buy finance companies' commercial paper. This is pushing up the borrowing costs for finance companies just as revenues are falling and their assets are being written off. The consequences, like gravity, are inevitable. The strength in the Thai market today presents another excellent opportunity to exit from what remains a high-risk investment.

It is always tempting at the end of a bear market to proclaim that the bad news came as a surprise and nobody could have foreseen it coming. The complete meltdown of the Thai credit system was very apparent at least eight months before the authorities were forced to devalue the Thai baht exchange rate and almost two years before the price of Thai equities stopped falling. This of course was no ordinary business cycle or credit cycle. But that it was to be something that challenged the very solvency of the financial system was already fairly evident by the second half of 1996.

I had attended the presentation in Edinburgh for the IPO for Somprasong Land just a few years before. We received a detailed list of the property the company owned and some delightful artist's impressions, they always are, of the buildings they would build there.

Over lunch, the company's chairman and managing director, Prasong Panichpakdee, discussed a wonderful piece of land that the company owned not far from the Mandarin Oriental in central Bangkok. I was confused that such a prime piece of real estate had not been mentioned in the presentation we had just seen. At this stage, the chief financial officer of the company intervened to explain to the chairman and managing director that the company did not own that piece of land but that he owned it personally!

That the apparent rainmaker behind the company did not understand the difference between company property and personal property was a real red flag. We did not partake in the IPO. On 28 October 1996 the Thai police announced that they were looking to arrest Prasong on fraud charges.

While financial market practitioners could see that something was wrong in Thailand – we didn't know how wrong – other analysts continued to produce incredibly optimistic analysis on the outlook. As late as October 1996, the World Bank had published a report entitled *Thailand's Economic Miracle: Stable Adjustment and Sustained Growth*. Within a year, Thailand was at the door of the World Bank's sister organisation, the IMF, seeking an emergency bailout!

It seems unfair to single out anyone specifically, but chosen at random from the bookshelves in my study, I present the titles of two books: *Time for Thailand: Profile of New Success,* published in 1996; and *Thailand's Boom*, also published that year. The authors of *Thailand's Boom* were nothing if not entrepreneurial. By 1998, the book had been updated and sold as *Thailand's Boom and Bust.*

Having your cake

29 October 1996, Malaysia

The currency jitters come just when Malaysia needs them least. Figures released yesterday showed that loan growth continued to power ahead at 28.5% while M2 growth remained much lower at 19.9%. The loan-to-deposit ratio of the banking system is rising rapidly through 90% and loan growth will have to slow. This will be exacerbated if Bank Negara's recent intervention to buy back ringgit is sustained for any prolonged period of time. In short, liquidity is already tightening up.

Sometimes economic slowdowns come over prolonged periods in which both debtors and creditors become gradually more cautious. The slowing in credit growth that follows negatively impacts economic activity and asset prices. However, sometimes the credit system is going full steam ahead and is stopped very suddenly by a sudden change in perception.

While the deterioration in credit conditions was already impacting growth and asset prices in Thailand, a full-steam-ahead credit boom was still underway in Malaysia and elsewhere. Despite growing caution among foreign investors that Thailand's problems were not unique, the locals in Malaysia continued to add to their gearing.

How likely is it that a banking system growing its loans at 28.5% per annum, as the Malaysian banking system was as late as October 1996, is focused on the credit quality of those loans? Is it possible to find 28.5% more loans every year that have the same high credit quality as the loans you made the year before?

One of my first meetings as a young fund manager had been with a banker from the US Midwest. This was in 1991: things had been tough in the Midwest for a long time and a US recession was then underway. Realising that I didn't know much about banking, he passed on what he considered to be the most important advice to any investor in bank equity: "If it grows like a weed, it is a weed." The Asian banking systems had grown like weeds for many years and by late in 1996, with the exception of Thailand, that growth still showed no signs of stopping.

Ourselves alone

30 October 1996, Indonesia

Can Indonesian authorities afford to continue to milk foreign investment for private gain? It may seem an irrelevant consideration for equity investors in Indonesia, but it is the crucial question to be asked by all long-term investors. The arrival of FDI in Indonesia has been the most important key variable in lifting the Indonesian economy from its sick bed.

This capital inflow has reduced the prospects of a currency crisis, reduced interest rates and increased economic capacity. Without it, Indonesia would struggle to finance a current account deficit which will be around 8.5% of GDP this year (second only in magnitude in Asia to Thailand). Without significant capital inflows, these three positives would be reversed. Yet despite the essential nature of such capital flows, the authorities in Indonesia continue to milk such capital inflows for private gain.

The debacle at Astra has brought Indonesia into conflict with two of the world's largest companies (GM and Toyota) and the world's three largest trading blocs (the EU, the United States and Japan). Daewoo Motors has already cancelled an extension of its facilities in Indonesia. Another money-spinning ruse now threatens to bring Indonesia into conflict with Fedex and UPS, and hence the US administration.

The Ministry of Transportation has announced that no foreign cargo plane may land in Indonesia – with the exception of Batam Island. All cargo will then be transhipped from Batam to other areas of Indonesia by local carriers (no prizes for guessing who owns these airlines).

Reaction from the United States is likely to be swift and the impact on economic efficiency is clearly not positive. But wouldn't any tenant seek to maximise rents from a property as their tenure becomes increasingly short? If this is the motivation behind these recent moves, then there is more to come and FDI approvals and realisation rates are unlikely to increase from the current high levels.

Asia was rife with crony capitalism, but it was a practice that was largely ignored by foreign investors. Indeed, many foreign investors considered that they wanted to invest in such 'well-connected' companies likely to get the key deals and franchises from government that usually assured supra-normal returns on capital.

The Chinese population of Asia had a name for such a form of capitalism, *guanxi* capitalism, with *guanxi* loosely translated as 'connections'. In Indonesia, President Suharto and his family were ensconced at almost every nexus of the economy. As the piece above shows, there were almost no lengths they could not go to to extract another form of 'commission' from the trade and capital flows that made up the life-blood of the economy.

The same foreign investors who not just tolerated but endorsed such behaviour in the economic boom, labelled it as crony capitalism in the economic bust. This was a very different form of capitalism where rule by one person was more important than rule of law, but foreign investors treated it as if it entailed the same risks. Foreign capital was at best amoral and perhaps immoral as it sought to ride on the coattails of such rent-seeking activity and hypocritical in condemning it when things went wrong.

How the Suharto family business interests were to be dealt with in the economic crisis severely complicated the bailout plan proposed by the IMF. The rent extracting was ramping up in late 1996 but nobody cared – until they did.

Changing of the guard

2 December 1996, Hong Kong

In Hong Kong's Pacific Place there is a shop called King & Country. The shop specialises in toy soldiers, in particular British and latterly US regiments. Two months ago, they introduced the PLA solider to their range. It is out-selling the British toy soldier by two to one.

The PLA soldier is trading at a 7% premium to the British equivalent. The price of a PLA solider is HK$200 (US$25), which is the equivalent of one month's wages for the real thing when joining the Special Administrative Region (SAR) garrison. So will there be any further changes at King & Country as we head towards the change in sovereignty? Yes. They had decided to discontinue the governor by July 1997. There's only one problem. The governor has already sold out!

All or nothing

3 December 1996, Thailand

OK, so corporate Thailand is now aware that there are increasing dangers in borrowing US dollars to fund investment in Thai baht assets. A new approach to funding is necessary. Phatra Thanakit, TPI Polene and Siam Commercial Bank are all launching yen-denominated Samurai bonds. In total, the three hope to raise 22bn yen to finance their investments in Thailand and shed that high-risk US dollar debt. Indeed a cunning plan.

Reality is not easily digested as a credit boom comes to an end. Any number of ways will be sought to extend it. The fact that leading Thai companies thought it could be extended by simply exchanging one form of foreign currency risk for another just showed how desperate things had become. They just could not afford to borrow baht at the then high prevailing interest rates.

With the consequences from the status quo of large US dollar borrowing increasingly looking like bankruptcy, doubling-up suddenly seemed like an attractive option. If the yen continued to decline then this bet on replacing US dollar debt with yen-denominated debt could solve the growing balance sheet problems in just one transaction.

The more corporate management's answer to their problems smacks of the last bet on red 36 at the roulette wheel, the more worried you should be. The yen did decline until August 1998, but by that stage Thai corporates had even more to worry about than the cost of their foreign currency debt.

A bang or a whimper?

6 January 1997, Japan

The recent events in Japan are positive for Asian and global equities if the BOJ/Ministry of Finance decide to remedy Japan's ailments in the tried and tested way. We have argued before that the current high level of global equity markets is due to the lax credit policy of the BOJ. It now appears that while this liquidity has been successful at inflating global equity prices, it has not succeeded in sustainably reflating the Japanese economy. So what do the Japanese authorities try next?

Should Hashimoto stick to his election pledges, then a fiscal solution is ruled out. This will leave the BOJ to either act further to combat the economic slowdown or watch while growth disappears and the problems of the banking system are amplified. Further action by the BOJ is thus likely and even more easy money is likely. (Significant market deregulation is an option but is politically sensitive and would probably not boost activity in the short term.)

Thus the BOJ is about to provide more easy money and is also probably less likely to be concerned about any further weakness in the yen (US politicians and businesspeople may be more concerned). With the BOJ having to work harder at the monetary pump, then global excess liquidity will remain high and global equity markets can continue to move higher.

There are two potential worries for Asia in the short term. If the BOJ provides further liquidity and asset prices in the United States suffer from further 'irrational exuberance', will Mr Greenspan pull the trigger on interest rates? A weaker yen may be targeted and this would compel the Asian governments operating currency policies to force their currencies up in line with the US dollar. However, on balance, the markets' indications on Japanese growth are a positive for global equities and Asian equities. If the markets' signals on growth are correct, then this global bull market in equities is set to end with a bang and not a whimper.

The more investors could see continued weakness in the Japanese economy, the more they could see yen weakness and the improved prospects of borrowing yen to profit from investment overseas. This weakness should have created an even greater flow of yen-leveraged money into Asia, but increasingly through 1997 the growing capital losses in Asian equity and fixed interest securities discouraged such trades.

That Japanese banks had increasing solvency problems played a role in now reversing the yen carry trade. With their capital positions threatened by bad loans at home and the value of their overseas assets growing, at least as reported in yen terms, Japanese banks were increasingly capital constrained.

The enforced caution in relation to any further offshore lending was another force driving the ebbing of the tide of capital from Asia. There was more to assessing the direction and magnitude of the carry trade from Japan than just the level of the yen exchange rate.

Banker pays

6 January 1997, Thailand

Evidence continues to mount that the commercial banker (and the shareholder therein) is expected to pay the price of reflating the Thai economy. As already highlighted, this will take the form of thinner net interest margins and possibly some government-directed borrowing.

Another strand to this 'banker pays' approach was outlined at the weekend. The BOT governor, Rerngchai, announced that a Thai equivalent of the RTC (Resolution Trust Corporation) will be set up to purchase non-performing loans from the banks. This will be at least partly funded by the banks themselves.

In other words, some of the capital of the strong banks will be used to alleviate the problems of the weak banks. The capital structure of this body was not announced, but any significant equity injections from the stronger banks would clearly be another negative for their shareholders.

The US authorities healed their ailing banking system via creating a steep yield curve. This was very beneficial for the banking sector as profits were boosted and low interest rates reflated asset prices. However, this remedy is not available to the BOT (due to the fixed exchange rate) and the need to reflate the economy will thus create negative repercussions for bank profitability.

Every day there is more evidence of this dynamic. This banking cycle will be very different from the US banking cycle – keep your powder dry.

A potential bank collapse will always bring forth government plans to shore up the financial system. Invariably a plan will be found that works, given the consequences of a collapse of the banking system. However, it is not always the first plan that works, and the plan that works is not necessarily good for those who own bank equity in either the weak banks or the strong banks.

In the 1980s, in the United States, the central bank kept short-term interest rates low and the steep yield curve that ensued allowed banks to borrow short and lend long at great profit. This was a form of surreptitious recapitalisation that met with little political backlash, required limited government capital and did not need to force strong banks to bail out weak banks.

The owners of bank equity capital benefited greatly from this mechanism. That mechanism was not available to the Thai authorities as in managing their exchange rate they had lost control of interest rates. Something more direct would be necessary.

Thailand proposed government intervention that involved a huge political choice as to how much capital to leave in the banks depending on what price the bad assets were bought for. The authorities proposed weakening the balance sheets of the strong banks by forcing them to fund the purchase of assets from the weak banks.

The uncertainty for investors in bank equity capital was now increased by this announcement and the prospect of raising further capital, at least until the price of the purchase of bad assets was announced, was all but eradicated. Things were to get much, much worse for the Thai banking system before a way was to be found to flush the system with fresh capital. Anything that delayed the arrival of that new capital was prolonging the agony. In January 1997 the proposed government action to solve the problem was making things worse, not better.

Follow the money

15 January 1997, Regional

One of the most important questions for the Malaysian equity investor is: what is the size of Malaysian long-term capital inflows? With an increasing number of foreign investment announcements, this capital outflow can be expected to increase. If this offsets long-term capital inflows, then Malaysia will be more reliant upon short-term capital inflows.

At a meeting with Bank Negara last week, a deputy governor revealed that long-term capital outflows could be around RM7bn in 1996. This will very likely exceed long-term capital inflows. In 1995, FDI approvals were just RM9bn. Thus long-term capital inflows would have to exceed 78% of FDI approvals to produce a surplus long-term capital inflow!

Indonesia's problem is too much capital. In September, there was a dramatic change in tactics by Bank Indonesia. With the rupiah moving constantly to the strong end of its new bands, it was decided that a more direct approach to currency management was necessary. As the widening bands failed to frighten away 'hot money', the authorities decided that a forced depreciation of the currency and a reduction in interest rates would produce the desired retreat.

Yesterday, we discovered the price of this tactic – foreign exchange reserves have risen US$2.7bn since the end of September to end December. Not surprisingly, overnight interest rates have tumbled from an average of 12.9% in October to 8.9% yesterday. This strongly suggests that any sterilisation of this intervention has been at best partial. This rise represents 2.5% of M2 and 11%

of M1. It is thus not surprising that an equity market which had gone sideways through 1996 to September has since risen 21%!

The key question for the equity investor is how long can this unsterilised intervention be sustained for? Answering that question is extremely difficult. Perhaps they can sustain the current policy for months or maybe it's just days – the one-month interbank rate fell 47bp yesterday! For the equity investor, this means that uncertainty is high and thus it is dangerous to take a large 'bet' on the Indonesian market.

It was no secret that Asian current account deficits were increasingly funded by short- and not long-term capital inflows. I brought this issue up constantly with investors, but they considered it to be a rather obscure piece of data that was irrelevant given how strong total net capital inflows were.

Just how strong total capital inflows remained in Indonesia was shown by the major jump in the country's foreign reserves in the final quarter of 1996. They were to continue to rise until the end of the second quarter of 1997, when Thailand devalued the baht. The growing travails of Thailand were not yet discouraging capital inflows to the region. The economist Herbert Stein famously said: "If something cannot go on forever, it will stop." It did stop in Asia, but even by January 1997 capital continued to pour into the region.

Meat and drink

15 January 1997, Indonesia

According to yesterday's *FT*, a corporation associated with the First Family will be given the exclusive rights to print labels identifying food as halal. Within the new system, the producers themselves will be given responsibility for certifying that the food has been prepared in the appropriate fashion.

This is disturbing Muslim leaders who see their own role in this process as integral. The price per sticker of Rp10 also appears on the high side. This is very delicate ground for any capitalist and certainly for the First Family. In 1857, the Indian army was rife with dissent but the catalyst for the Sepoy mutiny was the use of cartridges greased with cow and pig fat (the Sepoys had to bite the top off these cartridges).

Religion, politics and money are a volatile cocktail and they are increasingly mixed in Indonesia. Uncertainty and risk are rising in Indonesia.

Anybody who bought Indonesian equities unaware of the corruption at the heart of the economic system was not reading the newspapers. Perhaps they were reading the reports of stockbrokers who were loath to mention such activities. The president, his family and their chosen business associates were heavily involved in the stock market and could also be the source of lucrative capital issues for the financial community.

Many investors believe that they will only receive old information in the newspapers and thus they are not worth reading. Any investor who didn't read *The Jakarta Post* during this period was missing the main story.

Jardines no more

31 January 1997, Hong Kong

The Hong Kong police force has had a new insignia designed to reflect the fact that they will soon cease to be 'Royal'. The new insignia features the Hong Kong waterfront and its distinctive buildings. However, Jardine House has been removed. In an effort to remove all colonial connotations, it was thought appropriate that Jardine House be removed. So farewell then Noble House.

Jardine Matheson is a company owned by a British family that had seen many of its Chinese assets sequestered by the Chinese Communist Party (CCP) after world war two. It had moved its operations to Hong Kong but had recently restructured the legal ownership of those businesses through offshore companies in preparation for the handover of Hong Kong to the PRC.

Their HQ remained in Jardine House, however, a building that when completed in 1972 was the tallest in Asia. Being on the harbour and with large round windows, it is easily identifiable today though dwarfed by neighbouring buildings. Because of those round windows, presumably, it is known locally as 'the building of a thousand arseholes'.

The Midas touch

4 February 1997, Emerging markets

The most recent report from the Institute for International Finance (IIF) focuses on the prospective demands for and use of capital in emerging markets. While the IIF expects the current account deficits of emerging markets to rise by 40%

in 1997, there will also be an acceleration in capital inflows. On the IIF's figures, there will be US$240bn in capital inflows to finance the US$150bn of current account deficits plus domestic capital outflows.

It is interesting that the IIF has calculated that 30% of all capital flows into the emerging markets go towards boosting the foreign exchange reserves of the respective central banks. While the foreign investor receives physical and financial assets priced in the emerging market currencies, the local central bank gets foreign currency (usually US dollar) assets in return. Should the emerging market central banks not intervene in the currency market, the impact would be to push local currencies higher rather than accelerate the accumulation of foreign exchange reserves.

In the broadest sense and in the long term, it is arguable that the foreign investor must suffer from the Midas touch when these exchange rates are fixed. In the initial stages, when too much capital hits a fixed exchange rate regime, a rapid monetary and economic expansion usually ensues. This is a positive for equity and property prices. However, to the extent that these phenomena attract even further capital inflows, there is too much liquidity with inevitable consequences for inflation and competitiveness.

King Midas initially enjoyed his new-found powers, but came to renounce them in due course. However, in this case, the fault lies not with the greed of Midas, but rather the inflexibility of emerging market politicians with regard to currency stability. If this structural analysis of the problems with emerging market equities is correct, then it is clearly important for the foreign equity investor not to overstay their welcome. In short, perhaps emerging markets (with fixed exchange rates) are not the excellent long-term investment we assume, but a series of liquidity parties with ensuing hangovers.

The asset allocation of the Foreign & Colonial Investment Trust for 1868 is published in a new *FT* publication, *Investing With the Grand Masters*. It is interesting that two-thirds of the fund was invested in equity markets which are still considered emerging markets today, 129 years later!

Anyone in the financial markets could see that investors were beginning to reconsider their commitments to emerging market equities. This did not necessarily mean that they would stop investing, but the IIF forecast that the huge capital inflows would continue and also easily finance current account deficits was wildly optimistic. The IIF was ideally placed to make forecasts on such capital flows as it was owned by the very banks that were instigating much of that capital inflow.

Sometimes even being close to the source of something isn't enough to help you see that Stein's law is invariably correct – but when? The sudden stop and the reversal of these flows, by portfolio investors but also by the banks that owned the IIF, were now only a few months away. By Christmas 1997, these same banks would be locked in meeting rooms contemplating the bankruptcy of South Korea – then the world's 11th largest economy.

Of course, there was more to capital inflow than just portfolio flows and credit provided by foreign banks, and Asia had been a major beneficiary of FDI. However, this too was already clearly slowing and the accelerated opening of the Chinese economy to foreign investment was redirecting capital inflows to China.

In 1994, annual FDI inflows to China were US$33bn, but they had jumped to annual inflows of US$45bn by 1997. If China was to get an increasingly large share of capital inflows, this left other emerging markets, with already very large current account deficits, struggling to maintain their exchange rates while running monetary policy supportive of economic growth.

China may have been a small portion of the Asian equity indices and thus have attracted limited portfolio flows, but FDI flows were unconstrained by the tyranny of benchmarks. As more and more FDI flowed into China, the rest of Asia sought capital from less stable sources.

A key problem for the investor focused on liquidity analysis in a managed exchange rate is, of course, that it is very difficult to track capital flows in real time. The external account data is reported quarterly and often comes with a large lag. The composition of those capital inflows disclosed as part of the external account data is very important but not always easy to discern. The data is not always clean and can be severely distorted.

There are numerous tax incentives, usually associated with foreign investment, that create arbitrage opportunities for local investors who want to dress up their investments to look like foreign investment. Analysing capital inflows and capital outflows is essential but still fraught with difficulty. Throughout the Asian crisis I focused on the monthly foreign exchange reserve data as the best proxy through which to track capital flows.

When a country manages its exchange rate, its foreign reserves rise if it is intervening to prevent the exchange rate appreciating and decline if it is intervening to prevent the exchange rate from falling. The foreign exchange reserves are thus the balancing item in the balance of payments and tell you whether there is more buying or selling of the local currency at the targeted exchange rate.

This data comes out monthly and provides some early indication as to whether the net capital inflows are improving or deteriorating. Changes in the monthly foreign exchange data became a bit of a fixation for me during this period and it took a while for institutional investors, focused on selecting equities, to grasp the importance of this monthly data.

The plateauing in foreign reserves and then their decline were very clear indications that the IIF was way too optimistic regarding net capital inflows. In any period of market history, one data series usually rises to prominence as the key indicator of the flows that count. In the Asian economic crisis, following monthly foreign exchange reserve numbers became imperative.

Of course, it is possible to lie about the value of one's foreign exchange reserves and this is exactly what the BOT did in this period by reporting its foreign exchange reserves on a gross basis. This is akin to a company reporting a balance sheet that deliberately chooses to ignore its liabilities. It entirely misrepresents the company's position and the BOT, by failing to report its foreign currency liabilities, did exactly the same thing.

While it was true that the bank did own the foreign currency reserves it reported, it had also been racking up foreign currency liabilities. Through various transactions, the BOT had effectively borrowed US dollars to bolster its war chest to intervene in the defence of the Thai baht. Any borrower of course has to one day pay back their liabilities, but the BOT did not report their liabilities and it looked like their foreign reserves were in robust health.

By early 1997, no market practitioner could be in any doubt that the BOT was very actively involved in defending the Thai baht exchange rate, but reported reserves were not declining. This was causing me some problems with institutional investors. The more I stuck to the dynamics outlined in the research highlighted in this book, the more anyone could point out that I had to be wrong because Thai foreign exchange reserves were not declining.

My assertion that net capital flows would cause downward pressure on the exchange rate and a defence of the exchange rate, leading to a decline in foreign exchange reserves, a tightening of liquidity and lower equity prices, did not add up. It almost added up, as all of those features had become part of the Thai market, but I could not understand why the foreign exchange reserves were not falling.

The idea that the BOT would misrepresent these figures seemed to be the only reasonable explanation, but to say that in public would have caused real problems for CLSA's operations in Thailand. I had no specific evidence that the reserves figure was misrepresented beyond the mystery of how we could watch the BOT spend US dollars to defend the exchange rate without their foreign reserves declining.

The Thai financial community is fairly small and the BOT had to borrow these US unreported dollars somewhere. Slowly news began to leak out, presumably originating with the counterparties to those BOT liabilities, that the bank was engaged in such operations. The rumours further undermined faith that the BOT was capable of defending the exchange rate as nobody knew exactly the extent to which their net reserves had already been depleted.

The authorities did not reveal the true position of their foreign exchange reserves until after they had moved to float the baht and even then they were only revealed under pressure from US policy makers through the IMF. Uncertainty is the enemy of stability and the BOT had just turned a key certainty, the level of the country's foreign exchange reserves, into perhaps its greatest uncertainty. This shift further exacerbated the capital outflows.

In the years since the Asian economic crisis, the world's central bankers have signed swap agreements that allow them to borrow foreign currency from each other. In a swap arrangement two central banks exchange currencies at the prevalent exchange rate. As both organisations are free to create as much of the local currency as they require, this is a quick and easy way for a central bank to effectively borrow foreign currency. The bank's assets rise, in the form of the foreign currency they now own, and their liabilities rise in the form of the new local currency they have just credited to the foreign central bank. This is not a commercial transaction with the risk that the access to foreign currency credit is pulled or will expire. It is a form of almost unlimited backing that few in the financial markets would bet against.

When those attempting to prevent an adjustment in market prices can create, with the stroke of a pen, virtually unlimited financial firepower to do so, most investors accept that they will succeed in halting an exodus of local capital seeking to cover its foreign currency liabilities. They don't always do so, but few investors have the financial resources and institutional fortitude to bet against such immense resources.

Would the existence of such swap agreements, particularly between Asian banks and the US Federal Reserve, have made a difference to the outcomes in Asia in this period? Would investors have seen such backing from the US Federal Reserve as making a devaluation of the local exchange rates almost impossible? Would capital have fled at the pace it did, leading to the economic chaos that ensued? Would the exchange rates have been devalued? Assuming that these swap lines created the stability in the exchange rate, what was the prognosis for the economies given that they still had huge current account deficits and their competitiveness was steadily being undermined by China?

The ability to borrow almost unlimited US dollars from the US Federal Reserve would probably have changed the nature of the economic adjustment in Asia and indeed a crisis situation may have been avoided, particularly in South Korea. However, it would have left the region likely suffering a death by a thousand cuts, stuck with increasingly larger current account deficits and a commitment, through borrowing ever more US dollars at the official level, to prevent the decline in domestic prices that would restore their competitiveness.

To act to effectively suspend internal price adjustments during this period of growing mobilisation of cheap Chinese resources would have likely produced a prolonged economic agony, particularly for Southeast Asia. Had Asian central banks had access to swap lines with other central banks during this period, particularly the US Federal Reserve, the Asian economic miracle would still likely have ended, but more with a whimper than a bang.

Should it stay or should it go?

11 February 1997, Thailand

Commentators on the current Thai baht currency battle continue to cite the size of Thailand's foreign reserves as underwriting currency stability. This argument puts the cart before the horse. The ability of the central bank to defend the currency is not in question, but the key issue is whether they are prepared to pay the price for defending it.

We have argued for over a year that the dynamics of the fixed exchange rate were likely to put upward pressure on interest rates, just as the economy needed lower rates. The current battle to sustain the exchange rate further exacerbates this problem and overnight interest rates briefly reached 30%! Yes, the BOT can continue to buy back baht, but this will result in sustainable, very high real interest rates. Even if interest rates move to just 10%, Thailand will be labouring under high real interest rates at a time when non-performing loans in the banking sector account for 7.7% of total loans and asset prices are still falling.

Investors appear to take it for granted that periods of pain are necessary in developed economies at certain stages in the economic cycle. In Asia, it has been a long time since investors have had to experience any of this pain, but that does not mean that an easy way out must be available. Forget the ability to sustain the current exchange rate regime; it does not matter. Further pain for equity investors is on the way whether the current currency policy stays or goes.

Developed world investors are not very familiar with 30% overnight interest rates. Brought up and educated in economics and finance in jurisdictions with flexible exchange rates, they expect interest rates to reflect inflation expectations.

In Thailand in early 1997, inflation was stable to falling and investors expected it to move lower: by 1999, Thailand was reporting deflation. Many of those investing in Thailand still expected interest rates to decline as inflation expectations declined. This mistake was based upon an analysis that transferred their understanding of economics from the developed world, with floating exchange rates, to the emerging world, with managed exchange rates.

One might have thought that lessons would be learned from using the same rules in two very different monetary systems. Perhaps for a while the lesson was learned, but in 1999 a new system of managed exchange rates was fixed in place through the creation of the euro. From 2011 to 2012, interest rates soared in key Eurozone member states while their inflation rates collapsed. That this could happen and would likely happen is something I had discussed in Hong Kong in 1998 with some of those proposing the creation of the euro.

It was during the Asian economic crisis that I met with a committee of the French Senate and concluded that the creation of the euro would not only create great economic damage in Europe, but also great social and political damage. The committee of about 16 had arrived in Asia to investigate the causes and consequences of the Asian economic crisis. I was asked to present to them – possibly because I had just been voted Asia's best Asian equity strategist, but much more likely because I happened to work for the subsidiary of a French bank.

I prepared a presentation along the lines chronicled in this book that put the blame for the massive imbalances, which had then been unwound, on the attempt to manage exchange rates. As most of Europe had already been running such policies and was about to solidify them through the creation of a single currency, I thought it would be informative to mention how the new single currency zone could create an economic disaster similar to the Asian financial crisis.

To put it mildly, this presentation did not go well. It was a long time ago now, but I remember that one member of the Senate rose to his feet to reply as he felt so strongly on the matter. He explained that someone who had not lived through war in Europe could not really understand the need to create a single currency. This single currency, he argued, would act to iron out economic inefficiency across Europe and make Europeans much more like each other, reducing any prospect of a future European war.

Living through the Asian economic crisis, I could not have disagreed more with his belief in the mechanism through which a single currency could breed harmony among disparate peoples. By the time of our discussion, people had already died in riots in Malaysia and Indonesia and the political turmoil seemed far from over. The crisis threatened to wipe out a form of Asian economic system that, for all its problems, was a product of the local culture and replace it with an alien, more Anglo-Saxon business system.

I suggested to him that the eradication of what he and economists liked to call 'inefficiencies' would mean eradicating what many people in Europe referred to as their culture. A single currency straitjacket aimed at creating efficiency would, through destruction of the inefficient, such as perhaps small businesses to the benefit of large businesses, lead to greater social tension within states and also between states. It seemed a policy likely to destroy rather than create peace and stability.

As soon as the translator had finished translating these comments, two other members of the Senate now stood up and started clapping and I was asked to leave the room. Outside the room, I asked the French consul who these two members were who seemed to also be concerned that a single currency would lead to less peace and cohesion in Europe. He replied that I should ignore them as they were representatives of the communist and fascist parties! I will never forget that a shiver went down my spine. It became clear to me then that if I was right on the economic consequences of the creation of a single currency, then the political beneficiaries of those consequences were likely to be Europe's political extremists.

Since then, the attempt to create a single currency has caused untold economic, financial and social damage across Europe. It has stripped millions of people of opportunities through high unemployment, created mass immigration of the young and materially depleted the power of local democracy. The extreme political parties have indeed benefited from the powerful eradication of inefficiencies that a French politician so accurately predicted would be reduced by the iron fist of a single currency.

What a tragedy that this man of such high and noble ideals had chosen a mechanism to enact them that continues to act to destroy them. There were key lessons for politicians to learn from the Asian financial crisis, but they were ignored in Europe and the consequence was a series of financial crises that continue to create a dangerous political backlash that threatens the socio-political stability of Europe.

Thar she blows!

13 February 1997, Global

The Great Sanhedrin, the early supreme judicial and legislative body of the Jews, consisted of 71 members. It had a rule that unanimous verdicts were invalid. The idea was that it could only be possible for its 71 members to agree in unanimity with each other if so induced by outside pressures, bribery or exceptional emotional circumstances.

Marc Faber, *The Great Money Illusion*, 1988

The cry of 'Thar she blows!' was instantly met with a unique mix of fear and greed on the whaling ships of yesteryear. Fear because many men lost their lives in pursuit of the whale, but greed because each man profited from every pound of flesh, bone and oil.

That mixture of greed, fear and frenzied activity is now more commonly found in the global financial market dealing rooms than the great whaling routes of the Indian Ocean. Today, the cry of 'Thar she blows!' refers to a further rise in the value of the US dollar. While few sailors ever lost respect for whale or sea, the sailors on the financial markets currently show an unhealthy lack of fear and a focused love of greed.

While the US dollar continues its rise, even the cabin boy continues to increase his profits. Yesterday, the lack of concerted effort by the G7 to depress the US dollar produced a cry of 'Thar she blows!' that rang out around the world. The cabin boy reached for his buy tickets. Global equity markets blew: Japan +1.3%, Singapore +1.3%, Malaysia +1.0%, Germany +0.9%, Netherlands +1.0%, Switzerland +0.8%, Hungary +1.7%, Turkey +1.2%, USA +1.5%, Mexico +1.4% and Brazil +4.3%!

The tipping point had not yet come. A strong US dollar had its negatives in terms of lower competitiveness for Asian countries and tighter liquidity as local central banks intervened to force their currencies up in line with the US dollar, but it also brought the prospect of even more yen 'carry'. It was only when the weakness of the Japanese banking system and capital losses on Asian investments undermined the flow of yen leverage to Asia that investors focused on the downside from the rise and rise of the US dollar. On the eve of Valentine's Day 1997, that downside was still not the focus of attention.

The mighty have fallen

13 February 1997, Thailand

Morgan Stanley Capital Indices continue to award the Philippines a smaller weighting than Thailand in the Far East ex Japan Free Index. A reasonable portion of the Philippines market cap is not considered appropriate for inclusion in a 'free' index. However, in market capitalisation terms (Datastream figures), Thailand has already become the smallest equity market in Asia, after China and Pakistan.

Based on these figures, the total capitalisation of the Thai equity market is now less than the US$63bn market capitalisation of HSBC Holdings! Indeed, HSBC's market cap is only marginally smaller than that of Indonesia and the Philippines. Remember, HSBC has a 100% free float, while Indonesia and the Philippines do not!

As the market capitalisation of Asian countries declined to remarkably small levels relative to other financial markets, it became a mantra among some to state that they must now be a buy. Why not buy the listed equity of a whole country for the same price you could buy the equity of one Hong Kong bank?

Given the major declines in equity prices that were to come, this approach to analysis proved to be deeply flawed. Equity is not an asset per se, but rather a bundle of assets and liabilities. While most of the assets, particularly the physical assets, survive recession and even depression, equity need not do so. When a company is unable to cover its interest expense, ownership of its assets can and often does pass to its creditors and equity is wiped out or suffers massive dilution.

There are very good reasons why the value of equity can collapse to incredibly low levels, relative to the market capitalisation of other equity markets, and still offer no value for investors. Equity is just that fine sliver of hope between assets and liabilities, and that sliver can be eradicated. If the price of assets unencumbered with debt or other liabilities looks incredibly cheap relative to other assets, then a good case can be made for investment.

Sometimes selected equities, with negligible liabilities, can have those characteristics, but in most cases the liabilities are large enough that the market capitalisation of the equity represents just a hope that title to the assets is retained and not the certainty that it is. Smart investors can make money investing in equities that have really become just options on asset ownership, but for most of us this should be classified as a dangerous sport.

The Citibank experience

14 February 1997, Thailand

Many analysts are proclaiming that yesterday's provision by TFB symbolises a recognition of the problems impacting the Thai banking system. Correct. Further, they assert that this is a buy signal for the banks. We beg to differ … in Thailand, there is no prospect of a recapitalisation as yet but equity prices and property prices continue to fall. Thus, the provisioning at TFB takes us beyond the denial stage, but it does not yet take us to the desperation stage.

How many fund managers will be queuing up to take Thai bank rights issues in eight or nine months' time? Not many, and particularly not those who bought on the news of higher provisioning in February 1997. However, it is when the banks are desperate for capital and when nobody wants to provide the capital, that bargains are to be found. Ask that gentleman in the Middle East who bought Citibank shares at US$12 in 1991; current price US$123!

In my first book, *Anatomy of The Bear: Lessons from Wall Street's Four Great Bottoms,* I looked at the four times in the 20th century when US equities became incredibly cheap. We know they became incredibly cheap because the returns in ensuing years were wonderfully high. All four of those bear market bottoms were associated with not just a regular recession, but also deflation or the expected deflation that threatens bank solvency.

In 1921, bank balance sheets remained solid as they were – post world war one – heavily invested in government debt, the price of which rose in a deflationary recession. In 1932, banks went bankrupt and closed and, in an era before deposit guarantee schemes, people's deposits were destroyed.

In 1949, the banks were once again full of government debt, the market price of which was held at non-market rates by intervention by the US Federal Reserve. Investors wondered what would happen to the price of these bonds and bank solvency when the US Federal Reserve stopped acting to inflate their price. In 1982, US banks had almost certainly eradicated their capital had they marked to market their loans to lesser-developed countries (LDCs), later rebranded as emerging markets.

Distress in the banking system has always been part and parcel of why a recession risks tipping into a depression. In recessions, investors worry that banks can no longer provide the credit that any economy needs and even, in extremis, that they cannot repay their depositors. These are both important factors in assessing the role of banks in a recession and a crisis, but banks play an even more important role in the reflation dynamic that creates and reverses a financial crisis.

As we have seen, it is commercial banks that create the money that is the life-blood of the economy. Without capital, banks cannot legally expand their balance sheets and create money. TFB's provision in February 1997 was finally a recognition of reality, but it did nothing to rebuild the capital base that was the essential step if Thailand were to enter a period of stability and then reflation. The time when Thai banks would be in a position to grow their balance sheets, create money and reflate the economy was still a long way in the future.

It is not easy to assess when commercial bankers are able and willing to extend their balance sheets. Commercial bankers are highly incentivised not to reveal the true scale of their capital depletion during a crisis. Should they do so, their creditors, in the form of those who lend them money on financial markets or even their depositors, are likely to ask for higher interest rates to compensate them for the growing risks of default or refuse credit at any price. A bank already suffering from a decline in the value of its assets and the likely ensuing decline in its capital will likely be in dire straits if it then also has to pay higher interest rates on its liabilities.

Throughout the crisis I was to focus on the imperative for bank recapitalisations before investors could expect to see the economic stabilisation that might augur expanding bank credit, expanding money supply at the end of the crisis and a rise in equity prices. The recognition of losses by banks was not a signal that they were on the verge of financing the credit expansion and reflation that would most likely bring the equity bear market to an end.

Those investors who bought shares in TFB following that first major provision for bad debts in February 1997 were to lose 80% of the value of their investment in local terms and even more in foreign currency terms by the time the equity market bottomed in 1998. Yes, it was true that the share price by the start of February 1997 had already fallen over 40% from its 1996 high, but when dealing with highly geared corporations, such as banks, such major declines in equity prices tell us very little about value.

In 2020, the price of TFB, now renamed Kasikornbank, traded just below the level it had reached at the time of that first major provision against bad debts in February 1997. The well-timed investment in Citibank mentioned in the above piece continued to be the gift that kept on giving as the share price rose to US$557 by 2006 – before declining to US$10 by 2009!

The equity owners of banks are often relaxed about or even unaware of the high level of gearing inherent in their investments. It was very clear in Thailand in February 1997 that there were many more negative impacts from that gearing to come. Management's dawning recognition of their balance sheet weakness was not of itself a buy signal for their equity.

Regional debt

19 February 1997, Regional

Increasingly, many fund managers are wary about building sums of US dollar debt in the Asian corporate sector. When significant sums of such debt are combined with a fixed exchange rate, it can lead a country into a monetary corner; witness Thailand.

There are therefore two risks for the investor. Firstly, to what extent does accumulating foreign currency debt take a country towards the Thai situation? Secondly, to what extent does the accumulation of foreign currency debt boost reported earnings growth at the expense of higher risk? Table 2.4 shows outstanding foreign currency debt maturing within one year divided by foreign reserves (figures as at end June 1996 according to the Bank for International Settlements (BIS)).

Table 2.4: Outstanding foreign currency debt maturing within one year divided by foreign reserves

	Short-term debt divided by foreign reserves debt	% of debt in private sector
South Korea	1.89	94.3
Indonesia	1.85	86.9
Thailand	1.21	96.2
India	0.37	78.3
Malaysia	0.36	88.5
China	0.23	83.5
Taiwan	0.22	97.5

There are two clear groupings shown in Table 2.4: South Korea, Indonesia and Thailand have foreign currency debt well in excess of their foreign reserves. Perhaps surprisingly, Indonesia not only falls into this section but has the second-highest ratio of one-year maturing debt to foreign reserves of all the Asian countries except South Korea.

More importantly for investors, these levels of US dollar debt in Indonesia also appear high in relation to the size of the economy and the listed corporate sector, to the extent that domestic corporates borrow US dollars and escape the strictures of the domestic yield curve and inflate their returns on capital (while accepting higher risk due to the currency exposure). However, it is more difficult to calculate the range of such profit distortion by market as one could equally argue that such debt levels should be compared to GDP or market capitalisation, as shown in Table 2.5.

Table 2.5: Private sector foreign currency debt in relation to GDP and market cap

	As % GDP	As % market cap
South Korea	16.8	57.2
Thailand	40.1	68.0
Indonesia	21.6	48.2
Taiwan	7.9	7.9
Malaysia	19.7	5.8
India	4.3	10.9

On this measure, Thailand and South Korea clearly stand out. However, whether on a GDP or market capitalisation basis, Indonesia is the market where the next highest levels of profit distortion are occurring. In Indonesia, few corporates manage to secure returns on capital above the risk-free rate. It appears that even the current returns on capital are being inflated by borrowing extensively in US dollars.

Clearly, the situation is not as bad as Thailand, but with limited evidence of any hedging of US dollar debt, the Indonesian corporate is being tempted by the 'honey pot' of cheap US dollars to inflate its return on capital. Needless to say, higher rewards come only at the expense of higher risks.

That all the commentary so far has focused almost exclusively on Southeast Asia will come as a surprise to most readers. It was driven by my belief that what came to be known as the Asian financial crisis was a crisis for Thailand and would trigger a crisis for Southeast Asia.

However, as I began to look at the foreign currency debt figures for all the countries in Asia, there was a growing concern that this could be more than just a Southeast Asian crisis. This piece in February 1997 clearly suggested that there could be problems in South Korea. I did not fully grasp the implications of this, which was a bad mistake.

Like many others, I reasoned that the South Korean economy could support higher levels of foreign currency debt than other Asian economies. The South Korean economy was dominated by very large export-orientated companies that earned most of their revenues in US dollars. It was normal for them to borrow in US dollars as they had US dollar revenues to meet their US dollar debt liabilities. Further investigation would have been a better approach when the data flagged up that South Korea's foreign currency debt levels, relative to GDP, were higher than even some of the countries in Southeast Asia.

What was even more alarming was just how much of the foreign currency debt was short term in nature. South Korea had been opening its capital account as part of the package of reform that allowed it to become only the second emerging market, after Mexico, to become an OECD (Organisation for Economic Co-operation and Development) member in December 1996.

Policy makers, business leaders and even the people of South Korea were concerned that opening the capital account might allow the takeover of local corporations by foreign entities. Thus the form of capital account opening pursued encouraged short-term capital flows, often in the form of offshore borrowing by local corporates, rather than the long-term capital inflows such as FDI or the takeover of local corporations.

The South Korean corporates had taken full advantage of the partial opening of the capital account by borrowing in foreign currency, primarily US dollar debt, and they were organisations already used to operating with high debt levels. The country's growth model was based on Japan, where commercial banks focused on providing very cheap funding for selected business groups known in South Korea as *chaebol*. This created a very concentrated business structure as the groups with access to cheap finance could out-compete those without such a subsidised cost of debt.

The top 30 *chaebol* accounted for around 85% of the country's industrial production and had an average debt-to-equity ratio of over 500%! That was quite a debt burden given that the debt-to-equity ratio for Japan was 193% and for the United States 154%. As the analysis above shows, it was known in February 1997 that a large portion of this debt was denominated in foreign currency and was of short-term duration. The general belief was that the *chaebol* would always be supported by both their captive commercial banks and the South Korean authorities, and that thus they could not face either liquidity or solvency issues.

That the *chaebol* could struggle to service their debt burdens was something that was becoming more evident. On 23 January 1997 the market learned that the 14th largest *chaebol*, Hanbo Steel, was in financial difficulties because of its over-close relationship with the government and the fraud inherent in that relationship.

By March 1997 Sammi Steel, the 26th largest *chaebol*, found itself with liquidity and solvency issues. A key driver of both companies' problems was also the massive overinvestment in steel production and the ensuing overcapacity in the industry they had been able to fund with cheap credit.

The South Korean system of subsidised lending from captive banks was supposed to ensure that these groups would never find themselves facing liquidity and solvency issues, but now they were. Foreign lenders had to reconsider the credit risk inherent in lending money to the *chaebol* if the lesson from the problems at Hanbo and Sammi was that the credit quality within the *chaebol* system was not as strong as previously assumed.

I was not the only one paying insufficient attention to the very large foreign currency borrowings by the South Korean corporate sector. When the Thai baht was finally devalued and the full force of the crisis unleashed in Southeast Asia, prices in the Korean Stock Market did not decline. Indeed, in those early months South Korea was one of the countries that pledged financial aid as part of the IMF support package for Thailand.

It was not until October 1997 that the market came to ask the question this research report should have triggered in February: 'How reliant is South Korea on the ability to roll over its US dollar debt and attract foreign capital?' In October 1997, the answer to that question was that it had lost the ability to refinance its short-term US dollar debt. The prospect was that the world's 11th-largest economy was about to go bankrupt. The vulnerability of South Korean corporates to collapse, evident from data long publicly available, turned what had been an Asian crisis into potentially a global crisis.

Anatomy of a bull market

20 February 1997, China

What are the defining characteristics of a bull market in equities? At the core of any bull market are two cyclical forces: the liquidity cycle and the earnings cycle. These rarely coincide for any prolonged period as the central banker usually likes to spoil such parties due to the potential inflationary consequences. However, during periods of structural change, strong corporate earnings growth and abundant liquidity can collide without panicking the central banker. The current bull market in US equities is built on the belief in such a major structural alteration.

In Hong Kong, there is no independent central banker to prevent the regular and explosive combination of the liquidity cycle and the corporate earnings cycle. As each day passes, these two key drivers become more supportive for equity prices in Hong Kong. Each day, China's (and hence Hong Kong's) economic recovery becomes stronger. Each day there is continued evidence that inflationary pressures in the United States are muted and thus the US central banker will not act to hinder the positive liquidity trends. The crucial question for investors is: does the death of Deng threaten to alter the outlook for the liquidity cycle or the corporate earnings cycle?

Political events in China can alter these two fundamental bull market building blocks. Following the Tiananmen 'incident', the animal spirits of consumers and investors in Hong Kong were so badly impacted that economic growth and earnings growth slowed. There were thus fundamental causes for the end of the bull market.

Can Deng's death produce a similar shock to Hong Kong's economic activity as the shocking and threatening events of 4 June? The potential repercussions for the Hong Kong people in June 1989 were of a much more serious and profound nature than they are today after the death of 'the paramount leader'. While the Tiananmen incident was a shock, the death of 92-year-old Deng cannot be described as an unanticipated event which will alter the behaviour of consumers and investors.

In June 1989, uncertainty increased dramatically, but Deng's gradual demise over the past few years has resulted in a limited rise in uncertainty on his death. If Deng's demise does not impact the outlook for economic and earnings growth, then it does not impact the key cornerstones of the current Hong Kong bull market. With no alteration in our economic outlook, recurrent Hang Seng EPS growth is forecast at 20.6% this year and 15.9% in 1998.

In short, the key building blocks of a bull market are intact in Hong Kong. The equity market appears fair value relative to its historical relationship with bonds. The PE ratio at 13× 1997 earnings remains among the lowest in the world, as the uncertainties regarding the transition to China decrease every day.

Elsewhere in Asia, investors fret over the high levels of corporate gearing, dangerous balance sheet currency mismatches and poor-quality management. In Hong Kong, gearing levels are at historically low levels, the peg to the US dollar is rock solid and Hong Kong management has delivered on the Asian growth miracle with a 17% compound annual growth rate (CAGR) in EPS over the past 23 years. While foreign competition threatens returns on equity across Asia, the power of Hong Kong *guanxi* in China is likely to continue to assure decent returns on equity for the foreseeable future. The Hong Kong bull market continues and Hong Kong equities remain attractive on a regional basis.

Deng Xiaoping died on 19 February 1997, just a few months before the handover of Hong Kong to the PRC. There was a sense of loss in Hong Kong. Deng had been a victim of the Cultural Revolution in China as had many of the people of Hong Kong who had fled that terror. That much of the prosperity of the colony emanated from the growth of the Chinese economy was apparent to everyone and everyone knew of Deng's key role in delivering the economic reform that had enabled that growth.

For many years investors pondered what Deng's death might mean for the continuation of that reform, the growth of China and the growth of Hong Kong. When it finally came, the answer was that it meant nothing. That this was so was perhaps Deng's greatest achievement.

The death of Deng occurred as a China mania raged in Hong Kong. In November 1995 I had written that it seemed a major capital inflow to Hong Kong was likely as Chinese corporations were instructed to buy Hong Kong assets. By 1997, there was also a stream of Chinese assets flowing into Hong Kong via a mechanism that became known as 'red chip' investment.

'Red chip' was the title for a mainland Chinese company that had achieved a listing on the Hong Kong stock market. These companies, it was argued, were the future as the colony of Hong Kong would very soon be transformed into an SAR of the PRC. From the summer of 1996 to the peak of the Hang Seng Index in the summer of 1997, investors could not get enough of red chips.

There had been mainland companies listed on the Hong Kong stock exchange for many years. In 1992, the Chinese regulatory authorities began to approve certain PRC corporations for listing on the Hong Kong stock market and these were known as H shares. Since 1992, foreign investors could also buy B shares of mainland companies listed on the Shenzhen and Shanghai stock exchanges.

Red chip stocks were something different from H and B shares as they were overseas-registered companies that had Chinese business assets injected into them. The crucial thing for their investors was the price that these new assets had been injected at and would continue to be injected at. While the H shares were part of a process strictly controlled by the Chinese authorities, the red chips were, it was argued, run by new Chinese entrepreneurs who could be relied upon to inject better-quality assets into the companies they owned.

The bulls argued that these new overseas registered and listed vehicles would see a prolonged period of asset injection at low prices. They were controlled by mainland investors with good *guanxi* who would ensure that the assets were both good and cheap, and thus they would see their own wealth, in the value of shares beyond China's strict capital controls, rise and rise.

With details on the quality and the true value of these injected assets very limited, anyone could speculate as to their true value and the speculation was that Chinese assets were going cheap. The index that tracked Chinese stocks listed in Hong Kong doubled in 1996 and then doubled again from January to July 1997. Even that spectacular rise did not do justice to the scale of the boom that was focused on IPOs.

The red chip IPO boom in Hong Kong was astonishing in its fervour. On listing, the price of these red chips usually soared – in late January 1997, the IPO for GZI Transport was 529 times oversubscribed and the share price closed 51% higher on its first day of trading. Other transactions consisted of using existing listed companies, often little more than shells, as the repository for asset injections. Investors who realised that Silver Grant would be transformed into a red chip could buy the shares at just HK45¢ in June 1996 and see the share price ascend to HK$5.95 by late August 1997!

I well remember the disgust at the phenomenon among experienced investors; one visiting senior investment professional described it to me as "That China nonsense – whatever they are calling it this time". From 1992 to 1996 there had already been booms and busts in H shares and B shares, and the unlucky who bought at the peak of the China mania saw the value of their investments more than halve. To most investors red chips were just old wine in new bottles, being low-quality companies dressed up, somehow then transformed into proxies for the future economic and profit growth of China.

By the time the fervour peaked the index of red chip shares was trading on 52× earnings and even the privatised H shares were trading on 30× earnings. The speculation in Hong Kong spread beyond the China story and in the two years running up to the handover of sovereignty to China, residential property prices rose 80%!

I saw the red chip boom as confirmation that investors would continue to pour money into Hong Kong to benefit from the combination of high levels of Chinese economic growth and the low US interest rates transmitted into the domestic economy through the operation of the currency board system. If the red chip boom attracted more capital into Hong Kong, then it would only add more fuel to the fire in terms of liquidity creation, as the HKMA was forced to intervene to create more Hong Kong dollars to prevent an appreciation of the exchange rate.

That portfolio capital had been pouring into the colony was evident to anyone in the stockbroking business, but it was also clear from Hong Kong's foreign reserves, which rose by 23% in the course of 1996. There was much more to come and those reserves rose a further 33% in just the first eight months of 1997, while the stock market boom continued. This was reflexivity on a grand scale. The more foreign funds were attracted to the local stock market, the greater the purchasing of Hong Kong dollars and the more Hong Kong dollars the HKMA had to create. The lure of China hardly seemed to be a passing phase and, despite the clear problems brewing in Southeast Asia, this positive reflexive relationship, I thought, could last a long time:

> The red-chip bonanza is thus likely to continue for some years and significant profits can be made as they have been by early investors in CITIC. The longevity of this particular boom does not mean that it is any different from any other. The profits reported are based on issuing high PE paper to buy low PE paper. The underlying assets can only produce growth in the hands of the correct management. In the absence of good management, when the game ends, the conglomerate will be only an accumulation of poor quality, low growth businesses. Many investors may not wish to participate in this current bonanza due to the risks involved.
>
> **Author's opinion**

That was an opinion I proffered in March 1997 and the boom ended in July! Given the likely ultimate denouement for this boom it was a recommendation based upon the greater fool theory. There was a clear lesson from the red chip boom that it just wasn't possible to work out when the world would run out of greater fools. According to Adam Smith:

> The really old generation, the greybeards, they're the ones with General Motors, AT&T, Texaco, Du Pont, Union Carbide, all those stocks nobody has heard of for years. The middle-aged generation has IBM, Polaroid and Xerox, and can listen to rock and roll music without getting angry. But life belongs to the swingers today. You can tell the swinger stocks because they frighten all the other generations. Tell him, Johnny, Johnny the Kid is in the science stuff.
>
> "Sir!" Johnny the Kid said, snapping to. "My stocks are Kalvar, Mohawk Data, Recognition Equipment, Alphanumeric, and Eberline Instrument."
>
> "Look at him the middle-aged fogey. He's shocked," the Great Winfield said. "A portfolio selling at a hundred times earnings makes

him go into a 1961 trauma. He is torn between memory and desire. Think back to the fires of youth my boy."

It was true I could hear the old 1961 Glee Club singing the nostalgic Alumni Song. "I loved 1961," I said. "I love stocks selling at a hundred times earnings. The only problem is that after 1961 came 1962, and everybody papered the playroom with the stock certificates."

Adam Smith, *The Money Game,* **1967**

Perhaps the advice I gave in June 1997 was more accurate:

The greybeards survived and made it to retirement with their GMs and AT&Ts. The middle-aged generation ended up owning what became the Nifty-50, but presumably sold too early as they were transformed into greybeards by the early 1970s. However, the swingers had one hell of a party and then one hell of a hangover. But what a party!

So with the Kalvars, Mohawks and Alphanumerics, run the Founders, COSCOs and Silver Grants. The only way to outperform in this market is to employ a swinger to buy stocks and a greybeard to tell them when to sell. At 32, I was already well progressed into the middle age of Asian investments. In my opinion this game is still on, but to be safe you'd be better off asking a swinger.

I was clearly too old for the greater fool game at 32 and not yet a greybeard, but time does march on. Even by 2020, the index that tracks the performance of the Chinese-affiliated stocks listed in Hong Kong remains well below the level it reached at the peak of the boom in late 1997. Looking back I would have thought that even by 1967 Adam Smith would have been aware that 'swinger' was perhaps not the best term to use to describe these new investors. Of course, maybe that just shows that he was already a greybeard.

The only way is up?

21 February 1997, Malaysia

Mastercard International publishes a bi-annual survey of consumer confidence in the Asia-Pacific region. This survey focuses on the employment outlook and quality of life issues, but respondents also reply regarding their outlook for the stock market. According to Brian Thom, senior vice-president for marketing, "Malaysians are certainly more upbeat about the stock market compared with respondents in the other countries surveyed, with most scoring in the region of 60 or less."

The Malaysian respondents' score for the local stock market was 84.7. With domestic sentiment towards equities so positive and foreign fund managers weightings close to all-time highs, this further suggests that this is not the time to be increasing exposure to the Malaysian equity market.

There are any number of sentiment surveys published regarding consumption and investment. They are always worth looking at. It is always easy as a financial professional to assess sentiment from those who surround you.

Among professional investors in Asia I could sense that sentiment was souring. What the sentiment indicators showed is that perhaps with the exception of Thailand, the people of Asia had no foreboding about what was to come. While it was true that some equity markets had already fallen significantly, could they really be buys if local sentiment was still riding high? Could we see the end of an economic downturn without first the average consumer and investors changing their behaviour to reflect a more conservative approach to their spending and investing?

The animal spirits of investors in some markets may have been dimming, but among the population at large the good times were very much seen as being here to last. On my travels in the region I would fly over the countries of Southeast Asia and wonder whether the tens of millions of people below understood the magnitude of what was likely to come. Could it really be possible that I knew something that would so profoundly impact their daily lives that they did not know?

For almost all of them, life was going on as normal and there was every reason to expect, as there had been the year before and the year before that, that they would become more prosperous as each year passed. Meanwhile, the capital that had financed the prosperity and forced excess money creation was increasingly ebbing away.

At last, synergy

25 February 1997, Malaysia

Chronicling the continued growth of Malaysia's overseas corporate empire has become a sad fascination for me. Why are Malaysians so keen to invest overseas while the world's emerging market investors continue to increase their investments in Malaysia? Are the investors best placed to know, suggesting that all is not rosy in the Malaysian garden?

While some of corporate Malaysia's forays overseas are clearly questionable, George Town seems to have hit upon the obvious geared investment based upon these current trends. George Town has just paid US$41m for the Swiss private bank Banque Financière de la Cité de Geneva and its associated bank in the Cayman Islands.

Capital flight comes in all shapes and sizes. The average citizen may have been blissfully unaware of the storm to come, but the cognoscenti seemed to be accelerating their capital outflow. Where such flows exist there will always be agents to facilitate them. In any country, but particularly in emerging markets, it is always worth befriending a few private bankers.

In my professional life I spent time mainly with investors who were managing large institutional funds for pension funds or life assurance funds. There was thus a veil between the end owner of these funds and me. When you spoke with private bankers the veil was partially lifted. They often did not run aggregated funds but discrete portfolios. They ran these discrete portfolios for locals and these were often very wealthy locals. While they advised their clients where the bank thought they should be investing, the end client often played a key role in deciding where to invest.

Private bankers are best placed to understand how local savers are reacting to economic changes. Their clients are often very well connected and understand the economic/political nexus much better than foreign analysts. In my experience they often have tales that would make your hair turn white about the degrees of risk their clients are prepared to take in bull markets. They also can tell you about shifts in local capital that the institutional fund managers and stockbrokers simply miss. What is even better, they are individuals who know how to entertain and they usually pay for the drinks!

It's year-end day!

27 February 1997, Japan

Following the excitement of Groundhog Day on 2 February, the next major event in the international calendar is 31 March – Japanese financial year end. Investors watch the Japanese corporate with the same acuteness that lunatics and newscasters gaze upon the movements of the groundhog. Will the Japanese corporate see its shadow and rush back into the yen or see sunshine ahead and maintain its US dollar positions? The first indications suggest a shadow. Mitsubishi Heavy Industries (MHI) announced yesterday that it will be repatriating US$700m into yen.

Japan is an incredibly large economy that never runs current account deficits. A country with a permanent current account surplus and a flexible exchange rate must be a net exporter of capital every year. It is tempting to believe this means that Japanese capital will always arrive to bolster non-Japanese asset prices.

However, the destination for Japanese capital can shift quickly, particularly when things start to go wrong. In aggregate, Japan was a net exporter of capital to the world in both 1997 and 1998, but its lack of enthusiasm for Asian assets played a key role in exacerbating the Asian economic crisis even as the country remained a large net exporter of capital.

Like Topsy

28 February 1997, Malaysia

Regular readers are about to be bored by yet another story regarding the mighty corporate empire being built by Malaysia. Mega Meisa, a vehicle trading company, will build a US$1.3bn coal-fired power station in Kazakhstan. The company will have a 70% stake in the project. Westmont Land is following up from its power barge in Mombasa by plunging into the Kenyan hotel business. It will also be bidding for power projects in Bangladesh and the United Arab Emirates. Renong also announced an interest in a project in Bangladesh.

There are thus two new countries which can be added to corporate Malaysia's growing empire (Land & General is already active in Kazakhstan). The list of 37 countries in full: United States, Cayman Islands, Guyana, Brazil, Chile, Argentina, Cook Islands, Liberia, Nigeria, Ghana, South Africa, Zimbabwe, Madagascar, Sudan, Kenya, United Arab Emirates, United Kingdom, Denmark, Switzerland, Croatia, Bosnia, Russia, Kazakhstan, Azerbaijan, India, Pakistan, Bangladesh, Thailand, Cambodia, Myanmar, Singapore, Indonesia, the Philippines, Papua New Guinea, Australia, New Zealand and Mongolia.

Some other facts about Malaysia. Malaysia has a population of 20 million. Of the total workforce, 20% is imported. The current account deficit is 4.5% of GDP. Loan growth is 27% and nominal GDP growth is 13%. The loan-to-deposit ratio of the banks is 95% and deposit growth is 20% and loan growth is 27%.

There is a property over-build in the hotel, office and condominium markets. The price to book ratios of the banks are approaching 3.5× as we near the top of the economic cycle.

The second section of the stock market has doubled in one year. Foreign investors' weightings in the market are approaching all-time highs in absolute terms and are at all-time highs in relative terms. Mastercard's Asian survey of consumer sentiment shows 84% of Malaysian respondents are bullish on the equity market; no other country in Asia has levels above 60%. The yen appears to be strengthening, thus threatening to raise the price of Malaysia's imports.

Many investors focus on the ability of this market to defy the gravity of value. Perhaps the value of gravity is already reasserting itself. Among the Asian markets, only Hong Kong, Thailand and Sri Lanka have produced lower returns than Malaysian equities year to date.

You can perhaps sense a growing degree of frustration in these comments. The macro data was absolutely screaming that Malaysia was on the verge of a major economic crisis, but the stock market was still marginally higher than when I had arrived in Asia in May 1995. Despite what I thought were very obvious signs of excess and the evidence of how such excess could be unwound coming daily from Thailand, investors in Malaysia just did not want to know.

The country had somehow got itself included in the MSCI Asia indices, the Emerging Market Index and even the Developed World Index! Portfolio investors allocating capital to Asia had equities from Malaysia, a country of just 20 million people, coming out of their ears. Their refusal to act on the macro data partially reflected the reality that they probably could not exit their commitment to Malaysia due to a lack of liquidity. Even individual savings institutions had holdings that were so large it would take them months to fully liquidate them.

Investment driven by benchmark considerations was proving to have some of the characteristics of a lobster pot about it. In a bull market, secondary market turnover is high and there is a plethora of primary market issues, and investors can build up large positions. When the tide turns, it is much more difficult to sell positions than it is to buy.

Given the sheer pain of attempting to liquidate in such a situation, most investors prevaricate and convince themselves that everything will be alright 'in the long term'. The decline in liquidity is an excuse to alter time horizons to justify an existing position despite clear evidence that it is not meeting expectations.

The decline in liquidity changed investors' mental state for the worse in Asia as they held on with Micawberish expectations that something would turn up. Indeed, something was to turn up, it was not what they expected and it was now just four months away.

Of the dust

3 March 1997, Thailand

On Saturday, Thai newspapers reported that the government has instructed Thai Danu Bank (the country's 12th largest bank) to bail out Finance One Plc. (The source for this information was given as "Officials in the BOT and at Thai Danu".)

All are of the dust, and all turn to dust again.

Ecclesiastes 3:20

All Thai finance company and bank shares were suspended from trading today. In a televised address, Amnuay announced the names of ten finance companies which had been given permission to raise capital. If the market would not provide sufficient capital for these ten companies, then the rehabilitation fund would be a purchaser.

Amnuay's measures fall far short of a cure for the problems in the Thai financial system. Only three of these ten finance companies are large enough to be listed and thus there has been no attempt to provide a cure for the financial system's ills. He also announced that all bank and finance company shares would remain suspended until "market conditions stabilised".

This indefinite restriction in the free market of the banking system's capital does not sit easily with Amnuay's policy of raising fresh capital for the Thai financial system. This suspension is a regrettable action which must compound investor fears that the Thais will resort to more formal restraints on capital outflows should the position worsen further.

Recognising the reality that you have an overvalued exchange rate that needs to be devalued very rarely comes quickly. It is an adjustment that brings its own form of pain – usually associated with the inability of the local private sector to repay the foreign currency obligations they used to finance their local currency investments.

Governments and central bankers will jump through many hoops to avoid being the central banker or the finance minister who has to devalue the currency. The problem for investors is that they have to predict what these 'many hoops' might be. The suspension of trading for Thai financials was a 'hoop' that most investors had simply not seen coming.

It was a desperate measure because by suspending share prices it lessened the prospect that investors could establish the correct price for providing fresh capital to the financial system. It was the sort of administrative response to a financial crisis that raised uncertainty for investors. What other such measures could come? What other negative impacts could flow to investors from the fiat of government? Given the increasing uncertainty associated with the actions governments would take to prop up their exchange rates, wouldn't it be better to move one's capital somewhere else?

Governments rarely understand how the measures they take to shore up certainty, usually by fixing the price of something, actually create the uncertainty for the investor that repels capital. The administrative measures that were implemented during the Asian financial crisis acted more to repel than attract capital. This was a major problem when the stability of the exchange rates, given the large current account deficits, relied upon attracting very large capital inflows. Rather than accept policies that might encourage capital to remain, government action often unintentionally served to expel it.

The hole in the balance sheet of the Thai financial system was just too big to be filled by raising new capital in March 1997. This was not a liquidity crisis; it was very much a solvency crisis, but it was clear that neither the commercial bankers nor the central bank understood that it was the latter. Nothing the BOT did created the scale of financial system recapitalisation that was already necessary.

That more capital was urgently needed was a lesson the Thai authorities were too slow to learn and ultimately they would still have almost certainly been required to devalue the exchange rate. More than ten years later the authorities of another country had to make the same call – were their banks suffering from a liquidity crisis or a solvency crisis?

On 13 October 2008, the US secretary to the Treasury brought the CEOs of the biggest US banks together and handed each of them a piece of paper. It explained how they would be selling shares to and accepting capital from the US government. They were supposed to sign it before they left the room. When the problem is a solvency crisis and not a liquidity crisis, it is capital that is needed and by March 1997 there was still no sign of new capital for Asia's banks.

CLSA received its fair share of opprobrium as part of the Asian governments' attempts to shore up their exchange rates. As the company that had flagged up the likelihood that the Asian exchange rate policies would eventually have to be abandoned, we were seen as conspiring against the local governments and peoples. I was advised by the heads of our local offices in both Thailand and Malaysia that I should avoid visiting either country as much to avoid civil suits as to avoid the attention of the local authorities.

It was not just that the governments were angry about the role the company was playing in warning about exchange rate instability, but many individuals, particularly in Thailand, had lost significant sums of money and were looking for someone to blame. At the height of the crisis the company had to increase security at its office in Bangkok; there were arrests at the office in Kuala Lumpur, but of course no charges; and some staff at foreign brokers in Jakarta were evacuated due to the rising social unrest. As time progressed, the phrase 'don't shoot the messenger' seemed to become a bit more than an aphorism for those of us responsible for advising investors in Asia.

Meanwhile, in March 1997, at the CLSA offices in Hong Kong, we had a visitor as the Oscar-winning actor Jeremy Irons walked into the office. He was in Hong Kong to film Wayne Wang's new movie, to be set at the time of the handover to China, called *Chinese Box*. He was playing a journalist and was apparently meeting a lot of people to help define his character. I'm not sure what he was doing in the office of a Hong Kong stockbroker, but it was run by a former journalist. With the handover of sovereignty to China just a few months away, the eyes of the world were increasingly upon Hong Kong in its final days as a British colony.

Liquidity problems

10 March 1997, Indonesia

According to the *Harian Ekonomi Neraca* journal, Prajogo Pangetsu (listed vehicle Barito Pacific – market cap US$1.3bn) is having trouble raising enough cash to keep its petrochemical, sugar and timber businesses afloat. Citing unnamed sources, the journal claims that the cabinet discussed last week whether it should continue to provide loans to Pangetsu's companies from the state-owned Bank Bumi Daya.

Institutional investors and their advisers focus primarily on what is happening to listed companies. This is a natural focus, but it is also a dangerous one. The unlisted private sector is a key part of the economy and trends in that sector are always important. In the Asian financial crisis, tracking trends in the unlisted corporate sector was particularly important.

In the form of capitalism that then existed, particularly in Southeast Asia, the families that controlled major listed companies often also controlled large unlisted companies. The links between these companies were often extensive and designed to transfer wealth from the listed vehicle, partially owned by institutional investors, to the unlisted entity often owned entirely by the family. Most investors knew that these wealth transfers were underway but accepted it as part of the cost of doing business in Asia. Some investors liked being aligned with the well-connected locals who could still sometimes create deals that could make money for the listed vehicle.

However, what none of us knew was just how much debt was in these unlisted vehicles. What collateral had been pledged against such debt? Could the shares of the listed vehicle have been pledged as collateral for the loan to the unlisted vehicle? Would the family be forced to liquidate their holdings in the listed vehicle to satisfy the collateral calls from their bankers? Would the family accelerate the process through which wealth was passed from the listed vehicle to the unlisted vehicle to shore up the balance sheet of the unlisted company? These were not factors that developed world analysts usually had to contend with and most emerging market investors had not fully considered the consequences of the links between listed and unlisted companies in an economic downturn.

In a country like Indonesia, writing about the links between the listed and unlisted vehicles was dangerous territory to venture into and physical violence against analysts who got too close to the truth was not unknown. With information thin on the ground, it was worthwhile reading the local newspapers. They were interested in all local stories and, unlike the investment community, did not care whether these stories concerned listed or unlisted companies.

Again and again throughout the crisis stories appeared in the newspapers concerning balance sheet distress in unlisted companies that did not register widely with the investment community. These stories were very important in explaining a growing distress in the system, but because they did not directly impact a listed company, they were ignored by most professional investors. Reading the local newspapers, some of which were available in English, provided an ample flow of information that distress was spreading across the economy.

The best local stockbrokers in any market will be on top of all local stories and the implications they have for the listed sector. Many foreign analysts, unfamiliar with the linkages between the listed and the unlisted sector and unfamiliar with the implications of high levels of corruption, will simply not understand why such stories are important. In emerging markets in particular, things are rarely as they seem and imposing a developed world template is fraught with danger. It is important to connect with and listen to locals who understand the political economy of their home nations.

More than once I was in a room to hear a foreign fund manager explain to a local management team how capitalism actually worked. The locals listened, as they were paid to do, but they knew that their form of capitalism worked very differently indeed. One of the greatest shocks for younger foreign fund managers in Asia during this period was to discover that the tools of analysis they had imported from a business school education ultimately brought little added value to understanding the *guanxi* or crony capitalism, depending upon one's opinion, extant throughout Asia. There were also greybeards among the investment community who knew how the game was played and their advice proved much more important than anything that could be generated through an Excel spreadsheet.

Minding the store

11 March 1997, Thailand

One of the key questions for investors in Thailand is: just how large is the property over-build? This will give an idea of how large a government bailout plan will have to be to reliquify the system. According to JLW, vacancy rates in Bangkok retail space had risen from 19% in June 1996 to 21% by year end. In suburban areas, the company estimates that vacancy rates may be as high as 50%.

The situation is unlikely to improve quickly in Bangkok with 400,000 square metres of space to be added in 1997, compared to 297,000 added last year. The expected economic slowdown is likely to lead to a slowdown in the take-up of retail space in 1997. An important part of any government bailout plan will involve greater control of the real estate market. If the property developers are simply flush with cash and left to their own devices, the temptation will be to rush to complete projects. This will further exacerbate the situation.

Should the bailout package permit the property companies to reduce their debt to the banks and cover their working capital expenses, there will also be a need to reduce supply and shore up property prices. Based on the JLW statistics for retail vacancy and supply statistics, there will be a lot of shoring up to be done.

I remember visiting Thailand in 1993 as a fund manager. The extent of the office property over-build was very evident and lots of people were very concerned about what this meant for the local economy and local bank balance sheets. That it took another four years for those chickens to come home to roost was something that I would never have forecast at the time of my visit. That it took so long was probably due to the fact that the bank lending boom continued and as long as there was plenty of money sloshing around the system, the value of property remained stable.

The banks were incentivised to lend even more money against property to play a role in keeping prices up and thus avoiding the write-down in the value of the property collateral that backed many of their loans. That I arrived in Asia in 1995 and began writing about the likely bust in Thailand was probably more to do with luck than anything. Had I arrived a year earlier, I would probably have written the same opinion then on the likelihood of a bust.

Who really knew when the veil would be lifted and the scale of the mal-investment and ensuing shocking credit quality be revealed? Would I have kept my job for that extra year when the crisis did not develop and the Asian economic miracle continued? I was lucky to arrive in Asia in 1995 when the unsustainable, more certainly by the summer of 1996, was beginning to look like it could not be sustained.

3 am Monday, 18 August 1969

18 March 1997, Global

In February, David Bowie successfully securitised the future income stream from his back catalogue and sold the resulting security for US$55m. Now Crosby, Stills and Nash are approaching the market (it was 3 am on Monday, 19 August 1969 by the time the band, then including Neil Young, made it onto the stage at Woodstock).

When global risk premiums are low and the spread on junk bonds is approaching new lows, this is the ideal time to securitise uncertain future earnings streams. The lower the interest rate which investors are prepared to accept, the higher the capital value for the new security. Thus the growing appetite for risk is likely to produce further such securitisations, and the Rolling Stones and Pink Floyd are also rumoured to be coming to the market.

As with global emerging markets, the quality of issuers is likely to deteriorate as the bull market progresses – what price the future earnings stream of the back catalogue of Country Joe and the Fish? The time to sell this market is probably when the catalogue of every performer from Max Yasgur's dairy farm in August 1969 has been securitised. What price the basket derivative Woodstock?

The ability of Bowie to pull off this deal seemed to herald that we had reached the extremes of how far the securitisation business could go. I had no idea that the securitisation of uncertain future income streams was still in its infancy. It continues to rage today despite a few hiccups along the way associated with some US mortgage instruments that brought the global financial system to its knees in 2008.

Ever falling interest rates have forced many investors to consider more uncertain income streams in pursuit of the yield on investment that they desire. That rates would still be declining more than 20 years after the Bowie bond was issued is something that few people could have foreseen. For those in the securitisation business, this continued decline in interest rates has been the gift that kept giving. Much of the future long-term decline in inflation and interest rates that fuelled the boom in the creation of such instruments was to stem from the consequences of the capital exodus and ensuing economic bust then brewing in Asia. Far from undermining the appetite to purchase uncertain future income streams, the consequence of the credit crisis in Asia would be to super-charge it.

Cheaper still

20 March 1997, Indonesia

Indonesian equities have been one of the biggest beneficiaries in Asia of the spread in global 'irrational exuberance'. The faith in the rupiah as a quasi US dollar has produced a significant inflow of interest rate arbitrage funds. This arbitrage has intensified with the widening of the currency bands as the interest rate differential looks even more attractive when the rupiah is strengthening.

In a recent visit to Jakarta, I came across three private individuals who had borrowed yen to put on rupiah deposit. Last year's bull market in emerging market debt has produced a wave of buying of rupiah paper and emerging market bond funds continue to be launched. Despite an annual current account deficit running around US$5bn, the country has reported a rise in foreign exchange reserves of US$3.4bn in the four months to the end of January.

The BIS shows a US$4.7bn increase in Indonesia's foreign currency debt to the BIS reporting banks in the first six months of 1996 alone. Borrowing

US dollars to invest in Indonesia or to buy rupiah paper has become the only game in town. However, investors should not be concerned that this is another Thailand as the central banks' widening of the currency bands shows that they are prepared to deter such arbitrage.

We expect the currency bands to be widened from the current 8% to 20%! The arbitrage game will end with one almighty thump when such an announcement is made. The risk characteristics of the rupiah will be changed dramatically and the arbitrageur will no longer consider the rupiah a quasi US dollar. A blow-off in financial asset prices is inevitable as this flow of 'hot money' at least slows down and may be diverted to safer arbitrage activities.

Investors should thus remain extremely cautious about the outlook for Indonesian equities. The markets must begin to build in the correct risks of doing business in Indonesia and this is likely to reduce valuations. This fall in prices will produce one of the best buying opportunities in Asia. While the initial move by the authorities would act as a 'cold bath' for the speculators, the widening of the bands would be a major positive for the economy and the stock market over the longer term.

The Thai experience should convince investors that equities in an economy operating a flexible exchange rate policy deserve a premium rating to those operating in a fixed exchange rate system. Over time, this premium will build up, but in the initial act of pricing in real business risks, the equity market is highly likely to take a significant tumble. Keep your powder dry and prepare to move in as the speculators move out. Stay clear.

That carry trade that saw investors borrow in one low-yielding currency to invest in a high-yielding currency had spread from hedge funds to individuals. The people I met in Indonesia who thought this was a good idea were of above average wealth, but they were not particularly wealthy. When such a risky investment opportunity was being pursued by such people, it was legitimate to question how much more of this 'carry' capital could really flow into Indonesia. That they did not fully understand the risks in their 'strategy' was all too apparent to me and yet another area of ill-informed risk taking joined a growing list of such practices.

When you meet investors who do not really understand the nature of the risk they are taking, it is time for caution. Borrowing yen cheaply to invest in high-yielding Indonesia rupiah paper had become an incredibly dangerous activity, but one that was increasingly popular.

Sadly, the plan to widen the currency bands for the rupiah had come far too late. The stability of the rupiah had already created massive imbalances in which foreigners and locals using foreign currency debt had come to rely upon the stability of the rupiah. That the rupiah was trading at the strong end of its trading band in late March 1997, just more than three months before Thailand was to devalue the baht, showed how unconcerned investors were that the Thai malaise could spread beyond Thailand. I was right that a move to allow greater exchange rate flexibility would mean that things in Indonesia would end with a 'bump'. It was to be a big bump.

Not Thailand

21 March 1997, Philippines

When any economic improvement is associated with a surge in activity in the real estate sector, alarm bells start ringing. When a growing proportion of economic activity is financed with foreign currency debt, the degree of alarm is further increased. The economic renaissance in the Philippines has been accompanied by both phenomena. While extrapolation is an easy forecasting tool, it is inevitably flawed. Simply viewing Asian markets through the looking glass of Thailand is at least likely to produce significant errors in market timing and potentially also in long-term market direction.

An equity market analyst in Asia could sometimes best be described as a party analyst. The liquidity waves which blow through the domestic economies, primarily driven by the operation of currency policies, can produce wonderful liquidity parties. Within the 12-month time frame within which most fund managers now operate, the existence or otherwise of such a party will be more important than company fundamentals. Such prolonged parties in any economy produce prolonged hangovers.

Thailand is witnessing such a hangover. However, it is important to remember that the party comes first and, as in the case of Thailand, can rage for many years and be extended for many more years than anyone believes. The property over-build in Thailand and associated bank collateral problems have been a fact of life for some years. However, it was only in a period of economic deceleration that these problems came home to roost.

The two positives for the Philippines are that the economy is nowhere near the top of the economic cycle and the local authorities are fully aware of the price to be paid for letting the party rage too long. The Philippines is at a much earlier stage of its economic development than Thailand, with GDP per capita of US$1,173 compared to US$3,000 in Thailand. With economic policy on track, we see a steady acceleration in economic growth in the Philippines for at least the next two years. Thus, even if the Philippines were currently delighting in a party of the Thai magnitude, it is unlikely that an economic slowdown would bring it to an end for at least two years. We would contend that such a party is not in progress and thus the outlook for the Philippines is bright.

Given the Philippines' stage in the economic cycle, any end to the current bull conditions for the stock market is likely to be some years away. However, many would argue that the potential for the development of a Thai scenario should be sufficient to persuade investors not to adopt an overweight position in the Philippines, even at this stage. It is not always easy to remember to leave every party at midnight.

While many see only dread in the Thai example, it in fact contains a great deal of hope for equity investors. The Thai fiasco is producing a new realisation among Asia's politicians that the slavish adoption of a currency policy will inevitably produce economic problems. In the past, it may have been difficult to explain to politicians that soaring economic growth and asset price inflation were bad things. The downside is now clear. Indonesia's widening of the currency bands is the first significant sign that these lessons have been learned.

In the Philippines, also, the politicians are now more likely to heed the advice of the central bank regarding the problems associated with strict currency policies. We believe that the Philippines central bank has been actively sterilising the significant sums of foreign exchange intervention which it has had to undertake to prevent an appreciation of the peso, relative to the US dollar. What has been underway has been a prudent accumulation of foreign exchange reserves in preparation for the more flexible exchange rate policy, which will reduce the prospects of the Thai situation developing in the Philippines. The equity market will suffer further setbacks as global risk premiums rise; the Philippines Brady bond yield premium is now less than 100bp! For any investor with a time frame of more than just a few months, this will present an excellent buying opportunity.

The tyranny of the benchmarks was now in operation to create a capital outflow from the Asian equity asset class as a whole. It did not really matter that the Philippines had not had the scale of credit boom and overinvestment that the rest of Southeast Asia had enjoyed. The local authorities were targeting the value of their exchange rate and there was about to be downward pressure on that exchange rate as institutional investors liquidated their equities – almost regardless of any better fundamentals in the Philippines. Their opinion on Asia had soured and withdrawing capital from Asia meant, given the focus on following benchmark equity indices, selling both the equities and the currency of the Philippines.

Most analysts I know who have visited the Philippines develop a very soft spot for the people and the country. In some way I think we all come to root for their economic success and an escape from the poverty that inflicts the people. While elsewhere in Asia there were booms and busts, the booms always seemed to be smaller in the Philippines and to have had fewer positive impacts on the mass of the people. Despite this, the country and its people seemed to suffer just as much as everyone else when the busts came.

It would be nice to think that we all analysed the outlook for the countries of Asia with complete impartiality, but this was not true. I had already discovered very strong home bias among my colleagues in the CLSA regional offices. No decisions are without bias and I, and others, wanted the Philippines in particular to succeed, and this may have clouded our judgement in assessing the likelihood that the country would weather the brewing storm. I had no illusions that the Philippines was only home to wonderfully friendly people. One day while boarding a plane for an internal flight from Manila I passed a sand pit. A sign above the sand pit read, "Please Discharge Weapons Here"!

In the piece above I mentioned that the authorities in the Philippines had been acting to sterilise their intervention in the foreign exchange market. As we have seen, any intervention to prevent exchange appreciation leads to the creation of more money by the central bank, in the form of commercial bank reserves, created to fund the purchase of foreign currency. That creation of local currency can, if it is sustained, lead eventually to higher domestic inflation.

Recognising this risk, the local central bank can sell newly created bonds in return for local currency. This mechanism removes from circulation the local currency it had created via its exchange rate intervention. The idea is that this allows the central bank to target the exchange rate while stopping this policy from leading to excessive money creation and inflation. The adoption of a sterilisation policy showed that the authorities in the Philippines at least recognised the problem, but I did not think that sterilisation was likely to work.

Some years before I had read a paper by a man with the unlikely name of Beryl Sprinkel. Sprinkel was a monetary adviser to Ronald Reagan and had been part of the Second Armoured Division at the Battle of the Bulge, so I don't imagine that most people focused on the peculiar nature of his first name! His damning analysis of sterilisation was that it would only act to keep interest rates higher than they otherwise would be and likely attract more yield-seeking foreign capital inflows that would have to be monetised. The policy was therefore just creating a vicious circle. With all the 'carry' trades flowing from Japan, that seemed to me an accurate diagnosis of what would happen if the Philippines conducted a sterilisation programme.

I had already seen a sterilisation programme fail in the early 1990s in Malaysia. A central bank can only sell bonds to investors if it provides them with a market rate of interest. The more bonds it sells, the more its outgoings rise in paying that interest. As the local interest rates were much higher than US interest rates at the time, the bank would be paying more in interest on local bonds than it was earning in interest on its growing holdings of foreign bonds.

Taken to its extremes, the policy could lead to the central bank making a loss. In Malaysia just a few years before this dangerous dynamic had forced the central bank to end its sterilisation programme. Sterilisation is a policy that, while recognising a problem, is unlikely to solve it as it does not discourage the large capital inflows that are usually the cause of the problem.

It turned out that the authorities in the Philippines never got to discover whether the policy could be sustained or not. In just a few months there was massive capital outflow from the country and they were not intervening to suppress the value of the currency, but desperately trying to support it.

The piece above also references the yield on the Brady bonds of the Philippines. These bonds were named after Nicholas Brady, the 68th secretary to the US Treasury. They were an innovative financial instrument created to help clean up the legacy of the financial crisis in emerging markets that had erupted in 1982. That they were still around when the next crisis came suggests something about the financial stability of emerging markets.

In later years I came to know Nicholas Brady and some of the team who worked with him in solving that particular financial crisis and achieving much else. I have on my desk a quotation attributed to Alexis de Tocqueville that Nick likes to hand out to visitors to his office. He kindly signed my copy:

> The American Republic will endure until the day Congress discovers that it can bribe the public with the public's money.

Dangerous signals from Singapore

21 March 1997, Regional

The most worrying aspect of the export data from Singapore is what it augurs for the rest of Asia. Japanese import data for February reveals significant year-on-year declines of imports from all Asian countries, with the exception of the Philippines. While imports from Singapore declined 28% in February, there was an identical decline in imports from Taiwan and Hong Kong. Japan's imports from South Korea declined 20% and from Thailand 13%.

This is an across-the-board slowing in exports from January. It appears increasingly clear that the expected recovery in Asia's export growth is being pushed further and further into the future. This creates a dangerous hiatus for the Asian markets. An export recovery must now wait until 2H 97. Thus, significant current account improvement is probably also postponed. In the absence of such an improvement, those economies running current account deficits and adopting currency policies will have to see an acceleration in capital inflows if the current poor liquidity conditions are to improve.

If the market consensus is correct that US interest rates are rising, this would mitigate against an acceleration in capital inflows. Already Asia is not attracting significant new equity portfolio inflows and this will continue as long as momentum remains in Latin America and Europe. In recent meetings with global asset allocators, it has become clear that Asia's many documented problems are filtering up to the most senior levels.

UK global asset allocators, with twice as much money in Asia as in the United States, are questioning whether Asian equities are really a long-term warrant on economic growth. Some reductions in weightings could occur if the current accounts do not begin to improve and provide the liquidity momentum to satisfy such investors. In this scenario, Singapore, with a current account surplus of 13.5% of gross national product (GNP), and with equities cheap relative to interest rates, will provide significant outperformance against its Asian peers. Batten down the hatches, we're in for a blow.

That Japanese imports from Asia should turn so negative was particularly alarming given that the growth in Japan's total imports was still above 10% in the first half of 1997. Japanese imports from China had grown at over 20% year on year in 1994 and 1995, and by over 30% in 1996. In 1997, a year of economic crisis, the growth in Japan's exports from China still exceeded 15%.

The evidence grew and grew that China, with its massive mobilisation of resources and exchange rate devaluation in 1994, had undermined Asia's competitiveness. That was not just a fundamental, it was the most important fundamental of all. As this reality dawned, UK asset allocators had still twice as much money committed to Asian ex Japan as they had to US equities. The fundamental case supporting growth in Asia was being undermined by an Asian country they had almost no investments in – China.

As for the recommendation that investors should invest in Singapore, well, it did fare better than the rest of the Asian markets, but from its level of 21 March 1997 to its low on 4 September 1998, the MSCI Singapore Index fell almost 54%. That's what outperformance can look like in a full-blown crisis.

Don't bank on it

25 March 1997, Malaysia

Today's *FT* provides some useful data regarding the scale of the property over-build brewing in Malaysia. Since 1991, the CAGR of office space in Kuala Lumpur has been 6.2%. Kuala Lumpur office space now stands at 38m sq. ft, but a further 37m sq. ft will be added by 1998. The CAGR over this two-year period will be 34%. The annual take-up rate has been 3m sq. ft per annum. Thus, to keep occupancies at current levels, the take-up will have to rise to 6× the average annual level.

The situation would deteriorate even further if the prime minister were ensconced in the new city of Putrajaya as early as September 1998, as the government is forecasting. Lending for construction, real estate and housing rose 27% last year and 60% of total bank lending is for property-related activity. Last year, loan growth approached 30% while real economic growth was 12%. This growth in lending is particularly worrying given that the financial system in Malaysia is already developed and M2 as a percentage of GNP is already 106%. Risk would clearly seem to outweigh reward in this scenario.

In the minds of the general public, the professional investor is in possession of some informed opinion that gives them an edge when it comes to investment. That can often be true. Sometimes, though, the information that should inform opinion is on the front page of the newspapers, as it was in 1997. That Malaysia had been involved in property mal-investment was absolutely no secret. That the government was shifting most of its employees to a newly created city called Putrajaya was unlikely to help with demand for commercial property in the capital and centre of the property over-build, Kuala Lumpur.

The Petronas Towers, then the world's two tallest buildings, were to be topped out early in 1998. They were not constructed in secret either. Evidence of the over-build in Malaysian property, both commercial and residential, was evident everywhere. Nobody it seemed thought that this could lead to lower property prices or to problems for the financial system. In the period from 1993, when the first signs of a property over-build were already showing, the share price of Malaysia's leading bank, Maybank, had risen by over 350%! In April 1997, the price remained close to its all-time high set in February of that year. That ignoring these obvious excesses was dangerous is evidenced by the fact that by 2020, the price of Maybank was still at a level it first reached in February 1997.

That I was capable of writing anything quite so coherent on Tuesday, 25 March 1997 is quite amazing, given I had spent the weekend drinking with Ian Botham. Ian Botham is one of the greatest cricketers to ever play the game and has a reputation – rightly, as I was to discover – as a bit of a party animal. That was the weekend of the famous Hong Kong Rugby Sevens tournament and this year, just a few months before Hong Kong was to be handed back to Chinese rule, was the World Rugby Sevens.

We heard that Ian Botham was attending, so we booked him to speak at a lunch the company hosted for clients the day before the tournament began. My colleague Donald Nimmo and I spoke first, on something only partly related to investment, and Botham spoke next. Over a beer or two after lunch, he asked if he could bring a few friends along to the CLSA box at the stadium the next day. We obviously agreed and the next day he turned up with, among others, one of the world's greatest ever rugby players, Gareth Edwards.

What happened after that is a bit hazy, but I know it did not end until the Sunday night and I was indisposed on Monday. I do remember, however, that a charity fundraiser tried to persuade Botham to parachute from a plane in the New Territories. Botham asked how much this might raise and the fundraiser guessed that they might expect to raise £5,000. On the spot he offered her £5,000 if I would jump from a plane in the New Territories. I was still in a condition to refuse to participate, having the greatest of respect for gravity, something I have maintained to this day. As we partied in the bars of Wanchai that evening, a different form of gravity, financial gravity, was creating even greater problems in Southeast Asia.

By the pricking of my thumbs

8 April 1997, Regional

Something Wicked this Way Comes for the Asian equity investor. Returning from a week's holiday, one is supposed to be full of new enthusiasm. There is one main reason to be cheerful for the global equity investor and that is that the timing of the reduction of yen leverage in the global system appears to have been postponed. With the US$/yen rate around 120–122 and a sell-off in US treasuries underway, there is real reason for concern.

Had the US dollar weakened from this position, it was likely that many arbitrageurs would have been selling US dollar debt to repay yen liabilities. However, Robert Rubin's comments last week combined with a weak Tankan survey and a rally in the US dollar and Japanese government bonds suggest that we have taken a step back from that particular precipice. The unwinding of yen leverage still hangs over global financial markets like the Sword of Damocles, but the thread now appears a little more secure. However, this does not mean that it is time to adopt a more aggressive investment stance.

Rising US interest rates not only have direct impacts on Asian interest rates, but they have historically impacted portfolio flows from the United States. When the yield on the US long bond yield has exceeded 7%, there has been a drying up of flows into international mutual funds. Already, Asian mutual funds have been witnessing net redemptions for the past four months and rising interest rates suggest that redemptions will continue.

In 1996 a significant escalation in foreign currency debt accounted for an increasing proportion of capital inflows into the region and this is also likely to recede as US interest rates rise. It is also increasingly clear that the bulls of Asia – the UK pension fund managers with twice as much equity money in Asia as the United States – are increasingly disillusioned. This growing disillusionment has yet to be reflected in disinvestment, but judging from recent conversations with asset allocators, such action is increasingly likely.

A reduction in weightings by this investor class would occur just when Asian equities are at their most vulnerable. Returning from holiday, one is supposed to be more optimistic and a 2.22% fall in the MSCI Far East ex Japan Index and a lessening threat from Japan should help. This is not the case. The next six to nine months are set to prove very difficult and our strategy remains the same as it was going into this year – concentrate overweight positions in Singapore, India and China, and underweight in Malaysia and Thailand.

A week in a beach hut in Koh Phi Phi Lai in the Andaman Sea with my wife and some friends from the UK had clearly not lightened my mood. Now on the eve of the devaluation of the Thai baht, foreign investors had still only begun to reduce their exposure to Asian equities. The redemptions from Asian mutual funds forced them to sell Asian equities.

The problem was that the numbers for their redemptions were publicly available. One of CLSA's most popular publications simply reported these statistics and its release each month was eagerly awaited by institutional investors. The fact that mutual funds had had redemptions yesterday did not mean that they would have them tomorrow. It did not mean it would happen, but it increased the prospects that it could. In theory, lower prices encourage more buying, but for mutual fund investors, declining prices often triggered greater selling and Asian equities were not doing well.

The retail investors' attention was being increasingly drawn to a dotcom boom that was picking up pace in the United States. It wasn't just the jump in US short-term interest rates from 5% to 5.5% and 10-year bond yields above 6.5% that were attracting retail investors to US investments. An exciting new dotcom stock was coming to the market on 15 May at a price of US$18, and there were those who thought it was undervalued. The new listing was called Amazon.

Recommending, as I did, that clients invest in China and India in May 1997 was really a bit of a cop-out. These were tiny markets in the index due to the restrictions on foreign ownership then in place in both markets. Combined they still represented a lower weighting in the Asia ex Japan Equity Index than Taiwan and were less than half the index weighting of Malaysia. It was simply not possible to move funds in any scale from the then large Southeast Asian markets into the tiny and illiquid markets of India and China.

There was the obvious issue of finding sufficient liquidity, but once again the tyranny of the benchmarks played a key role. No fund manager would risk their clients' money and their job by having as much money in China and India as they had in Southeast Asia. That would have been so far away from the weightings in the benchmark index as to have been called up in front of senior management to explain your 'risky' behaviour. It was too dangerous for portfolio investors to invest in the world's most and second most populous countries – not because they had poor prospects of future returns, but because they still had half the index weighting of Malaysia!

The risk of any investment depends very much upon the incentive of those making the investment. For those managing equity portfolios in 1997, it was too risky to avoid investment in small Asian countries very clearly coming to the end of a credit boom. It was also too risky to allocate any significant amounts of capital to benefit from the continued economic reform and growth of the world's two most populous countries.

The incentives were wrong and as a result the assessment of risk was wrong. As the crisis approached, the slavish focus on the benchmarking of portfolio capital to the index kept institutional investors invested where they increasingly knew they shouldn't be invested.

A key reason for recommending investment in Chinese and India equities was that they were not widely held by foreign investors and, thus, when capital retreated from the region, they were more likely to be supported by local buying. The exodus of foreign capital was also less likely to create the tightening of liquidity conditions that was already evident in Thailand. This was bad advice. The MSCI China Index was to fall 73% from its level in April 1997 to its lows at the end of August 1998. China's GDP growth did slow through this period, but it remained above 7%. It did not have a credit crisis and it did not devalue its exchange rate.

This proved to be irrelevant in the short term as foreign investors assumed that China would have to devalue the currency to remain competitive with its Asian neighbours. This fear of a devaluation of the Chinese exchange rate hung over the outlook for Asia and was probably at its most intense in August 1998, just as the stock markets were to bottom.

China continued to be an economic miracle and surpassed in economic growth terms even the forecasts of the most bullish commentators in 1997. That equities are not necessarily a good way to benefit from a country's high economic growth is clear from the performance of the Chinese equity market. The MSCI China Index in 2020 remains below the level it was at when the index was launched at the end of 1992! If proof were needed that there is more to investing than buying equities in fast-growing economies, then this prolonged period without any increase in the capital index of Chinese shares is probably it.

Investors did fare better sheltering in India, but the MSCI India Index still declined by almost 20% from its levels in April 1997 to its lows in November 1998. Few foreign investors had jumped the legal hurdles that allowed them to invest directly in the Indian market and their exposure was gained through offshore securities issued by Indian companies. For most institutional investors it was simply not practical to shelter from the coming storm by investing in Indian equities.

That there were fortunes to be made investing in Chinese equities was an opinion that was widespread in investment magazines and among the investing public from an early stage in China's economic reform process. In 1992, not long after the first shares in Chinese companies had become available to foreign investors, I had journeyed to China to visit some of the listed companies and those that proposed to list.

The stockbroker who arranged this tour asked me if I minded if some other investors joined in and I was happy for them to do so. What I did not appreciate was that the other potential investor was a retail investor. It seemed that he had made quite a bit of money selling a business in California, from memory it was a sound stage, and he had read in *Time Magazine* about the economic boom in China. I don't know how much of the proceeds of the business sale had been invested in Chinese equities already, but it was clear that some of it had.

Travelling with him was his pregnant wife, who also attended most of the meetings. The companies then available for foreign investment had all recently been 100% owned by the Chinese government and it showed. We visited the factories as well as the offices and it became very clear very quickly that these were not the sorts of companies we would contemplate investing in anywhere else in the world. I remember visiting a company in Shanghai where there were employees, each with a set of hedge clippers, cutting the grass outside the management offices. The man and I asked the standard questions of management that one would ask of any company, but it was his wife who often asked the real zinger that exposed just how inefficient the company was.

China was just opening up in 1992 and who wouldn't want to be in at ground level given the potential for any company operating in the world's most populous country? My advice to my employer at the time was to stick to investing in China by buying companies in Hong Kong invested in China and not to invest in the former state-owned companies then offering shares to foreigners.

I often wondered whether the couple from California followed through on the conclusions they had reached which I thought were probably very similar. Being in on the ground floor of the Chinese economic miracle was indeed a great thing for many investors. However, it was primarily a great thing for direct investors who chose which industries to be involved with and which managements were worth backing, and not those who bought the shares of former state-owned companies that the government had decided to bring to market.

The fate of Mr William Brodie

12 May 1997, Malaysia

In 18th-century Edinburgh, Deacon William Brodie designed cabinets for the gentry. However, in the evenings he used his expertise as a locksmith and his inside information to burgle his clients. When finally brought to justice, the Deacon suffered the final ignominy of being hanged on a gibbet of his own design.

There is often a similar macabre rationality to financial markets and the price-boosting activities of yesterday, best summed up by the Japanese term *zaitech* (financial engineering), can become a tool of dispatch in due course. In particular, the so-called 'conglomerate game' has the brutal inevitability of a Swiss watch.

The mechanics of the game involve issuing high PE equity to purchase companies with low PEs. This transaction boosts EPS growth. If the PE of the acquiree is actually lower than that disclosed, then investors will be surprised by the strength of EPS growth. The market may not only begin to focus on the cheap price of these assets, but also come to believe that there is underlying earnings growth in the acquired assets. Sometimes the market awards a higher PE to the acquirer as a result of this growth perception. A management premium may even accrue. However, at some stage, market conditions reduce the acquirer's PE and/or there are fewer things to acquire at a low PE. An inevitable deceleration in earnings growth and PE derating ensues.

At least one investor claims to have profited from this brutal inevitability: "The first time I used my model systematically was in the conglomerate boom of the late 1960s. It enabled me to make money both on the way up and the way down" (George Soros, *The Alchemy of Finance*). The model to which Mr Soros refers is that of reflexivity. Simply put, this theory expounds that the fundamentals of a financial instrument can be altered by the very act of purchase. The buying of conglomerate shares, which advances the PE, makes the next acquisition even more EPS enhancing.

The key problem for Malaysia is that the conglomerate boom combines a macro and micro reflexivity. The capital inflow to purchase the conglomerates acted to depress interest rates and boost money supply growth as Bank Negara acted to prevent currency appreciation. This capital inflow was thus instrumental in boosting economic growth/earnings growth, reducing interest rates and boosting PEs. The problem is that with domestic low PE assets in short supply (the government is running out of things to sell), the conglomerates are now pouring money overseas in an attempt to keep the conglomerate bandwagon rolling.

With PEs contracting in Malaysia, they are forced to buy ever lower PE paper overseas and thus they are currently mining the high-risk seams for prospects: South Africa, Croatia, Madagascar, Myanmar, Sudan, Yemen, Kazakhstan and Azerbaijan. However, this significant long-term capital outflow has the impact of reducing the net purchasing of the ringgit and potentially placing upward pressure on interest rates. As foreign investors see the end of the conglomerate boom, there is a growing prospect that they will reduce their significant exposure to this capital-lucky (Malaysia is weighted in all global, Asia and emerging market equity indices) country. Further upward pressure on interest rates is likely. Macro and micro reflexivity begin to work simultaneously to reduce share prices.

On Edinburgh's Lawn Market stands Deacon Brodie's Tavern, a reminder to all of the fate of the Deacon. The forthcoming conglomerate end game has few positives for investors, but may in due course significantly boost the number and quality of watering holes in Kuala Lumpur.

Bubbles are wonderful things, but they burst. Working out how and why they burst is more a job for the psychologist than the investor. There does come a stage in any bubble when capital begins to get diverted to somewhere else. The smart money is often early, but it departs – and in Malaysia it was departing very quickly. While I had already written about the impact this would have on the macro variables, it occurred to me in May 1997 that Malaysia had also been a beneficiary of the great PE conglomerate game that Soros had flagged up in *The Alchemy of Finance* and that Adam Smith (aka George Goodman) had so wonderfully exposed in *The Money Game*.

The control of most of these conglomerates was in the hands of politically well-connected business people who were benefiting from the New Economic Policy that was supposed to move wealth towards the Bumiputra section of Malaysian society. That they would be doubly impacted by the forthcoming recession, through worsening economic conditions and the end of the profit inflation that acquisition accounting can bring, indicated just how big a problem Malaysia would have.

Could the political class really allow these conglomerates to fail and risk allowing their assets to fall into the hands of foreigners or the local Chinese population? The end of this conglomerate game in Malaysia had more than just economic consequences and made it more difficult to estimate the policy choices that would be implemented when the crisis came.

The day the PE died

15 May 1997, Regional

Today your in-tray will be full of the assembled musings of the broking community on the future of the baht/US dollar exchange rate. Clearly speculation increased yesterday that the Thai authorities would take the Lamont (ex-member for Harrogate) option. It would appear that yesterday the emphasis altered among market participants, with the word 'if' being replaced with 'when'.

The answer to either of these questions is now of only passing interest; it was of much greater importance when Thailand was 13% of the MSCI FE Index rather than the current estimated 4.3% weighting. Regardless of the answers to 'if' and 'when', yesterday will begin to bring into focus the real issue facing investors in Asia: the use of the US dollar risk-free rate in valuing investments is now over.

While many pin their hopes for Asian equities on the current low ratings on their PE band charts, events yesterday in Thailand must show that faith in this indicator is increasingly dangerous. There are two reasons. The currency policies in Asia can and have produced the monetary policy which has pushed equities to overvalues. At some stage in the cycle, it is almost inevitable that it will have the impact of pushing equities to undervalues.

Regardless of what happens to the currency regime in Thailand, the events of the past 12 months have revealed the terrifying dynamic of what can happen when liquidity is squeezed for too long by the operation of an exchange rate intervention policy. Last year's Thai bulls sought relief from the central bank, but the central bank's hands were tied. The dangers of the currency policies to equity valuations on the cyclical downside are now more apparent to all. Assessing the value of equities based upon their historical PEs is thus increasingly dangerous. Previous valuations were inflated in the liquidity rush produced by the currency policies and the reverse could now occur.

Regardless of what happens to the Thai currency regime, the Thai experience is likely to lead to structural changes in Asia. Our key call at CLSA for some time has been that this would not just be the downswing of a liquidity cycle. During this cycle there always appeared to be a high probability that the authorities in Asia would proactively or reactively seek to move away from the currency policies. The good news about events in Thailand is that policy makers are increasingly likely to move proactively.

The downside of the current monetary regimes is now as obvious to politicians as it is to investors. Thus investors in Asia must now begin to factor in the domestic risk-free rate when valuing equities rather than the US dollar risk-free rate. Hopefully yesterday's events will mean that you will never again have to listen to any equity sales people expound on why Indonesian equities are 'cheaper' than Singapore equities because the PE is lower. "One small step for ...."

Market movements across Asia suggest that this new reality is already beginning to be priced into equity markets. So how far are we from fair value? The honest answer is that it is difficult to tell. When historical returns have been so comprehensively distorted by a degree of monetary illusion, it will always be difficult to correctly adjudge future value. However, using the historical equity risk premium over the past five to seven years and using the domestic risk-free rate, Table 2.6 shows the implied terminal rate of dividend growth currently priced into equity markets.

Table 2.6: Implied terminal rate of dividend growth priced into equity markets

Hong Kong	21.1%
Indonesia	18.3%
India	21.9%
Malaysia	14.7%
Philippines	22.6%
Singapore	2.5%
Taiwan	16.3%
Thailand	8.1%

Asian corporates in these countries have to be capable of producing these levels of long-term earnings growth to be considered fair value. It is important to stress that the mathematics of value themselves have been distorted by the money mania of yesterday and it can be argued either way whether this means that the above implied growth rates are too high or too low. Money mania probably boosted the performance of equities, thus raising the equity risk premium, but it probably also inflated historical growth rates etc. However, Table 2.6 might give some indication that when it comes to PE analysis, "there are more things in heaven and earth, Horatio, than are dreamt of in your philosophy" (Shakespeare, *Hamlet*). Whatever the outcome of the current battle of the baht, yesterday will probably be remembered in the history of the Asian equity markets as 'The day the PE died'.

By this stage, the CLSA stock analysts across the region had either got or been forced to get the message. They were co-operating with the bearish top-down forecasts and producing analyses that showed the potential scale of downside for corporate earnings and share prices when economies contracted and risk-free interest rates rose. I well remember that the first collaborative element in this regard was named *The Death of PE*, a title derived from this shorter piece I had written in May 1997.

My own calculations, noted above, were very much back of the envelope, but even these showed the impossibility of earnings growth and dividend growth matching the expected growth rates then priced into equities. For many years, many forms of investors – whether corporate management, direct investors or institutional investors – had decided to discount the future cash flows of their Asian investments using the prevailing yield on 10-year US government bonds. Of course they had added a premium to that rate to account for the greater risks associated with investment in Asia, but the building block had still been the risk-free rate of the world's largest economy.

They were using the risk-free rate of an economy with a sophisticated commercial infrastructure, a high-quality rule of law, an independent judiciary and a democracy that had weathered many economic cycles and two world wars. To import that US risk-free rate into an economy such as Indonesia was nuts, but it is what happened, and none of the risk premiums added to that risk-free rate came anywhere close to the rupiah interest rates that developed once the currency was allowed to float.

Choosing to value investments using the US risk-free rate developed because at this stage in their development very few Asian economies had issued long-dated government bonds in their own currencies. There simply was no local currency bond market from which investors could take their lead to find the appropriate discount rate. What there was though were exchange rate links to the US dollar. Those links seemed inviolate as all the pressure for many years now had been for Asian currencies to appreciate. It thus seemed reasonable to use US interest rates as the first building block in calculating the appropriate rate at which future income streams should be discounted.

The calculations above that indicated huge downside for Asian equities used local currency short-term interest rates as long-term interest rates were mostly unavailable. These rates gave shocking answers as to how overvalued equity prices still were in May 1997. What was more concerning was that if I were right, these short-term interest rates were likely to go sharply higher and the devaluation of the exchange rates would divert a very large portion of corporates' domestic cash flow to service their now much more expensive foreign currency debt. The adjustment in the exchange rates would bring much higher discount rates and much lower corporate earnings simultaneously. That's a combination for a major downward adjustment in share prices.

Since I had arrived in Asia I had constantly been confronted by institutional investors wielding PE band charts. These charts simply charted the PE ratios of the Asian stock market indices back as far as the data was available. At CLSA, we had these charts of PEs going all the way back to 1990!

A PE calculation divides the share price of a company by its earnings per share. It calculates how many years' earnings an investor is paying to own the earnings power of the company. A PE calculation has its place, and the PE charts for Asia, particularly Southeast Asia, had been declining from a peak reached at the end of 1993.

The constant question was: how could these equities not be a buy given how cheap they had become by historic standards? The first obvious answer was that we only knew the PEs back to 1990 and that was far too short a period over which to judge whether equities were either cheap or expensive. There were also more compelling reasons for caution than just the short period over which we had measured the PE ratio.

In arguing that PE ratios should be ignored, my reasoning was that valuations were meaningless because it was a money and credit bubble and the so-called fundamentals were as much a product of that bubble as the share prices themselves. That investors had insisted on utilising US interest rates to assess just how attractive these meaningless earnings numbers were just compounded the overvaluation.

But how should an investor value Asian equities when we did not know how high local currency interest rates would go or how far corporate earnings would fall? Given the structural change and the uncertainties associated with it, all previous valuation data was irrelevant. Along with the stock analysts and the clients, we set out to find something – anything – that would tell us when Asian equity valuations were truly cheap.

The first stab at this in the piece above came up with outrageously high expected dividend growth rates implied by existing share prices. This did not tell us how much equities were overvalued by, but it certainly suggested that the recent PE history was a poor way to value equities and they had a long way still to fall. It was now just a few weeks until the structural change would be upon us and the need to find a new way to value Asian equities would be essential.

Thailand or BT

16 May 1997, Regional

The MSCI weightings have once again altered significantly with the further adjustments. Taiwan is now the third largest market in the index with a weighting of 13.9%; it is now larger than Singapore at 13.2%. The Thai weighting was 5.2% at the beginning of this month, but due to relative underperformance is probably now around 4.3%.

Should a currency adjustment actually occur, a further contraction in weightings would take place. The market capitalisation of Thailand is currently US$66bn and the prospects of a currency adjustment appear to be increasing. Some scenario analysis on a fall in the value of the currency reveals the incredibly low market capitalisation of the Thai market, as shown in Table 2.7.

Table 2.7: Thai market capitalisation given currency adjustment scenarios

−10%	US$59bn
−15%	US$56bn
−20%	US$53bn
−25%	US$50bn
−30%	US$46bn
−35%	US$42bn
−40%	US$40bn

For this price, you can buy the financial, industrial and communications backbone of a country with a population larger than France. Should even a 30% currency correction be forced, the entire market would be cheaper than British Telecom. This is not to say that the market is a buy today.

For those unable to hedge their currency exposure, the risks of significant capital loss remain high. Indeed a currency adjustment is likely to result in bankruptcies in the listed sector in Thailand and a complete loss of capital. Caution is still advised. However, for the hedged investor, selected opportunities may already be appearing in those corporates which can weather the storm.

That a low market capitalisation must indicate long-term value proved to be wishful thinking. It really wasn't relevant that you could soon buy the equity of the Thai listed sector for less than the market capitalisation of what was then British Telecom. As equity is the fine sliver of hope between assets and liabilities, the first decision is to assess whether that fine sliver survives a crisis before estimating just how much one might pay for it.

Thailand did devalue the exchange rate and did eventually reflate the economy and much of the listed equity survived. That long-term returns from Thai equities have since been so poor, even from their already low levels of May 1997, indicates that they were still significantly overvalued even though the stock market's total capitalisation was seemingly incredibly small.

Many years later for Greece, during the European sovereign debt crisis of 2011–12, no such remedy of currency devaluation and reflation was available given the restrictions of euro membership. The pain inflicted by that fixed exchange rate regime reduced the stock market capitalisation of Greece, a country with a population of 11 million, to just US$25bn by 2012. As at the end of 2020, the local stock market index was still below its 2012 crisis level.

The wrong monetary policy can play such a major role in distorting stock market valuations that establishing true value can become incredibly difficult for investors. While Thailand painfully abandoned the wrong monetary policy structure in July 1997, Greece continues to labour under the same structure that led to its rescue from bankruptcy that began in 2010.

The choice to adopt a new monetary structure is ultimately a political choice. Investors in any stock market with the wrong monetary policy structure have to assess when the country is politically ready to make such a major choice for change and what its implications might be. While Greece did not ultimately make the choice to adopt a new monetary structure, by May 1997 Thailand was just a month away from such a momentous decision.

Perhaps if all Thailand faced in May 1997 was a normal business cycle, the low market capitalisation of its local stock market might have indicated that good long-term returns would follow. However, as Thailand faced a major structural adjustment that unveiled the excesses wrought by the wrong monetary policy, the small stock market capitalisation said little about the level of likely future returns.

IF97: Cabbages and kings

27 May 1997, Regional

"But he has nothing on!" said the whole people at length. And the emperor shivered, for it seemed to him that they were right; but he thought within himself, "I must go through with the procession." And so he carried himself still more proudly, and the chamberlains held on tighter than ever, and carried the train which did not exist at all.

Hans Christian Andersen, *The Emperor's New Clothes*, 1837

The chamberlains were clinging on more tightly than ever at CLSA's 1997 Investors' Forum (IF97). The questioning was tougher and the facts, as well as management opinions, were debated with equal intensity. Across most markets, investors see things very differently from management.

Following three years of poor market conditions, it would be encouraging to report that fund managers found themselves surrounded by golden nuggets of value and were dancing for joy like Walter Houston in *The Treasure of The Sierra Madre*. They weren't. Investors singled out Siam Commercial Bank as purveying a unique unreality, but there were numerous other examples where management and investors remained on different wavelengths.

It was not surprising that the red chip management could put little flesh on the bones of the basic asset injection concept. Such is the nature of any asset injection story. However, it was perhaps surprising that nobody seemed to care that much. Despite scepticism running high throughout IF97, the quality issues concerning the red chips are currently considered secondary, given their almost unique momentum status in Asia. While the focus on value intensified at IF97, there seemed every prospect that most investors would be prepared to play the Asian liquidity-driven markets again, should improving external accounts produce easier money in the region.

While investors have always been prepared to question Asian managements' opinions, there was increasing disagreement as to the facts. In particular, few were prepared to believe banking management regarding property exposure and there was general scepticism as to the sustainability of property prices. Some managements were honestly shocked by the degree of disbelief.

The disagreement is as to the facts and only one side can prevail… It was difficult to come to any other conclusion than that IF97 attendees are more likely to return home sellers than buyers of Asian equities. Though convinced that he is fully clothed, the shouts were loud enough at IF97 to produce a shiver down the spine of the emperor. The chamberlains' clutch tightened.

Each May CLSA hosted its Investors' Forum in Hong Kong. Corporates came from around the region to present the case for investment in their companies and institutional investors flew in from across the world looking for investment ideas. There would be many corporations presenting at the same time and if any meeting was a bit light on institutional investors, then CLSA staff would be sent to the meeting to make things look a bit better.

It was fascinating to see which meetings were well attended and which were not. More savvy investors sought out the poorly attended meetings hoping to find a company whose shares might be cheap because they had not already been pushed to giddy valuations by the attention of the institutional herd. This tactic was often successful.

In 1997 the chief speaker at 'The Forum' was President Fidel Ramos of the Philippines. To a packed ballroom at the Grand Hyatt he was introduced by Gary Coull, who thanked him for coming and for also bringing his lovely wife Imelda. There was a very audible large intake of breath across the room. Imelda was the notorious wife of a former president of the Philippines called Ferdinand Marcos. Fortunately, President Ramos laughed first.

What a swell party this is

16 June 1997, Regional

There is no better testimony to the powers of inflation than the lyrics to Cole Porter's classic *Who Wants to be a Millionaire*. When Porter wrote the lyrics in 1956, a millionaire was able to afford a country estate, a yacht, a supersonic plane, "flashy flunkies everywhere" and still have change to "wallow in champagne".

According to a recent private banking survey, there are now 6 million US dollar millionaires worldwide. Not many of today's millionaires can stretch to such essentials. Of course the powers of inflation mean that a 1956 US dollar millionaire is the equivalent of a US$6m millionaire today. Unfortunately, the dynamics of wealth mean that the price of the requisites of the rich have a nasty habit of at least advancing in line with inflation. Who would ever have thought that the leader of the UK Labour Party would be selling his family home for US$1m!

There is no doubt that Mr Porter would have to alter the word millionaire for billionaire if he were alive today. The list of billionaires is rather shorter than 6 million. According to *Forbes* magazine there are 447 billionaires worldwide, of whom 82 are in Asia ex Japan. In a new publication, *Asia's Wealth Club*, Geoff Hiscock lists the top US dollar billionaires in Asia (Mr Hiscock finds 93 in Asia ex Japan). Mr Hiscock's league table of the super-rich is shown in Table 2.8.

Table 2.8: Mr Hiscock's league table of the super-rich in 1997

	No. in top 100	Total net worth of top 100 billionaires
Malaysia	15	US$34bn
Indonesia	15	US$37bn
Hong Kong	13	US$53bn
Thailand	13	US$27bn
Philippines	12	US$22bn
Taiwan	8	US$28bn
South Korea	7	US$23bn
Singapore	6	US$14bn
India	3	US$4.2bn

In Hong Kong, one person in every 460,000 and in Malaysia one in every 1.2 million is a billionaire. However, in India, only one in every 300 million is a billionaire and Mr Hiscock could find no billionaires in China at all. It is interesting that only four of the Malaysian billionaires are indigenous Malays (Halim Saad, Rashid Hussain, Tajudin Ramli, Estate of Yahaya Ahmad). The concentration of wealth among the billionaires is highest in Hong Kong, but Malaysia runs a very close second. Table 2.9 shows the billionaires' wealth as a percentage of their respective countries' GDP.

Table 2.9: Billionaires' wealth as percentage of GDP in 1997

Hong Kong	34%
Malaysia	33%
Philippines	23%
Indonesia	17%
Thailand	14%
Singapore	13%
Taiwan	9%
South Korea	4%
India	1%

The number of billionaires in the world, according to *Forbes*, has risen from the 447 reported in this piece in 1997 to 2,095 in 2020. Today it is not difficult to find more than 100 billionaires in Asia ex Japan – *Forbes* listed 468 as of mid-2020. Just replicating the data for the top 100 billionaires in Asia ex Japan illustrates the shift in the distribution of the ultra-wealthy – to China (see Table 2.10).

Table 2.10: The top 100 billionaires in Asia ex Japan in mid-2020

	No. in Asia's top 100	Total net worth
Malaysia	4	US$37bn
Indonesia	2	US$36bn
Hong Kong	14	US$207bn
Thailand	3	US$34
Philippines	0	N/A
Taiwan	0	N/A
South Korea	3	US$30bn
Singapore	4	US$52bn
India	12	US$201bn
China	58	US$863bn

And as a percentage of their respective country's GDP, see Table 2.11.

Table 2.11: Billionaires' wealth in Asia's Top 100 as percentage of GDP

Hong Kong	55%
Malaysia	10%
Philippines	N/A
Indonesia	3%
Thailand	7%
Singapore	14%
Taiwan	N/A
South Korea	2%
India	7%
China	6%

In China there are now 200 billionaires. As Table 2.12 shows, the number of billionaires may have risen in Asia, but this has not been true in every country.

Table 2.12: Number of billionaires in 1997 and 2020

	Billionaires in 1997	Billionaires in 2020
Malaysia	15	8
Indonesia	15	13
Hong Kong	13	64
Thailand	13	29
Philippines	12	14
Taiwan	8	16
South Korea	7	34
Singapore	6	25
India	3	60
China	0	200
Macau	0	1
Vietnam	0	4

Asia's economic miracle turned into the Asian financial crisis of 1997–98. In that crisis, many people lost large percentages of their wealth and some lost all of it. However, economic growth did return and fortunes were still to be made. China, a market which few portfolio investors could invest in in 1997, was to be the country where the greatest fortunes of all were to be made. Achieving good returns in Chinese listed equities may have been difficult, but there were plenty of people who were able to make fortunes from what became the Chinese economic miracle.

Keeping track of the number of US dollar millionaires in the world is no mean feat, but by 2020 there were estimated to be about 50 million, quite a few more than the estimated 6 million of 1997. In 2020 purchasing power terms, you would now need US$9.5m to have the same purchasing power as a 1956 millionaire. The price of "flashy flunkies" it seems never does run cheap.

Plus ça change, plus c'est la même chose

18 June 1997, Thailand

Raja Finance had been one of the stars of the 1977–78 bull market in Bangkok and its shares were among the most actively traded on the market. It was also one of the principal providers of margin finance for stockmarket investors. When Raja failed at the end of 1978, the Bangkok bubble burst.

The bubble had indeed grown very big. From a level of around 80 throughout 1976, the market (as measured by the SET Index) took off at the beginning of 1977 and had breached the 200 mark by the end of the year – a rise of around 150%. Toward the end of 1978, it had scaled the peaks of 260 – a rise of well over 200% in two years. Half-way through 1979 it was back down to around 160 and bottomed out at around 120. It was to languish between there and around 160 for several years.

Anthony Rowley, *Asian Stockmarkets: The Inside Story*, 1987

Anthony Rowley's description was of another time but not another place. The 1978 peak was not surpassed until May 1987.

On this occasion, the 1994 peak for the Thai SET index was not surpassed, and then only briefly, until 2018. By the end of 2020, the index was below the level it first reached in January 1994. As the rise in the number of billionaires in Thailand shows, it has been possible to invest in Thailand and secure very strong returns over the past few decades.

Investing in listed equities was not the way to do that. At the peak of the Thai SET in early 1994, investors were investing in the equities of what they thought was a high-growth country and they were paying a price earnings ratio of 27× to do so. It turned out that it was a very high valuation for earnings that were largely illusionary.

Field of dreams

20 June 1997, Malaysia

Earlier this week, Hock Seng Lee announced it has been awarded a new reclamation and development contract. The company has gained approval from the Kedah government to reclaim 16,300 hectares of land and link together nine islands off Malaysia's north-western coast.

The reclaimed area alone is the equivalent of 163 sq. km and is 2.2× the size of Hong Kong island! While Hong Kong has a population density of 5,677 people per sq. km, the Malaysians have slightly more elbow room, with 58 people per sq. km. This makes Malaysia about as land short and claustrophobic as Ireland, where there are 51 people per sq. km. Should Ireland require a similar development, this would involve building an island one-third the size of the Isle of Man.

The announcement of the new island comes a day after the announcement of another new mega-project – the construction of a bridge between Malaysia and Sumatra. Our best estimate of the current schedule of mega-projects is as follows: the world's two tallest buildings (the Petronas towers), the world's longest building (Giga-city), Asia's biggest hydro-electric dam (Bakun), a new administrative capital (Putrajaya), a new airport, new sports arenas (Commonwealth Games), a new industrial zone with its own capital (the Multi-Media Super Corridor and CyberJaya), the city on stilts (off Johor), the world's biggest reclamation project (off the north-west coast) and a 22km bridge (Malaysia to Indonesia). You may be sceptical, but remember the success of Kevin Costner in *Field of Dreams*: "If you build it, they will come."

They did only build some of it, but they did come – it just took a while and too long, in most cases, to create the cash flow to service the debt associated with the investment. Based on my conversations with investors in the first half of 1997, none of these grand plans created particular cause for concern. That these 'fields of dreams' were to be financed largely with foreign currency debt also seemed to be irrelevant. These opinions were about to change quickly.

This time it's personal

24 June 1997, Thailand

According to leaks from a confidential report by one of Thailand's leading commercial banks, the BOT bears a grudge. According to the leak in *The Nation* newspaper, the BOT wishes "to destroy George Soros". The confidential report states that Soros is short US$4bn of baht and that this position matures at the end of August. If this story deserves credence then there may be tactical reasons for believing that any significant depreciation of the baht will be delayed until after the end of August.

To state the obvious, it is a matter of some concern that punishing an investor would rank higher than the conduct of monetary policy. While the end of August may seem near, it seems like a long time for the banking sector to wait for relief from the ever rising level of interest rates. Bangkok Bank now lends three-month money into the interbank market at 17.5%.

When the currency adjustment occurs, probably every Asian broker will be screaming "buy". The market will rally very quickly on low volume and could certainly offset the depreciation in the value of the currency. However, after this initial rally there will be a significant sell-off in the finance and property counters as the extent of the bad loan position becomes increasingly clear and major rights issues are announced. It is even possible that the government would attempt to sustain the currency at a new level, and interest rates may not fall as rapidly as at first expected. Volumes will be low during the rise in stock prices and low at the top. For most investors the trade in the Thai financial stocks will be completely impracticable.

Not for the first time George Soros was to become the figure the authorities came to blame. They had to blame someone and in Malaysia the blame game played upon Soros's Jewish ancestry. I did not fully understand why Mahathir Mohammad, the prime minister of Malaysia, chose to blame

George Soros in particular until one day I was in the bookshop at Malaysia's very impressive new airport in 1998.

Among the usual thrillers on sale for holiday reading I also found piles of a book called *The International Jew*, a notorious anti-Semitic tract and the front cover of this locally printed version bore the name of its original promoter, Henry Ford. As a regular frequenter of bookshops, I had never seen this publication before and I have never seen it since. That was shocking enough, but the bookshop also proudly displayed copies of *Mein Kampf*!

When looking around for scapegoats, the authorities were playing to a receptive audience. The ebbing of the tide of capital would reveal more than just ugly financial fragilities in Asia.

A farewell to arms

26 June 1997, Hong Kong

Last night, at the Hong Kong Stadium, the British Military Garrison gave their last marching band display. Not surprisingly, it was a feast of military and British classics. However, there was one concession to the modern idiom as the combined bands of the Gurkhas and Black Watch played a medley from *Les Misérables*. In particular, several rousing choruses of 'Do You Hear The People Sing?' rang around the stadium. For the remaining few who have not seen *Les Misérables*, a reminder of that chorus may be in order:

Do you hear the people sing?
Singing a song of angry men?
It is the music of a people
Who will not be slaves again!
When the beating of your heart
Echoes the beating of the drums
There is life about to start
When tomorrow comes.

Herbert Kretzmer, *Les Misérables*

Song sheets were not provided. Now why couldn't they have played something by that frightfully nice Lloyd Webber chappie?

There had been a production of *Les Misérables* in Hong Kong in 1996. Was it this or was it that concert on 25 June that planted a seed that has grown? 'Do You Hear The People Sing?' is now a key protest song sung by Hong Kong's democracy protestors.

There were just a few days to go before British rule was to end. I was amazed to see some local Cantonese people standing to salute the British military band as they marched past. There were even a few locals with tears in their eyes. However, this was a territory of over 6 million people and the vast majority of them just wanted to get on with their lives, which primarily meant in Hong Kong getting on with business. A then recently published book in Hong Kong had been called, only partially satirically, *Let's All Shut Up and Make Money!*

The third option

27 June 1997, Thailand

It is not a closely guarded secret that the IMF is currently visiting Bangkok. Speculation is thus rife that discussions are current regarding implementation of a package which would prevent Thailand from having to make that onerous choice between devaluation and deflation. One or other of these eventualities had increasingly seemed a certainty and the market's slump illustrated the increasingly limited prospect of escape.

As deflation threatened to destroy the financial system, we have believed for some time that an adjustment in the currency policy would be the more likely option. Now overseas investors are salivating as perhaps with IMF assistance a middle way can be found. At current market prices (market cap just US$61bn), equities are cheap for the long-term investor if the avoidance of deflation or devaluation becomes a probability.

In the short term, it may indeed appear to be the case that a middle way can be found. However, the assistance of the IMF is always at a price. The price is the policy alterations which the IMF believes will ensure that the crisis will not happen again. On this basis, the IMF can provide a loan in the belief that that loan will not become a gift. Flexible exchange rates are so central to current IMF economic orthodoxy that it seems highly likely that greater currency flexibility would be at the top of the list...

In the initial enthusiasm, the finance/property/banking sector may well outperform. However, we expect those sectors' woes to continue as the economic situation continues to deteriorate and huge rights issues will be called at higher levels. As the market cap is just US$61bn, it is unlikely that any institutional investor will find the liquidity to trade this movement in finance/property/ banking. The preferred strategy is to accumulate those companies which seem most likely to survive most eventualities and hold them, and accept whatever short-term underperformance this might lead to. Trading such a small market in the forthcoming period of volatility is only for the brave and the nimble.

The IMF had arrived and we were now just days away from the devaluation of the baht. The arrival of the international lender of last resort would lead to a flexible exchange rate, but it also provided a backstop regarding the form that future economic policy would take. As we shall see, the Asian authorities, even at the darkest hour, did not submit easily to the policy prescriptions of the IMF.

At various stages investors feared that the international lender of last resort would refuse support. The prospect, should that happen, was for policies that would almost certainly lead to capital controls and very probably money printing aimed at generating the inflation to inflate away the excessive debts of the private sector. With so much of the accumulated debt priced in US dollars, it would also have meant default on most of the foreign currency debt the region had borrowed from the developed world banking systems. The IMF was in town and their arrival reduced the prospects that Asia would fall into the abyss, or at least what would have been an abyss for foreign investors.

Even on the verge of the now-expected devaluation, an Asian stockbroking company was expected to recommend stocks to buy for those investors that could not reduce their weightings to zero – that tyranny of benchmarks again. Our Thai office did indeed come up with some survivors, but in the storm that was to sweep across Asia, Thailand was to go from centre stage to side-show. Investors in the region would very soon have very many more important things to worry about than selecting the least bad Thai equities.

A US$41,000 bargain

27 June 1997, Global

Yesterday, Lady Diana's dresses were sold in New York for US$41,000 each. This was perhaps the best-value purchase in Manhattan for some years. Although most focus on 'fame' associated articles with a view to profiting from capital appreciation, the yield prospects are often ignored. The success of the Hard Rock Cafe and Planet Hollywood indicates that 'fame' articles can act to boost turnover and margins at venues where they are deployed.

So what are the potential annual leasing revenues from a dress of Lady Diana's from a restaurant, dress shop, department store, etc? Anything in excess of US$685 per annum would result in a gross yield higher than US equities. How many owners of venues do you know who might be prepared to pay US$1.87 per day (US$685/365) to display Lady Diana's dresses with a view to attracting a few more customers? At a price of eight bucks a day, the dresses will have a gross yield higher than the government 30-year bond.

So for the price of a couple of beers, the venue owner could lease a dress with the prospect of boosting turnover and perhaps profit margins. Sounds like a bargain, so US$8 per day is probably too cheap. Thus the gross yield on the dress is probably well in excess of 6.78%. A yield double this seems easily possible and perhaps triple could be achieved. The investor thus has a prospect of significant yield enhancement while also participating from capital gain.

In December 2019, one of Lady Diana Spencer's dresses sold at auction for US$290,000. It was not disclosed whether the owner had been receiving a monetary yield on the dress over the course of their ownership.

PART THREE
Devaluation and crisis

The Timeless Explosion of Fantasy's Dream

3 July 1997, Thailand

W hen the controlling shareholder of the largest commercial bank in Thailand publicly forecasts bank runs, times are not normal. This is exactly what Chatri Sophapanich did on Wednesday, 18 June. This was the clearest possible indication that the financial system could not survive a deflation and thus the authorities would have to opt for the only other alternative – a devaluation.

The tumble in the market up to that date had been caused by a growing belief that the Thai government was prepared to follow the deflationary option. So is the stock market's reaction to the devaluation an overreaction? Yes.

The currency movement augurs a more accommodative monetary policy. With the currency peg straitjacket removed, interest rates can be adjusted in line with domestic economic conditions. However, the currency adjustment produced an 1100bp rise in overnight baht interest rates! Such an initial reaction is not surprising as many domestic actors have been genuinely surprised by the government's announcement.

Interest rates should begin to subside from current levels over the next few weeks. However, the government is now targeting interest rates and not the level of the currency. History would suggest that real interest rates will need to be reduced towards zero if the banking system is to be rescued and an economic recovery prompted. With inflation at 4.4% (possibly on a rising trend following the currency move), the current 27% overnight rate indicates just how aggressive the authorities will have to be to produce an accommodative monetary policy.

The work can be done, but only by resorting to the printing presses (inherent in the government's pledge of cheap loans to corporates) and thus a further decline in the external value of the baht. Should any capital flight from Thailand occur, then the battle to lower interest rates will be a tough one unless significant further currency downside occurs. The pledge to provide subsidised lending to corporate Thailand (assuming this is baht denominated) is an inherent recognition that the authorities will resort to the printing presses.

Given the dynamics above, it seems unlikely that the next few months will see a dramatic decline in interest rates (from Monday's levels) and the defeat of the forces of deflation. An orderly retreat from the currency peg means a gradual decline in interest rates and it will be some time before bankers' spreads have been rebuilt to such a level that results in the recapitalisation of the financial system. Within this adjustment period, credit growth will continue to slow and financial distress will accelerate. Listed companies will go bankrupt.

Yesterday was a move in the right direction and a further fall in the currency and interest rates is on the cards. However, we are at the stage of the cycle where financial distress will be at its extreme and failures in the listed sector mean that caution is essential, especially in the banking and finance sector. CLSA can find 33% of the market capitalisation which we believe has the balance sheet strength and the resilient cash flow characteristics necessary to survive the last down leg of this credit cycle. For the other 67%, it is a touch and go situation.

In total, 23% of market capitalisation is in the survivor category and also offers reasonable valuations. Our strategy is to buy that 23% of the market only and if possible move to a market weighting in Thailand or above buying the survivor stocks. The market capitalisation of that quarter of the market is just US$12.9bn! That US$12.9bn (less than Bill Gates's personal net worth) represents the commanding heights of an economy of 59 million people. With the outlook for the MSCI Far East ex Japan Index constituent markets still looking restrained, the purchase of this low-risk 23% of the Thai market should provide a reasonably low-risk strategy for providing index outperformance. Why take high risks in the banks/finance companies and marginal survivors when you don't have to?

In Hong Kong at midnight on 30 June, the former colony was handed back to China. I attended a party in a hotel suite with a view across Hong Kong harbour. We watched the ceremony live on television and for me the most dramatic moment was when members of the PLA, now just a few blocks away from where I stood, marched onto the stage of the Hong Kong International Convention Centre.

The PLA has a particular form of marching that is at the same time frightening and comical, and now they were here to display it. We watched the *Royal Yacht Britannia* carrying Prince Charles and the last governor, Chris Patten, sail out of the harbour and then life went on. As I left that night I walked out of the elevator on the ground floor and, looking up rather than down, fell straight into the lap of a man in a wheelchair.

I was rapidly raised to my feet by some security guards. I had fallen upon Deng Pufang, the son of Deng Xiaoping, the former premier of China. Deng Pufang had been confined to a wheelchair since 1968, when he was thrown from the third floor of a building by the Red Guards. I was not given the time to ask him for his thoughts on the evening.

The next day, 1 July, was a holiday. It was a new holiday that continues to this day and is gloriously named – Hong Kong Special Administrative Region Establishment Day – but perhaps it sounds better in Cantonese. The Thais chose the early morning of 2 July to announce the devaluation of their currency.

It was a very strange feeling when I heard the announcement. In some ways it was a vindication of opinions I had held for the past few years. However, it was also clear that the economic, social and political consequences of the move would be terrible for the people of Thailand, not just for investors in the Thai stock market. It was not as if this move by the Thais meant a victory lap and retirement, it meant even more work.

As Mike McCoy remarked at our morning meeting, investors who had been playing chess in two dimensions, because the exchange rate was fixed, would now have to learn to play in three dimensions. I am no mathematician, but the number of possible moves when the chessboard changes so dramatically creates an exponential rise in the potential moves. My quarterly report to clients, published in early April 1997, had been called 'The End of Certainty'. It had proclaimed rather ominously:

> The end of certainty produces volatility. When historical relationships break down, market participants find themselves without guidance and looking for the new relationships which are the new certainties. In the intervening period of flux, most established relationships are

likely to be challenged. At some stage there will appear to be few certainties, and great opportunities are created.

That proved to be an accurate statement, but the problem was that my job was to find some of those "new relationships" and to ring the bell when those "great opportunities" materialised. While some of the old skills I had learned could be useful, there were new skills to be learned if I was to have any chance of advising institutional investors what was to happen after 'The End of Certainty'. So far all we had come up with was some basic discount analysis that suggested the Southeast Asian markets were grossly overvalued. However, the two key inputs in those calculations, the discount rate and corporate earnings growth rates, were themselves now subject to huge uncertainty.

At least the early advice about Thailand had been correct. The baht had devalued and the first reaction was for the stock market to go up. In the three trading days that followed, the Thai SET Index rose 25%. In the same three days, the baht had declined by only 19% relative to the US dollar. Many thought that the removal of the straitjacket of the exchange rate policy would produce easier monetary policy and an economic acceleration that would be positive for the price of Thai equities.

In this first piece I wrote following the devaluation, I questioned whether this would be correct. On 3 July I published a piece called 'Thai Devaluation: Beware The Old Maid', which quoted from Keynes:

This battle of wits to anticipate the basis of conventional valuation a few months hence, rather than the prospective yield of an investment over the long term of years, does not even require the gulls amongst the public to feed the maws of the professional; it can be played by the professionals amongst themselves. Nor is it necessary that anyone should keep his simple faith in the conventional basis of valuation having any genuine long-term validity. For it is, so to speak, a game of Snap, of Old Maid, of Musical Chairs – a pastime in which he is a victor who says snap neither too soon or too late, who passes the Old Maid to his neighbour before the game is over, who secures the chair for himself when the music stops. These games can be played with zest and enjoyment, though all the players know that it is the Old Maid which is circulating, or that when the music stops some of the players will find themselves unseated.

John Maynard Keynes, *The General Theory of Employment Interest and Money*, 1935

The music had stopped and we knew there was more than one Old Maid circulating. We thought that two-thirds of listed equity could go to zero but were prepared to venture that 23% would remain solvent and would be worth investing in. To venture such an opinion was a mistake. The team in the Thai office did successfully pick the stocks that would survive, but when certainty ended in Thailand, all stocks were going down.

Keynes himself underwent a damascene conversion from what he called a 'credit cycle' investor – we might call a macro investor – to a value investor. Keynes's conversion happened at a fortuitous time in the early 1930s when equities proved to be very cheap. Both Keynes and the endowment fund of Kings College Cambridge, which he managed, reaped the rewards. But in July 1997 in Thailand, things were not just as simple as adopting a bottom-up value investing approach. The surge in interest rates and collapse in corporate earnings that threatened mass corporate bankruptcy made it very difficult to establish which Thai equities, if any, were offering good value.

This instant commentary above on this momentous event, written in haste on the morning of 2 July 1997, said nothing about the likely impact on the rest of Asia from the devaluation of the Thai baht. That would largely depend upon whether the baht devaluation would impact the direction of the short-term capital flow across the region. It did.

Déjà vu all over again

7 July 1997, Malaysia

Purchasers of Malaysian equities today must assume that the corporates have avoided the errors of the last cycle. They must assume that, unlike other recent examples – Japan, the United States, Australia, France and Thailand – there has not been significant mal-investment associated with the massive credit expansion in Malaysia. It is crucial that such mistakes have been avoided, otherwise 3× book is an expensive price to pay for the Kuala Lumpur Composite Index just as we enter an economic slowdown!

If the net assets of a company are worth US$100 and the share price trades at US$300, the company is said to be valued at 3× book value. To pay such a premium for corporate capital assumes an ability among management to achieve returns well in excess of the returns any investor can achieve by putting their capital in a relatively risk-free investment such as a bank account. The premium is paid while recognising the risks that management may also fall short of producing such returns, while the depositor can often lock in a fixed yield for some years to come.

By paying 3× book for Malaysia's corporate equity in July 1997, investors were showing a huge degree of confidence that corporate Malaysia was up to the task of producing such returns. The evidence that Malaysia had been the scene of huge overinvestment was there for all to see on the streets of Kuala Lumpur or in the pages of the local newspapers.

The price-to-book ratio was probably a better indicator of just how overvalued Asian equities were than the PE ratios that made equities look cheap by their recent standards. Even after the devaluation of the baht there was plenty of time to sell what remained very overvalued equities in Malaysia and also elsewhere in the region.

Danger

9 July 1997, Taiwan

It looks as if the monetary rush which has pushed Taiwanese equities up 32% this year is running out of steam.

It is increasingly likely that we are in the closing days of the great liquidity bull run in Taiwanese equities, and with price-to-sales ratios stretched to new highs, there is little fundamental value to support equities when liquidity dries up.

There is a risk to the liquidity-driven bull market and with price-to-sales ratios stretched for the cyclical sectors, this suggests that there is limited fundamental underpinning for the current price of equities.

Interestingly, this piece warning of danger for investors in Taiwan makes no reference to the impact from the devaluation of the baht. There remained a general view that there could be a capital exodus from the Southeast Asian markets, but portfolio investors would not rush for the exits in the other Asian markets. Across the meeting rooms of the developed world though, institutional investors were deciding to reduce their commitments to 'Asia'.

Reducing the Asia commitment meant reducing investment in the constituents of the MSCI Asia Index. While that could mean selling particularly aggressively in Southeast Asia, it also meant selling a bit of everything. We all should have expected the tyranny of the benchmark to trigger a more general capital outflow. More importantly, we should have contemplated how foreign bankers, who had huge US dollar loans across the region, might respond to the end of the Thai economic miracle. It turned out that they also were acting to reduce their exposure to that thing called 'Asia'.

On 11 July I took off on a two-week trip to visit institutional investors in Japan and the United States. In that period the downward pressure on many Asian exchange rates became irresistible. The Philippines devalued on 11 July and between 11 and 14 July, the defences of the Malaysian and Indonesian exchange rate targets were also abandoned. The Singapore dollar was also allowed to decline.

There was now a growing list of countries in the region where we were dealing with the end of certainty and playing an investment game in three dimensions that had previously only been played in two. The fixed variable that I believed made it easier to solve the liquidity equation had gone. The exchange rates of the key North Asian markets – Hong Kong, South Korea and Taiwan – remained stable.

Hong Kong's foreign exchange reserves continued to rise, partly as a result of the capital still flowing in for the 'red chip' boom. In Taiwan, foreign reserves were to peak at the end of June and in South Korea, at the end of July. The capital exodus in these early months of the Asian financial crisis was very much a Southeast Asian affair. It was not until October that it was to begin to force policy changes and bring the crisis to North Asia.

The four elephants of Houston

28 July 1997, Regional

> I never could succeed as a merchant. I have tried unsuccessfully several times. I never could be content with a fixed salary, for mine is a purely speculative disposition, while others are just the reverse; and therefore all should be careful to select those occupations that suit them best.
>
> **PT Barnum, *The Life of P.T. Barnum, Written by Himself*, 1855**

Day five of a marketing roadshow when suddenly our taxi is halted by a policeman with a sidearm on his hip. Clearly there is some trouble up ahead and the visitor to the United States relives a thousand episodes of *NYPD Blue*. Just as the cop starts to move slowly towards the taxi, an elephant appears, then another elephant and then two more.

The cop explains that the Barnum & Bailey circus is in town and the elephants are crossing the road to their new home – the underground car park of a nearby office block. The evolutionary pressures of the jungle have shaped an animal which may be the king of that jungle, but is clearly unsuited to life in an underground carpark.

As with animals, so with companies. To adapt and survive, companies evolve to meet their economic environments. During the hyper-inflationary period in Latin America, business adapted to provide good real returns; in Japan, cheap capital and booming asset prices resulted in high returns as *zaitech* evolved; and in Russia, a unique form of business has evolved to cope with a de facto legal vacuum. In Asia, businesses have evolved around the currency pegs which have provided a surfeit of cheap capital and an inflation in asset prices. Two weeks ago, the economic environment changed for good.

Four corporate elephants will now have to adapt to life without the currency policies, cheap capital and inflating assets: Malaysia, Thailand, Indonesia and the Philippines. The catalyst for this forced evolution is a rising cost of capital in all four markets and a falling return on capital in Malaysia and Thailand. Even in Thailand, where the pain of the adjustment is most advanced, there is no evidence that the fundamental realignment of capital necessary to adapt to the new environment is taking place.

Although the new pressures are painful, they have not yet been painful enough. The key question for investors is whether they want to participate in this adaptation of capital or assess it from the sidelines. Price will drive that decision.

A reworking of Gordon's dividend discount model reveals that the markets are only fair value if the terminal dividend growth rates are as follows: Malaysia 15%, Indonesia 19%, the Philippines 23% and Thailand 8%. While Thailand looks cheap for long-term investors, the evolutionary process is about to condemn certain companies to extinction in that jurisdiction.

From a micro perspective, all four markets have negative capital spreads (the weighted average cost of capital is higher than the return on that capital). The bad news for investors is that management's capital destructiveness is currently rewarded with high price-to-book ratios: Malaysia 2.7×, Indonesia 3.2×, the Philippines 2.5× and Thailand 1.2× (for Thailand, there is considerable doubt as to the accuracy of book value). Simply put, it is difficult to argue that investors are being paid to take the risks inherent in the evolutionary process.

For investors looking for sectors to avoid during the capital realignment process, the conclusion remains the same as it was in September 1995:

PT Barnum's capitalist nomenclature extends to just merchants and speculators. The cyclical pressures in Asia (as strong US$ and slowing capital inflows) have squeezed the speculator already. The structural adjustment in monetary policy will further squeeze the speculator as monetary policy will henceforth become more appropriate for domestic economic conditions. Who better than Mr Barnum to have the final word on how to outperform during this structural adjustment: "All should be careful to select those occupations that suit them best."

Author, *The Solid Ground*, 1995

Now there were four markets where the old form of analysis was redundant. With the adjustment already begun, the very rough calculation of the growth rate in dividends that the stock markets would have to produce to vindicate the current stock prices still indicated gross overvaluations. At least now we were getting a better understanding of the premium that domestic interest rates might have to reach above US interest rates, though there was great uncertainty as to their future path.

Utilising these new higher interest rates, the implied dividend growth rates priced into equities, with the exception of Thailand, were astronomical. Thailand may have looked cheaper, but we could not really know how much corporate earnings might shrink as interest rates rose and foreign currency debt became ever more difficult to service as the baht exchange rate declined.

In the United States, a country with a long history of operating a very successful capitalist system, the annual rate of dividend growth over the long term has been 3.7%. It seemed highly unlikely that the Asian markets could produce long-term dividend growth rates anywhere near the levels priced in – even after their declines following their exchange rate devaluations.

It was far too optimistic to expect that stocks in the Philippines and Indonesia would only be negatively impacted by the rise in interest rates. Those rising rates were also to bring economic distress and in many cases large losses for local companies. One thing was clear though, this was not a time to invest in the shares of banks and property companies in any of these four countries. The adjustments underway made it almost impossible to assess whether these companies had any book value at all.

Good capital, bad capital

5 August 1997, Malaysia

Governments regularly denounce the market. This denunciation is indeed less prevalent than it used to be, but is still practised by every government in the world, perhaps to prove that the sovereign state is still in existence. Thus the government's manipulation of the market is a common day occurrence.

The very adoption of currency policies within Asia was a renunciation of market forces and an assumption that a government-determined level for the currency would be more beneficial than one determined by market forces. The legacy of this hubris is now apparent in the carcasses of empty office blocks scattered across Thailand and accumulating in Malaysia.

Not surprisingly, governments have denounced that part of the market which creates negatives and championed those elements which create positives. Indeed, at different stages of the business cycle, governments may denounce the very market mechanisms which they championed at a very different stage of the cycle. Thailand boasted of high capital inflows but created a dual currency system to prevent high capital outflows.

The history of government interventions in markets is not a pretty one. Whatever price was manipulated, it invariably impacted another important element of the supply/demand equation, thus altering prices and capital allocation. In short, once you start tinkering with the market's machine, the serious repercussions are likely to occur in another market where such impacts were unforeseen. Having intervened in the price of domestic commodities for many years in Malaysia, the authorities have now decided to intervene in the free market for capital.

Last Friday, the domestic cost of money was deemed too high in Malaysia, so there was a unilateral declaration that it would rise no further (the base lending rate pricing mechanism was rescinded for the month of July). On Monday, the authorities decided that short-term capital outflows were injurious to the economy, so they have acted to prevent them. While intervening with the price of chickens was serious enough, to intervene with the price of money and the freedom of movement of capital is even more dangerous. The authorities have once again moved the goal posts for the providers of the international capital which has for so long financed their current account deficit and funded domestic investment.

Like Thailand, they seek to delineate between the bad capital and the good capital and in the process increase the risks for any investor committing capital to Malaysia. One attack on a market mechanism which permits an outflow of capital has been made. There are other ways of making negative bets on the direction of the ringgit. It seems unlikely that the government would stop short at attacking this particular method. With a high degree of uncertainty regarding the future freedom of movement of capital, the authorities are deterring all forms of capital flow, not just the short-term outflows which particularly perturb them.

In Thailand, the authorities altered one market mechanism and then another and then another as they ran around putting their fingers in the dike to prevent capital from escaping. In the end, the Thais ended up with a dual exchange rate which dramatically drove interest rates higher and heightened the problem they had tried to prevent. The Malaysians stuck their finger in the dike yesterday and the result is more likely to be a higher price of capital rather than a lower price. As the authorities will not permit the banks' lending rates to rise, this rise in money market rates is likely to squeeze banking and particularly finance company margins.

To list the potential distortions from the intervention in the swap market and the lending markets is probably sufficient scope for a book or a thesis. Only in retrospect will many of the impacts be determined. It is unclear just how far the authorities will pursue the persecution of 'bad' capital, but the chances are high that a continued chase will negatively impact the providers of 'good' capital.

Equity investors purchased Malaysian ringgit assets under one set of rules of convertibility but are increasingly operating under a different set of rules. In Thailand, one branch of capitalists (the equity investor) watched while another branch (the currency investor) was attacked by the authorities. However, it was the equity investor who lost significant sums of money as the markets reacted to the authorities' actions by driving interest rates up and equities down.

With the price of equities already high in Malaysia (2.7× book value), investors are simply not being paid to take the risk that the authorities' distortionary intervention in the ringgit market will not have negative impacts on the value of equities. Who is to say that equity investors repatriating funds will not themselves in due course be designated bad capital? Somebody is drawing a line in the sand between good capital and bad capital – 'Which side are you on?'

The prime minister of Malaysia launched his first tirade against 'rogue speculators' on 24 July 1997. This was a warning for investors that the rules in force when capital was flowing into the region may not be the same as when capital was flowing out. There were still investors who expected to play the investment game by the same rules that applied when they first invested. They simply could not believe that a government could change those rules. This was a form of apostasy that was just not possible.

This inability to see the world as a politician sees it was the cause of much distress in 1997 and 1998, and it continues to be so. Investors in Asia did not believe that the likely socio-political turmoil from the economic adjustments could lead to the rulebook being changed. Local policy makers had more to worry about than the sanctity of contract and if changing the rules could alleviate some of the pain inflicted on their peoples, then they would be sorely tempted to rip up the old rule book. This conflict between the owners of capital and local policy makers was to seriously complicate the business of establishing those 'new relationships' and 'great opportunities' it was my job to try to identify. The general impact, however, when governments start tinkering with the rules, is for investors to classify local investment as just too uncertain and uncertainty leads more likely to liquidation than accumulation.

Jockeys and knackers

6 August 1997, Thailand

At Downpatrick Racecourse, at the foot of the Mourne mountains in Ireland, the quality of the field is rarely good. It seems that everybody in the country who made some money on the dogs upgrades to a horse. However, these same turf investors sometimes pay top dollar to get the best jockeys.

The uninitiated punter often commits their hard-earned tenner to back a Dunwoody regardless of the quality of his mount. The punter believes that the owner must believe their horse to be a winner or otherwise why would they pay for a good jockey? The owner pays for a good jockey because they can and the punter waves goodbye to their tenner. Similarly, in Thailand, there is a belief that a new jockey (the IMF) can whip the bank and finance stocks into a dramatic outperforming run. Unfortunately, many of these mounts are set for the knacker's yard and not the winning post.

Even if the Thai authorities had been minded to bail out private capital, the IMF conditions make it clear that the principle of 'punter pays' is still in operation. The good financial institutions will now be expected to swallow the bad ones. In theory, Finance One was the best capitalised finco in Thailand, but its 'merger' failed because it had a negative net worth!

As things stand at the minute, it looks as if the good bankers will be forced to buy the bad banks with negative net worth. There will be an instantaneous decline in a book value which is already shrinking rapidly. Perhaps as the process continues, this dilution of bank capital will be seen as unpalatable – but what is the alternative?

This is not to say that bank and finance counters in Thailand will never be a buy. However, given the surge in share prices and the current premium-to-book values, the market is not accounting for the risks associated with mass bankruptcy in the sector and the need for the good capital to be used to bail out the bad. At this stage, neither the potential winners nor the potential knacker's fodder could be considered a value bet. With this sector so seriously overvalued, the SET Index can retest its lows of June.

In the early days it was if the fairy godmother had arrived in Asia in the shape of the IMF. A magic wand was to be waved and all the mal-investment would somehow be made good and shareholders would be made whole. While the arrival of the IMF strongly signals that a country will not take the path of hyper-inflation and default, it does not mean that suddenly all is right in the world of corporate capital.

Since 1997, we have come to believe that bailouts from government or supranational institutions are always just around the corner and a free lunch is thus available for those who buy in a crisis. This was not the case in the Asian financial crisis. A crucial part of the problem was the excessive level of US dollar debt across the region. Simply printing more local currency and lowering interest rates might have been good for the stock market initially, but the decline in the exchange rate would have made the foreign currency debt situation even worse.

The IMF was there primarily to stop such a policy from being implemented or capital accounts being closed, both moves that would have forced mass defaults on the US dollar debt provided by the developed world banking system. There were long-term positives from these policies for foreign investors, but there was also very considerable short-term pain.

The people of Hong Kong were fascinated by horse racing and it was the only legal form of gambling. One evening, on a junk on the way back from a company event on Lantau Island, I got talking to a man who turned out to be a jockey. He was Irish so I asked him if he had ever raced at Downpatrick. He had and we discussed what might or might not happen in that period when jockeys and horses are behind the hill in the middle of the track and beyond the view of the crowd.

I mentioned to Gary Coull the next day that one of our guests was actually a jockey who had even ridden at Downpatrick. Gary smiled and explained that he had not just ridden at such giddy heights, but had also won the Derby and several classics. He was to win two more Derbys and a few more classics. The jockey's name was Mick Kinane.

Sir Cliff, the King and Singapore

7 August 1997, Singapore

It is often said that Singapore is boring and that there is a general lack of lateral thinking. The very success of the economy and its constant ability to reinvent itself is sufficient testimony that such assumptions are incorrect. On a recent visit to Singapore I picked up another piece of evidence which attests to that long history of lateral thinking.

In November 1961, Cliff Richard (now Sir Cliff) and The Shadows played their first concert in Singapore. This was soon followed by Cliff's cinematic masterpiece, *The Young Ones*. Not surprisingly, the young man's talent sent shock waves through Singapore and suddenly on every street corner there was somebody doing a Cliff Richard impersonation. By early 1962, a local radio station decided to capitalise on the phenomenon by holding a Cliff Richard impersonation competition – the first of many. *The judges, carried away on the wave of hysteria, awarded the prize to a local man who was actually doing an Elvis impersonation.*

Underestimate such a nation at your peril. "Once in every lifetime, comes a chance like this…."

A local fund manager in Singapore once explained to me that foreign investors suffered from something he called 'Changi fever'. On arrival at Singapore Changi Airport, they marvelled not just at the efficiency of the airport relative to then chaotic Asian standards, but it was also clearly much more efficient than their home airports. According to my local expert, this dose of visible efficiency was not replicated throughout the economy.

However, as most fund managers did not get beyond Changi Airport and the Central Business District, these created enough of a good impression to add quite a bit to the annual flow of portfolio capital into Singapore each year. Despite the warning, I had clearly been impacted by 'Changi fever' and, I think, remain so. It is possible as a visiting investor to never have any real contact with the economy or local business practices, and I know one investor who proudly boasted that he never left property owned by the Jardines Group whenever he visited Hong Kong. The world of an international portfolio investor can be a rarefied one and it was not just in Singapore that a visitor could be deceived by appearances if simply moving from luxury hotel to meeting room and back.

Badgers, skunks and killer whales – again

8 August 1997, Regional

In August last year, we advised investors to beware of buying skunks and stick to badgers and if necessary killer whales. This nomenclature referred to the black and white business of lending money. As a guide to species' delineation we offered the Moody's credit ratings. In retrospect, credit ratings appear to have provided a reasonable guide to subsequent performance. Table 3.1 shows the credit ratings and percentage price falls since 6 August 1996 as at 7 August 1997.

Table 3.1: Credit ratings and percentage price falls since 6 August 1996

	Credit rating	% share price fall since 6 August 1996
Local share price		
Bangkok Bank	A2	−37%
IFCT	A2	−57%
Thai Farmers Bank	A2	−46%
Krung Thai Bank	A3	−77%
Bank of Ayudhya	Baa1	−52%
First Bangkok City Bank	Baa2	−52%
Siam City Bank	Baa2	−77%
Thai Military Bank	Baa2	−72%
Bangkok Metropolitan	Baa3	−71%
Bank of Asia	Baa3	−72%
Foreign share price		
Bangkok Bank	A2	−24%
IFCT	A2	−54%
Thai Farmers Bank	A2	−53%
Krung Thai Bank	A3	−78%
Bank of Ayudhya	Baa1	−59%
First Bangkok City Bank	Baa2	−47%
Siam City Bank	Baa2	−81%
Thai Military Bank	Baa2	−75%
Bangkok Metropolitan	Baa3	−59%
Bank of Asia	Baa3	−72%

Almost all investors are trained to look for bargains when share prices fall precipitously. Even at the earliest stages of the Asian financial crisis, precipitous falls had already occurred. It proved to still be a very bad time to buy equities in general, and bank equities in particular. These banks were not impacted by a normal downturn in an economic cycle.

They had seen their habitat of excess liquidity created by the operation of managed exchange rates destroyed overnight. One of the strengths of companies is that they can adapt to new environments, although that is often painful. The problem for banks is that the sales they made in the past regime, their loan book, remains the key driver of their future earnings. Any investor in banks in Asia in the summer of 1997 was not buying the future, they were buying the past.

As most people were to discover to their shock, that past had been even more corrupt and dangerous, in terms of what it meant for credit quality, than even the biggest bears had understood it to be. Most balance sheets in Asia were in trouble when the exchange rates devalued, but some were in more trouble than others. Owners of the equity of banks, inherently geared institutions that borrow short to lend long, were exposed to almost all of the mal-investment under the old monetary regime. For bank investors in particular, the sins of the past are visited upon the future.

Sending the boys round

12 August 1997, Thailand

I have said that lending to pay interest is more properly the domain of loan sharks than of commercial banks. When a loan has deteriorated so far that the borrower can no longer even meet the interest payments, you've got to get a tough, insensitive goon to go out and protect that new money. Since the Polish crisis, the banks have found such a goon – a powerful bringer of bad tidings to the embattled Third World called the International Monetary Fund.

SC Gwynne, *Selling Money*, 1986

Yesterday, the IMF, together with a dozen nations, got together to provide the finance which will keep Thailand's head above water. The appearance of individual nations as donors should not be surprising as these nations represent a cross-section of the commercial bankers who have financed the great Thai economic boom. The same dozen nations, probably coincidentally, cover the key nationalities of portfolio investors who have also committed significant funds for investment. The outstanding commitments from BIS-reporting banks (does not include Asian commercial banks) to Thailand are shown in Table 3.2.

Table 3.2: Outstanding commitments from BIS-reporting banks to Thailand

	US$bn
Japan	37.5
Europe	19.1
Germany	6.9
France	4.6
UK	3.1
North America	6.2

When the IMF came to Asia, they were not that interested in the plight of foreign portfolio investors. They were very interested in the plight of the foreign banks that had lent excessively in the region. In 1982, the Mexican sovereign default and the numerous defaults by other LDCs had eradicated the capital of some of the world's biggest banks. That sudden evaporation of bank capital threatened to create a credit crunch that would grind developed world bank capital even lower and reduce bank lending and global economic growth.

In response, Paul Volcker, Chairman of the US Federal Reserve, abandoned his broad money targeting regime, interest rates collapsed and something even worse than a recession was narrowly averted. However, cleaning up the commercial banks' balance sheet mess from the LDC defaults lasted for many years. By August 1997 the scale of the problem in Asia seemed to be much more limited, but the impact on Asian and developed world banks from the problems in Thailand was a key issue driving IMF intervention.

The countries providing finance to supplement the IMF programme were all Asian: Japan, Australia, Hong Kong, Malaysia, Singapore, Indonesia, South Korea and China. That so many Asian countries contributed to the Thai package indicated that they were largely unaware that the Thai crisis was rapidly morphing into an Asian crisis. The United States did not provide financial support because it seemed unlikely that Congress would support a financial contribution. The flexibility for the executive, acting alone, to use the Exchange Stabilization Fund to provide support had been restricted after the Mexican crisis.

That neither the United States nor any European country contributed to the Thai package was something that would not be forgotten in Asia. As Table 3.2 shows, their commercial bankers had large credit exposures to

Thailand, but it would be primarily money from Asian governments that might act to prevent major losses for all banks in Thailand.

Developed world policy makers could see the risk that the crisis in Asia would produce the same risks for developed world growth as it had in 1982. They needed to do something to stop that, but they were less interested in the plight of institutional investors who had bought Asia's listed securities.

Portfolio investors, in the form of mutual funds and pension funds, unlike banks, are largely unleveraged. When they lose money, this represents a decline in the value of someone's savings. A decline in the value of savings could, *in extremis*, result in a constraint on consumption and negatively impact developed world growth, but that was unlikely. The plight of these savers in Asia was not the key reason why the IMF rode into town. They were there to try to minimise the damage to the global banking system. The policies designed to do that would not necessarily promote the interests of the portfolio investor.

In Mexico, the combined US and IMF bailout of 1995 had in effect bailed out portfolio investors, particularly those holding fixed interest securities. That the United States had contributed in scale to that programme was probably because the key policy risk then was mass immigration to the United States from Mexico should the local economy have collapsed. There was no such risk to US borders from the economic collapse in Asia and it was thus not clear that portfolio investors could expect the same scale of actions in 1997 that had bailed out portfolio investors in Mexico in 1995.

The silos in finance still precluded the portfolio investor from fully understanding that the role of the IMF in Asia was to primarily protect a financial crisis spreading from Asia, through developed world bank losses, to global economic growth. Those who thought a Mexican-style bailout for the portfolio investor was coming to Asia were to be sorely disappointed.

In the institutional investment silo, the focus was on the damage that liquidating portfolio assets might have on the price of financial assets, interest rates and exchange rates. In South Korea and Taiwan, there was limited involvement by foreign institutional investors, a legacy of restrictions on foreign ownership of local equities, but the foreign banks were large lenders of US dollars. It was the decisions of the bankers to cut their Asian exposure that spread the crisis to Taiwan and South Korea.

By late August 1997, Thailand, the Philippines, Malaysia and Indonesia had devalued their currencies and both Thailand and the Philippines were receiving support from the IMF. In South Korea, further liquidity issues had already forced Ssangyong Motors to seek to sell itself to a stronger partner, and Jinro Group, Dainong Group and Kia Motors had all required emergency loans orchestrated by the government.

That foreign bankers might have been reconsidering their exposure to South Korea as well as Southeast Asia should have been something more widely recognised by portfolio investors. However portfolio investors still saw North Asia as the port in this particular storm, an opinion that was not to change until October.

Farewell then Tamagotchi capitalism

15 August 1997, Thailand

The fund provided by the IMF will be at the disposal of the central bank of Thailand to replenish reserves … If the balance of payments is not covered by the long-term capital, this money can be used as and when necessary. The fund will absolutely not be used to clean up the finance sector.

Hubert Neiss, IMF, 13 August 1997

The Tamagotchi is an electronic virtual pet. Apparently the virtual pet needs constant care and attention, otherwise it becomes the equivalent of virtual compost. While most equity investors would not be seen dead with a Tamagotchi, many have committed significant funds to the Thai equity market in a belief that the government would succour and sustain their 'virtual' company with public funds. Many see the IMF package as the provision of public funds to bail out the owners of private capital. The words of Mr Neiss above make it absolutely clear that Tamagotchi capitalism is dead in Thailand. The implications go well beyond the current stage of the economic cycle.

For the past six months, the battle cry of the Thai bulls has been: "Well they can't let all the banks/fincos/cement companies/property companies [delete as applicable] go bankrupt." Well it is true that Thailand will continue to have banks etc., but it is simply not true that the ownership of those assets will go uninterrupted through this particular stage of the economic cycle.

There are numerous banks in Texas today, but none of the large banks are still in the hands of those owners who steered them into the 80s. When the net worth of these banks went negative, foreclosure was instituted and public funds were utilised to take control of the bad assets while the good assets were sold to out-of-state bankers. Public money was not committed to save the shareholders who were made to take the risk, having taken some substantial rewards of the ownership of equity capital.

Throughout the Asian financial crisis there were significant amounts of wishful thinking, probably because detailed analysis to establish value was so difficult. Much of what passed for analysis was trying to assess which companies would 'have' to be saved and which could be let go to the wall. A simple analysis would say that the arrival of the IMF would improve the chances that equity would survive.

The Thai government suddenly had access to the funds that could be used to sustain what would otherwise be the unsustainable. It was not to be so easy. The IMF were to insist that some companies, particularly banks and finance companies, were closed. As the crisis developed, their demands were to become more extreme, demanding the type of root and branch reform that would have destroyed the existing form of capitalism, particularly in Indonesia and South Korea, and significantly increased the risk of mass bankruptcies. Even by the summer of 1997 it was evident that the IMF's arrival in Asia would augur some form of structural change, but few investors considered whether such reforms were compatible with what had been previously lauded as Asian values.

What none of us appreciated until much later in the crisis was that behind the IMF, exerting considerable influence, was the US Treasury Department. The secretary of the Treasury, Robert Rubin, and his deputy, Larry Summers, saw an opportunity to open up the Asian economies for international, for which read US, business. The more pain felt by the supplicant governments, the greater the prospect that they would accede to such demands to open their economies.

This was an Asian financial crisis, but very soon it developed into an attempt to bring a different form of capitalism to Asia. Investors who had been aware of the agenda of the US Treasury may have been more cautious on investing based on the belief that the capital inflow from the IMF would act to save the remnants of equity in the region remaining post the devaluations.

As the crisis developed, a drive for a form of business regime change became evident. Those who were invested in listed companies were invested in the old regime. That regime was now threatened with extinction by the very organisation some investors thought had arrived to save it.

The luxury and excitement of Southeast Asia

9 September 1997, New Asia

At this point in history, the investor is in a luxurious position in regard to analysis using the domestic risk-free rate. Equities in Southeast Asia (ex Singapore) are so overvalued that risk-free rates would have to fall significantly below the pre-'Mekong' crisis levels before fair value could begin to be established. At this stage the investor's position is straightforward.

With interest rates very unlikely to return even to pre-Mekong crisis levels over the next 12 months, these markets are sells now. (A fall in interest rates below these levels is only likely to be achieved due to considerable currency weakness.) At a future date there will need to be a more careful assessment of exactly what risk-free rates are to be used. However, as was suggested in *The Solid Ground Daily* yesterday, the market machine has changed, leaving equities overvalued, and this is much more important at this stage than any of the variables one feeds into the machine.

That investors had switched from using a risk-adjusted US Treasury yield to value Asian equities would seem obvious given the change in the exchange rate regimes. It wasn't. Some clung onto US interest rates as the correct variable for equity valuation. Ralph Waldo Emerson in his essay 'Self-Reliance' was right to remind us all that "a foolish consistency is the hobgoblin of little minds". When a fixed variable in an equation is removed, never underestimate the ability of any human being to simply continue to act on the basis that it is still there.

My attempt to label the Asian crisis as the *Mekong crisis* failed. It was not a name chosen to reflect the name of that long river that forms a large part of the Thai border. It was a name that reflected the tequila crisis, the name for the Mexican crisis of 1994, but this time it was the epithet of the Mekhong whisky brand of Thailand. I can only guess that not enough people had sampled its delights to endorse the comparison.

Musical chairs

15 September 1997, New Asia

The focus is now on the Asian foreign currency debt binge. Foreign investors are pointing at local corporates and questioning their competence in running up such currency mismatches. For every borrower, there is a lender. According to BIS statistics, the BIS banks have increased their exposure to Asia by US$87bn in the 18 months to the end of 1996. Of this, US$51bn has been loaned by European banks, US$10bn by Japanese banks, US$15bn by US banks and US$10bn by other banks.

As the data shows, it has been an alteration in lending behaviour by the European banks in particular which has driven the build-up in foreign currency debt exposures in Asia. European banks have lent US$37bn more than the Japanese banks into Asia. The BIS debt tables only include data up to the end of 1996. The best indications of the trends in 1997 are provided by the International Financing Review (IFR).

According to the IFR, there has been US$82.7bn in syndicated credits arranged in the first eight months of 1997. Of course this will not represent a net addition to the sums outstanding, but will partially represent refinancing of maturing debt. However, in the first nine months of 1996 (as the net debt exposure mounted rapidly), there was a total of US$87bn arranged. Thus assuming an even maturity profile in 1996 and 1997, it would appear that the pace of foreign currency debt build-up has remained rapid during 1997. The currency adjustment and associated rising risks would appear to have been a surprise to borrower and lender alike in mid-1997.

The makeup of the top arrangers of these syndicated credits provides interesting reading. One has to get to the 13th most active arranger before one encounters a Japanese bank. In total there are just five Japanese banks in the top 25 arrangers for 1997. In the top ten there are four US banks (Chase, BankAmerica, Citibank, JP Morgan) one Asian bank (HSBC – in first position), one Australian bank (Westpac) and four Europeans (CSFB, UBS, SocGen, ABN AMRO). There have been few significant changes in the activities of individual arrangers over the year, apart from HSBC's move from sixth largest arranger at the end of September 1996 to the number one position by September 1997.

One of the problems for the Asian equity investor is that the outlook for Asian markets is now inextricably linked with the reactions of the foreign currency lenders to their Asian risk. The sums above represent debts that are currently being offered to foreign bankers. Should foreign bankers continue to provide financing, there will continue to be the capital inflows which will assist in stabilising the currencies and maybe even permit downward pressure on interest rates. However, if the credit quality committees of Frankfurt, Amsterdam, Geneva, Paris and Zurich decide that they wish to reduce their exposure to Asia, then there is likely to be steady downward pressure on the Asian currencies. Table 3.3 shows the sums that are maturing within 12 months of the end of 1996, according to BIS data.

Table 3.3: Sums maturing within 12 months of the end of 1996. Source: BIS data

	US$bn
Indonesia	33
Malaysia	11
Philippines	8
Thailand	45

Asia is currently flooded by European fund managers seeking to quantify the downside from the current currency adjustment. It is ironic that the key imponderable in quantifying the downside is the decisions of the credit quality committees in Europe itself.

The more these publicly available numbers for foreign currency lending in Asia were seen by portfolio investors, the more horrified they became. Virtually nobody had bothered to look at these numbers and those who did simply concluded that Asia would always be able to roll over foreign currency, primarily US dollar, credit lines.

I had more phone calls and emails about this data than on any other subject in the second half of 1997. Investors often refused to believe the numbers and then they would state, without any particular evidence, that the local corporates must have hedged their exposure. A currency hedge would have indeed reduced their risk from the devaluation of their exchange rate relative to the US dollar, but it would also have massively increased the price of their US dollar borrowing. None of us knew how much of this US dollar debt was hedged and none of the stock analysts I asked could provide me with any answers from the companies' annual reports and accounts.

It was this lack of disclosure that led institutional investors to believe that the aggregate data for foreign currency lending had to be wrong. I suspected that very little of the foreign currency debt was hedged, given the cost advantages of not hedging it. The fact that the companies' balance sheets made no mention of foreign currency debt or foreign currency hedging did not inspire confidence that a prudent path had been followed. The bottom line though, is that we just did not know which companies were dangerously exposed to such forms of borrowing and which were not.

This piece of analysis from September 1997 includes a huge error. It does not even report the foreign currency debt exposure of South Korea. It was a very large number, but I, along with just about everyone else, thought it was irrelevant. It never occurred to us that South Korea, a country with some of the world's largest US dollar earning export-orientated companies, could find itself struggling to roll over its foreign currency debt. That foreign banks were already refusing to roll over their short-term US dollar loans to South Korea was something of which we were entirely unaware. As we were 'looking under the stones' in Southeast Asia for credit disasters, the biggest credit disaster of the whole crisis was already unfolding in the world's 11th-largest economy to the north.

Back to the future

16 September 1997, Thailand

Last week's *FT* attempted to solve the conundrum of whether Thai manufacturers would see a major jump in export orders following currency devaluations. According to the exporter they interviewed the answer was easy. "No way, Jose. I'm swamped with new orders for Christmas but there's no liquidity to expand," lamented Thailand's key economic hope.

Many manufacturers have seen their working capital frozen in the 58 finance companies. It is a criminal offence to sell these finance companies' promissory notes at a discount in an attempt to free up that capital. With the manufacturing business very working-capital intensive, there are more basic problems for the Thai exporter than securing fresh orders. The deterioration in the credit quality of the banking system and the undermining of faith in the banking system are the first hurdles which Thai manufacturers must surmount.

Despite the arrival of funds from the IMF, there are no signs as yet that the cash crunch is easing. If Thailand's exporters are barred from expanding due to this crunch, then the situation is likely to get very much worse before it gets better.

Yesterday's *Bangkok Post* reports other consequences from the closure of the 58 finance companies. The paper reports barter trade is now increasing in Thailand and cites the following examples:

- B Grimm Engineering said several customers had asked to pay in goods and services. One hotel has offered the use of conference facilities. One hospital company offered its own shares. Property companies had offered condos, golf club memberships or use of sports club facilities.
- TPI Polene admitted that they had approached suppliers with a view to paying them in cement.
- Media companies are being offered the use of hotel rooms or meal vouchers in return for airtime debts. One company was offered tickets to an amusement park as payment. A tuna canning factory offered to pay in tins of tuna.
- Banks are being offered property and shares as settlement of outstanding debts.

The barter system is partly forced on creditors as the legal system is unlikely to provide any rapid ability to force cash payments. An executive of B Grimm made the following statement:

> We don't want goods or services. The company wants to be paid in cash. But it's a difficult situation worsened by the current laws. Bringing the clients to court for the debts could take up to three years, in which time we would only be able to gain interest of 7% as fixed by the law.

The collapse in credit will in due course present wonderful buying opportunities for the foreigner who can pay cash. These opportunities are more likely to fall to the direct investor who is able to buy distressed assets from companies and the receiver. The equity investor is faced with a different risk profile. They have to be satisfied that the value of their equity will not go to zero due to the credit implosion now underway.

There is a crucial difference in distressed situations in the risk for the portfolio investor and the direct investor. The portfolio investor is buying a bundle of assets and liabilities and thus the ability to wipe out equity during a credit crisis is high. The direct investor is often in a position to buy assets unencumbered by liabilities. The direct investor is usually buying assets from the banks who have seized them because liabilities significantly exceeded assets and interest default occurred.

The risk of the *equity* falling to zero in such a situation is radically reduced even if the acquisition is partly debt financed. Risk/reward has now swung dramatically in favour of the direct investor in Thailand. For long-term funds seeking to access Thai assets at good prices, at the bottom of the economic cycle, even now portfolio investment remains too risky.

This was the first indication that the IMF package was backfiring. The IMF insisted that numerous bankrupt finance companies were closed but did not take into account what this meant in terms of liquidity provision to Thai companies. The companies that were impacted were the small and medium enterprises that comprise the backbone of almost any economy.

The IMF package insisted on higher interest rates to drive a contraction in aggregate demand, create a current account surplus and stabilise the exchange rate. Did it really have to drive up interest rates to crush domestic demand when the financial system was already refusing credit to just about everyone and some key credit providers had closed under IMF direction? How could a country, even with a much more competitive exchange rate, export its way back to economic stability if funding for the export-orientated companies had dried up? Key IMF prescriptions were starving the economy of liquidity at a time when a collapse in aggregate demand and an improvement in the external accounts were already guaranteed.

This is also the first mention in the contemporaneous writings of the likely importance the direct investor was likely to play in this crisis. As none of us portfolio investors really had any idea of what horrible surprises lurked on the balance sheets of Asia's listed companies, how could we value the equity?

Direct investors had a much better chance of making a detailed assessment. Any such investor contemplating the purchase of a local company would have much greater visibility on the condition of the business, its cash flow and its balance sheet through the necessary due diligence process. If the direct investor, given this advantage, would not buy at current prices, then how could the portfolio investor chance their arm with such an investment?

With no real value compass anymore, I decided that the Asian economic crisis would not be over, at least for those invested in listed equities, until there was evidence that direct investors were prepared to invest. It was very much the case of choosing any port in the storm as a valuation metric in the storm then raging for those trying to determine what the end of certainty meant. It was to be almost another year before the scale of direct investment in Asia seemed to warrant a call that the crisis, for equity investors, was now over. Charting that flow of capital and trying to talk to those who controlled it now became an essential part of assessing just how much downside there still was for equity prices.

The quality of capital is not strained

24 September 1997, Regional

Since April of this year, *The Solid Ground Daily* has been boring readers with stories relating the potential problems associated with the building levels of foreign currency debt in Asia. In particular, it was seeking to draw attention to the fact that it is the European banks and not the Japanese banks which are likely to pay a high price for this most recent international banking act of indulgence.

How international bankers now assess Asia risk will play an important role in determining how tight liquidity can get in Asia. If the foreign bankers decide not to roll over their credit lines, then we are at the beginning, not the end, of a difficult period for currencies and interest rates.

However, perhaps most worrying is the mix of funding for Korea's external accounts. As the current account deficit deteriorated last year, many analysts were surprised by the stability of the currency despite the absence of FDI. The BIS data suggests that the funding for the external deficits was largely conducted by borrowing US$22.5bn from the BIS banks in that 12-month period.

The country increased its foreign currency debt exposure by 30% in this 12-month period to cover its funding gap! The sourcing of those loans is particularly alarming if you are an investor in European banks. Of the total US$99bn lent to Asia, two-thirds have been lent by the European banks (remember this does not include the loans from the Swiss banks, which are not BIS members). Of the net US$22.5bn increase in exposure in the 12 months of 1996, a cool US$18.5bn was lent by European banks.

Finally, the scale and importance of the short-term US dollar borrowing by corporate South Korea was something to focus on. At this stage it would have been wise to have been much more vociferous on the risks to South Korea should the country struggle to roll over its short-term US dollar borrowing from banks.

That that struggle was already underway in September, we did not know, and by November, the South Korean president had approached the IMF for a support package. A measure of how quickly this shock was to develop was the fact that the MSCI Korean Index, measured in US dollar terms, was, by mid-September 1997, unchanged from the level at which it had started the year. Three months later it had fallen 73%.

The knight has a thousand ayes?

24 September 1997, Hong Kong

> You can put all the sincerity in Hollywood into a flea's navel and still
> have room for three agents' hearts and a caraway seed.
>
> **Fred Allen**

It is not often that either party to a contractual arrangement pauses to consider how much they mean to each other. No doubt our lives are all the more empty due to this lack of consideration. However, it would eventually become tedious if you had to write a note of thanks to every counterparty to your sell transactions in Malaysia.

In the modern world, civility is jettisoned in the need for haste. With a view to ending this shallowness in contractual agreements, Sir Gordon Wu has bought a full-page ad and written a public letter in yesterday's *South China Morning Post* entitled 'In Praise of Bankers'. It is addressed to the 125 international banks which have assisted his numerous ventures over the years. Sir Gordon discusses the honesty of the banker and his delight in placing them in the correct order of payment as stipulated by his contractual obligations:

> Over the years I've found them to be a very honourable bunch of people,
> and in return I've done my utmost to be decent and honourable back.
> I've always paid interest payments on time and when we've made a few
> dollars on a project, they're the first people I visit.

Now why couldn't more commercial arrangements be conducted in this friendly and relaxed manner? Sir Gordon even goes so far as to print a photograph of his favourite banker, Sir William Purves of HSBC. In concluding his panegyric address, Sir Gordon remarks:

> So I raise my glass to you (mug of tea actually). With the kind support of
> such fine people, anything is possible.

Given such kind words, surely only a banking charlatan of Scrooge proportions would consider not providing the necessary financing for Sir Gordon's future ventures (in today's paper, Sir Gordon has taken another full-page ad to explain to his bankers what he describes as the "bankability" of roads). In law, 'consideration' must be deemed to have passed before a contract is in existence.

With such evident consideration from Sir Gordon, which banker will now risk the public approbation of failing to renew his contractual relationships?

So three cheers for chivalry, the new land of knights and Camelot. In these difficult days, even the bard himself would be touched by this bold new approach:

These times of woe afford no time to woo.

William Shakespeare, *Romeo and Juliet* (Act 3, Scene 5), 1597

I still think that this is one of the most remarkable ads I have ever seen and I have kept a copy. That a high-profile businessman such as Gordon Wu would resort to such a public plea to his bankers seemed bizarre in the extreme. It was no surprise to anyone that the company was having problems securing further credit, particularly as it was committed to build the doomed Bangkok Elevated Road and Train System (BERTS).

To put it mildly, the very public plea did not inspire confidence among investors regarding the liquidity situation at Sir Gordon's Hopewell Holdings. By 2020, the litigation between the company and the government of Thailand regarding payments due relating to the contract to build BERTS still remained in the courts. Roads may indeed be bankable, but the government partners that are involved in them may not be.

Bagehot and elephant identification I

26 September 1997, Regional

One thing is certain, that at particular times a great deal of stupid people have a great deal of stupid money ... At intervals, from causes which are not to the present purpose, the money of these people – the blind capital, as we call it, of the country – is particularly large and craving: it seeks for someone to devour it, and there is a 'plethora'; it finds someone, and there is 'speculation'; it is devoured and there is 'panic'.

Walter Bagehot, 'Essay on Edward Gibbon', 1856

Bagehot's description of the self-destructive nature of capital is perhaps one of the best descriptions of the vagaries of the modern banking cycle. Bankers' targeting of low-risk assets for loan collateral actually begins the process of transforming them into risky assets. When the bankers move in herds, suddenly there is a "plethora" of capital allocated to such assets. The arrival of such a "plethora" of capital to target such assets produces the rise in price of those assets and the "speculation".

In due course, and usually when speculation is high, a shock occurs which informs the banker that they are lending on risky, not low-risk assets. Suddenly, a reversal of bank lending occurs and the ensuing panic devours the capital of those bankers not nimble enough to leave the party early.

These dynamics are in operation in Southeast Asia and the reaction of bankers is typical, if disappointing. Some weeks ago, we visited a major Malaysian bank where management informed us of their new-found love of conservative banking practice and their recent rejection of property assets as a form of collateral. As a result, they were slowing loan growth from 40% to around 10% and this would largely be achieved by the new approach to collateralisation. These same bankers express undinting faith that the collateral values on their existing loan book are secure. If only it were true that bankers could turn off the spigot of liquidity pointed at one asset class, and sit back and watch collateral values stabilise. This is not the real world.

The rush by bankers to shun property collateral will in itself produce the collapse in value which will devour bank capital. The inevitable shrinkage in bank capital based upon such 'collateral damage' (appropriately a term used in the Gulf war for the massacre of civilians) has a geared effect on reducing the supply of 'blind capital'. Whatever spurious numbers a banker chooses to report to the world, they are conscious of the real size of their capital base.

While not able to precisely quantify the bank's existing capital, their knowledge of the quality of the loan book is such that they know what their core capital probably is; and then there is a grey area of capital which they may have but is subject to uncertainty. The banker will then have to act to adjust their asset base in line with this diminished capital base, even if they are telling the public that their capital base is expanding. Thus the destruction of the banker's 'blind capital' has a geared impact on the total sum of 'blind capital'.

The equity investor should be stepping up to the plate for asset purchases as the devouring process is nearing its end. If 'blind capital' is at least as prevalent today as it was 100 years ago, then there is every probability that we shall see it again. The secret for the investor seeking to buy assets based upon supply and demand conditions is to buy on the eradication of 'blind capital' and sell when the 'blind capital' is once again in abundance. It may sound simple, but clearly it is not or there probably wouldn't be any blind capital in the first place!

Given the commercial bankers' key role as a provider of 'blind capital' and the geared nature of their activities, a study of the commercial banks is likely the best method of determining the existence or otherwise of the 'blind capital'.

When the bankers' capital base has shrunk to such an extent that loan growth is contracting, a rapid destruction of 'blind capital' is most likely. In the 1990s, a massive transfer of property collateral to the banks in the United States, Japan and Australia – quaintly called OREOs (Other Real Estate Owned) in the United States – occurred as the 'blind capital' was destroyed and the property market squeezed.

The movement of property assets into the hands of such unnatural owners – Westpac was allegedly the largest landlord in Australia – and natural sellers further depressed prices and began to bite through the fat of 'blind capital' and into the sinew of real capital. When the transfer of property was completed, the capital destruction process was nearing its end.

This slowdown in property transfer also provided confidence to the banks' owners that the commitment of more long-term capital (rights issues) would not be further devoured. Gradually, bank capital began to build. This was the beginning of the new cycle which would end inevitably in the targeting of a new low-risk asset as a form of collateral and its inevitable transformation into a high-risk asset subject to speculation and the avarice of 'blind capital'. The maniacal pursuit of residential property as low-risk collateral by the recovering Australian banks in 1990 was a good buy signal for Australian residential property.

In assessing when the domestic demand for assets is once again about to accelerate, one must attempt to see through the mist to the actual capital base of the commercial banking system. When the transfer of property from owner to lender is almost complete, the prospects for equity capital raising are significantly increased and bank capital will once again begin to expand. The clear problem in Southeast Asia is that we are a very long way from reaching such a stage of the cycle. In Thailand, where the destruction of 'blind capital' is most advanced, the transfer of property assets is only just beginning. Indeed, there are well-documented peculiarities in the Thai legal system which may result in such transfer being prolonged. Elsewhere in Asia the destruction of 'blind capital' is only a few months old.

The end of a bear market is a bit like an elephant – it's very difficult to describe what it looks like but you know it when it steps on your foot. In short, it's usually best to wait to see one rather than attempt to forecast months in advance what it will look like when it comes along. However, for those seeking a guide to the appearance of a bear market bottom, the eradication of 'blind capital' through the gearing inherent in the banking system is as good a guide as is available. When such capital destruction is complete and the supply of monies for asset purchases depleted, then it is highly likely that the equity market is approaching 'fair value'. Let's hope we reach that stage in Asia in 1998.

How do you invest in an economy when it is devoid of bank capital? As banks are the key creators of both credit and money, they are, usually by law, barred from extending credit when they know they have no capital. Should banks shrink their balance sheets to fit with their new lower capital base, both credit and money are destroyed and a country has entered what Irving Fisher once described as a *debt deflation*.

There was no sign of new capital for the remaining Thai banks and finance companies, and there was nothing in the IMF package that dealt with such recapitalisations. The problem with the package was that it demanded a very high level of interest rates that was acting to worsen credit quality problems and further reduce, probably eradicate, commercial bank capital. Even at the time it seemed that such action would further delay the ability of the banks to raise further capital.

The three biggest banks in Thailand – Bangkok Bank, Thai Farmers Bank and Siam Commercial Bank – accounted for 60% of all Thai banking transactions. All three were listed companies and conversations with the investment community strongly suggested that capital raisings were highly unlikely to be successful. The price of Thai bank equity may have collapsed, but all the evidence was that there was plenty of blind capital in Thailand still to be 'devoured' as they were forced to shrink their loan books due to their lack of capital. The debt deflation was far from complete.

Bagehot and elephant identification II

29 September 1997, Regional

For better or for worse, blind capital is once again now free to roam the globe. In Bagehot's day, there was already a high degree of capital mobility and a 'devouring' of foreign capital was common. Significant losses occurred in Britain when the states of Pennsylvania, Mississippi, Maryland, Indiana, Arkansas and Michigan all defaulted on their interest payments in the 1840s (to this day, Mississippi remains in default on those issues). In 1873, European investors lost US$600m (approximately US$5bn in today's US dollars) in the collapse of the railroad stocks alone. When economic development is low, the role of foreign 'blind capital' in Bagehot's process is likely to be high as foreign savings seek the high returns partly due to the lack of domestic capital.

Clearly in Asia, such a wave of foreign capital inflow has been occurring. In estimating the scale in Southeast Asia, we add together the current account deficit over the past ten years with the rise in the forex reserves over the same period (see Table 3.4). This covers the ten years from end 1986 to 1996 during a period of currency stability and is thus a proxy for net capital inflows over that period. If anything, this methodology underestimates the sums of foreign capital involved as it assumes no capital outflow from domestic savers.

Table 3.4: An approximation of foreign capital inflows (US$bn)

	10-year CA deficit	10-year rise in foreign exchange reserves
Indonesia	35.1	12.2
Malaysia	24.2	20.4
Philippines	19.9	9.5
Thailand	68.5	35.0
Total	147.7	77.1

This suggests that in these four economies of Southeast Asia, there has been a net inflow of foreign capital of US$225bn over the past ten years. By comparing these sums to the deposit base of the domestic banking systems, one gets some conception of the importance of foreign capital in the forthcoming 'devouring' process (see Table 3.5).

Table 3.5: Comparison of net inflow of foreign capital with deposit base of domestic banking systems, 1986–96

	A: M2 in US$bn end 1996	B: Total foreign capital (US$bn)	B/A
			(%)
Indonesia	94.3	47.3	50
Philippines	33.4	29.4	88
Malaysia	96.0	44.6	46
Thailand	154.8	103.5	67

Note: All M2 currency calculations are pre-currency adjustment.

While the numbers in Table 3.5 distort the debt-to-equity mix of foreign capital in Asia, it is still clear that debt accounts for a significant portion of the capital that must retreat before equilibrium for listed capital is obtained. The equity investor has the advantage of liquidity and may thus be able to retreat with the same semblance of order that Rommel achieved on the long road from El Alamein to Tunisia. Something similar to Napoleon's retreat from Moscow now faces the foreign banker in Asia.

Of the total sums of foreign currency debt outstanding in the four Southeast Asian nations, the following proportions are maturing within 12 months: Indonesia 62%, Thailand 64%, Malaysia 54% and the Philippines 58%! With a liquidity crisis already in effect, few foreign bankers can afford to roll over their commitments when the next banker may refuse such an indulgence and suck the remaining liquidity from the borrower. While the foreign banker must await their maturity date to withdraw liquidity, the equity investor has the very valuable option to get out before the banker. The banker is leaving and risk/reward clearly favours leaving before them.

It would be easy to criticise the pace at which portfolio investors, sometimes referred to as the 'electronic herd', sought to exit their investments in Southeast Asia. If only they had beat a more orderly retreat, then perhaps the Asian economic crisis would not have created the massive economic contraction that followed in 1998. The problem they faced was a massive overweight position, relative to their benchmarks, but even more importantly, the prospect that the foreign banker would be beating their own retreat.

Portfolio investors have much more liquid positions than bankers, but a very large proportion of US dollar bank loans to Asia were short term in nature. A portfolio investor who did not expect those short-term loans to be rolled over could expect very large capital outflows to be driven by bankers, and who really knew when that might end. There was a clear incentive for portfolio investors to use the liquidity available in the financial markets to exit their exposure to Asia before the bankers were able to do so.

What was happening in Asia was in effect a modern form of a bank run involving foreign bankers and portfolio investors instead of bank depositors. It had been a similar problem that had impacted Mexico in 1995 and Newt Gingrich, then speaker of the US House of Representatives, had described as "the first crisis of the 21st century". It was indeed true that the role of portfolio investors, in a new era of free movement of capital, made this crisis very different from the others that the IMF had dealt with since its inception in 1945.

In the past, policy makers had been able to co-ordinate commercial bankers, albeit with difficulty, to stabilise credit provision and prevent the pulling of credit from distressed creditors. However, there were myriad portfolio investors holding Asian equities and debt instruments and they were spread across the world. Even if these holders could be identified, it was not clear that any policy maker had the legal powers to force their co-ordination to prevent capital outflow from Asia.

The reopening of global capital accounts, underway since the 1970s, had indeed created a new form of crisis. As the tools to tackle such a crisis were lacking, it raised the prospect that closing capital accounts might be one quick fix that would appeal to Asian policy makers. The fear of the imposition of such controls further amplified the drive to remove capital from the region.

As the piece above shows, there were truly huge sums of capital that might seek to exit. By the end of 1997 the IMF was realising that simply providing more US dollars to the Asian authorities was unlikely to stabilise the situation unless the foreign banks stopped pulling their short-term US dollar loans to the region. It was the global central bankers, backed by the authority of their governments, that finally stopped the retreat of the foreign commercial banks from Asia. What seemed certain to be the financial equivalent of Napoleon's retreat from Moscow for foreign bankers turned into something much more benign.

Few portfolio investors, however, could afford to bet that such a stand-still agreement and debt restructuring could be forged among the bankers and, in the case of South Korea, it was to be Christmas Eve 1997 before even an outline agreement was reached. Had that agreement among bankers been forged earlier, it is likely that the collapse of the South Korean equity market in Q4 97 and the near 11% contraction of GDP in 1998 would not have occurred.

Stand-still agreements among foreign banks could have been put in place in Southeast Asia much earlier, but it was argued at the time, by both the IMF and the US administration, that such agreements could not be arranged or enforced given existing legal authorities. Not for the first or last time, a policy that was ideologically anathema and theoretically impossible to policy makers at the beginning of a crisis ultimately became essential to its solution.

In early October 1997, the crisis spread to North Asia. The Hang Seng Index of Hong Kong, which had reached a new all-time high as recently as August, was falling rapidly. On 10 October the authorities in Taiwan stepped away from intervening to support the New Taiwan Dollar and suddenly a North Asian currency had fallen victim to the capital exodus.

The currencies of Thailand, Malaysia, the Philippines and Indonesia had already devalued, but these were countries running substantial current account deficits. Taiwan was running a current account surplus that was greater than 3% of GDP and it had still been forced to devalue its currency.

Taiwan had the third-highest level of foreign exchange reserves in Asia, after Japan and China, almost triple the level of South Korea and almost double the level of Hong Kong. If a country with such a large current account surplus and some of the largest foreign exchange reserves in the world could be forced to devalue, then which Asia exchange rate would not devalue in this crisis? If a country with such strong fundamentals could not maintain the value of its exchange rate due to the capital stampede, who could?

From that moment investors feared that South Korea, China and Hong Kong would follow suit and devalue their exchange rates. They were right about the South Korean won and its decline accelerated markedly from 24 October. They were to be proved wrong about the Hong Kong dollar and the Chinese renminbi, but fears of the devaluation of those currencies would increasingly dominate investors' perceptions of risk for the next year. In particular it became a consensus view that China would devalue the renminbi and that you could not invest in Asian equities until that devaluation had occurred.

In a report called *Speculator Beware: How Does The HK$ Peg Work* published in December 1995, I had concluded: "speculators cannot break the HK$ peg". That speculators disagreed with those conclusions became clear in early October 1997. On 13 October the Hong Kong overnight interest rate was at 5% and very much in line with the corresponding US interest rate at the time. By 23 October the overnight rate had doubled to 10%. At one stage on Thursday, 23 October the lending rate for Hong Kong dollars reached 280%! From 5 to 28 October the Hang Seng Index fell by 40%.

I had long been forecasting that the exchange rate management policies of Southeast Asia would be abandoned and many investors expected that I would now focus on the likely failure of the same policies in Hong Kong and China. Throughout the crisis, however, I held the view that both Hong Kong and China would retain their managed exchange rate regimes and not devalue. This opinion was now being tested in October 1997 and fear of a devaluation, particularly among foreigners, was high.

One day, Gary Coull came to my office and said that if I really believed this so strongly, I should write an article for the *South China Morning Post* explaining my reasoning. The article I wrote was published by the *South China Morning Post* on 27 October, the same day the Dow Jones Index posted its largest ever points decline to that date, driven by expectations of further exchange rate devaluations in Asia and the consequences for both global credit quality and economic growth:

The six million people of Hong Kong represent the services economy of 1.2 billion people of China. That hinterland is still the home of the world's cheapest labour. Following the recent adjustments in Southeast Asia the hourly wages of Shanghai are 90 US cents per hour, still only half that of Indonesia and a third that of Thailand ... It seems to be going largely unnoticed that one of the world's great economic powers has just altered its macro-economic policy with the aim of supporting a minor currency. We are talking about the decision by China to reduce interest rates and stimulate demand to support the Hong Kong dollar. China's aggressive cut in lending rates shows the political willingness to reflate and the belief in the need for easy money ... In this rich man's panic nobody seems prepared to ask: 'What happens if the foreign investor stops selling?' The answer is that we probably revert to net buying of Hong Kong dollars as the proceeds from the labour of Hong Kong's seven million mainland employees continue to flow into Hong Kong dollars ... In a world where deflation looms shouldn't you align your wealth with those companies who benefit from access to the world's cheapest labour? The commanding heights of the financial capital of these 1.2 billion people are now going for a song.

South China Morning Post, 'HK economy is living in a different world', 27 October 1997

That article was well timed and by 30 October, the *South China Morning Post* declared 'Bullish brokerages fuelled bungee rebound' citing that 27 October article among other similar optimistic commentary. By 31 October the overnight deposit rate in Hong Kong was back to where it had been on 5 October, very close to US levels. This first serious battle to defend the peg had been successful, but there was to be another and much more serious battle in the summer of 1998.

I had noted in this article in the *South China Morning Post* that a key reason to invest in Hong Kong was that China was cutting interest rates to stimulate growth in China and to support growth in Hong Kong. That this would not lead to a devaluation of the renminbi did not seem to be an outlandish forecast as China already had a large stockpile of foreign reserves and a current account surplus that was 4% of its GDP.

China was in a very different position from when it had last devalued its exchange rate. However, as the October 1997 crisis passed and 1998 wore on, investors began to lose faith that China could provide economic stimulus while also maintaining a stable exchange rate. That change in opinion was to produce another major surge in Hong Kong interest rates and another major decline in the price of Hong Kong equities. Even from its lows in October 1997, the Hang Seng was to fall a further 33% before it bottomed on 13 August 1998. Why it bottomed on that Friday in August was one of the greatest surprises of the entire crisis.

Nerves were frayed by the attack on the Hong Kong currency. In mid-November there was a run on deposits at the International Bank of Asia (IBA) and some smaller Hong Kong banks also saw deposit flight. The HKMA publicly proclaimed that they stood behind IBA and the bank met all demands from its depositors, even allowing those with time deposits to redeem early. The run stopped.

That people remained jittery became evident in late November 1997, when office drawers were suddenly emptied of cake vouchers. It was a tradition to receive cakes on your birthday in Hong Kong and to solve the problem of having too much cake on the one day, not too big a problem for some of us, people often presented you with cake coupons. There were estimated to be as much as US$40m of cake coupons circulating, mainly sitting in office drawers, in the Hong Kong economy.

On 25 November a rumour began to circulate that the Saint Honoré Cake Shop was in financial difficulty. The cake run began and some of the company's 43 outlets had to stay open until midnight to satisfy the rush to redeem coupons. A run on the tokens used in the Whimsy amusement arcades also developed. Other runs were to follow and in 1998, one bakery had to close its doors, unable to redeem its coupons in full, and a video rental company was driven to the wall by a run on its coupons. In Hong Kong, money was a serious business, but money and cake were very serious business indeed.

CLSA by now had become one of the biggest brokers in Asia, but it had only a small foothold in the primary issue business. This turned out to be a blessing in disguise as the company did not find itself holding a dangerous inventory of securities with the attendant credit risk when the Asian financial crisis broke out. However, the company always had ambitions to increase its primary issuance business and decided that it would be good for the research team to visit the crisis-hit countries and explain what we thought the new valuation parameters were going to be for equities.

The inputs one could put into valuation models were all over the place so I structured my presentation around a sensitivity analysis with discount rates down one side and return on capital across the top. The grid of numbers allowed anyone to combine the risk-free rate and the return on equity and where they intersected see the prospective stock market decline for each country.

The CLSA offices in Jakarta, Manila, Kuala Lumpur and Bangkok were told to assemble as many senior corporate officers for these meetings as possible, and these presentations took place between 4 and 10 November 1997. As the regional offices had been heavily involved in creating the sensitivity analysis, they cannot have been too surprised at what happened next.

Every business manager and owner who attended these meetings focused on the line of the sensitivity analysis showing the current interest rates. The sensitivity analysis showed at least 60% downside for share prices in all cases and up to 90% in some cases. I suspect many of those present had a much better idea of what their current return on capital really was, and they may have been looking at even bigger suggested share price declines than us outsiders. I heard a few gasps, quite a lot of laughing and my memory was that in Jakarta quite a few of the corporate executives walked out of the presentation. The apparently ridiculous numbers turned out to be not that far from the truth. I am not aware that the four-city jaunt generated any business for the capital markets operation of the company!

This was to be my last visit to Indonesia. I took the opportunity to buy a large bundle of 100 rupiah bank notes. I was able to buy 60 of those notes for a pound sterling, but had I waited until June 1998 it would have been almost 250 of these bank notes to the pound. I supposed the cost of production must have been less than the face value, but it must have been getting close by June 1998?

This might account for why the country stopped printing 100 rupiah notes in 2000. Years later, I founded a business and financial history library in Edinburgh and these 100 rupiah banknotes now paper the bathroom walls at The Library of Mistakes. Without faith, paper, even if described as a currency, is just paper.

Snap and the banker

22 October 1997, Regional

It is a bias of this author, as an ex-lawyer, to place perhaps an undue importance on the rule of law in any society. In particular, the ability of the individual or a corporation of such persons to protect their assets from thieves and governments plays a key role in bolstering investment. The rule of law is something we take for granted in the West, apart from in some of the nether regions of Montana, and we generally accept that the law provides such protection for our assets.

However, generations of Asian savers and investors can have built up no such touching faith in the protection of their assets by the adjudication of independent third parties. The history of Asian capital is the history of appropriations and thefts. The notorious pirate Mrs Cheng was able to put 50,000 pirates afloat in the South China Seas by 1805 and the state was powerless to protect any citizen or their business. While in the 19th century the Chinese businessman was powerless against the thieves, in the 20th century he is powerless against the appropriations of his own government.

Given this background, the attitude towards asset utilisation in Asia is likely to be radically different from that which has developed in the West. It will be much more difficult for an Asian investor to consider long-term fixed assets as a sound form of investment. Indeed, any such investment will have to be quickly securitised, and hopefully flipped at a profit, to reduce the inherent risks given the legal vacuum which protects such assets. With no practical judicial system, an alteration in the helmspersons of government threatens the ownership of assets.

When it is a case of rule by person rather than rule by law, it is important to hire the best gunslingers. However, even William H Bonney (aka Billy the Kid) had but a brief career – arriving in New Mexico in the mid-1870s to fight in the Lincoln County war, he was dead by 1881. This lack of legal protection may lie at the root of the poor returns on listed capital in Asia, but it is also the dreadful dynamic which may unfold as the foreign investor retreats from Asia.

The foreign banker, who has played an important role in *bankrolling* the game of Snap, may now begin to demand they be repaid. The longer they wait and the longer the asset prices fall, the lower the chance that they will get their money back. Snap!

The foreign investor in Asia had been brought up and educated in jurisdictions where it never occurred to them that their property would not be protected by the rule of law. There were actually few Asian countries where such certainty under law existed. Even where it existed on paper, there were key inter-linkages between business and politics that could see valuable business franchises suddenly destroyed without the owner having any reasonable prospect of recourse to law.

When Asian business owners were at such risk, it made sense to create liquidity in their assets by listing them on the stock market. They could control the company without owning all of it, but just as importantly they could trade and liquidate formerly illiquid assets should the necessity arise. These liquefied assets, part of a broader portfolio that included less liquid assets, now played an important role in wealth preservation for the Asian families that owned them.

In Indonesia, in particular, there was significant capital flight from the local business owners who were ethnically Chinese and were close to the Suharto regime. They feared what regime change might mean for their business franchises and also their personal safety. It was not just foreign investors who were rushing for the exits. Asian families knowing of the thin protection their legal systems offered to their property rights were also seeking to sell their liquid assets.

In some cases they had created the liquidity in their assets in case just such a breakdown in their cosy relationships with the political hierarchy occurred. The lower protection for their property rights and fragility of their politically connected business franchises had many Asian business owners selling equities and then rushing to sell the local currency to move funds offshore. Foreign investors were used to panic among portfolio investors, but this form of panic by business owners, concerned about the socio-political collapse of their own countries, was something they did not expect to encounter when they invested in the Asian economic miracle.

For Asia there was also some good news, as on 31 October the government of Indonesia signed a letter of intent with the IMF. There had been significant losses for investors in Thailand since the letter of intent was signed with the government there on 14 August 1997, but perhaps things would go better in Indonesia? Meanwhile, the country was burning.

In October 1997 forest fires started in Indonesia. It was not just the trees that burnt; the topsoil was a peaty substance that also burnt and smouldered for weeks on end. Perhaps up to five million acres of forest burnt in the last months of 1997. The result was that a great pall of smoke hung over not just parts of Indonesia, but also Singapore and Malaysia.

The Air Pollution Index in Kuching, Malaysia, rose to 800, with 200–300 being the equivalent of smoking 20 cigarettes. More than 200,000 people in the region may have been hospitalised as a result of this smoke. The smoke blocked out the sun and the smell got into everything. For some in business, the economic collapse made it feel like the end of the world. In some parts of Asia, it looked like it also.

That there was another Asia under the surface was brought home to us in September 1997. Our friend Emma Slade had been visiting Jakarta as a debt analyst when she ended up being held hostage at gunpoint in a robbery gone wrong. She was eventually freed by the police and came to stay with us while she recovered in Hong Kong. Emma's recovery took her down many paths, but eventually to Bhutan and Buddhism, and a new life as the Buddhist nun Pema Deki. Many lives changed course as a result of the Asian economic crisis, but few of them in such a dramatic and dangerous way as Emma's changed that day.

The buck stops here

12 November 1997, South Korea

The game of international banking is best described as a game of pass the parcel between international banks. Major defaults at various stages in the economic cycle should come as no surprise. We expect major defaults in the developed world economies at economic troughs, but for some reason expect that emerging market borrowers will always satisfy their international bankers.

When the economic music stops and the final layer of packaging is removed, some international banker has to be left with the lemon of a loan. For whatever peculiar reason it is widely assumed that the Asian lemon will fall squarely into the hands of the Japanese. For most of this year, *The Solid Ground Daily* has been boring readers with tales of the profligacies of European commercial banks in Southeast Asia. But now South Korean corporates are headed into default on their international loans and once again the finger is pointed at Japanese banks as the key losers. Once again, this is not correct. The data in Table 3.6 from the BIS shows the exposure of the commercial banks of each developed country to South Korea.

Table 3.6: Exposure of commercial banks to South Korea (US$bn)

	End of 1996	% of total loans to Asia	% growth year on year
Japan	24.3	20	+13
Germany	9.9	24	+36
France	7.6	23	+27
UK	5.6	22	+48
Belgium	3.7	35	+91
Netherlands	1.9	15	+70
Italy	1.2	29	+20
Austria	1.2	23	+139
Europe	31.1		
US	9.4	27	+23

European banks are significantly more exposed to the travails of South Korea than Japan, and the BIS data does not include the exposure of the Swiss banks! Notable for their exposure to South Korea are those plucky Belgians who, ever since the creation of the Maginot Line, have delighted in being even more exposed than the French!

From a very early stage it was clear that the European and Japanese banks would have heavy losses to bear in this crisis. As an Asian stockbroking company, we spoke to institutional investors who covered Asia ex Japan. It might sound like the easiest thing in the world to get this information about European and Japanese bank exposure to the institutional investors who covered those markets. It was not.

The Eurostoxx Banks Index had risen 42% from January to October 1997 as investors got excited about the rise in profitability for banks that they theorised the move to a single European currency would create. From October 1997 to July 1998, the Eurostoxx Banks Index was to rise a further 83%. It was not until July 1998, when the impacts from the Asian financial crisis began to impact Russia, that the share prices of European banks began to decline.

In the next few months the index declined by 45% and bank share prices were back to where they had been in January 1997. Any investor who sold or shorted European banks when their huge exposure to the Asian financial crisis became apparent did not prosper. They missed a very large rise in the price of European bank equity and the crash, when it came, only returned share prices to roughly where they had been in early 1997, when investors in Asia first realised the scale of their exposure to the growing credit risk. As for the prospect that European banks would prosper from the introduction of the euro, in 2020 the Eurostoxx Banks Index was almost 40% below the lows reached in early 1997.

Things were very different in Japan, where the balance sheet weakness of the commercial banks was well known if difficult to precisely assess. A decline in the price of Japanese bank equity had been underway since the peak of the great Japanese asset bubble at Christmas 1989. The reversal of the gross financial engineering of that period and the overhang of bad debts on the balance sheet of Japanese financial institutions were problems that did not go away, even with the passage of time.

By November 1997, the Japan Topix Bank Index was well below its 1989 high, but had traded sideways for many years and was still at its 1992 level. In April 1997 Nippon Credit Bank was bailed out by a deal arranged by the

BOJ that involved the injection of capital by both the BOJ and private sector institutions. This injection of capital was ultimately to be insufficient and eventually Nippon Credit Bank was nationalised. The Japan Topix Bank Index was to fall 40% from November 1997 to late 1998, under the influence of growing bad debts in Asia but also as investors realised just how weak the balance sheets of Japanese commercial banks had become.

Following the bailout of Nippon Credit Bank in April 1997, Sanyo Securities, Yamaichi Securities, Hokkaido Takushoku Bank and Tokuyo City Bank all failed in October and November 1997. By February 1998, US$230bn of public funds were mobilised to provide capital for the banking system. The Japanese banking crisis was not caused by the Asian financial crisis, but the growing realisation that the banks would also face major losses on their Asian loan books accelerated the country's own banking crisis.

Foreign investors had long worried about the balance sheet condition of Japanese banks and the premium these banks had to pay for US dollar borrowing had been rising, reflecting the growing concerns. As the Japanese banks did not have large US dollar deposit bases, they financed their US dollar lending primarily through such borrowings. As the cost of borrowing these dollars rose, it became less profitable to lend US dollars in Asia.

With Japanese banks now failing, even higher premiums were demanded when they sought to borrow US dollars. As Table 3.6 shows, they may have slowed the growth of their Asian US dollar lending before the Asian crisis erupted but this allowed the European banks, not afflicted with a rising premium for their own US dollar borrowing, to fill the gap left by the Japanese banks. Foreign bankers had continued to grow their foreign currency loan books aggressively in Asia right up until the devaluation of the Thai baht. Their retreat from foreign currency lending in Asia was probably only just beginning.

Snippets

13 November 1997, Global

Last night I attended the Chartered Financial Analyst (CFA) presentations in Hong Kong. The guest speaker outlined the success of the Association for Investment Management and Research (AIMR) in attracting new students and professionalising the industry globally. In 1990 there were 10,000 students enrolled for the CFA exams and they are now expecting 50,000 to enrol for the 1998 exams. The growth in the number of students has been compounding at 22% per annum for the past eight years. The bull market in CFAs has even outstripped the bull market in US equities. There are currently 27,000 CFAs worldwide and the AIMR expects that one-third of all those taking the Level I exam will eventually earn the CFA designation.

Thus as half of all students are taking these exams, there will be around 8,000 new CFAs joining the ranks every year in the near future. Even assuming a static growth rate at 8,000 per year, this would be a CAGR of 20% for the next five years. Indeed, in five years from today there will be more CFAs in the world than the entire population of Bangor, County Down! Food for thought.

The last time I did a crane count anywhere was in Sydney in 1992, and I didn't get beyond one. I think that one crane was building Governor McQuarrie Tower and construction activity in the city had stopped due to the recession and oversupply. On Sunday evening, I drove from Bangkok airport to the Marriott Hotel and in a fit of boredom began a crane count. However, tension mounted as we neared the hotel. Relief – yes there are more than 100 cranes (I spotted 104) on the road from the airport.

While things were tough in Sydney in 1991 and 1992, I don't remember there being a problem with the non-acceptability of credit, the involvement of the IMF and mass bankruptcy of the non-bank financials. A friend who recently visited Wellington tells me that they are building their first office block since the end of the great 1987 boom. Crane spotting in Thailand may have the same future as Dodo hunting in Mauritius.

By 2020, the number of CFA charter holders had increased to 154,000, posting a CAGR rate since 1997 of almost 8%.

Two Renongs don't make a right

19 November 1997, Malaysia

So can it really get any worse? Yes. On 1 December Malaysia will present a list of currency curbs to a meeting of the ASEAN finance ministers and recommend they be adopted across the region. It seems unlikely that there will be such success, although the Malaysian press is suggesting that Jacques Chirac favours the move – "Hurrah!" However, even if this move fails, there remains the risk that Malaysia will seek to introduce unilateral currency curbs. So there is yet another potential event out there which could even further undermine confidence in Malaysia.

The prime minister of Malaysia was not the only person who supported the introduction of capital controls. At the annual meeting of the IMF and World Bank in Hong Kong in September 1997, Joseph Stiglitz, then chief economist of the World Bank, had also recommended their introduction. Before the year end, both the governments of the UK and Canada were recommending that capital controls might be part of the answer for the growing Asian crisis.

Portfolio investors in Asia knew nothing of this and Mahathir was seen as isolated on this issue, but it was to be almost another year before he acted unilaterally despite the fact that he had publicly raised the prospect of capital controls in late 1997. The longer he raised the spectre of capital controls and nothing happened, the more unlikely it seemed that they would be imposed – until they were. His intentions however had been made fairly clear in his speech in Hong Kong on 20 September 1997:

> I know I am taking a big risk to suggest it but I am saying that currency trading is unnecessary, unproductive and immoral. It should be stopped. It should be made illegal. We don't need currency trading. We need to buy money only when we want to finance real trade. Otherwise we should not buy and sell currencies as we sell commodities.

Eisenhower, Shangri-La and the symbol

21 November 1997, China

> There are some causes which are entirely uniform and constant in producing a particular effect ... Fire has always burned, and water suffocated every creature; the production of motion by impulse and gravity is a universal law, which has hitherto admitted of no exception. But there are other causes, which have been found more irregular and uncertain ... When we transfer the past to the future, in order to determine the effect, which will result from any cause, we transfer all the different events, in the same proportion as they have appeared in the past ... As a great number of views do here concur in one event, they fortify and confirm to the imagination, beget that sentiment which we call belief.
>
> **David Hume, *An Enquiry Concerning Human Understanding*, 1748**

The term 'Asia' made its first appearance in the English language in 1563. Presumably, until that time, Asia did not exist. For before the West discovered Asia, it was not considered an amorphous whole by other nations or races. But now in the minds of Westerners there is a region of the world which is known as Asia. It seems to begin close to India but stops short of the Pacific islands.

In the current reasoning, within that newly created region (just 434 years vintage), every country is suffering from identical economic problems which have been simultaneously revealed to the world. This is an incredible coincidence which the creators of Asia could no more have foreseen than could James Hinton have foreseen that his mythical paradise of Shangri-La would one day become a hotel chain.

In 1954 Dwight Eisenhower brought another Western concept to the region called 'Asia' when he coined the phrase the 'falling domino' principle. So now the Westerner has the concept that these geographically and economically diverse nations are somehow linked together in a mystical 'domino effect'. In this sense, we transfer the past to the future in the same proportions to create a 'belief' about 'Asia' as Hume espoused. Are these 'beliefs' rational? Had economic problems developed in 'Asia' 434 years ago, would we have been so certain that that entire region would be simultaneously contaminated?

The Solid Ground Daily has been boring readers for years with the concept that 'Asian' equities are not an asset class. 'Asia' is an agglomeration of economies at different stages of development operating different types of economic systems at different stages of their economic development. In recent years the export-orientated economies of Southeast Asia have added to the illusion of an Asian asset class by their blind pursuance of US dollar currency policies. These days, too, have passed.

The operation of these currency policies in Southeast Asia has led them into the current trap where they cannot reduce interest rates without creating a fall in the value of their currencies. (Unless they adopt the radical reform programmes which they currently seem loath to contemplate.) This problem does not extend to China and thus it is not part of a so-called 'domino effect' in 'Asia'.

The lack of convertibility of the Chinese currency allows the authorities to run an independent monetary policy without producing downward pressure on the currency. When interest rates fall, there are no foreigners to rush out of the domestic debt markets and thus renminbi, and locals are legally barred from investing overseas. Forget the 'domino effect', the much sought-after reflation in Asia can be provided by China. Elsewhere in Asia it will require acts of political courage which are not yet evident – perhaps with the exception of the Philippines.

Another term of conventional wisdom talks of the renminbi as the 'last man standing'. This is not correct, for the following currencies have also failed to devalue against the US dollar in the past six months: UK pound, Argentine peso, Brazilian real, Estonian kroon, Irish punt, Danish krone, Lebanese pound,

Lithuanian litt, Norwegian krone, Saudi riyal, Slovakia koruna, Vatican City lira. There are an awful lot of last men standing out there.

Since the 1 July devaluation of the baht, China's foreign exchange reserves have risen by US$13bn. With a current account surplus of US$36bn in the first ten months of 1997 and foreign exchange reserves of US$134bn, it is difficult to see the renminbi as the most vulnerable currency among 'the last men standing'. Of course, it has one major disadvantage in that it is situated in the middle of what Westerners refer to as 'Asia'.

The impact of recent currency depreciations in Asia, combined with a lack of growth in Japan and the increase in cheap labour globally, is creating increased strain on exchange rates around the world. China too will be under such pressure as its surpluses are likely to slowly diminish, but the 'last man standing' is another illusion of geography. Other currencies are likely to be under greater pressure and much more quickly.

For over two years we have discussed the coming problems for Asia as it would be forced to abandon the currency policies, thus forcing equity markets to adjust to more reasonable valuations. It would be intellectually easy to suggest that the same dynamics will act to depress equity valuations in the whole of the region referred to as Asia. It would also be dangerously akin to rolling forward the misconceptions about 'Asia' which have been building for the past 434 years.

Those investors who are searching for reflation in Asia, for growth in Asia and for good returns from equities can rely upon the flexibility of the Chinese system and the political impetus for lower unemployment to see such attributes in China. Death to 'Asia', death to the 'domino', death to extrapolation and life to the freedom of belief.

At one stage, the MSCI Far East ex Japan Free Index was weighted at around 1/3 to the markets of Thailand and Malaysia. The events of the past year, hopefully, show that following index benchmarks, particularly in the emerging markets, is fraught with hazards. The events of 1997 may bring a new approach towards investing in the region. In future, perhaps, at least as investors, we will come to address this region with the prefix currently only accorded to a diminutive US recording artiste. Welcome to: 'The region formerly known as Asia.'

There are many things that readers may find peculiar about the historical reporting on events in Asia during 1995–98. Surely one of the strangest is the limited comment on China. The clients of CLSA were primarily interested in the large equity markets that dominated the benchmark index and were liquid enough to trade. The Chinese stock market was just too small and the tyranny of the benchmarks meant that it was too dangerous, for those paid to deliver performance relative to those benchmarks, to have all but a token amount committed to the Chinese stock market. Thoughts of Malaysia filled much more of the working day of the investor in 'Asia' than thoughts of China.

Looking back it is also peculiar that investors were so convinced that China would also devalue its exchange rate. The piece above focuses on the strong external accounts and rising foreign exchange reserves that powerfully suggested that no such devaluation would be necessary. Throughout the crisis, I argued that China would not devalue and that, partially related to this, the Hong Kong dollar would also not be devalued. That proved to be correct, but I remember the derision those opinions were held in by many institutional investors. The prospect of a devaluation by China hung over the Asian financial markets like the sword of Damocles throughout the crisis and it became a consensus opinion that a Chinese devaluation would occur.

No matter how quickly Asia's external accounts improved, its banking systems were recapitalised or its corporates acquired by multinational corporations, it was probably correct to argue that there was a further major downside for Asian equities should China devalue the renminbi. There were many investors who were to miss out on buying Asian equities at incredibly cheap valuations in 1998 because they retained this view that the renminbi would be devalued.

Historians often miss the importance of the things that did not happen, but were expected to happen, that have huge influences on the behaviour of key players at the time. The stability of the renminbi exchange rate throughout this period was the equivalent in this crisis of Holmes's 'dog that didn't bark'. To commit capital to Asian equities when the bottom finally came, one was taking a strong view that the Chinese exchange rate would not devalue.

Asian equities bottomed in early September 1998 just as the belief in the devaluation of the renminbi had probably reached its zenith. It was policy changes in the United States, assumed to be part of a package to weaken the US dollar and strengthen the yen, that finally convinced markets that Chinese interests had been appeased and that the renminbi would not be devalued.

The governments of Asia may have linked their exchange rates to the US dollar, encouraging their citizens to borrow US dollars in the process, but the US Federal Reserve had no commitment to act as a lender of last resort to this US dollar block. Assessing when the lender of last resort of US dollars would do something to alleviate a financial crisis far from home was incredibly difficult.

It was possible to speculate from November 1997, when the crisis had spread to South Korea, the world's 11th largest economy, that the US Federal Reserve would have to do something given the consequence for the global financial system of mass defaults by South Korean borrowers. It was not until September 1998, when the impacts from the Asian financial crisis had reached US shores, that the lender of last resort of the US dollar decided to reduce interest rates. Investors in Asia who knew such relief must come finally had a long and painful wait for it to arrive.

At last Torschlusspanik

24 November 1997, Malaysia

> Revulsion and discredit may go so far as to lead to panic (or as the Germans put it, Torschlusspanik door-shut panic), with people crowding to get through the door before it slams shut. The panic feeds on itself, as did the speculation, until one or more of three things happen: 1) prices fall so low that people are again tempted to move back into less liquid assets; 2) trade is cut off by setting limits on price declines, shutting down exchanges, or otherwise closing trading; or 3) a lender of last resort succeeds in convincing the market that money will be made available in sufficient volume to meet the demand for cash.
>
> **Charles P Kindelberger, *Manias, Panics & Crashes: A History of Financial Crises*, 1978**

If the period of revulsion is characterised by the panic selling of assets below fair value, it is very difficult to argue that we are witnessing revulsion in Malaysia. Currently, investors are paying a 60% premium to net asset value (NAV) for listed capital in Malaysia. It is now widely recognised that this listed capital is about to witness a period of falling returns and potential distress due to significant overcapacity in the country and slowing economic growth.

Interest rates have now risen to 10%. Even in the good times, Malaysian corporates did not secure returns in excess of 15% on their capital. Thus, despite the recent collapse in prices, it is difficult to argue that revulsion is underway as investors are being asked to pay a significant premium for capital which has produced sub-par returns.

If the value investor can see no signs of revulsion, the liquidity investor would agree. Liquidity investors begin to salivate when they see an unduly tight monetary policy. They buy knowing that, in a fiat money system, the authorities will, in due course, attempt to reverse this dynamic and provide the easy money they crave. While such dynamics are operative in China, the reverse is true in Malaysia.

In analysing the liquidity cycle in Malaysia, we would come to the conclusion that we are at the beginning of a credit-tightening period rather than at the end of one. The collapse in asset prices in Malaysia is occurring at a time of loose monetary policy! With nominal GNP growth of 12% this year, it is difficult to suggest that M3 growth of 20% and loan growth of 28% in September represents a tight monetary policy!

At some stage the authorities in Malaysia will realise that the easy money policy is only creating greater long-term problems while failing to provide the cheap funds for asset price support they currently seek. At this stage, monetary policy will have to be tightened from its current very loose levels. Thus liquidity investors looking at the monetary data would be very concerned that we are about to enter a period of monetary tightening and would be very wary of concluding that the 55% fall in equity prices has been driven by monetary conditions at all. The tight money and its negative impacts on equity valuations are yet to be witnessed.

It seems unlikely that the events of last week represent revulsion in the absence of banking distress.

A study of financial history proved to be very useful to investors during the Asian financial crisis. While some investors thought that something like this had never happened before, others picked up their financial history books. Kindelberger's classic, *Manias, Panics & Crashes: A History of Financial Crises*, may have dealt in the history of panics and crashes in very broad brushstrokes, but it was still essential reading for investors in Asia during this period.

In this period I often quoted from Keynes, Bagehot and Kindelberger, and although some appreciated that they had something to add, the general feedback was that these old guys had no value to add in a crisis like this one that was so 'modern'. Kindelberger's book in particular showed a consistency in behaviour during 'Manias, Panics and Crashes' over many centuries and I had no reason to believe that that consistency was about to disappear.

It is often said, usually by those with a business school education, that 'all available information is in the price'. It was clear in 1997 that whatever information may have been in the price was fairly irrelevant compared to the role of sentiment in determining the price. A reading of financial history proved of great value in assessing what was actually going on in relation to investor sentiment and under what conditions sentiment would likely become more positive.

A tighter monetary policy did indeed come to Malaysia, and the growth in broad money collapsed from a peak of 23% year on year in December 1997 to just 1.5% year on year in December 1998. That it kept growing so strongly for six months after the devaluation of the Thai baht was testimony to the country's determination to ignore the impact of capital exodus and continue to attempt to pursue a high-growth policy.

That policy failed and in 1998 the economy contracted by 7.4% in real terms. The Malaysian equity market bottomed in September 1998, when monetary policy was very tight, but by that time the country had imposed capital controls, making Malaysian equities an uninvestable asset class for most foreign investors.

Where the value is

25 November 1997, Singapore

With the death of the liquidity-driven markets in Asia, it is often said that there is currently no 'value' in the region. Preliminary work at CLSA on the market-average intrinsic value calculations for the adjusting Southeast Asian markets suggests that this is indeed the case. However, in Singapore there is an increasing body of evidence which suggests that market participants are significantly underpricing the listed capital of Singaporean companies.

In the current environment, Asian investors are dumping the baby out with the bathwater as they fret over the 'contagion' effect from Indonesia and Malaysia. While not doubting that there will be a 'contagion' impact from Malaysia and Indonesia, it would appear that the market is discounting a scale of contagion which is both immense and prolonged. Already Singaporean equities have shown their defensive qualities during Asia's economic crisis and this relative outperformance seems likely to continue with equities trading below fair value while looking extended elsewhere in the region.

With Singapore continuing to amass significant current account surpluses (we estimate 14% of GDP this year), we expect three-month interbank rates to trend back below the 4% level. At that level of interest rates, equities are trading below intrinsic value. During the course of 1998, we expect the downward pressure on interest rates to continue and three-month interbank to reach the 2.5% level. If this interest rate scenario is correct, then the intrinsic value model suggests that there is 58% upside for Singaporean equities if the corporate return on equity (ROE) remains unchanged.

There were no prizes for recommending Asian investors seek shelter in the purchase of Singaporean equities during the economic and financial storm that was blowing through Asia. The city-state had a strong economy and strong banks. The banks did lend across the region, but their reported capital expanded by 13% in 1997 and 6% in 1998, and they did not report losses during the Asian economic crisis.

Even in 1998, the Singaporean economy expanded, if only by 1.5%. Despite this stability, investors who held stocks in Singapore from their peak in early 1996 to their nadir in late 1998 lost 69% of their money in US dollar terms. If you bought shares in one of these stable Singaporean banks in November 1997, you would have lost half your investment by September 1998. Had you bought in November 1997 and held to the end of 1999, you would have doubled your money. Were they cheap by November 1997? They were cheap, but they were to get significantly cheaper in the next 12 months.

The buck stops here

26 November 1997, Regional

"Who lent how much and to whom?" This is probably the question which I receive most often from fund managers. Given the private nature of business between borrower and lender, it is impossible to get the precise data. However, using the data from the IFR, we can make some very broad calculations which may at least point the finger in the right direction.

The IFR data provides information on all foreign currency syndicated loans, bonds and a limited selection of non-syndicated loans. The problem in trying to analyse this data is that it is impossible to work out exactly the exposure of each bank on each transaction. The database includes the sum borrowed and lists all arrangers and all managers, but the proportion of each loan taken by each bank is not included.

In an attempt to make a broad indication of where the 'buck stops', we have run two calculations: 1) divided all the syndicated loans pro rata among the 'arrangers' and totalled this up for all banks; and 2) divided all the syndicated loans pro rata among all the 'managers' and totalled this up for all the banks. There will clearly be distortions in this data as some banks may consistently take below their 'market share' in every syndicated loan in which they participate. Thus the data shown in Table 3.7 should be read in the light of this major caveat and the numbers provided should be treated with appropriate caution.

Table 3.7: List of the 20 largest foreign currency lenders to Asia ranked by 'arranger' and 'manager' classification

	Arranger (US$bn)	Manager (US$bn)
HSBC Holdings	7,349	3,497
Korea Development Bk	6,960	3,872
IBJ	6,864	4,612
Sumitomo Bank	6,817	5,322
Bank of Tokyo	6,549	5,474
Sanwa Bank	5,998	5,045
Dai-Ichi Kangyo	5,936	6,386
Fuji Bank	5,751	6,188
Chase Manhattan	5,739	2,652
Sakura Bank	4,803	4,829
Citicorp	4,723	2,106
Korea Exchange Bank	4,423	3,292
Bank of America	4,336	2,292
Soc Gen	4,314	3,198
LTCB	4,100	3,798
ABN AMRO	3,726	3,421
Commerzbank	3,277	2,470
Chung-Ho Bank	3,207	2,469
Credit Lyonnais	3,110	3,453
Dresdner Bank	2,809	2,407

The discrepancy in amount between the two sums provides a good indication of the 'fuzzy' nature of this data and thus the degree of caution with which it should be treated. However, on either measure of exposure, it reveals a consistent pattern of Japanese and South Korean banks as the most aggressive lenders of foreign currencies in Asia. When we analyse the lenders by their geographic region, there are some alarming statistics.

Of the ten Asian banks (on the all arrangers' measure) which have lent the greatest sums of US dollars in Asia, eight are South Korean: KDB, KEB, Cho-Hung,

Hanil, Commercial Bank of Korea, Korea First Bank, Seoul Bank and Industrial Bank of Korea. Currently, the disclosed sub-standard loans of the top 25 South Korean banks are US$19bn. Based on our all arrangers' total, just these top eight banks could have made US$24bn in foreign currency loans in Asia.

As the South Korean banks are not natural takers of US dollar deposits, they have had to fund such lending. According to BIS data, they have borrowed US$66bn from the BIS reporting banks. Based on the average maturity schedule of South Korea's BIS bank borrowings, US$48bn of these moneys are due for repayment within the next 12 months! The other point of interest is that the two other banks in the top ten lenders are DBS (US$2.6bn by arranger) and OCBC (US$1.2bn by arranger). (HSBC is counted as a European bank by the IFR.)

There are really no surprises in the US data. The three largest lenders are Chase, Citicorp and Bank of America, and they are all included in the top 20 in Table 3.7. There is then a smaller second league of lenders beginning with JP Morgan (US$2.0bn), Banker's Trust (US$1.5bn by arranger) and NationsBank (US$890m).

Table 3.8 shows the same basis for the top ten European lenders as these banks have been the most aggressive new players in Asia over the past few years.

Table 3.8: Top ten largest European foreign currency lenders to Asia ranked by 'arranger' and 'manager' classification

	Arranger (US$bn)	Manager (US$bn)
HSBC Holdings	7,349	3,497
Soc Gen	4,314	3,198
ABN AMRO	3,726	3,421
Commerzbank	3,277	2,470
Credit Lyonnais	3,110	3,453
Dresdner Bank	2,809	2,407
Deutsche Bank	2,794	1,952
BNP	2,706	3,219
ING	2,676	2,120
Westdeutsche Land	2,543	2,469

The good news for UK investors is that you have to get to number 12 on the list before a UK clearer appears – Barclays (US$2.3bn calculated by arranger). However, Royal Bank of Scotland does come next among the UK banks with

US$1.2bn (calculated by manager), but the exposure slips to US$510m if ranked by manager.

The IFR data may be particularly misleading for merchant banks given their predilection to lead deals while not necessarily taking significant exposure. With this caveat in mind, it is worth remarking on J. Henry Schroder's position as 14 on the list (US$2.1bn by arranger and US$1.0bn by manager). Of the top 30 European lenders, seven are German regional banks. It is commonly assumed that the high exposure of Dutch banks in the region is due to the activities of ING. The data in Table 3.8 suggests that ABN AMRO has been more aggressive.

The Asian malaise will spread out of the region. One of the key causes of contagion is the falling price of tradable goods in the global marketplace and the impact this has on emerging economies attempting to maintain the value of their currencies. The other main transmission mechanism is the problems for the global banking industry based upon mounting bad debts in Asia. In particular, European banks appear exposed.

That the South Korean banks were in trouble was not widely accepted and the president of South Korea had only called in the IMF, just before South Korea's general election, on 22 November 1997. The IMF quickly established how much the South Korean banks had borrowed in foreign currency and were shocked to discover just how much of it had been borrowed at short maturity. Their counterparties were not rolling over that credit and as the South Korean banks had lent at longer maturities, they could not realise sufficient US dollars to meet these US dollar liabilities.

There were bigger shocks to come when the IMF discovered that the offshore branches of the South Korean banks had borrowed a further US$70bn of foreign currency. Then came the revelation that a high proportion of South Korea's foreign exchange reserves were on deposit or had been lent to South Korean banks. At a time when these banks were already scrambling to access US dollar funding, the central bank could not pull their US dollar deposits from these banks and use the proceeds to defend the exchange rate.

That very large loans of public money from the IMF were being negotiated in Seoul without the disclosure of these key facts was shocking. Portfolio investors were also ignorant of these problems and there was a temptation to believe that the IMF had arrived with a bailout and it was time to buy.

It turned out that the IMF financial support package for South Korea, the largest package it had so far put together, was too small and there was more pain to come. By the time the capital outflow from South Korea was stemmed, it was possible that the country's usable foreign exchange reserves had been reduced to less than US$1bn. By Q4 1997, it seemed increasingly likely that South Korea was on the brink of defaulting on its foreign currency liabilities.

The United States that can say no

27 November 1997, Regional

Policy reactions in Asia since the currency depreciations make it clear that most Asian governments expect to export their way out of the current economic crisis. To some extent the delay in making necessary reforms may be based on the principle that if they wait, then a current account surplus will come along putting upward pressure on the currency and downward pressure on interest rates.

It has already been a long wait and the argument is flawed anyway, as an improvement in the current account may not offset the capital outflow as foreign banks withdraw their credit lines from the region. While the Asian authorities wait for the export bailout, the Americans have other ideas.

Commerce Secretary Daley has already made it clear that he believes Asia should not be permitted such an exit. Last night on CNBC the CEO of Micron Technology, the last dynamic random-access memory (DRAM) manufacturer in the United States, questioned whether US tax dollars should be used to bail out the commercial mistakes which had produced the dumping of DRAMs in the international marketplace.

For years the South Koreans have made non-commercial decisions in underpricing their competitors in the developed world and it would be peculiar if the IMF now acted to support those non-commercial decisions. So last night the last chip maker in the United States complained. For the next year it will be the makers of the following items who will have plenty to complain about: TVs, videos, mobile phones, chemicals, cars, trucks, steel, plastics, ships, computers, etc.

The crisis seemed like a threat to many US businesses, but there were also those who those who saw opportunities too. As time went on the IMF started demanding things that seemed different from what they had previously demanded in return for their support. Such demands included the opening of the local financial service sector to foreign competition and the dismantling of local monopolies and cartels that had favoured well-connected individuals.

These peculiarities of the local business system were offensive to many, but they had little to do with how stable the financial system was or how quickly the countries might make it back to large current account surpluses that would stabilise their exchange rates and bring interest rates down. What we did not know in November 1997 and were just beginning to pick up on was that the US Treasury was playing a crucial behind-the-scenes role in influencing IMF policy. Robert Rubin, secretary to the US Treasury, was a former Goldman Sachs executive and he had very decided ideas as to what was necessary to end the crisis in Asia:

> If the markets wanted Indonesians to wear blue shirts, would blue shirts become essential to the restoration of confidence? My view was that by and large the markets tend to shine a spotlight on real economic problems, although they may exaggerate the importance of those problems at times (as well as ignoring them at other times). In a situation like Indonesia's, foreign investors and creditors might become preoccupied with a symbol, such as the ending of a specific monopoly or the removal of a single corrupt official. But those symbols weren't just blue shirts; in most cases they related to significant underlying issues: monopolies, corruption, mismanagement, and weak financial systems.

Robert Rubin, *In an Uncertain World: Tough Choices from Wall Street to Washington*, 2003

The scale of changes that were demanded were huge and for President Suharto, in particular, threatened his political survival as they involved allowing subsidised prices of consumer necessities to rise. Everyone knew that ending such subsidies would hit the poor particularly hard in Indonesia and would probably lead to social unrest. The reforms demanded as part of the IMF support package would strike at the socio-political stability of Asia.

I was already focused on how important FDI would be in creating stability for Asian exchange rates and establishing clearing prices for Asian equities. It was now becoming clearer that this was a war between two very different business cultures. Was this more than just an economic crisis? Was this the defeat of Asian capitalism, a form of business formerly thought to be the bedrock of an economic miracle and a victory for the particular brand of free market capitalism practised in the United States? Given how intertwined business and politics were in Asia, could such changes occur without political change? Investors were not the only ones wondering about some of the reforms being asked for by the IMF:

"What did spice monopolies have to do with restoring financial stability?" Volcker demanded of IMF officials when he arrived at Jakarta. "They said, 'You don't understand. It's run by Suharto's son and if we don't do anything about it, nobody will say we're serious'," recalled Volcker, who was still not entirely convinced of the merits of the Fund's approach. "People have different philosophies", he said. "The Fund's business is macro policy, and that's the stuff you can get changed. How programmatic you can be, in things that go into basic cultures and economic structure – whether that's productive or counterproductive, well it's a continuing issue, that's all I'll say."

Paul Blustein, *The Chastening: Inside the Crisis that Rocked the Global Financial System and Humbled the IMF*, 2001

That something bigger was at stake in the IMF negotiations than a 'bailout' was just becoming visible, and it would play a crucial role for portfolio investors in assessing when it was time to buy Asian equities. Could the local corporations survive in the new habitat that the IMF might impose and compete with the new foreign competitors more skilled in survival in such a habitat? To what extent would the Asian authorities be allowed again to intervene to undervalue their currencies with the risk that entailed for their competitors in the rest of the world? These became key questions to answer, but finding the right answers lay in an understanding of politics and not economics.

Lord Keynes and Santa Claus at the casino

28 November 1997, Malaysia

All acts of government to date in Malaysia indicate an unwillingness to accept the need for slower economic growth and the necessary associated economic pain. Only a few months ago, the chicken farmers of Malaysia slaughtered their flocks as the ringgit depreciation pushed up the grain price, but the government prevented them from raising prices. A rise in the chicken price was not permitted as it would cause painful inflation. The government is now proposing that PLUS will not get their toll increase but instead will be given an offsetting tax perk. Inflation is not permitted and PLUS will not suffer economic pain either.

With the assistance of capital controls, a government can target currency stability while having an independent monetary policy. Currently, Malaysia's ability to provide the low interest rates which reduce the pain of recession is restricted by the downward pressure on the currency. A move to capital controls would allow the authorities to adopt a policy of currency stability and falling interest rates. China has adopted just such a policy quite successfully. Increasingly, this course may become more tempting to the authorities as the worst of the business cycle has yet to develop.

It is to be hoped that should the Malaysians decide to implement their capital controls, holders of equities will find themselves denominated as investors rather than speculators. Wherever the line is drawn, some restrictions on the convertibility of the currency are increasingly likely as the authorities seek the 'painless' option of targeting both currency stability and interest rate flexibility simultaneously.

So are you an investor or a speculator? It is increasingly likely that such a definition will be provided by the Malaysian authorities, presumably based upon the same thought processes which occur when 'Santa Claus is Coming to Town'. Have you been naughty or nice?

Few investors were equipped with the skill set that would allow us to second-guess the acts of a government's desperation to protect the status quo. As the crisis intensified, key political players were indeed replaced, sometimes through the ballot box and sometimes not, and the new players, on the whole, endorsed the rules of the IMF. Which politicians would be replaced and which would not was not easy to forecast, but it was crucial.

Malaysia proved to be the place where the political status quo did not change and where capital controls were implemented as the solution to maintain the socio-political status quo. There was though considerable doubt as to whether that would be the case. There was strong political dissent from within the ruling party and it was led by the deputy prime minister, Anwar Ibrahim.

Foreign investors were enamoured with Anwar whom they thought could shift Malaysia, both economically and politically, to something more akin to a Western system. Few had any doubts that such a shift would have also been positive for capital. Within a year, Anwar was in jail and Prime Minister Mahathir had imposed capital controls on Malaysia, trapping foreign investors in local currency assets. Second-guessing political change in Asia during the crisis was a dangerous game for which few investors were properly equipped.

You will not find many pieces of research in this collection written in December. From early December to Christmas I was always travelling to visit the company's clients. December was always thought to be a good time to be in front of clients as they would be reassessing their asset allocation for the following year and might be generating some transactions and of course commission for CLSA.

I was delighted to be travelling at this time of year as I saw Christmas in many different cities and all of them were more festive than Christmas in Hong Kong. One night I remember having a drink in a bar on the Nyhavn in Copenhagen as the snow came down outside. I struck up a conversation with a fellow customer and we had far too many beers together. When his phone rang he answered it and then explained to me that he had to go. He put on his oilskins and walked out into the harbour. A ship needed oil and he was driving the oil tender!

Being in the UK for Christmas meant spending time with friends and family. Part of this was helping my dad in his butcher's shop on the Crumlin Road in Belfast in the very busy run-up to Christmas. Sometimes I would sleep over in the shop to make sure that our turkeys did not fall into the hands of turkey rustlers. Turkeys stolen in the evening could be liquidated quickly at low prices in markets the next morning. Arbitrage comes in many forms, legal and illegal, but I had the near-perfect defence against this form – a meat cleaver beside my camp bed. Its deterrent value was always enough.

432 Titanics, Warren Buffett and the price of the bun

8 January 1998, Regional

With the Indonesian market falling 32% in US dollar terms in four trading days, it is probably time to reassess exactly what remains of Asia. Table 3.9 shows the approximate market caps of the Asian markets as of yesterday.

Table 3.9: Asian market capitalisation in US dollars on 7 January 1998

	US$bn	% of total
Pakistan	12	1.0
China*	11	1.0
Indonesia	29	2.7
Thailand	32	2.9
Philippines	30	2.7
South Korea	83	7.5
India	111	10.1
Singapore	118	10.7
Malaysia	119	10.8
Hong Kong	243	22.2
Taiwan	306	28.0
Total	**1,094**	

* China A share market is US$165bn

You have to get to the sixth-largest equity market in Asia before you can find a market larger than British Telecom! Thus today, for the market cap of General Electric (GE) (US$243bn), you could buy the entire market cap of China (H and B shares), Pakistan, Indonesia, Thailand, the Philippines and South Korea – and still have loose change to pick up a majority stake in India.

These markets (excluding India) are the listed capital which represent a population of 1,568 million people or 27% of the world's population. All these markets can be purchased for the same price as the Australian equity market – a country of 17 million people. For the price of GE, if you include the controlling stake in India, you can buy the listed capital of nations comprising 2,487 million people or 44% of the world's population.

China's A share market has a market cap of US$163bn and is now the third-largest equity market in Asia.

At the end of 3Q 1996, there were 1,316 companies in Asia (Hong Kong, Indonesia, Malaysia, Singapore, Taiwan, Thailand) with market caps in excess of US$200m. As at the end of last year, the number had fallen to 823. This is a 36% fall. If you exclude Taiwan from the figures, where the market has risen over the period, the numbers are even more depressing. Where once there were 915 companies with market caps over US$200m, now there are 483, a fall of 47%. The movie *Titanic* cost US$200m to make. Thus over the past year, Asia has watched the submergence of 432 such vessels.

In February 1997, Geoff Hisock wrote a book called *Asia's Wealth Club*. The precision in the mistiming of this book was only surpassed in 1997 by the publication of *Education of a Speculator* just months before the author's hedge fund was reported to have moved to a negative NAV (the 1996 honours fell to Thailand's economic boom). *Asia's Wealth Club* purported to list Asia's 100 US dollar billionaires. Assuming that all entrants' wealth has deteriorated in line with the US dollar fall in the value of their local stock market (it may be less if they are holding cash, or a lot more if they are geared), the changes shown in Table 3.10 in Asia's wealth club have occurred within the past 12 months.

Table 3.10: Number of billionaires in the key Asian markets

	1997	1998
Hong Kong	13	8
India	3	3
Indonesia	15	2
Malaysia	11	3
South Korea	7	3
Philippines	12	3
Singapore	6	4
Thailand	13	1
	80	27

These statistics are not aimed at inspiring purchase. As *The Solid Ground Daily* has suggested over the past few days, most values are illusory while the Asian governments pursue policies which threaten to eradicate the domestic banking system. That policy will change and bargains will abound, but at this juncture the governments have the ability and the seeming will to pursue the economic equivalent of a 'scorched earth' strategy.

The last time this author looked at the *Forbes* list, the world's richest man was Warren Buffett, who had amassed US$43bn from the splendour of Omaha. Should Mr Buffett choose, he could thus be the majority shareholder of every listed company in Thailand, Indonesia and the Philippines. Just another few days of downside and he could add Pakistan to his shopping list. Mr Buffett was last spotted conducting an investment appraisal in Asia in Hong Kong in October 1995.

Warren Buffet ordered a Big Mac, fries and a Coke at a McDonald's in Hong Kong just about midnight between October 1 and 2nd 1995 … Then Bill Gates walked up and Warren introduced Gates to me and my brother. I had to scrape my jaw off the floor.

He [Buffet] picked up the bun a little and looked at the bun and the meat and said "the bun is the same [whether in the US or Asia], the meat is the same and the fries are the same. And the price is about the same," Buffett told the group …

Buffett paid for the meals with McDonald's gift certificates and gave the Langdon brothers what certificates were left over … After Buffett handed over the gift certificates, he cracked, "You don't have any frequent flier coupons do you?"

Andrew Kilpatrick, *Of Permanent Value: The Story of Warren Buffett*, 1996

Thus no doubt when confronted with the knowledge of his Asian purchasing power, Mr Buffett would retort with one of his favourite aphorisms: "Price is what you pay. Value's what you get."

For a while investors did think that the comparisons made in this piece of research were valid. A major rally in Asian equities began in January 1998 and the MSCI Asia ex Japan Index rose 45% by March. That may have only taken the index back to its December 1997 level, but it was the first sustained rally that equities had made during the crisis.

I had forecast that the crisis could not be over before currencies stabilised, banks were recapitalised and foreign direct investors established a clearing price for Asian equities. It now looked like this analysis was wrong as the equity markets rose strongly and many investors thought the crisis had ended.

The greatest transformation of wealth in Asia since the dark days of 1998 has come in China. By 2020, the combined wealth of the four richest men in China exceeded the entire market capitalisation of the Chinese A Share Index in January 1998. The Asian financial crisis represented a hiatus in wealth creation in the region and in particular in China.

Availability bias meant that investors in 1998 were focused on that narrow portion of wealth represented by the price of listed equities. It was easy to miss that a new form of capital and new capitalists were ready to benefit from the chaos. However, these direct investors were yet to emerge and for those in the Asian financial system, and in particular for stockbrokers, that chaos came particularly close to home in mid-January 1998, when Peregrine Securities failed.

The falcon and the falconer

12 January 1998, Hong Kong/Global

Turning and turning in the widening gyre
The falcon cannot hear the falconer;
Things fall apart; the centre cannot hold;
Mere anarchy is loosed upon the world,
The blood-dimmed tide is loosed, and everywhere
The ceremony of innocence is drowned;
The best lack all conviction, while the worst
Are full of passionate intensity.

William Butler Yeats, 'The Second Coming', 1919

Can the centre hold? The bad news is that only governments have the answer.

The move to a perilous condition by Peregrine Securities was the second-most important event for Hong Kong on Friday. For although it may not have seemed so on Friday night and well into Saturday morning, the collapse in US equities and the rally in Treasuries is a more ominous portent.

For many months Asian commentators have wondered how long the US markets could continue to ignore the winds of deflation blowing from the east. The US markets have constantly focused on those companies directly trading with the United States rather than the major impact on prices when the problems associated with the huge overcapacity in Asia are then intensified by a collapse in what had been the fastest-growing source of demand. Companies which have never traded with Asia in their history will be impacted by the ensuing fall in price when demand and supply suddenly alter so rapidly.

The best-case scenario now is that the signs of global contagion from Asia produce a firmer policy response from the G7. In particular, it is to be hoped that the Japanese realise the heavy onus on them to use the power of fiat money to produce the surge in demand which can help to alleviate the negatives associated with overcapacity in the global system. Greenspan is at least partially constrained in providing easier money due to the tightness in his domestic labour markets and the Bundesbank is concentrated on the political goal of creating a single currency within 12 months. Sadly, we are particularly reliant upon the most incompetent G7 monetary authority to fight the powers of deflation.

So in the short term, the best that can be hoped for is that the events of Friday and the ensuing storms of today may persuade the G7 or the G3 to provide some currency intervention in Asia and thus some short-term relief. Then it is to be hoped that the Japanese can come up with the measures which finally turn the Japanese economy into a major source of consumption growth. Then will the fiat money system have fulfilled its role as a tool for alleviating the worst impacts of deflation. Time is ticking away.

In the meantime, the HK dollar will be under continued attack as investors worry about the contagion from the downturn in US equities. The currency board system will continue to operate and Hong Kong's reserves will once again be used to buy back the HK dollar and shrink the amount of HK dollars in the system. Interest rates will rise once again and the equity market will react negatively.

This pressure will not abate anytime soon while there are signs of nervousness in the major global capital markets. Once again, the only major alleviating factor would be a government policy announcement. Should the pressure in Hong Kong intensify, the Chinese government could make significant progress in restoring confidence should they announce intensified moves to reflate their own economy.

It is crucial to remember that the Chinese authorities are one of very few global emerging market governments who also command a fiat money system. Around the world, most emerging market governments have handed control of domestic monetary policy to the markets by operating currency policies and open capital accounts simultaneously. Perhaps more by luck than judgement, China has retained sufficient capital controls permitting the government almost complete monetary flexibility.

Thus while the bulk of global emerging markets are now reliant upon actions by the G7 – and more specifically Japan – to offset deflation, the Chinese have command over their own destiny. At this stage, they have shown only limited willingness to use such flexibility. However, as the global situation deteriorates over the next few weeks, this may provide the catalyst for the Chinese to utilise the fiat money system in an attempt to prevent the 'D' word becoming prevalent in China.

For China, the stakes could not be higher. Should a collapse in Hong Kong equities continue, it is increasingly unlikely that China will be able to continue to access global capital. In the absence of such capital, the state-owned enterprise (SOE) reform process in China will be slower than was to be expected. Perhaps more importantly, without access to global capital it will be increasingly difficult to roll out economic growth to the inland provinces through significant infrastructure improvements.

Thus a collapse in Hong Kong may augur a significant rise in urban unemployment in China due to more SOE closures and continued population drift to the coast. At this stage, China would have to provide a fiat money response anyway. Why wait? It is not an exaggeration to say that the long-term political legitimacy of the CCP would be threatened should Hong Kong cease to fulfil its role as a source of global capital. The stakes for China are very high indeed. The aggressive use of the fiat money system at this stage would provide major relief for Hong Kong.

So we are now in the business of betting on governments. If the right decisions are made by the G7, then this will be good news for all markets. Investors in Hong Kong have the added advantage that the Chinese government has a very major political incentive to utilise its fiat money system to shore up the outlook for Hong Kong's markets. So now that we have to bet on governments, Hong Kong is still the best bet. When we are so reliant upon government response, it should be no surprise that:

> The best lack all conviction, while the worst
> Are full of passionate intensity.

This proved to be just a wobble for the US financial markets, and the rise of the S&P500 soon continued and the decline in Treasury yields ended. The hoped-for intervention in foreign exchange markets did not materialise until June and the US dollar had much further to rise. From an Asian perspective it seemed inevitable that the crisis would produce dire economic impacts in the developed world. A significant portion of developed world bank loans in Asia seemed likely to be written off with negative impacts for bank capital.

The devaluations of the Asian currencies had intensified the deflationary pressures that were putting downward pressure on the price of globally traded goods. As early as the summer of 1996, US import prices were falling. A steep decline began in 1997 and by January 1998, US import prices were declining by 6.2% year on year. These ever cheaper prices symbolised the growing competitiveness of Asia, at the new exchange rate level, and suggested to the forecaster that developed world jobs would be lost to the new Asian competition.

What seemed obvious from Asia was not obvious to G7 policy makers. These policy makers were active in Asia, supporting the IMF with numerous multilateral back-up loans, but they did not alter their domestic monetary policy to account for the impact the Asian economic crisis might have on their domestic economies.

The Japanese authorities were working hard to prevent the recent collapse of large financial institutions from dragging their growth even lower and it proved a vain hope that they could stimulate higher domestic consumption.

It was not until September 1998, when the crisis led to a devaluation and default in Russia, that the G7 policy makers delivered the policy response that played probably the key role in preventing the Asian economic crisis from becoming a global financial crisis. It was incredibly difficult to forecast when they would be triggered into such a move and there were large losses for investors who bought equity in Asia in January 1998, betting on co-ordinated G7 policy change to ward off the growing deflation.

The collapse of Peregrine Securities of Hong Kong on Monday, 12 January 1998 was one of those moments that defined the crisis. The company was a regional stockbroker that had been active in raising capital for Asian corporations. As part of that business it would often use its own funds to provide such loans while it sought to sell the credit risk, in the form of bonds or commercial paper, to institutional investors.

One way in which firms competed for such business was in offering to take ever larger portions of this credit risk onto their own balance sheet as part of the capital raising. The borrower was thus assured rapid access to credit and often at a guaranteed price. As the crisis progressed it was of course becoming ever more difficult to sell this debt to institutional investors and those behind such deals found themselves effectively providing loans to companies with ever worsening credit quality.

Many of the most aggressive firms in this business were the Asian subsidiaries of the world's largest banks. Such large institutions could survive the major losses of capital that occurred when the issuing companies defaulted on their debts. Peregrine Securities was a locally listed Asian stockbroking company without a well-capitalised parent company. In the case of Peregrine, the straw that broke the camel's back was the default on its loan to an Indonesian taxi company ironically called Steady Safe.

Along with much of the financial community, I headed to Lan Kwai Fong, an area in Hong Kong renowned for its bars and nightclubs, on the night that Peregrine failed. It was a remarkable atmosphere and there were plenty of newly unemployed ex-employees of Peregrine in the bars and drinking on the streets. These people had lost their jobs and many of them had lost a significant portion of their savings that they had invested in the company's shares.

I do not remember seeing any tears, but a wide-eyed stare that betrayed a stunned disbelief was common. By this stage, I had gained a certain reputation in Hong Kong as someone who might know when the pain might stop. Many people, some ex-employees of Peregrine, asked me when it all might end. Perhaps I should have lied, but nothing I said then alleviated the fear and pain among those drowning their sorrows in Lan Kwai Fong that night.

It was not just the employees of Peregrine who were alarmed. Many of those present had a significant portion of their savings invested in the shares of their employers – including me. With financial institutions in Thailand and Indonesia closed and Peregrine Securities now bankrupt, who would be next?

China still did not respond to the growing Asian crisis with a change towards a more relaxed monetary policy. Perhaps worried that somehow the capital exodus could impact its own ability to manage its exchange rate, the People's Bank of China (PBOC) did not act to reduce interest rates any further in 1998. If the South Korean won and the New Taiwan Dollar, the currencies of two economies with very large current account surpluses, could be forced to devalue, there was probably concern in Beijing that they should err on the side of caution and not reduce interest rates or stimulate domestic economic growth.

However, as each month passed, despite a decline in the size of the country's current account balance, there was no decline in China's foreign exchange reserves. The mechanism through which capital outflow would force the PBOC to utilise its reserves to support the renminbi and, in the process, tighten domestic monetary policy did not materialise. While these numbers remained positive, it was increasingly likely that Chinese policy makers would not revert to a devaluation to support economic growth.

The thread that held this particular sword of Damocles did not break, and the best guide to the fact that it would hold is that China's foreign exchange reserves were not declining. This did not prevent another run on the Hong Kong dollar in January 1998. By 13 January the overnight interest rate had risen to 12%. In just over a week Hong Kong's interest rates were back close to US levels. The currency board system worked again to maintain the exchange rate, but the Hang Seng Index declined 17%.

Twice now those selling the Hong Kong dollar had seen the currency board mechanism act to produce higher interest rates and produce a decline in equity prices. It was an indication of the strength of the mechanism that such adjustments happened quickly. It was also to prove a mechanism that drew the attention of investors who thought they could profit from it. This was not to be the last attack on the Hong Kong currency board system and the next one, when it came in August, had a new angle that many thought would likely guarantee its success.

To recommend that investors buy Hong Kong equities on 12 January 1998, the same day that its leading independent stockbroking company had gone bankrupt, may seem reckless. Perhaps it was. The Hang Seng Index was to go lower, but crucially the Hong Kong currency board system held fast. From its lows in January, the Hang Seng Index was to fall a further 18% in US dollar terms before it bottomed in September 1998.

From the January 1998 lows, the Hang Seng Index would more than double by March 2000. The bankruptcy of Peregrine Securities was not to be the moment of maximum revulsion towards Hong Kong equities, but it was to prove to be a time when Hong Kong equities had become cheap for the long-term investor.

For currencies yes, for equities no

15 January 1998, Regional

The risk characteristics of currencies and equities are very different. It would be very possible to see a strong currency and weak equities. The currency markets have now, correctly in our opinion, begun to worry less about debt moratoriums. Over the coming weeks and months they will receive confirmation that the reform process is underway. Having gone to the brink of pricing in debt moratoriums, there will be significant upside, as it is clear that the reverse is occurring. Equities too had been partly discounting debt moratoriums and/or hyper-inflation and they too will see a rise in price. However, that will be a dead-cat bounce.

On the announcements of liberalisation there will be a continued flow of short-term capital into the currency. This may be sufficient to put some downward pressure on interest rates. However, it will not stop the process of equity diminution currently underway in Southeast Asia. Interest rates will not fall to levels that will save the banking system and reflate the economy.

As equities represent a bundle of assets and liabilities, there remains every prospect that the value of equity can go to zero in this environment. The equity market will not have bottomed until we begin to see the inflow of long-term capital which can directly recapitalise Asia's ailing corporates and simultaneously push interest rates to more reflationary levels.

Thus equity prices will bounce on the announcements of liberalisations, but this is unlikely to signal the end of the bear market. Following the announcement, an anxious wait will begin for the arrival of the direct investor. With the legal impediment to ownership removed, the next important hurdles are quality and price. It will take many months before direct investors have made their judgements on quality and negotiated their deals on price. During that period, the equity markets can give back the gains made on the announcements of the liberalisations. The withering of equity continues during that period.

Between 23 December 1997 and 12 January 1998, the baht, peso, won and ringgit all reached their lows for the Asian financial crisis. The IMF's arrival had reduced the prospects of a resort to the monetary printing press and default on foreign currency obligations as the likely path for Asian policy makers. The rapid slowdown in the economies was quickly leading back to current account surpluses. Crucially, none of these countries had resorted to the printing press before the arrival of the IMF.

Things were very different in Indonesia and by the first quarter of 1998, year-on-year broad money growth was 77%. The decline of the rupiah had much further to go. With the exception of the rupiah, it proved a great time to buy Asian currencies as investors benefited from their appreciation relative to the US dollar, but also the very high interest rates available on short-term deposits at that time.

On 15 January Michel Camdessus, managing director of the IMF, stood with his arms folded watching as a seated President Suharto signed a new 'strengthened and reinforced economic programme' with the IMF. This was supposed to be the deal that finally brought stability for the exchange rate, the financial system and the economy. The rupiah kept falling. The plan said nothing as to how the country's large US dollar debt would be dealt with nor how the banking system would be recapitalised.

The government guarantee on bank deposits was capped at what proved to be too low a level, and people continued to remove their deposits from the banking system. On 27 January the government announced that all bank deposits would be guaranteed. Later, as in South Korea and Thailand, agreements would be reached to allow a rescheduling of some of the US dollar debt owed by Indonesian corporations.

These additional measures were crucial in ending the crisis in Indonesia. The IMF programmes that Suharto signed up to were not magic bullets, but slowly the additional measures were being taken that would bring stability to the financial system and corporate Indonesia.

By January, Indonesia's problems were no longer being confined to government offices and boardrooms. The decline in the rupiah was acting to produce a dramatic rise in food prices. Riots now broke out in the country and often the Muslim population targeted the food stores owned and run by the Chinese population to vent their anger at the growing chaos.

Our local office reported that street vendors preferred payment in Marlboro cigarettes rather than rupiah. The president was looking for answers other than capitulating to IMF demands for the structural reforms that would undermine his grip on power. One of these answers was the creation of a currency board system to stabilise the exchange rate. Some investors got excited about this, given that so far the Hong Kong currency board system had held firm.

To me it seemed like a ridiculous idea for a country with limited foreign exchange reserves to operate a currency board system. Indonesia had a financial, social and political structure that was already fragile and seemed unlikely to survive the very high interest rates that a currency board system would very likely, at least initially, entail. For a few weeks though some investors recommitted capital to Indonesia in the belief that the currency board system would be established and somehow end the crisis.

The United States was against the plan to create a currency board to stabilise the Indonesian rupiah and pressure was put on Suharto to abandon it, which he did. This attempt to find a solution to Indonesia's problems independently of the IMF further undermined confidence that the Suharto regime would be prepared to implement the reforms that it had signed up to. Increasingly, investors focused on whether stability could only come to Indonesia on the departure of President Suharto from office. What we did not know was that similar opinions were now circulating among key global policy makers.

Death of PE revisited

22 January 1998, Regional

As we look at the equity indices today, they are overvalued. However, the liberalisation process will transform the ROE for those companies lucky enough to be recapitalised, while for the rest we have gone beyond the 'death of PE' and onto the 'death of equity'. A winnowing of equity is about to take place in Southeast Asia.

There is wheat among the chaff, but the market indices will prove to be largely composed of chaff. Do not be tempted to buy the victors of the last cycle. These financiers or asset traders were creatures of fixed exchange rates and ensuing liquidity bubbles. That chaff is about to blow away; buy the wheat which represents the domestic consumption/distribution assets, with good balance sheets. They look expensive but let's assume that the new US (?) management can lift the ROE to the same levels they have achieved in the United States! Does it still look expensive?

There was now little faith in the same Asian management that had once been lauded as a key ingredient of the Asian economic miracle. Very well capitalised foreign firms, mainly from the United States, stood ready to compete with these firms assuming that the liberalisation programme imposed by the IMF was implemented. Could the domestic firms, badly managed and with weak balance sheets, cope with this form of competition? The best scenario for an Asian equity investor seemed to be that the assets of local companies would be so attractive that the company would be bid for by foreign corporations. By January 1998, there was still limited evidence that those foreign corporations would be interested at any price.

By this stage, I was beginning to describe myself as the Rhinestone Cowboy, "getting cards and letters from people I don't even know". Having been ranked as the number one Asian equity strategist in polls towards the end of 1997, other people were interested in employing me. I did get a call from Goldman Sachs, so decided to go along out of curiosity.

My interviewer explained that I would work as part of a team and other members of that team would forecast interest rates, currencies, economic growth and just about any other important variable I could think of. I raised the question that given that all these inputs would be provided to me by other people, perhaps there might not be enough for me to do all day. My interrogator didn't smile at the question. We parted company.

Bill, Larry, William and bovine flatulence

23 January 1998, Regional

If extrapolation was all that was necessary, then the secret to investment success would be determined by the possession of a pencil and a ruler. Not for the first time, and I suspect not for the last, it is worthwhile to quote from Fred Schwed Jr on the issue of market dynamics as opposed to the laws of dynamics as expressed by physicists:

> It is a fair thing to say of a piston, an elevator, or a golf ball at a certain moment, that it is "going up". This suggests not only that it has been going up, but that it will probably continue to go on up, for a little time at least, because whatever impulse started it is still operating to some extent. But it is not a fair thing to say of the stock market, which, not being a physical thing, is not subject to Newton's laws of propulsion or inertia. Unfortunately most of us unconsciously credit this false analogy.

Thus we are not tempted to buy unless they are "going up" or to sell unless they are "going down".

Fred Schwed Jr, *Where Are All the Customer's Yachts?*, 1940

In the mystical certainty of extrapolation, madness lies. A topical example. If the list of President Clinton's alleged paramours continues to double on a daily basis, then he will have been 'linked' with all the 135 million women of the United States by the end of February! As the number of alleged paramours increased by 100% yesterday, it is thus logical to assume that this trend will continue and it is thus logical that President Clinton will find himself eventually 'linked' to the entire female population of the United States.

Sounds like madness? Well of course it's madness, but it's a form of analysis which is conducted in financial markets every day. Those same commentators who proclaimed a rupiah/US dollar rate at 6,000 last week are today suggesting that it may not stop at 25,000. The only key difference is that the direction of the exchange rate has changed. Thus should you know any Americans involved in this methodology of prognostication, bet them US$100 that if they phone their mothers, Bill picks up the phone. It's always worth US$100 to advance the cause of reason.

In the absence of reason surrounding the rupiah, it is time for a 'reasonable' conspiracy theory as to why the rupiah will trade nearer 6,000 than 25,000. Now I am highly sceptical of conspiracy theories with regard to the actions of government. The same taxi driver who will tell you that the CIA shot JFK will tell you how the US government once set aside US$21m per annum. for the study of flatulence in cows. It was the same government which didn't really put a man on the moon that was the same government which funded a research programme in Massachusetts aimed at increasing the average size of the American dwarf – not coincidentally creating employment in Tip O'Neil's constituency.

The preceding are two real examples of government spending taken from Hedrick Smith's *The Power Game*. As an ex-lawyer, I prefer the admissible evidence of government incompetency to the hearsay of conspiracy perfection. Anyway, this conspiracy theory is in no way as outlandish as suggesting that the US government would assassinate the leader of the free world, spend money on the smell of a cow or seek to improve the welfare of the perpendicularly challenged. The theory is that the US government will assist in the support of the rupiah.

The United States does not want an Asian country of 200 million people lapsing into anarchy. There are a lot fewer people in Bosnia, but even there prevention would still have been politically easier than military intervention. In the space of just a few days these dynamics were outlined to the current president of Indonesia by the president of the United States (Bill Clinton), the

US defense secretary (William Cohen) and the deputy US Treasury secretary (Larry Summers). The present incumbent's stewardship of Indonesia was secured against a background of a growing communist movement and an increasingly ardent anti-US predecessor:

> Foreign policy took a decidedly anti-western tone. Sukarno intensified efforts to wrest control of Irian Jaya from the Dutch and launched an ill-fated military campaign against Malaysia to protest the establishment of the Malaysian states of Sabah and Sarawak on the island of Borneo. Relations with Beijing and Moscow improved while ties with the USA became increasingly strained, particularly with the CIA … For Sukarno, still imbued with notions of revolutionary grandeur, economics took a back seat to the political struggle. In a famous speech on 25 March 1964 Sukarno told the United States to "go to hell with your aid".

Adam Schwarz, *A Nation in Waiting: Indonesia's Search for Stability*, 1994

At 9 pm on 1 October 1966 Sukarno was gone and a General Suharto explained to the nation why the army was now in de facto control of the country. These events took place in an era when President Lyndon Johnson was famously to explain of another US ally: "Well he may be a son of a bitch but at least he's our son of a bitch."

Following last week's discussions with Bill, William and Larry, a Frenchman, Michel Camdessus, arrived in Jakarta to witness President Suharto sign a franchise agreement for Western capitalism. Well perhaps Larry Summers' grandiloquent oration on the benefits of the free market system impacted the president in a similar spirit to that which embraced St Paul on the road to Damascus. On the other hand, it does seem more likely that a US commitment to economic and political stability in Indonesia was the minimal price to be asked for the elimination of crony capitalism and a decidedly frosty air around the dinner table in the Suharto household.

Strangely, both goals – political stability and liberalisation – coincide with US interests. Only politicians really know the real cost differentials between monetary and military reserves. The United States may be spending wisely and as yet "In God We Trust" has not been printed on the rupiah.

That an Asian equity strategist should be so speculating on such affairs of state further indicates just how uncertain things had become in Asia. We now know that the US Treasury was behind the plan to enforce root and branch reform upon the Indonesian economy and the US defence establishment was very concerned about the prospect of instability in Indonesia and perhaps the rise of Muslim fundamentalism.

There is little doubt that there were some in the US administration who thought the best chance for stability would come with the resignation of Suharto. That final act in what had morphed from an IMF support package into a drive by the United States for regime change was something I did not foresee. The rupiah was at 12,750 to the US dollar when this piece was written and it was to reach 16,650 by June 1998. By year end, the rupiah traded at 8,000 to the US dollar.

For currency investors in Indonesia it had been a year of living dangerously, but good profits were made by buying the Indonesian rupiah in January 1998 in the belief that the United States, working behind the scenes with the IMF, would act to prevent Indonesia lapsing into anarchy. In his memoirs Robert Rubin reveals that by this stage of the crisis the almost daily meetings to discuss US policy involved the US Treasury, the National Economic Council, the National Security Council, the State Department and the Department of Defense.

There were more than economic considerations influencing US decisions on the degree of support that should be provided to Asia in general, but to Indonesia in particular. The US administration stayed engaged with President Suharto and Indonesia despite a growing lack of trust in the president. That anarchy in Indonesia was avoided is now a matter of record, but the slide towards such a condition only intensified from January to May 1998 and in that chaos, over 1,000 people were to lose their lives. It seemed likely by late January 1998 that the United States and the IMF would not walk away from their support of Indonesia, but it was to be many months before financial markets were reassured of that continued support.

The victory of quality

5 February 1998, Regional

It's the style that gets you; technological ugliness syruped over with romantic phoniness in an effort to produce beauty and profit by people who, though stylish, don't know where to start because no one has ever told them there's such a thing as Quality in this world and it's real, not style. Quality isn't something you lay on top of subjects and objects like tinsel on a Christmas tree. Real Quality must be the source of the subjects and objects, the cone from which the tree must start.

Robert M Pirsig, *Zen and the Art of Motorcycle Maintenance*, 1974

For investors in Asia, never has the style/quality dichotomy been of greater significance. The calculus of pain has forced most Asian governments (Malaysia is the clear exception) to choose economic liberalisation rather than the cataclysmic road to the printing press and debt moratoriums. Great news for the economy, but not necessarily good news for that bundle of assets and liabilities we know as equity.

The move towards liberalisation has produced an enthusiasm for equities in Southeast Asia which is not surprising given that the alternative was too dire to contemplate. As part of the capitalist infrastructure, it would be surprising if brokers and fund managers did not cheer the decision by Southeast Asian governments to announce liberalisation, which is simply to 'let the markets work'.

However, the euphoria surrounding the embracing of the market masks the reality that the United States/IMF has created this victory for markets to unleash the forces of 'creative destruction'. Investors do not always cheer the operation of market forces. It was market forces that produced the great equity and bond bear markets of our time and market forces that put Asia into such a dire predicament in the first place. In the long term, it is good news that market forces are being fully unleashed but at this stage, those forces are destructive and are about to chew up and spit out great swathes of equity across Southeast Asia.

The turnaround in the Asian situation coincides with the direct involvement of the US administration. That administration realised there was a real risk that Asian capitalism was drifting into a dangerous half-life where it would continue to survive by selling goods at ever cheaper and cheaper levels. This unique form of zombie capitalism would develop in the absence of a liberalised economy which created the ability of both government and capitalists to subvert the creative destruction process. Producing appalling returns on capital and barely cash-flow positive, these zombie capitalists would live on selling products at prices which would be uneconomic for real-life capitalists.

Most of these real capitalists reside in the United States. While Congress rages over the presumed benevolence of US funding of the IMF, they are missing the key point – after many years of effort (previously concentrated in Japan), the United States is finally killing the zombie capitalist. While this may be yet further bad news for US labour, it is extremely positive news for US capital. It is crucial for equity investors to remember that the alacrity of US involvement in Asia is due to this desire to expunge certain Asian capital. You might own that capital.

This is where the style/quality dichotomy is essential. Like the great plague which swept across Europe in the 14th century, the great purge which will sweep across Asia will not eradicate all organisms. In fact, part of the liberalisation process entails the ability of foreign capital to intervene for the resuscitation of mendicant capital. It appears that many equity investors see the 'liberalisation' process as an opportunity to seize the equity of those companies which outperformed in the last bull market and 'gear' into the recovery. This is an incorrect strategy.

The last economic and equity market upswing in Asia was characterised by a victory of style over quality. No better example need be given than the thin patina of opulence laid upon the premises of Finance One and others of Asia's asset financiers. There was never any quality here, but it produced the style that was essential to build confidence in the chimera of easy money and rising asset prices. As fish had to develop gills to survive underwater, so has capital to develop weak limbs but a pretty face in an easy money environment.

The stylish assets associated with easy money will one day also be back in fashion. One day Southeast Asia will see another burst of excess liquidity when quality will be of secondary consideration to style. Many investors believed that the 1929 US equity market crash would forever preclude a return to favour of the common stock whose value was built on style rather than quality. By the late 1950s there were already signs that style was back and there was a great bull market in style from 1963–67 as the conglomerate boom and the REIT booms took place. However, in the 30 years between 1929 and 1959, quality outperformed style. It took another generation to buy style and shun quality.

As mentioned in *The Solid Ground Daily* of 23 January, it is increasingly clear that China, the United States and Japan have reached some form of agreement on currencies. China has demanded a strong yen and higher demand in Japan in return for promising renminbi stability. The Japanese seem finally to have realised that their local difficulties threaten to produce a global downturn and thus are inclined to provide the Chinese and the Americans with the rise in demand and stronger currency which they demand.

These are the key external conditions for a sustainable bull market in Hong Kong. If China chooses currency stability, then reflation will have to be achieved through monetary and/or fiscal methods. Hong Kong faces the combined positives of a stable HK dollar, falling HK dollar interest rates as the currency board brings interest rates to equilibrium, a stable renminbi, falling Chinese interest rates and/ or fiscal stimulus and a weak US dollar. If you were to make a checklist for bullish external conditions for Hong Kong, then you could wish for little more.

The zombie company was of course to go from strength to strength – on a global basis. The subsidy of such companies in Asia by the local authorities was something that the developed world was subsequently also to embrace. The Asian form of capitalism was not erased but modified, and it was enfranchised as hyper-competitive by the decline in the Asian exchange rates and the crucial intervention in currency markets that followed and locked in that competitiveness.

The theoretically victorious form of capital in the developed world would have to respond to Asia's hyper-competitiveness by cutting costs and investment and often adding – ever cheaper – financial gearing to boost returns. This forced adjustment stemmed directly from the fact that by late 1998, the Asian governments were back intervening in foreign exchange markets to prevent the appreciation of their currencies.

Those policies continue until this day. This new post-crisis global financial architecture was to ensure that developed world governments and central bankers would one day also have to intervene to prevent the full forces of creative destruction falling upon their economies. The result would be the proliferation of zombie companies and not their extinction.

The strength of capital is that it evolves, but post-Asian crisis, the evolution of global capital, driven by the perverse incentives in place, was towards financial engineering. There was no victory for one form of capitalism over another in 1998. The old Asian system, saved primarily by locked-in cheap exchange rates, forced the developed world system to change. How it changed and the consequences from those changes are the story of the age of debt that we are still living through.

Whatever Japan, China and the United States may have agreed in early 1998, Japan proved itself unable to deliver. While the large Japanese government capital injection did save the local financial system from collapse, it did not lead in 1998 to any acceleration in economic growth. Japan launched a US$120bn fiscal stimulus package in April 1998, but by June was reporting its first economic contraction in 23 years. The weakness in the yen continued during the year and it was not until market participants began to bet on declining US interest rates in August 1998 that the US dollar began to decline relative to the yen.

The key developed world central bankers, *primus inter pares* the US Federal Reserve, then delivered interest rate cuts. The Hang Seng Index, trading at 10442 when this piece was written, did not rally to the 14000 level I then forecast – it declined to a low of 6660 first! In due course it became clear that the renminbi would not be devalued, the HK dollar/US dollar peg would hold, US interest rates would decline and the US dollar would weaken. However, betting on such a combination in February 1998 was to be a costly mistake.

Investors often have to read the runes to establish what agreements have been made between governments and central bankers in pursuit of economic stability. It is rare for such agreements to be announced publicly. Larry Summers visited China in January 1998. According to one of the journalists who travelled with him, he had come to 'grovel' before Zhou Rongji, China's premier in waiting, and ask that China did not devalue its exchange rate. Whatever happened at that meeting and whatever the United States promised, on its own behalf or in agreement with its partners, the renminbi was not to be devalued. In January 1998 the financial markets were speculating that such an agreement had been reached, but nothing was announced and faith in any agreement was not to last.

Don't fear the reaper

11 February 1998, Hong Kong

Seasons come and seasons go. Weakness comes and weakness goes but as Blue Oyster Cult reminded us a long time ago: "Seasons don't fear the reaper.
The layers of doubt surrounding the probability of a stable HK dollar and lower HK dollar interest rates are gradually falling away. However, I continue to encounter among investors a deep lurking fear which appears to be almost primordial in its origins. There is a belief in a werewolf, a bogeyman, a banshee who will prevent such stability. While those were some of his guises in previous generations, today he is called the hedge fund manager.

In the history of mankind we have thought it necessary to create such a dangerous omniscient villain. This social history has been repeated in the markets. There is always a 'they' in the markets who know more and thus move prices. Back in the 1960s it was the gunslingers; in the 1970s it was Arab money; in the 1980s it was the wall of Japanese money; and today it is the hedge fund manager.

The reasoning goes that if interest rates return to too low a level in Hong Kong, then hedge fund managers will be back shorting the currency and the equity market and minting money for themselves. Nobody pauses to ask why we have one market participant who is all powerful against all others. Nobody pauses to ask why such activities are the unique preserve of one nomenclature of investor while others are forced to watch powerless. Nobody pauses to ask whether this omniscient predator couldn't work that magic trick in reverse and profit on the long side of the equity market?

These questions are not asked. In the mind of the mainstream institutional investor, the hedge fund managers hunt in packs, they are omniscient, they only short things and they force movements in markets. This is a modern myth. Hedge fund managers go to great lengths to conceal their movements from their competitors, like any other investor. They are market participants like others and thus they do get it wrong. They buy as well as sell. Most crucially, they exploit fundamental weaknesses to move markets and gain profits.

Their biggest coups have all been based upon the probing and revealing of such weaknesses. Profit is made in markets from exploiting weaknesses, not running headlong against strengths. We are increasingly reaching a situation where there will be significant net buying of HK dollars based upon fundamental flows of money. The hedge fund manager or any other sensible investor will not be in the business of fighting those flows. There are situations of weakness to be exploited elsewhere.

The building strength behind the HK dollar is based upon dynamics for equilibrium necessitated by a currency board system. In short, when there is net selling of the currency, interest rates rise and growth slows and costs fall. This reduces imports and restores export/services competitiveness until the external accounts turn around and there is net purchasing of the currency. Above these P&L movements of cash, there is the steady swing of capital into and out of the currency. The speculator (for proprietary dealing desks of stockbrokers are just as aggressive as hedge fund managers) saw a weakness in this situation in Hong Kong.

In Hong Kong, the P&L account (current account) was probably in significant deficit back in October. Also, the foreign fund manager had placed significant short-term capital in Hong Kong. The opportunity for the speculator, against a background of concerns regarding competitiveness, was to increase interest rates in the SAR and watch the provider of short-term capital run for cover. Nobody could have believed how easy it would be.

But now things are very different. The dramatic rise in interest rates has acted to reduce growth and reduce asset prices, and thus the P&L situation is steadily strengthening. Many of the providers of short-term capital have departed the scene. The weakness has been exploited and the currency board system is now working to produce an increased position of strength. This return to strength will also be based on capital inflows.

It is my belief that this strength will be significantly boosted next month as Zhu Rongji clarifies his position on infrastructure spending, low-cost housing investment and easier monetary policy. Then the foreign investor will see a political commitment to sustaining and in due course boosting economic growth in China. It is irrelevant that such a turnaround in growth is very unlikely in 1998. A political commitment to growth will be sufficient to persuade the foreign investor that Hong Kong's companies will derive profit growth from China and a flow of short-term capital back to the SAR will be established.

Such flows will be based on the strong fundamentals of the prospect of the beginning of a new Chinese economic cycle in 1999. It will be backed up by increasing belief in the 'quiescence' of US interest rates and increasing evidence of a weak US dollar. The hedge fund manager who wishes to short the HK dollar will be betting against the political commitment to sustaining or boosting growth in China, the direction of US interest rates, the renewed China ardour of the foreign investor and a weak US dollar.

Simply, there are so many weaknesses to exploit in the world that any speculator would be verging on the lunatic if prepared to battle against a combination of what are probably the most powerful forces in financial markets today. Seasons come and seasons go. Weakness comes and weakness goes. "Seasons don't fear the reaper."

Investors were actually in the dark with regard to the condition of Hong Kong's external accounts. The colony, and now SAR, had long published a trade account, but not a current account. As the current account also includes the balance on the export and import of services, this was an important piece of data not to know. It was not until the year 2000 that the local government released data that showed the SAR's current account had moved from a deficit representing 3.6% of GDP in 1997 to a surplus representing 1.7% of GDP in 1998.

Just how far that adjustment had progressed by February 1998 we don't know, but a huge improvement in the external accounts was indeed underway as GDP growth of 7.5% in 2Q 1997 was already replaced by a GDP contraction of 2.7% in Q1 1998. This was already the third-largest contraction in GDP since Hong Kong GDP was first measured in 1974. The exit of capital continued through 1998, interest rates rose and the economic contraction accelerated. By 3Q 1998 the economy was shrinking at an annual rate of 8.3%! The currency board system was indeed operating to improve Hong Kong's external accounts.

There was in fact very good reason to fear the reaper in the form of the hedge fund manager. Even with a major improvement in Hong Kong's external accounts underway, the hedge funds did return both to short the

Hong Kong dollar and to short Hong Kong equities simultaneously. By doing this they drove up interest rates and this pushed the price of Hong Kong equities lower – a mechanism they had seen in action both in October 1997 and in January 1998.

I continued to think that it was 'lunatic' to short the Hong Kong dollar, given the rapid improvement in Hong Kong's external accounts, but I did not consider that this short would just be a mechanism through which profits were made elsewhere. The so-called 'double play' of shorting both the Hong Kong dollar and the Hang Seng Index created profits from shorting equities as interest rates soared, as the currency board system acted to ensure the stability of the exchange rate.

A devaluation of the Hong Kong dollar did not have to be forced to create a profit from the 'double play'. How the 'double play' was eventually thwarted by government intervention stunned the world of finance.

Is it rugs or fitted carpets?

13 February 1998, Indonesia

Now it is night and the barbarians have not come.
Or if they have we only recognize,
Harsh as a bombed out bathroom,
The frantic anthropologisms
And lazarous ironies behind their talk.

Of fitted carpets, central heating
And automatic gear-change -
Like the beached bones of a hare
Or a handful of spent
Cartridges on a deserted rifle range.

Derek Mahon, 'Poem Beginning with a Line by Cavafy', 2018

What the Asian investor is living through today will be a defining moment in the history of the 21st century. Now that the great ideological debate of the 20th century has been won (capitalism defeated communism), two great competing forms of capitalism or quasi-capitalism now come to battle. From the West, we have US capitalism with its belief in the sanctity of contract and a goal of achieving superior returns on capital. From the East, we have Indonesian/Chinese capitalism with its belief in *guanxi* and a goal of achieving superior returns for the controlling family.

The Indonesian/Chinese system has, through government *guanxi*, set up a system of protections and monopolies to achieve its superior returns. The United States sees the Indonesian/Chinese system as a 'bamboo curtain' designed to exclude its capitalists from obtaining superior returns in Indonesia. They see the absence of bankruptcy laws as permitting a form of zombie capitalism which threatens the superior returns for US capital in the global trading arena. They see this Indonesian/Chinese system as very similar to the impediments which they have been attempting to demolish in Japan.

Now Indonesian capitalism has collapsed as the local capitalists all committed the same error simultaneously – they all borrowed a hard currency to invest in soft currency income streams. They need more capital and this very probably has to come from overseas. The United States is prepared to provide that public but primarily private capital as long as Indonesia accepts a change to the US form of capitalism. Hence in early January the United States rode into Jakarta to back the IMF's programme with a combination of sanctions and promises. Full liberalisation (adoption of US capitalism) now appears imminent and the way will be opened for all foreign investors to exploit Indonesia according to the rules of US capitalism.

There had been an attempt to bail out Asia without resort to the IMF and thus an attempt to avoid the structural changes demanded by the US Treasury. Eisuke Sakakibara, Japan's vice minister of finance for international affairs, had attempted to create a new Asian Monetary Fund (AMF) in a proposal he put to the governments of South Korea, Malaysia, Hong Kong, Singapore and Indonesia in early September 1997.

This AMF, an idea that had been mooted long before the crisis, was not aimed at supplementing the work of the IMF, but would act independently. Sakakibara's motivations for such a move were not hard to find as in a book published in 1990, called *Beyond Capitalism*, he had put the case in support of the form of capitalism then practised in Japan – a product of the country's culture, more communal in design and very different from the rugged individualism that US-style capitalism was at least in theory based upon.

Sakakibara could see that the arrival of the IMF would bring demands for structural changes associated in particular with pressure from key players in the US Treasury Department. Sakakibara's plan would have amassed such a financial firepower, given the combined foreign currency reserves of its Asian members, that it would have been able to defend Asian exchange rates and economies from the destructive pressures then resulting from capital outflows.

The US Federal Reserve may have been restrained in acting as a lender of last resort for Asia's borrowings of US dollars, but between them the governments of Asia had hundreds of billions of US dollars in foreign reserves. There would be, Sakakibara hoped, no need for structural and cultural change and no external agenda to force such change in return for US dollars from the IMF if Asia's existing foreign exchange reserves could be pooled and, at least for a time, shared.

Some Asian countries refused to participate in the AMF and importantly China, the country with the second-largest foreign exchange reserves in the region, was one of them. Had it been possible to form an AMF with both China and Japan as key members, the financial firepower would have been greater than anything then available to the IMF. Such a pact between these two powers might also have changed their relationship, which was and is still scarred by their histories and ongoing territorial disputes.

Perhaps it was too difficult to put these disputes to one side or perhaps it was just too early for China, whose financial strength was still nascent, to take such a risk on the international stage. Even had China agreed to collaborate, it was not clear that Sakakibara could have persuaded Japanese politicians to endorse another bailout of financial institutions. The bailout for the Jusen home mortgage companies in 1996 had caused outrage in Japan and the appetite for further bailouts, especially far from Japanese shores, was probably limited. However, it was the US Treasury that was most opposed to the creation of an independent AMF and the idea made no progress at the annual meeting of the IMF and World Bank held in Hong Kong in late September 1997.

That intra-Asian government-financed bailouts could happen was rumoured in the financial markets. We knew that such a fund, to be credible, would have to come from Japan, a country with US$218bn of foreign reserves. South Korea, with then US$30bn in reserves and significant business interests across Asia, would probably also have to be involved. Had the AMF been created would things have played out very differently?

So much of the strength of such a fund would have relied upon the foreign reserves of South Korea; but South Korea, it turned out, was facing a run on its reserves due to the reversal of US dollar bank lending. Would a pact with Japan have stopped such an outflow? If it had, would the other Asian countries really have provided the scale of funds necessary to stabilise Indonesia with the very light conditions that the Sakakibara plan seemed to entail? Would the non-Asian commercial banks have agreed to the stand-still agreements and restructurings that were eventually reached if the AMF had acted unilaterally from the IMF? Given just how competitive China had become with its 1994 exchange rate devaluation, could such a fund really have restored stability and growth to the region without major exchange rate devaluations?

There were certainly investors at the time who speculated that just such an organisation could be created and thus that the powers of creative destruction in Asia could be largely suspended. Such optimism did not count upon the political power of the United States and its determination to not let this particular crisis go to waste. The clash of cultures left a mark on Asia and its leaders. It was a mark that played a huge role in influencing the policies they chose to pursue when the crisis ended.

That the Asian financial crisis could have created an Asian monetary fund dedicated, at least in part, to preventing the reforms pushed aggressively by the US Treasury is an intriguing prospect. Such unity within Asia was not possible, but a key lesson from the crisis for policy makers was that they needed ample foreign reserves to prevent outside forces from dictating changes in the structure of their local economies and societies in any future crisis. It was that drive that led to new monetary policies in Asia that built just such reserves and in doing so, played a crucial role in building the foundations for the global age of debt that was to follow.

Burning witches

25 February 1998, Regional

> To suppose that the value of a common stock is determined purely by a corporation's earnings discounted by the relevant interest rate and adjusted for the marginal tax rate is to forget that people have burned witches, gone to war on a whim, risen to the defense of Joseph Stalin, and believed Orson Welles when he told them over the radio that the Martians had landed.
>
> **James Grant, *Minding Mr Market*, 1993**

During the past week, I have been involved in a dangerous flirtation with what passes for the real world. Leaving the 'Ivory Tower' (at least better than 'Tower One', the new name for the Peregrine Tower), I have spent the past week visiting institutional direct investors, a major multinational corporation (MNC) and attending a two-day conference for Asian and MNC CEOs. So what reports from the battlefield for the control of Asian business?

The first reaction from MNCs and direct investors is perplexity concerning the recent rally in the equity markets in Asia. Their reaction to the price movements is best summed up in the quotation from Mr Grant above. They are now worried that investors in listed equity are about to recapitalise the listed sector, and that by bidding up prices they will add to the mispricing of businesses in the private equity market.

One direct investor phoned me in a panic last week wondering whether they should reallocate resources away from Asia given that the 'crazy' valuations in the secondary market would simply mean that the direct investor was never going to be able to buy at the right price. Thus the crazy situation we face at the minute is that the price of listed equities is being bid up as the move to liberalisation augurs major M&A activity by the direct investor/MNC. However, the listed equity investor seems to have already pushed prices to levels that the direct investor/MNC regards as unreasonable.

Of course, one must suspect that the price of the listed equity will have to fall in this scenario, but this may not be necessary. What worries the long-suffering direct investor is that the ball has finally been hit to their side of the court, but now there are any number of players suddenly appearing in their domain.

Asia is crowded with direct investors/MNCs seeking to do deals. Already Asia seems to face the same problem it has faced for the past ten years – too much capital. Thus this Mexican standoff between the direct investor, the MNC and the listed equity investor could act to keep prices high because too much capital has once again flowed to Asia. This is partly good news. With most of the foreign bankers simply taking their losses and going home, and new capital prepared to pour in, it appears that the private sector is more than capable of recapitalising even the very bankrupt systems of Asia.

The bad news is that this apparent surfeit of capital may mean that businesses never get to the rock-bottom prices that one associates with great liquidity seizures. While the US market remains buoyant and capital abundant, prices in Asia may not get really, really cheap. With GE and Procter & Gamble able to issue equity at 32× earnings, they may be prepared to pay higher prices for some Asian businesses than would otherwise be the case. So while the current indicated prices in the secondary market may be too high, there is already so much new capital in the field that prices may not really get to distressed levels.

As early as February 1998, one could see that a huge wave of private sector capital was lining up to pour into Asia. This was to be much more important in ending the crisis than the capital ultimately provided by the IMF. After a prolonged period of foreign currency debt lending and portfolio inflows, this was a very new form of capital entering Asia. It consisted of MNCs and direct investors.

This new inflow was very encouraging and essential for the recapitalisation of the system. It still created many potential problems for stock pickers. At this stage, the major acquisitions and investments' by foreign corporations were just a glint in their CEOs' eyes. How quickly would such a glint transform into real capital inflows? We still did not know, and there is many a slip betwixt cup and lip.

What I had not focused on enough is that foreign bankers were not taking their losses and going home as I mentioned in this piece. What I had missed was that on 18 January the foreign banks reached an agreement to reschedule their short-term loans to South Korean banks to longer-term maturities. As an outsider, it seemed impossible that the foreign banks could walk away from Asia without huge losses on their foreign loans. It looked like they had come to the same conclusions and, under the watchful eye of their respective central banks, they were rolling over their obligations.

Stuck between a rock and a hard place, they chose to extend and pretend, rather than recognising their losses by continuing to constrict credit to the region. Without this agreement it is very likely that South Korean banks would have been in mass default on their US dollar liabilities. The ability to persuade or cajole the bankers into such action was one of the most important actions that prevented this Asian financial crisis from spreading to become a global financial crisis.

This turning of the tide of these key capital flows met an incoming flood of new capital. Portfolio investors were largely unaware of these changes, fixated as they were with what was going on in their own capital silo and wondering when the liquidation would end. What brought the Asian financial crisis to an end was a stability in capital flows largely unconnected to the actions of portfolio investors.

The train which did not exist at all

27 February 1998, Asian banks

Whereas physical systems concern material objects, the central nexus of economics is value, which is not inherent in any physical object but rather derives exclusively from human desire for particular objects at certain peculiar times. Therefore, the ultimate subject of economics is not gold or savings accounts or money supply or houses or any physical goods whatsoever – but immaterial mental and emotional states. The fundamental difference between the values, or mental states, which are the subject of economic science, and the material objects, which are the subject of physical science is that mental states do not obey the Law of Conservation of Momentum … Unfortunately, mental states, and hence economic values, unlike physical phenomenon, do not remain constant with time.

Paul Macrae Montgomery, *Logical Limits and Practical Possibilities of Interest Rate Forecasting*, 1984

I have no opinion on whether the statements above of Mr Montgomery accurately describe the field of economics. However, in the field of investment they provide significant insight into the dynamics that establish the worth of an equity. If only Hans Christian Andersen's emperor had been fortunate enough to have had Warren Buffett as his chief minister he would have known that "Price is what you pay, value's what you get".

It is through the mechanism of price that the contesting mental states of a million investors wax and wane. However, there are some companies where the contesting mental states play a major role in determining the value of a company's assets as well as the valuation then placed on those net assets. For such companies, major price deviations from value are not only likely but highly probable.

In no form of investment does varying "immaterial mental and emotional states" play as major a role as in bank investing. The assets of these ventures are in effect intangible and subject to rapid revaluation based on macroeconomic developments. Valuing a bank's book is fraught with accounting difficulties that increase the uncertainty as to actual values. One's assessment of the real value of these assets is thus highly subjective.

The investor places a mental overlay of macroeconomic conditions on the accountant's assessment of book when they attempt to value the bank's assets. Given the amount of gearing inherent in the fractional reserve banking system, such alterations in asset values have a gross impact on shareholders' equity. The varying mental condition of the investor has a double whammy by impacting asset prices and also the price that should be paid for the equity itself.

While such assessments occur for other companies' assets, the gearing in banking and the intangible nature of the assets mean that the contending mental conditions play an amplified role in determining the value of bank assets. Geared balance sheets and geared mental conditions can lead to extreme volatility – ask Alan Bond.

It is my contention that the contending mental conditions are now acting to grossly overvalue bank stocks in Malaysia and Thailand and undervalue bank stocks in Hong Kong and Singapore. Table 3.11 shows the price-to-book ratios for a selection of banks in these jurisdictions.

Table 3.11: Price-to-book ratios of Asian banks

Thai Farmers Bank	3.4×
IFCT	3.1×
Bangkok Bank	1.4×
Thai Military Bank	1.5×
Maybank	1.4×
RHB Capital	1.2×
Dao Heng	1.2×
Dah Sing	1.1×
Wing Lung	1.1×
Wing Hang	1.1×
DBS	1.2×
OUB	1.1×
Keppel Bank	0.8×

To me this ordering of the premium-to-book is inherently flawed. Now clearly it would be different if Thai and Malaysian management had taken 'the big bath' with an enormous provision for their bad loans. However, it is very difficult to argue that their books have been even partially cleaned up. Maybe these premiums would make sense if investors believed that the risk-free rate in Thailand and Malaysia would settle at levels lower than Hong Kong or Singapore rates! This also seems highly unlikely.

Perhaps there is a belief that a majority foreign owner will take these banks out at such significant premiums to book or even above. This cannot be the case in Malaysia where such an alteration in ownership is not permitted. Even in Thailand, the government's selected attempts at recapitalisation of banks have so far resulted in massive dilution to existing shareholders. So how can one explain the facts that investors believe the books of Thai and Malaysian banks are more valuable than those of Singapore and Hong Kong banks?

From conversations with investors, it is becoming increasingly clear that they expect public support for their equity. The idea is that the government will have to save some commercial banks and thus it is safe to pay a large premium-to-book as the state will provide a de facto put which will limit your downside. Belief in such a de facto put would perhaps account for the high valuations in both jurisdictions.

When the contending mental conditions create such a restriction on share price downside, it is not surprising that the price is bid up. In particular, investors may be looking to the recent Mexican experience. In that situation, the loan books were so bad that government intervention was necessary to ensure that new capital flowed into the system. However, rather than taking control of the bank and wiping out the equity owner, government assistance was provided to the existing owners. Thus public funds were used to bail out private capital.

Of course, the experience in Texas and Norway was very different, with equity owners losing 100% when the government had to use public funds to shore up the banking system. So why did Mexico provide a de facto put to shareholders and are we likely to see such largesse in Asia?

Now it is likely that there are still some nasty earnings surprises to emanate from the Singapore and Hong Kong banking systems. This may produce further share price erosion. However, the recent crisis in Asia has shown how stable these banking systems are. Although EPS contraction is inevitable, we do not foresee any of the listed banks lapsing into loss. In short, there will be no capital diminution at all.

This is in dramatic contrast to Thailand and Malaysia, where the scale of capital diminution could be gross. Yet despite the fact that we expect retained earnings to continue to accumulate through the cycle, the market is valuing Singapore and Hong Kong banks at the same level or even a discount to banks in jurisdictions where capital is being rapidly destroyed. It is worth looking around the world to try to find where else you can find sound banks trading at small premiums to book!

In the increasingly distressed economic conditions in Asia it was becoming almost impossible to assess the true book value of that highly geared corporation we call a bank. The Hong Kong economy contracted in Q1 1998 and for the year as a whole, registered the largest annual contraction in GDP then recorded. The share price of HSBC, the colony's largest listed bank, declined from HK$70 in early March 1998 to just HK$41 by late September that year.

As it happened, HSBC made a profit in 1998, even after significant provisions for bad debts, and shareholders' funds increased. In Singapore, it was a similar picture, with lower reported profits and growing capital. That the banking systems of the two city-states in Asia performed so well given the scale of the crisis was a testimony to their credit quality standards. Investors were not of a mind to bet on that credit quality during the crisis and the share prices of both Singapore and Hong Kong banks declined through the summer of 1998.

When an economic crisis of a less severe magnitude came to the developed world banks in 2008, their credit quality decisions were proven to be of a lesser quality. They did report losses and many of them faced bankruptcy. They did require public support.

By March 1998, the IMF had now signed support agreements with Thailand, South Korea and Indonesia, and were increasing their existing credit provision to the Philippines. To many this seemed like a safety net, but the rally in Asian equities that began in January 1998 was running out of steam by the end of March. In Indonesia, in particular, it looked like the safety net was failing.

Has a panda mended your molars?

4 March 1998, Regional

If mankind eradicates the habitat of the giant panda, then the panda ceases to exist in the wild. Deprived of the ability to graze in the bamboo groves of Sichuan, the giant panda does not have the option to retrain as an orthodontist and move to Milton Keynes. The extinction of the wild giant panda is guaranteed when its habitat disappears and no number of visits to an out-placement agency can change this sad reality.

Some evolutionary departures are more rapid. Given the option, the dodo should probably have diversified its base of operations away from Mauritius. However, such prudent geographical diversification would not have prevented its extinction. A new stronger predator was swarming across the earth and the dodo could not defend itself and was hence doomed.

The indigenous corporation of the distressed jurisdictions of Asia now faces both threats simultaneously. At a time when the balance sheet is weakened due to currency speculation and economic contraction, the Asian corporate will be denuded of its environment and forced to confront the world's strongest predator on equal terms.

Anybody who has read the IMF package for distressed jurisdictions must be struck by the massive structural changes which it demands or implies. It is a mandate to eradicate the existing habitat for Asia's corporates. As all creatures are a product of their habitat, it is not surprising that Asian corporates have evolved unique characteristics to adapt to the Asian environment. Those key characteristics are as follows: cronyism, protectionism, asset price inflation, stable currency, cheap cost of capital, captive bankers, monopoly/oligopoly and limited threat of bankruptcy.

The new environment, which is part and parcel of the IMF programme, is as follows: free and open competition, asset price deflation, flexible exchange rates, a higher cost of capital, independent bankers and an efficient bankruptcy system. The indigenous corporates will have to adapt rapidly to this new environment. Such an alteration is tantamount to asking Asian businesses to make the changes in a year which it has taken UK businesses 20 years (1978–98) to make.

Investors in these companies must believe not only that they will survive the cycle, but that management is capable of rapidly adapting to the new cycle. This will probably involve dismantling the conglomerate, closing businesses with sub-par returns, focusing on core competencies and probably co-operating with the foreigner. In short, protectionism and fixed exchange rates have led Asian corporates into an evolutionary cul-de-sac which most Western corporates have been backing out of for many years.

In some businesses, such as asset trading and asset financing, the mass exodus from this evolutionary niche is likely to leave many crushed in the rush. For other businesses, however, there is still the possibility that they can emerge from the cul-de-sac and join the broad highway of corporate evolutionary progress. You have to bet that the management of your corporation is capable of such a dramatic and speedy manoeuvre.

This dramatic alteration in habitat is not the only challenge which faces the Asian corporate. The new environment is being introduced complete with a new and more powerful predator simultaneously. Whatever one's opinion of the organism known as the MNC, it is certainly larger and more powerful than any of the indigenous corporates in the distressed jurisdictions. Our indigenous corporations thus face the plight of the panda and the doom of the dodo simultaneously.

The good news for the MNCs is that they get to come to Asia complete with their own habitat. The bad news for the indigenous corporations is that they are now going to have to play by somebody else's rules. Of course with every threat there is an opportunity and the indigenous corporation may rise again – Borg-like – as a strong limb of an MNC. However, those not in co-operation will be in competition with a corporation with the benefit of size, experience in the new environment and a much lower cost of capital.

To buy equities in the distressed jurisdictions you are betting that the indigenous corporation will arise victorious despite the crushing pressures of the cycle, the alteration in habitat and the introduction of the new predator. Indeed you are backing the indigenous corporation at odds on. With these companies trading at average 50% premiums to book value, you are making a long-term bet that they will produce above-par returns in this new environment! If you don't believe in their ability to thrive in this new environment, then dig a hole in the ground, build your own capacity at a book value of one and do it yourself. Even if your business venture fails, you will not have paid a premium for the privilege of extinction.

Somewhere out there is a new genus of corporation which may be populated with creatures such as Guinness Philippines, GE Indonesia and Unilever Thailand. These mutants will demonstrate the best of both the Western and Eastern business strengths. The markets are already rewarding such MNC subsidiaries with premium ratings. If you believe you can find these mutant corporations, then there are major profits to be made. Otherwise, unless you've recently had a panda mend your molars, extreme caution is advised.

The accelerated evolutionary change in Asia did not have all the consequences I expected. The rollover and stand-still agreements accepted by foreign banks removed much of the heat from the feet of local corporates and allowed local owners to retain control of their corporations and eventually recapitalise them. More importantly, the central bankers of Asia were very soon up to their old tricks, some even before the end of 1998, acting to prevent the appreciation of their exchange rates and lock in their competitiveness.

Neither the IMF nor global policy makers took action to prevent a return to these policies. This act of exchange rate intervention, more than anything else, created a habitat of both a competitive exchange rate and a growing abundance of liquidity as growth in foreign exchange reserves resulted in the creation of more domestic reserve money. The full IMF package threatened to bring creative destruction to Asia, but that full package was not implemented as the crisis ended and recovery began.

It is remarkable to reflect that South Korea, a country very close to default just before Christmas 1997, was intervening to prevent the rise of the won by the first quarter of 1998. The country's current account went from a deficit equivalent to 2.2% of GDP in 4Q 1997 to a remarkable surplus equivalent to 9.5% of GDP in 4Q 1998. As early as April 1998 the government of South Korea was able to issue a bond priced in US dollars.

Initially, most of the external account improvement was driven by the contraction in the domestic economy and a contraction in imports. However, even after a significant rally in the South Korea won, it was to prove that the country was now blessed with a very competitive exchange rate; exports boomed and current account deficits were to be a thing of the past. The large surpluses the country was to rack up for many years were to be somebody else's deficits. These were conditions in which the old model of doing business in South Korea could be maintained. Through the course of 1998, similar conditions were to develop in the rest of Asia, with important implications for global financial stability and thereafter global debt levels.

There is no 'Asia' risk

11 March 1998, Regional

> Of all the stockmarkets of South East Asia, Indonesia's ranks last and seems the most unlikely – on the basis of past performance at least – to expand significantly. There are only 24 companies listed and their total capitalisation at the end of 1985 was just Rupiahs 132 billion roughly US$80m.
>
> **Anthony Rowley, *Asian Stockmarkets: The Inside Story*, 1986**

As the quote above suggests, what we as equity investors call 'Asia' changes significantly with every investing generation. In 1985, Indonesia was simply not part of 'Asia' as known to the equity investor due to foreign investment restrictions and its minute capitalisation. What we call 'Asia' today is something which is very selective and highly exclusive. There is a good reason why: for the past three years, *The Solid Ground Quarterly* has been emblazoned with maps of Asia which are area-weighted relative to certain economic/market measures. The rationale behind those maps is to show that what we call 'Asia' as equity investors is radically different from what we call 'Asia' as laymen.

In our red and green maps of Asia, whole nations are missing. The nations with the biggest populations regularly appear as having the least impressive economic aggregates or market capitalisations. A few small islands have an inordinate share of market capitalisation and economic wealth. This is the Asia that we invest in as equity investors, because this is the Asia that has prospered.

By definition, institutional investors only invest in the countries that have 'made it', otherwise the FT and the MSCI would not be including them in the benchmark index. Benchmarkers, like other historians, portray a very selected view that is written from the perspective of the successful. The unsuccessful or the defeated gain few chapters in history and have no place in the investment orthodoxy of benchmarking. Our maps have hopefully been thought provoking, but may not necessarily have provided any great investment insights (although they always suggested that shorts on Thailand and Malaysia were prudent).

However, now they may provide an important aide memoire as to the history of Asia and remind us that the history of the region is not a history of success, but rather a history of success and failure. Let's take a look at Asia as it exists in real life rather than on our pictorial version of how Asia looks to the equity investor. Just a few minutes pondering the difference may produce serious strategy consequences for those investors who believe the collapse of Indonesia will undermine the whole of the Asian investment story.

Some of the greatest economic success stories in Asia were kick-started by wars in the other Asian nations. The sourcing of materials for the Korean war from Japan certainly resulted in the acceleration of Japan's post-war recovery. The Vietnam war provided further boosts to the economies of those Asian nations which managed to escape associated political problems. In that period of history, we had whole Asian economies decimated while others boomed. The fact that these economies were in what we in the West call 'Asia' really didn't make any difference to their economic progress during this period. In fact, sadly, during the hot days of the Cold War, many 'Asian' economies actually benefited from the destruction of other 'Asian' nations.

I am not about to ascribe causes to the economic woes of Indo-China, but whatever the cause, nobody would characterise those nations as successful. But despite that region's economic collapse, the genocide in Cambodia, the sequestration of assets in Vietnam and the political despotism in Burma, there was a major economic boom in the neighbouring Kingdom of Thailand. Maybe I missed something, but I don't remember the rampaging of the Khmer Rouge and the setbacks to the Vietnam reform programme ever featuring in investors' perceptions of the Thai economic miracle.

Of course, it will be argued that Indonesia is a nation of almost 200 million people and thus its size makes it much more important. Well, Indo-China and Burma together comprise 136 million people, which at the time dwarfed the populations of the countries where foreign equity investors had committed the bulk of their funds (Hong Kong, Singapore, Malaysia, Thailand). Their economic and political disintegration went largely uncommented upon during the so-called Asian economic miracle.

Whatever the financial markets implied as 'Asia' risk, it is clear that the mess in Indo-China and Burma was ignored in determining those risks. It is simply a fact that as Asian equity investors we simply chose to take those disintegrating nations off the radar screen and focus on the successes and assess risk accordingly. Such is the nature of capital. It happened before and it will happen again.

So there is clearly a risk that a major Asian nation ignores the advice of the IMF, begins to print money and instigates a de facto debt moratorium. Surely this would produce a sea change in attitudes to Asian risk and ruin the outlook for the other nations? No, for this is exactly the situation which pertained in Asia in October 1983 as the Philippines went bankrupt and inflation peaked at 61% in October 1984!

The Philippines disappeared off the radar screens of international investors, not to return until around 1992, and the country earned the dismal sobriquet 'sick man of Asia'. The 'Asian' economic miracle did not appear to be upset by the absence of this nation of 70 million people even though the population exceeded that of Hong Kong, Singapore and Malaysia combined. It happened before and it will happen again.

One of the world's great bull markets took place in Hong Kong from 1969 to 1971. The PE multiple of the market reached almost 100× as the equity market rose 16.5× in a spectacular liquidity-driven bull run. Meanwhile, just a few miles north, the worst excesses of the Cultural Revolution roared on, and across the Pearl River Delta the government of Portugal offered to evacuate Macau! The social and economic disintegration of the PRC occurred as equity prices surged in Hong Kong.

Currently, consensus sees a political, social or economic disintegration in Indonesia as leading to a higher 'Asia' risk premium and thus producing a further setback for Asia's recovery. As enough people believe in this scenario, sufficient short-term capital flows will probably result to make such a rise in premiums occur. However, that will be a short-term movement. Then investors will segregate Indonesia from the rest of Asia in the same way they segregated Singapore from Vietnam in the 1960s, Hong Kong from China in the early 1970s, Thailand from Indo-China and Burma for most of the 1980s and the Philippines from the 'Asian economic miracle'.

Indeed, it is highly unlikely that Indonesia could pursue a debt moratorium and hyper-inflation and see its market share of global trade increase. Even should inflation not reduce their competitiveness, it is likely that the United States and the EU would bring dumping actions against any nation which pursued such rogue policies. Such behaviour may have been acceptable for US allies during the Cold War, but the rules have changed today.

In short, for investors looking beyond the short term, the disintegration of Indonesia creates opportunities for its trading competitors to gain market share.

The further any country is geographically away from Indonesia, the smaller the risk premium which the markets are likely to accord it in the initial wave of pessimism. Thus, in the first instance, Hong Kong and China are likely to be more insulated from any collapse in Indonesia. In the longer term, investors will also realise that the collapse in Indonesia creates another lease of life for China's export competitiveness.

A mixture of economic success and failure has been the norm during the Asian economic miracle. Throughout the period of the 'miracle', some nations experienced 60% inflation, sequestration of assets and even genocide. Clearly, there is now a significant risk that Indonesia drifts off into some form of economic or even political calamity. Given that the consensus seems so sure that this is bad for Asia, the short-term impact will be negative.

However, no 'Asia' premium will be permanently priced in due to the disintegration of Indonesia. In particular, Hong Kong will be unimpacted and as investors perceive that an extension of China's export boom may result, interest rates in the SAR will continue to fall. The history of capital in Asia is a history of major desegregation of risk. It has happened before and it will happen again.

At the time it seemed normal to assert that the rising risk premium associated with investment in Indonesia would push risk premiums in all markets classified as 'Asian' higher. I could not see why that would be true then and I cannot today, even with the benefit of hindsight, see why it made any sense. The key reason it happened then was because of benchmarking by portfolio investors that forced them to liquidate their holdings of Hong Kong equities if they were to reduce their exposure to 'Asia'.

In asset allocation meetings thousands of miles from Jakarta and Hong Kong, decisions were made to reduce 'Asia' risk that inflicted significant further economic pain on countries that faced virtually no prospect of the nature of socio-political collapse that seemed increasingly likely in Indonesia. That the business of managing the world's scarce savings is badly done under such a mechanism is, I think, very obvious. It continues.

Since 1998, this flow of blind capital has only increased, with more and more savings run, often by algorithms, to match the performance of market capitalisation weighted indices. I'm not sure what we call this system, but if Adam Smith – the economist from Kirkcaldy, not the journalist from St Louis – were alive today, I am sure that he would not recognise it as capitalism. This wrecking ball of global capitalism is still swinging and the only reason it appears to be doing less damage is because of the central bank swap lines that allow many central banks to access almost unlimited amounts of US dollars on demand.

Now when short-term capital stampedes for the exit, it is the balance sheet of the US Federal Reserve that often expands to prevent the sort of damage occurring that we witnessed in the Asian financial crisis. With access to such foreign currency, the local central bank can now act to offset or deter stampedes for the exits by capital with too short term a focus. That the people of the United States should permit their central bank to be so obliging is wonderful, but it would be healthier if we simply made a better job of managing capital for the long-term time frame of the ultimate owner of most global savings, rather than focus on chasing short-term returns focused on benchmark weightings.

There are still tens of billions of US dollars of foreign savings allocated to something we call 'Asia'. An increase in weightings to Asia brings indiscriminate capital inflows and outflows to the very different countries assembled under the Asia benchmark banner. In 1998 there was clearly cross-contamination from one crisis-hit country, Indonesia, to countries that faced virtually no prospects of a similar crisis. The reduction in 'Asia' risk by portfolio investors was on and all Asian equity markets continued to decline.

End or start of an era?

13 March 1998, Philippines

The news of the week appears to be that following a long desperate struggle against the pernicious forces of capitalism, the communist guerrillas of the Philippines have decided to surrender – in return for a share of a US$530m tranche of the sequestered Marcos' monies. You can just hear the cries of jubilation following the long, hard struggle for economic freedom – 'Vive la dollar, vive le mark, vive the numbered bank account in Switzerland'. With truly wonderful timing, the communists of the Philippines are buying into the whole capitalist thing just as the workers of Asia, for the first time since the Cultural Revolution, are showing their first inclinations to rise and seize the means of production.

For the contrarians among you, the sign of the Filipino communists chomping on a new Romeo y Julieta and handing in their AK47s alarmingly suggests that a bout of real social turmoil in Asia is now imminent. Following the announcement of the deal, all around the world revolutionaries are now renegotiating the terms of their own Transfer Operate Build (TOB) schemes.

In the TOB scheme, the guerrillas start by seizing control of the country's assets in the form of valuable pieces of property. Then that property is operated very inefficiently, usually as a low-yielding vegetable patch. Finally, the project is built with the money the government gives the guerrillas to discourage them from such socially disruptive and generally stupid behaviour. The TOB scheme appeals to the communist sense of justice as there is no interest rake-off by the international banker and, at least in the tropics, you can grow some 'wicked weed' on the vegetable patch. Of course, the government takes their cut when the project is sold to foreign investors, but there's usually enough left over for a trip to Havana and a replica *Dacha* near Cebu.

The key problem for the Filipino communists in particular is how to go about spending US$530m now that the struggle has ended and there is no need to pay the laundry bills on those Che Guevara T-shirts. One could provide shelter for the homeless or land for the landless, but then President Ramos may be persuaded to part with that gold-plated M-16 rifle which the vice president of Indonesia has just given him as a token of friendship!

Of course, the real risk is that they don't get their hands on the money before President Marcos is revived from his cryogenic slumber and uses his hard currency in Zurich to make a bid for most of what remains of Asia. In that case a gold-plated M-16 would still be nice, but a bit too heavy to carry around in the jungle.

The first time I heard a broker describing the case for investment in the Philippines, probably in 1991, I remember that following a full rundown of all the positive macro data he chose to highlight he finished with the final positive: "and the communists are coming down from the hills." This was clearly a very different form of investment proposition than I had learned as a US bank analyst!

Sadly, the truce with President Ramos mentioned above was not to last and the revolution resumed when President Estrada was elected later in 1998. One of the greatest surprises of the Asian financial crisis is that it left only a limited legacy of demands from the peoples of Asia for a more equitable economic system. There were political changes at the top in Asia, but the balance between capital and labour was barely questioned or even changed. There was no major demand for or increase in the social safety nets many of us take for granted in the developed world. An economic crisis of a similar magnitude was to come to the developed world ten years later and we are still living with the political legacy of that crisis.

That one Asian political leader can present another with a gold-plated rifle says just a little about why everything in Asia is never quite what it seems.

Saint Patrick, Sir John Cowperthwaite and the breakthrough to Northumberland

17 March 1998, Regional

Should but the Muse descending drop
A slice of bread or mutton chop
Or kindly when the credit's out,
Surprise him with a pint of stout.

Jonathan Swift, 'To Stella Who Collected and Transcribed His Poems', 1720

You may be asking yourself if there could be any possible connection between Saint Patrick and the current Asian economic crisis. Well, strange to tell, there is, and the tale of Saint Patrick provides yet another good reason why you should be overweight Hong Kong equities.

So, is there a modern capitalist equivalent of Saint Patrick? Yes – Sir John Cowperthwaite. Why is the current Asian crisis similar to those events of over 1,000 years ago? Because this crisis may mark an event as important for the future of capitalism as the Synod of Whitby of AD 664 was for the future of Christianity. Clearly some explanation is necessary.

Regular readers of *The Solid Ground Daily* will know that in my opinion what we are witnessing in Asia is a major structural alteration and no mere business cycle. In summary, the recapitalisation of the Asian systems can only be achieved rapidly and without hyper-inflation by importing foreign capital.

As anybody who has read the recent IMF packages can attest, the condition for the provision of public capital to secure the stability of the Asian systems is the introduction of free market capitalism. It is judged that the only way to secure such inflows, and a politically important exit mechanism for the IMF, is to introduce free market capitalism and thus permit and encourage foreigners to commit capital.

I have difficulty in assessing why any equity investor would seek to pay the current significant premium-to-book values to buy listed capital which is managed by managers who have never operated in such a system before. There are other people out there who are used to this system and they are your new competitors. So how do you make money from this frightening new environment? That's where Sir John Cowperthwaite and Saint Patrick come in.

Some contend that Saint Patrick's global fame is due to the fact that he is the only famous Irishman never to have had a drink problem. However, the real reason for his global notoriety is the role he played in preserving Christianity through the Dark Ages. A Roman/Briton, Saint Patrick ended up on the periphery of Europe as a Christian missionary while the Roman Empire collapsed and the very survival of Christianity was threatened. He preserved Christianity in Ireland and about 100 years later his followers, led by Saint Columba, grouping at Bangor (which happens to be near my hometown), set forth to introduce Christianity to the heathen Scot.

Within 100 years of establishing Christianity at Iona, the Celtic church met the reinvigorated Roman church coming in the opposite direction. This meeting confirmed the defeat of the heathen and Christianity secured its position as the dominant religion of Europe. A dominance which, unless one classifies materialism as a religion, it maintains to this day. This is where Sir John Cowperthwaite comes in.

The equivalent of the Dark Ages for the capitalist was the outbreak of communism. For capital anarchy reigned across large areas of the world under the name of communism. Even where such complete barbarism of capital was restrained, governments introduced legislation aimed at reducing returns on capital and distributing the proceeds among labour.

As with the collapse of Rome, even the very heartland of capitalism, arguably Northern Europe and its US subsidiary, saw an eradication of free market capitalism during these 'dark ages'. However, free market capitalism was not eradicated. It survived at the fringes of the global economy. Eventually, following decades of disorder, new disciples for free market capitalism appeared. One such disciple, Milton Friedman, claimed in his treatise *Right To Choose* that he had discovered the last working remnant of free market capitalism on a little island called Hong Kong.

So how did the free market system survive and prevail in the colony of a socialist country such as the UK and in a territory which bordered the world's largest communist country? Well, one man is widely credited with the preservation of the *laissez-faire* system in this colonial outpost: Sir John Cowperthwaite (financial secretary 1961–71). To quote Professor Alvin Rabhushka, Sir John was:

[b]rilliant, well-trained in economics, suffered no fools, and was highly principled. He wouldn't last five minutes in a similar post in Britain, since he was not predisposed to compromise on any of his principles – only the constitutional structure of Hong Kong allowed him that power.

Alvin Rabhushka, *Hong Kong: A Study in Economic Freedom*, 1979

To quote Frank Welsh, Cowperthwaite's philosophy was as follows:

Politicians and civil servants did not necessarily know more about business than did businessmen (a heretical thought in Britain at that time); nor did politicians have to suffer the consequences of business failures. They should therefore keep their noses to their own grindstones. Market mechanisms should be left to adjust fluctuations in the economy, and the government should concern itself only with sharply focused minimal intervention on behalf of the most needy.

Frank Welsh, *A History of Hong Kong*, 1993

Thus did Sir John preserve the spirit of free market capitalism on an island off China much as Saint Patrick preserved the traditions of Christianity on an island off Europe more than 1,500 years before.

Meanwhile, back in AD 664, when the two forms of Christianity met near Northumberland there was great confusion. The immediate problem was that somewhere along the line one of the regimes, or perhaps both, had moved Easter. This caused great problems for King Oswy of Northumberland because he celebrated Easter according to the Roman calendar, but his wife from the north insisted on using the Celtic calendar. She was still fasting when he wanted to eat. To cut a long story short, a synod took place at Whitby to establish which was the correct date for Easter, along with other issues. In a great loss to the world, the Irish did not prevail and ever since the world has struggled to get in sync with the Irish.

As with the meeting of the two Christianities, so with the meeting of the two free market capitalisms. Having vanquished the capital anarchy of communism, the last of the great 'barbaric' systems now seems to have collapsed. As the heathen Scots once separated the Celtic from the rejuvenated Roman church, the heathen crony capitalism once separated Hong Kong capitalism from the rejuvenated Northern European (now predominantly US-based) capitalism.

In that form of capitalism, politicians deliberately restricted the free market system with a view to increasing the returns on capital of their business associates. In that form of capitalism, the foreigner was restricted. In that form of capitalism, the power of the creditor was placed in abeyance and the risk/reward profile of equity capital distorted. With the collapse of that crony capitalist system, the breakthrough to Northumberland is now possible and the reunification of the free market capitalisms is now possible.

Not surprisingly, following decades of separation and near extinction from the mother capitalism, there are clearly some differences between the systems. In particular, the more unrestrained form of capitalism has developed a love of monopoly, just as Adam Smith had predicted. However, both forms of free market capitalism share a common heritage and common goals which suggest, as with the Celtic and Roman churches, they can now act to dominate that part of the globe which we in the West refer to as 'Asia'. Of the Scots heathen religions, only the worship of frugality survives. In the place of the heathen, the Celtic and Roman churches survive and thrive 1,334 years after the Synod of Whitby.

In Southeast Asia, a new form of capitalism is now ascendant. There is the one of the indigenous capitalist of that region who knows that system well; who knows how to maximise returns within that system while running acceptable risks. There is the one of the indigenous peoples, who will feel more at home in Asian business now than they have ever done before. These people are the free market capitalists of Hong Kong, the torch carriers of a form of capitalism which was almost extinguished in the 20th century.

It is these people who have the opportunities to thrive and prosper in the new Asia. Indeed, following many years of isolation, one could argue that they are purer in their practice of the art than the mother capitalism with which they will increasingly integrate. In the New Asia, it is these people who will generate the excess returns which investors seek. So tonight, on Hong Kong's first Saint Patrick's Day under Chinese rule since 1840, I will raise a glass to Sir John Cowperthwaite, the great reunification and the breakthrough to Northumberland.

The future for Hong Kong's business owners was not to lie primarily in restructuring the businesses of Southeast Asia. There was little need to go hunting for bargains in the south when they had China to the north. After a mild contraction in late 1998, the boom in Chinese exports continued through 1999 and into 2000. When China was allowed to join the World Trade Organization (WTO) in December 2001, the export boom accelerated even further. The capitalists of Hong Kong played a huge role in funding and managing that boom and local mainland business owners were soon as adept, if not more so, in the game of investing capital to maximise returns.

The 'great reunification' did occur, but it was between Hong Kong and China. Sir John's legacy, which created a colony with limited government interference in business, was to have a major impact in speeding up the economic development of China. That Hong Kong would be the major beneficiary from the continued economic reform in China was really not questioned by anyone in 1998, but it did not stop the drain and then flood of capital from the SAR through the end of spring and into summer 1998.

Investors were convinced that the devaluations elsewhere in Asia had left the Hong Kong dollar very overvalued and this consideration more than outweighed the positives that flowed to the SAR from its links to China. As spring turned to summer, investors increasingly thought the unthinkable that China, far from being an asset for Hong Kong, was a huge liability as it would have to devalue the renminbi.

It ain't over 'til it's over

18 March 1998, Thailand

In Thailand last week the king gave his royal assent to the new bankruptcy law. Anecdotally, it seems that almost on that day there arose a new willingness among the owners of companies in Thailand to talk to potential investors. The passing of the bankruptcy law has changed the nature of their ownership from that of an equity to that of a warrant. With the creditors now empowered, the time value of their paper is eroding and they must contemplate accepting lower levels of ownership to ensure their capital's survival.

The good news is that the flow of foreign capital into Thailand is set to significantly accelerate, but the bad news is that this new capital will be entering the system significantly below market prices. When the portfolio investor sees that the MNC and direct investor are only transacting at much lower prices, this will provide the catalyst for a downward lurch in the equity market. With the passing of the bankruptcy law it may only be a few months before such transactions occur.

The efficiency of local bankruptcy laws, something portfolio investors had never considered when they made their initial investments, was now seen as crucial. As long as bankruptcy could not be enforced, at least not without many years of proceedings in the courts, the existing controllers of listed companies could resist the forces of change. There was a prospect that they could retain ownership of their company and retain title to all the company's assets and wait for the economy to improve.

Whether it was a coincidence or not, the flow of direct investment into the region did not come until the bankruptcy laws were changed. Whatever ended the Mexican standoff between the Asian corporate and the foreign direct investor, it was to end in the summer of 1998 and suddenly clearing prices for Asian assets became significantly easier to establish.

Few if any foreign creditors wanted to pursue debtors through the local courts, but the risk that they might was enough to get things moving. Foreign direct investors were able to do deals with local creditors that reduced their risks of buying Asian businesses. In the bull market whoever asked about the ability of the local system to deal with the business of asset transference in an insolvency situation? In the downturn, portfolio investors realised just how much a hindrance to the clearing process a poor legal framework could be.

Investors knew the rules of the game for the first half of the match, but after half time, when the economies were contracting, they realised that they had not read all of the rulebook. Understanding the true status of equity in bad times as well as good times is worth the effort. Bad times do come.

Mescaline, convertible bonds and the Beardstown Ladies

19 March 1998, Regional

On 16 March the Consumer Affairs Ministry parliamentary-secretary said that egg prices would have to be controlled if they kept rising. There is already a long list of price controlled items in Malaysia, but the parliamentary-secretary declared that the ministry's approval would now have to be sought for egg price rises even though they are not on the list.

The Livestock Farmers' Association of Malaysia has therefore refused permission to raise the price of eggs. Thus the poultry farmers continue to make losses on their eggs as prices have not been allowed to rise to offset the rise in feed prices. According to the Veterinary Services Department, the farmers have now been forced to sell their eggs below cost prices since last July. Given this policy it is perhaps not surprising that the reported Malaysian Consumer Price Index remains so low.

Now there are all sorts of conspiracy theories about how Malaysia will continue to buck the market and even be successful at it. I have heard bullish fund managers tell tales of bank nationalisation using revenues from an oil-backed bond. There are also stories that the Sultan of Brunei will provide funds to support the system. It really doesn't matter. At every stage these funds are being used to take Malaysia away from the market. At every stage they are seeking to distort prices and then inevitably send all the wrong signals to the economic players.

Those who think that Malaysia can successfully buck the market and those who want to buy Malaysian equities would presumably also have been buying assets in Shanghai in 1947–48 as the plans of the communists became more evident.

Despite the positive noises from Anwar and Daim, every day the Malaysian authorities seek to subvert the market. Equity investors are well equipped to assess the laws of supply and demand and thus the appropriate pricing. However, when the government starts declaring the correct price of eggs, we'd better stop analysing the laws of supply and demand and take a degree in psychology.

Valuing equities when supply and demand is dictated by government fiat is a sport rather than a profession. Like all sports, some people are better than others and if you can second-guess where the government wants to push the wealth, then you may be able to make profits. Egg 'smuggling' from Malaysia is now very profitable and, I think, as the product is not on the controlled list, is not yet a criminal offence (all 'investors' should check with their own lawyer).

However, if I can second-guess whether Bernie Marcus is on form next week, I can make even bigger profits at Happy Valley. The difference is that the Jockey Board oversees the activities at Happy Valley and enforces the rules. However, in Malaysia the rules have to be changed to make sure the right horse wins. Those rules have just been changed so that the egg farmer must lose. Who is next? I don't know. You don't know. They don't know. Now who'd like to bet?

Words are cheap. It's about time that the Malaysian authorities told us the rules for their form of capitalism, assured us that those rules would not be changed and gave us an independent mechanism to dispute any such changes. Then at least we could begin to value the currency and equities under these unique rules. They'd still be making the rules, but at least with the rules fixed we could all get on with calculating the new values. Until we know the rules, the risks remain too high regardless of whether the government can source capital to continue to keep all the balls in the air or not.

I found it hard to believe that some institutional investors were prepared to invest in Malaysia because they thought that the country could 'buck the market'. That such legerdemain could restore exchange rate stability while also restoring growth was of course possible. However, in pulling off such a trick, the very basics of allowing price to be established by supply and demand were likely to be destroyed. It was perhaps too purist a view, but I did not foresee how capital could achieve good returns or how those returns could be forecast within such a capricious system.

A new government edict could be just as likely to destroy returns on capital, as it had done for the country's egg producers, as it would be to enhance them. On 1 September 1998 Malaysia introduced capital controls and those investors who had bet on the power of government intervention to prevent a further decline in share prices were hoisted on their own petard. Nobody could say that they were not warned that the rules relating to investment would be changed.

The rules of investing in Malaysia had already been changed numerous times since the crisis erupted in July 1997. The pain inflicted upon the poultry and then egg farmers of Malaysia was barely noted in the halls of 'high finance' when investors discussed the outlook for returns on Malaysian equities. The destruction of the returns of the chicken farmers was a clear sign that government diktat, not market forces, would be the key factor in assessing the outlook for future equity returns in Malaysia. Nobody seemed to care that the government had come for the profits of the chicken farmer until they came for their profits.

Back in the fold

25 March 1998, Indonesia

How does one begin to analyse the outlook for Indonesia? What good is micro analysis or macro analysis of a country where the authorities swing wildly from reform to the printing press sometimes on a daily basis? Thus the macro/micro outlook can vary from hour to hour, depending upon the latest proclamation from the government of Indonesia or the IMF. One has to make guesses as to how the political establishment will move forward in Indonesia. If you get that guess wrong you will lose a lot of money, and the reverse is also true.

It would be nice to pretend the right answers lie in the macro and micro data, but in Indonesia they don't. Either this country is headed for hyper-inflation and social turmoil, or it is in the arms of the IMF and heading towards liberalisation. In my opinion the latter is a more likely option.

It is already evident that the IMF is prepared to offer a degree of leniency to Indonesia in regard to at least the time frames for reform. This may simply be to recognise the volatile social situation which has been intensified by the drastic food price shortages caused by El Nino. Despite the fact that the Indonesian authorities have been at best tardy in introducing reforms, and at worst have flaunted IMF recommendations, the IMF keeps coming back to the table. It is not coincidental that President Suharto has been offered advice by President Clinton, Prime Minister Hashimoto and Chancellor Kohl. While the visit of Larry Summers to Southeast Asia in mid-January marks a turning point in the commitment to reform in the region, it must be remembered that US Defense Secretary William Cohen also visited Indonesia at that stage.

This visit was followed a month later by Walter Mondale and there was broad speculation that he had come to seek permission to create a US military facility in the country. The international community has remained heavily involved in Indonesia throughout the recent turmoil and there has been a willingness to bend. It really doesn't matter why this proclivity to flexibility among the international community exists. The simple fact is that it does exist and it is permitting a middle ground to be found between Indonesia and the IMF. For whatever reason of international politics, the Indonesians show every indication of being treated as the prodigal son.

It was only two months ago that rumours swept Jakarta that the president had already fled the city for Zurich. Just a week after this, the president met with Michel Camdessus and signed a further package for IMF support. With the currency spiralling downwards, there was a political need to do something quickly. The problems with inflation will be large enough this year without watching the currency fall back towards 15,000 to the US dollar and head even lower. Like the rest of the Asian establishment, President Suharto has had to live with the difficult choice between having 70% of nothing or 20% of something.

Without a stable currency and at least the prospect of some economic improvement, the simple political fact is that the president and his family have at best a very uncertain political future in Indonesia. If the economic ruin threatens tenure, then the value of the Suharto family's Indonesian assets is limited. Of course, if there were some other way to stabilise the currency and recapitalise the banking system other than using the IMF and accepting reform, then this would be preferable.

With this in mind, a currency board system was considered and non-conditional aid was sought from Singapore, Brunei and Taiwan. However, all the alternative avenues have now been exhausted. It's a simple political choice between a weak currency, economic/social collapse and political redundancy or the IMF, currency stability, economic/social stability and political survival. With all other options abandoned, it's back to the IMF.

In reading the political runes which determine chaos or stability in Indonesia, I foresee continued 'understanding' by the international community and the continued search for stability by President Suharto. This would appear to be a much more bullish scenario than the consensus foresees.

Walter Mondale's visit had opened up direct negotiations between the US Treasury and President Suharto, partially bypassing the IMF. Suharto, it seems, had concluded that the IMF was keen to oust him in pursuit of their economic programme. He thought that he could cut a better deal with the US administration given the geopolitical importance of the stability of Indonesia. Perhaps Suharto did not understand that it was the US Treasury that was pushing the IMF to secure the economic reforms he dreaded making. Perhaps he thought he could appeal to other interests in the US administration, perhaps more focused on defence issues; but the direct negotiations with the United States kept Suharto at the negotiating table.

One of the agreements that the US officials were able to agree with Indonesia related to a constraint on the supply of money. This, if enforced, was likely to be very good news for the exchange rate. In the first quarter of 1998 the year-on-year growth of Indonesian broad money had hit 77% as the central bank fed ever more funds to the distressed banking system! I was wrong that Suharto would do a deal that ensured his political survival and, although nobody knows for sure, he and his family almost certainly kept a lot more than 20% of something despite his departure from office which was to come as early as May 1998.

The rally in Asian stocks that had begun in early January ended on 25 March. Investors who thought they were joining the beginning of a new bull market and that the worst was over for equity prices were in for a rude awakening. From 25 March to the low on 1 September, the MSCI Asia ex Japan Index was to decline 46% in US dollar terms. The index finally bottomed 24% below the level it had reached when that early 1998 rally began in January. In US dollar terms, the Hong Kong stock market ended March 1998 above the levels it had first reached in 1996.

In the context of what was going on in Asia, it looked like a relative bastion of stability, despite the losses associated with two attacks on the Hong Kong dollar in October 1997 and January 1998. That stability was to be questioned one final time in the summer of 1998, in the final act of the Asian financial crisis.

Come talk to T-Rex

26 March 1998, Regional

Across Asia, the MNC is already buying out its joint venture partners. Because they are not conducted in the public markets, these deals are not as widely publicised. But apart from Toyota, I can think of similar deals done by BASF in South Korea, P&G in South Korea, P&G in China, GE in Thailand, GE in South Korea, Prudential in Malaysia and Dairy Farm in Indonesia. These, not the recapitalisation of listed parents, are the dominant transactions in Asia today.

With perfect knowledge of the operations, the due diligence process is short and the issue of pricing more certain. So while you continue to invest in the holding company, the high-quality foreign joint ventures may be sliced out beneath you. It is just such companies which are commanding high valuation premiums across Asia, but it is just such companies which are being jettisoned to preserve the financial integrity of the holding company.

The MNC here is clearly a threat. With greater flexibility than any investor, proceeding through the listed sector they can cherry-pick the best assets from the distressed corporates of Asia. You're investing in what's left. In the short term, the share price may even rise as such cash-raising exercises assure solvency. However, such exercises assure solvency at the expense of long-term returns as management follows a policy of selling the best businesses to prop up the worst.

The willingness for MNCs to buy out their local partners was an encouraging sign. It was the first sign of the form of capital inflow that was very necessary. Their local joint venture (JV) partners, likely in need of funds to save their other businesses, were willing to sell and, importantly, despite the chaos, the MNCs were willing to buy.

These foreign-managed businesses were often seen as the crown jewels of Asian business. A few minority stakes of such businesses were already listed on the Asian stock markets and they traded on very high valuations to reflect their higher quality. That there was a buyer for such assets was a good sign, but would there be foreign buyers for some of the companies we all knew were far from well run, with balance sheets shot to pieces, even if their local business franchises were strong?

Before the gates of the citadel of social capital

27 March 1998, Regional

For some time, I have been asserting that the business practices of Mitsubishi Heavy Industries puts more stress on employment than on profits. We pay absolutely no heed to such concepts as ROE, because they play no part in setting management targets. The main part of managing a manufacturing business is to use facilities and labour in a stable manner and at maximum capacity, and management tends therefore to focus first on the volume of orders it can pull in. If we look likely to make more money than we were originally expecting, we take on orders at lower prices in order to adjust the figure. It is absolutely essential that our business practices take social effects into consideration and due controls are maintained. That is why I publicly comment that MHI will not give its shareholders precedence. If the stock has no appeal, the investors can sell it off straight away, but our employees do not have such freedom of choice.

Kentaro Aikawa, chairman of MHI, 14 January 1998

Those investors who are wearied by the quality of Asian management and their inability to secure decent returns on capital may be cheered to know that things are worse in Japan. MHI is a US$13bn market cap company with US$8.6bn in shareholders' equity. According to the chairman the aim of this enterprise is full employment and full utilisation of facilities. Everything else is secondary.

The world is flush with capital. There is looming overcapacity in almost all global businesses. The Ford Motor Company itself estimates that there is 40% overcapacity in the global system for motor cars. The price of commodities is headed lower and the collapse in demand in Asia is already impacting capacity utilisation rates from the dairy sheds of New Zealand to the paper mills of Alabama.

Of course, such disruptions are perfectly normal and through the 'invisible hand' of price, such imbalances are corrected. Of course, as equity owners in Asia are finding out, that correction process which reads so quaintly in the textbook is actually a great rending destruction of capital when the current status is an oversupply of capital. Of course, the ability of the 'invisible hand' of the market to produce such equilibrium really depends upon whether the market is allowed to work properly.

The history of the 20th century has been one of concerted efforts by governments to corral markets for political ends. This experiment appears to have failed, and even the Soviets decided that price was a better allocator of resources than a million bureaucrats. So the hand of government is now being rolled back and the markets can act quickly through the mechanism of price to restore equilibrium. So the god of markets is in his heaven and all's right with the world. Mr Aikawa would disagree.

It should come as no surprise if certain people and cultures reject the principles of free market capitalism. After all, its wellspring is in a very narrow European section of the global population and need be no more culturally acceptable to the world than rugby football as a global sport. As Mr Aikawa is clear to assert, the goals which Japan seeks to achieve are very different from those dictated by the edicts of free market capitalism.

In a clear message to his shareholders, who value his equity capital at US$13bn, he has told them that his capital will be used for the service of 'society' rather than shareholders. The point of quoting Mr Aikawa is not to suggest that he is either wrong or right, but to point out the very dangerous dynamics for the world economy when the 'capitalists' of the world's second-largest economy ignore the 'invisible hand' of the market in an overcapacity situation.

So obviously when prices fall, the marginal producers see their cash flows squeezed and the viability of their business questioned. In due course, prices fall to a level where these producers have to close capacity or are bankrupted. Of course, if there are some players in the market who prefer to target other goals apart from returns on capital, then the road to equilibrium may be long and hard.

That is exactly the position which Japan is assuming in the global marketplace today. With the world in oversupply of capital, the global marketplace cries out for higher demand or the mothballing of capacity. While price will achieve such goals in certain parts of the global economy, Mr Aikawa asserts that they shall play no role in influencing the supply side in Japan. His goal is "to use labour facilities and labour in a stable manner and at maximum capacity". If Japanese capital views the world from this perspective, then the adjustments in supply dictated by price will all be forced upon the rest of the global economy, where returns on capital rather than full capacity utilisation are the key target.

Of course, the inability or unwillingness of Japan's capital to be triggered into adjustment by the mechanism of price is nothing new. However, we have reached a stage in the global economy when such intransigence to the 'invisible hand' of price is extremely dangerous. The death of communism has unleashed powerful new productive forces which at this stage are adding to the problems of oversupply.

Theoretically, such lower prices will trigger rises in consumption. This mechanism still works even if Japan refuses to play by its rules. However, Japan's capital intransigence will force the price disturbance to be even greater as they refuse to adjust their production regardless of price. Arguably, the structural impediments in place in Japan will act to prevent the full benefits of lower prices reaching local consumers and thus even the demand side in Japan may be impervious to the 'invisible hand' of price. If demand in the world's second-largest economy does not respond positively to price falls, then prices globally are just going to have to fall to even lower levels to stimulate demand elsewhere.

There are now three ways forward: Japan adopts free market capitalism, Japan collapses, or prices collapse. Arguably, if Japan were to adopt free market capitalism, the adjustment in their economy would make it feel like a collapse anyway! Given the social goals of the Japanese, it seems very unlikely that this culture will suddenly adopt this business system which up until recent years was even shunned by its European inventors. In the absence of such reform, the bulwark of Japan's capital intransigence must mean that either global prices collapse further or Japan collapses.

Free market capitalism is on a bit of a roll. Marching through Eastern Europe and Russia and defeating communism, it has swept through Southeast Asia and even appears to be making inroads into China. Now it stands poised at the gates of the citadel of social capital – Japan. Of course, we assume that free market capitalism wins for no other reason than we view this from a Western perspective and it seems safe to extrapolate recent victories. Should it be victorious, would the collapse of Japan augur bull market conditions for global equities? Well, the Japanese banking system would be sent into further shocks and the ability of Japan to keep buying US Treasuries would be undermined. It is difficult to see how the collapse of Japan would create bull market conditions for global equities.

Of course free market capitalism may lose, with the bulwark of social capital holding in Japan while capital all around the rest of the world is forced to melt or explode in reaction to falling prices. In that scenario, returns on capital across the free market system would implode and the current extended multiples on listed equities would be very extended indeed. In this scenario, a siege is waged on the citadel of social capital and unless the rest of the world is prepared to exclude Japan's goods from the global marketplace, the siege will be extended.

Whatever scenario turns out to be correct, it is difficult to see how this final showdown can create positives for global equity valuations. The collapse of Japan or the collapse of free market capital's returns is not an enviable choice. So the fall in prices has begun and the inevitable transfers of wealth are underway. As a holder of global equities in the free market system, that is likely to be your wealth being expended in the great battle between flexible and inflexible capital.

Wouldn't it be great to have the option of joining the capitalists' equivalent of the National Guard during this disturbance and viewing the battle from outside the free market system? Well in China one can do just this and rely on the authorities to create the domestic consumption demand which will actually be acting to produce rising capacity utilisation at a time when the free market system will be plagued by overcapacity. China's listed capital (H shares) is selling at around 12× earnings while multiples in Europe and the United States exceed 20×.

It was a long hard campaign against communism with returns on equities from 1929 to 1980 particularly depressed. It has been a rapid victory over crony capitalism. The campaign against social capitalism may be brief or prolonged – who knows. Capital knows no country. Time to join the National Guard.

This analysis was very right and very wrong at the same time. It was correct that Japan would not adapt its business system, would not cut capacity and thus would continue to export deflation to the world. By the middle of 2020 Japan's Export Price Index had declined 17% from its level of early 1998. The country's social capital system has adapted somewhat towards the US style of capitalism, but the changes have been slow and the words of Mr Aikawa of MHI are almost as true today as they were in 1998.

In South Korea the *chaebol* system, very much modelled on the Japanese system, survived the crisis with its social capital model largely intact and, combined with a very undervalued exchange rate, this allowed South Korea to also export deflation. The social capital system, with its prevalence to overproduction, did not just survive the Asian financial crisis, but was bolstered by the accelerated entry into the global trading regime of China.

What we did not know in 1998 was just how China would create a system that also never fully evolved from the social capital system to a system focused on return on capital. The remnants of its social capital system reduced in importance as the economy grew, but were not destroyed. This deployment of social capital, along with the massive mobilisation of China's cheap labour force, added to the downward price pressure on globally traded goods. The price of China's exports by 2020 were basically unchanged from their 1998 level.

Japan's reluctance to abandon its social capitalism was indeed a deflationary force for the world and China's choice to retain some of that social capital system exacerbated the deflationary pressure. The rest of the world has indeed, as I wrote in 1998, been forced to adapt to the social capital model.

What I did not understand is just how successful corporations, particularly US corporations, would be in making that adaptation, but ultimately how financially, socially and politically dangerous the consequences of such adaptation would become.

That the social capital system of North Asia did not collapse or significantly reform in the Asian financial crisis has played a crucial role in dampening inflation and depressing interest rates in the rest of the world. The result was that the other form of capitalism did indeed have to adjust in various ways to downward pressure on prices and downward pressure on interest rates. US corporations in particular adjusted through reducing costs in offshoring production and reducing capital investment. Corporations also adjusted by taking advantage of lower interest rates to boost leverage, often to juice equity prices through financial engineering.

Businesses outside the United States also adapted, but not with the same vigour and, it was to turn out, also without the same spirit of innovation that resulted in new US businesses rising to dominate the new digital age. The system that could adapt was forced to adapt, but that adaptation produced social changes and financial fragilities that would one day be dangerously exposed.

There have been a series of deflationary episodes post the Asian financial crisis which have brought the developed world to the edge of financial collapse and resulted in very material losses for equity investors. Outside of the United States and particularly in Europe, struggling to cope with deflation shocks while attempting to create a single currency, returns from equities have been particularly poor.

As recently as 2020 the MSCI World ex United States Capital Index was just below levels it first reached in 1998. That US corporations adapted more successfully to the deflationary forces emanating from North Asia is reflected in the fact that even at its lowest level in 2020 the MSCI US Capital Index had doubled from its peak level of 1998. The Hong Kong China Enterprise Index, composed of the shares of mainland Chinese companies listed in Hong Kong, was to rise 17-fold from its lows in 1998 to its all-time high in 2007. Even at its 2020 lows the index was 750% above its 1998 lows.

There have been good times and bad times to invest in Chinese equities since that option became available to foreign investors in 1992. It turned out that 1998 was one of those good times. Those investors who ignored the warnings of the chairman of MHI had, by 2020, seen the market capitalisation of the company fall by a further third since 1998.

That developed world politicians allowed these highly competitive exchange rates to be locked in, by China in 1994 but then by the rest of Asia in 1998, will go down in history as one of the greatest ever policy mistakes. It was of course an easy decision to make, as it reliquified and helped recapitalise Asia without further support from the IMF or developed world governments. It avoided the major political battles that would have had to be fought to force the Asian countries not to follow such currency manipulation policies.

The United States had already been waging a long political war with Japan to force changes in its social capital system and even as the Japanese financial system continued to weaken there were only limited successes. The politicians did not fight those battles in 1998 and beyond, and they allowed to be created a jury-rigged global monetary system that would create great socio-political damage in the developed world combined with unstable levels of leverage. We are living with the consequences of those decisions made in 1998 today and are likely to live with them for a very long time to come.

The battle between US-style capitalism and social capitalism did not end in victory for one side; it ended in a truce. In that truce it was the side pursuing the profit motive that was forced to make the greatest adjustments. The consequences of those adjustments continue to echo through the global economic, financial and political systems. I was wrong about Japan and social capital and the nature of the adaptation that it would force upon free market capitalism. There was a fourth option for the free market system and it was to involve assuming dangerously high levels of debt to keep returns to shareholders high through the use of ever more financial engineering.

Another March and another Hong Kong Rugby Sevens tournament had arrived. The name of the tournament had to be changed at short notice because the original sponsor, Peregrine Securities, had collapsed in January. The global financial behemoth CSFB was now the tournament sponsor and they were unhappy. The producer of the live video feed at the Hong Kong Stadium kept cutting to the CLSA box when a try was scored. This was not too surprising as it was well populated with cheerleaders bedecked in blue and yellow waving blue and yellow pom-poms. That there was so much blue and yellow, the colours of a competitor on the screen, led to the producer being asked by CSFB to stop cutting to the pom-poms.

I was sitting beside Gary Coull of CLSA when this news was relayed to him. He asked the company's head of marketing, Jodie Allison, how much these pom-poms cost. She answered, "HK$20" and he replied, "Order 5,000 for next year." At the Hong Kong stadium in 1999, there was a sea of blue and yellow which could not be avoided by any shot of the stadium.

Distressed market valuations – Catch 22

20 April 1998, Regional

All the evidence that I receive – admittedly largely anecdotal – suggests that the primary market will clear at much lower levels. Most direct investors contact me to ask the following question: "Are these secondary market levels sustainable and can Asia be recapitalised at these hefty valuations?" The reason they ask this question is because they want to know whether they are wasting their time or whether they will have the ability to invest capital at reasonable prices.

All discussions with direct investors suggest that they are not prepared to transact at current market prices. At the recent CLSA Emerging Markets conference in London, the MNCs indicated that the risk-free rate on which they base investment decisions is the cost of borrowing the local currency. As regular readers will be aware, when we use such risk-free rates in intrinsic value calculations, this also suggests that equities are very overvalued. There appears to be a high probability that the primary market will thus clear at lower prices.

That there was a huge pile of capital waiting to be deployed in Asia in April 1998 was very evident. This did not stop the decline in equity prices. The owners of Asian equities had been beaten about for almost a year. They were always prepared to believe the worst and the higher the pile of potential fresh capital, the more they argued that it would never actually be deployed.

It was at this stage that I began to hear opinions that suggested the crisis could not be over until certain businesspeople were bankrupt or even in jail. I can think of no rational reason why this had suddenly become a precondition for the Asian stock markets finally reaching their lows, but here it was.

I concluded then, and believe now, that in this period what we witnessed in the Asian stock markets was what is known as 'revulsion'. It is that stage in the cycle, that we noted earlier was identified by Charles Kindelberger, in which investors lose belief. Rational thought is replaced by something else, and I think this sudden focus on the need for legal and moral retribution across the region represented an emotional reaction that blinded portfolio investors to reality and, when it came, the growing good news. In 30 years in equity markets I would say I have only seen this revulsion twice again – in March 2009, in relation to equities in general, and in 2020, in relation to what are known as value stocks.

There are other ways one can pick up the evidence for revulsion. As a member of the research team of a stockbroking company, my place was not in the dealing room. In the dealing room the buy and sell orders of our clients were executed and I did not know what those orders were.

However, I would walk into the dealing room a couple of times a week, especially during particularly volatile periods, to see, more hear, what was going on without being aware of what stocks they might be selling or buying. Walking into the dealing room on one particularly hectic day in 1998, I asked our dealer Chris what was going on and he screamed back: "They're puking it up, they're puking it up." Yes, that is what revulsion feels like and it provided wonderful opportunities for long-term investors in the summer of 1998; but when you are surrounded by revulsion, it is difficult to be greedy when others are so fearful.

On 22 April I resigned from CLSA. I had never planned to remain in Asia for many years and by April 1998 I was exhausted anyway. We had bought a house in the countryside south of Edinburgh and that seemed to be a much better place to live than a small apartment in a tower block in Hong Kong.

I had tried to resign on 21 April on the steps of the Great Hall of the People in Beijing. I had flown up to support Gary Coull who was providing the keynote speech for a gathering of the World Economic Forum. CLSA had paid handsomely to sponsor the dinner that evening and Gary would no doubt not have wasted the opportunity to recommend the company's services. He never got the chance.

The acoustics in the Great Hall of the People are dreadful and nobody could hear him. Within just a few minutes people gave up trying to listen and conversations broke out at the huge number of tables and all was lost. Gary wisely simply wound up and sat down. He was not happy, to put it mildly, and this was not the time to resign. I said I'd like to talk to him about something when we got back to Hong Kong and so it was I found myself walking through Tiananmen Square almost, but not quite, on my way home.

The resignation went well. I had no plans for what I would do when I returned to Scotland and was surprised when CLSA offered me the opportunity to work from home as a consultant to the company. That was a remarkable offer, but when you've just resigned you are geared up to take a few weeks' down time. We compromised: I would stay in position full time until the end of September, but I would get to take the whole of June as holiday. Thus it was mainly by chance that I was not to leave the front line of daily prognostication and life in Hong Kong until after the Asian stock markets had bottomed on 1 September 1998.

Why it doesn't add up

23 April 1998, Regional

It is worth recapping on the movements of equities, currencies and interest rates during the recent improvement in the outlook for Southeast Asia. These movements make worrying reading for anybody considering a bullish position in Southeast Asian equities.

In local currency terms, the distressed markets of Southeast Asia have now given up a significant portion of the dramatic rises of the second two weeks of January. From their peak levels of 1998, the markets have corrected by the following percentages: the Philippines −10%, Indonesia −15%, Thailand −22% and Malaysia −16%.

From the peak of the equity markets around 2 February, currencies have done much better than equities, as shown in Table 3.12.

Table 3.12: Movement in currencies from 2 February to 23 April 1998

	2 Feb	23 April	% chg
Peso	41.2	38.3	+7
Baht	51.6	39.2	+24
Ringgit	4.19	3.76	+10
Rupiah	9,950	7,915	+20

Over the same period, only the Philippines has seen material declines in interest rates, as shown in Table 3.13.

Table 3.13: Movement in interest rates from 2 February to 23 April 1998

	2 Feb	23 April	bp change
Philippines	18.3	15.0	−330bp
Thailand	24.5	23.5	−100bp
Malaysia	10.7	11.1	+40bp
Indonesia	33.1	36.4	+330bp

The bull view on Southeast Asia was that the turnaround in the external accounts would result in an improvement in the outlook for currencies, interest rates and equities. However, somehow these pieces do not fit. The currencies have rallied throughout the improvement in the external accounts, but the transmission mechanism to lower interest rates and higher equity markets has not occurred. Yes, equities have rallied, but this has not been, with the possible exception of the Philippines, due to any material fall in interest rates. So why have interest rates remained 'sticky' and what does this mean for the immediate outlook for equities?

"OK, La. I've heard that Bank XYZ is bankrupt and I'm going down to take out all my deposits." "Oh don't be so silly, haven't you seen the export numbers?" This is a conversation which the bulls of Southeast Asia would have you believe is happening every day in Southeast Asia. It's not.

In the old Asia, a swing around in the external accounts would have produced more net purchasing of the domestic currency, and in an attempt to prevent an appreciation of the currency, the authorities would have been forced to pursue a looser monetary policy. In the old Asia, the bankers would have seized upon the ensuing increase in the deposit base to expand their loan books. Neither of these mechanisms is now operative. A swing around in the external accounts is very positive for the Asian currencies, but with the Southeast Asian nations targeting money supply growth and not currency stability, it need have no short-term impact on domestic liquidity.

More importantly, even should liquidity conditions ease, the capital in the domestic banking systems has been so impaired that the bankers may not wish to add risky assets (loans) to their balance sheets. The performance of currencies, equities and interest rates in Asia during 1998 suggests that just such a breakdown in the old transmission mechanism is underway – although the Philippines is exhibiting some of the old characteristics.

This is not to say that Asia will now languish in the liquidity doldrums. However, it is to say that the recapitalisation of the banking system is a prerequisite for a return to the old transmission mechanism and that money supply targeting should result in more limited swings in domestic liquidity than was once the norm. The movement in currencies, equities and interest rates in 1998 should thus cause significant concern for equity investors.

Many commentators criticise the so-called 'austerity' programme implemented by the IMF in Asia. Whatever term one chooses for that element of the programme, it has been crucial for the authorities in Asia to adopt a tighter monetary policy and prove they stand behind their currencies. Without such proof, the owner of foreign capital will be loath to sell their hard currency to buy an asset that produces a domestic currency income stream. Getting such capital flows into the distressed jurisdictions is exactly what the IMF programme is all about and thus the need for tight money.

Unfortunately, the Asian authorities proved themselves unwilling to initially accept the need for tight money and even clung to the restrictions on foreign capital inflow. The good news, and the reason for the bounce in equities in mid-January, is that they are now accepting the necessary medicine. It remains my contention that this continues to be positive for Asian currencies but negative for equities.

The longer any government pursues the tight monetary policy but does not receive the private capital inflows, the worse the economic outlook becomes. In the absence of recapitalisation, the outlook for corporate Asia actually deteriorates as interest rates remain high. So, by mid-January there was significant relief buying of equities as the Asian authorities took the right medicine. However, the problem has always been that there was likely to be a significant lag between the period when the authorities showed the commitment to their currencies and the period when capital flowed in.

Having flirted with monetary profligacy, it will take some time for the authorities to prove to foreign investors that they have seen the light. While we await this turnaround in foreigners' perceptions, interest rates remain high, the economy continues to contract and corporate cash flows are under severe pressure. The turnaround in the external accounts does not alter these realities.

That is exactly what has happened in Asia following the period of relief buying of equities in the second two weeks of January. Currencies have continued to rally as the external accounts improve, but interest rates have remained high and equity prices have come down. This process will continue unless one believes in an imminent clearing in the primary market. Such a clearing is delayed due to the flirtation with monetary profligacy and the institutional inertia of implementing the correct legislation.

It is a key lesson from the Asian financial crisis for portfolio investors that exchange rates can stabilise in a crisis long before equity prices. I had written in January 1998 that the Asian exchange rates had stabilised and that they offered good value. With the exception of the Indonesian rupiah, the real collapse of which was still to come in May, that proved to be correct.

Those who bought equities as the exchange rate stabilised in January got sucked into what became a dead-cat bounce. A key problem was that none of the IMF plans had yet brought any new capital into the banking systems. This was difficult ground for the IMF to be involved in directly as committing any public capital to bail out a private institution creates moral hazard on a grand scale.

In some countries in Asia the individuals who controlled these banks were often seen as the crony capitalists that the IMF thought Asia would be better without. So one reason interest rates tended to stay high was that people remained cautious about having money on deposit and any rush to banknotes tightened banks' funding requirements and forced them to pay up for funds in the interbank markets.

Deposit guarantee schemes are supposed to reduce the prospect of a run to banknotes from deposits, but often the sums guaranteed are small and local business owners are not reassured. When the Asian financial crisis erupted only South Korea and the Philippines had comprehensive bank deposit guarantee schemes in place. Had there been greater confidence in the deposit as a store of value, perhaps interest rates would have declined more quickly after exchange rates had stabilised from January 1998. Perhaps next time, if comprehensive deposit guarantee schemes are in place, equity prices might stabilise more quickly following the stability and rise of the exchange rates; but in 1998 those who thought currency stability would bring higher equity prices were very wrong.

Of masses and echelons

5 May 1998, China

BOC Group MasterCard Platinum Card, limited to those in the highest echelons of society – application by invitation only – is a true reflection of your achievements. Present it anywhere and there'll be no mistaking your status in life. Be seen for what you are with the BOC Group MasterCard Platinum Card. You deserve it.

Bank of China ad in Friday's *South China Morning Post*

We are empowered by the mass; we serve the mass; we die for the mass.

Mao Zedong

I first began to analyse China in 1990. In those days, the uninitiated were still expecting to see Mao suits on the streets of Beijing and following the 'Tiananmen incident', China was an international pariah. By 1991 the bold investor came to believe that perhaps Deng really meant it when he said that he didn't care what colour of cat he used as long as it caught mice. By 1992 even the cautious could see that there was an economic boom underway in China and that the private sector was ascendant. However, in 1993 the market got into wild speculations which foresaw market liberalisation in China, a smooth transition of Hong Kong to the motherland, the ascendancy of the technocrats and their leader Zhu Rongji, and general confirmation that there was no going back to communism.

Well the most incredible thing is that those wild speculations have been transformed into facts. Just imagine, even in 1993, had the Bank of China (BOC) taken a full-page ad in the *South China Morning Post* in an attempt to seek business from the "highest echelons of society"! Remember this bank is run by the state and the state is run by the CCP. Maybe I am off my rocker but the wildest speculations about China 1998 were not wild enough, yet the air of bearishness is growing by the day. In 1993 the outside possibility of such events was considered to be worth 18× earnings on the Hang Seng Index. Today you can buy the fact for 12×!

The ideological commitment of the CCP to more capitalism was fairly evident by 1998. Did the ad for this credit card available to only the "highest echelons of society" really tell us anything we didn't know? I think it told us how relaxed management of state institutions had become that the way of the 'capitalist roader' was a very safe road to follow.

It suggested to me that there was very unlikely to be any going back and if the BOC, an institution owned by the CCP, could issue such a Platinum credit card in Hong Kong, it was only a matter of time until the "highest echelons" in China itself would be benefiting from the Platinum service. That nobody in Hong Kong thought it peculiar that a bank owned by a communist party would issue a Platinum credit card just reinforced how the consensus could see that the SAR would benefit from the structural changes coming from China. This long-term positive consensus on China's shift towards a more market-orientated system did not prevent further capital drains from Hong Kong over the summer of 1998.

Markets and fetes

8 May 1998, New Asia

> Beware of the scribes, which love to go in long clothing, and love salutations in the marketplace.

Mark 12:38

It is possible that the authorities in the other distressed jurisdictions will heed the recent advice from Mahathir Mohamad and accept 'poverty' rather than seek aid from the IMF. If such a nationalistic backlash to the current policies occurs, then it is possible that interest rates will fall significantly. However, this would clearly be at the expense of weaker currencies and the cancellation of the recapitalisation process.

This is a clear lose scenario for the equity investor and thus clearly also for anyone who wishes to hold ringgit. The only other alternative is that the hard money and liberalisation policy continues. It is still likely to be many months before this produces the sustainable fall in interest rates that will stabilise equity prices. However, the currency investor will continue to see the authorities seeking to prove to foreign investors that they run a hard currency. During this period high yields are achieved and when foreign capital begins to flow in, capital gains will be made. So the advice of 15 January remains the same – "For currencies yes, for equities no."

The choice of poverty before the IMF imposed structural change, as argued for by Mahathir Mohamad, seemed increasingly likely to some to be the choice of President Suharto. In May things spiralled out of control in Indonesia. Suharto suddenly lifted the subsidy on petrol and the price rose by 71% overnight. People were really hurting and on 12 May four students were killed and many more injured as soldiers opened fire on an anti-Suharto demonstration.

On 15 May hundreds died in fires set across Jakarta. Foreigners were being evacuated by their employers and students occupied the grounds of the parliament. It looked as if Indonesia was descending into civil war when suddenly President Suharto resigned. It was 21 May 1998, the last day of the annual CLSA Investors' Forum. It must have been later in the afternoon because there were not many of us left in the Grand Ballroom when Pete Kline, the audio-visual genius behind these events, projected Suharto's resignation live onto the big screen.

Less than two years before, the president had been presiding over an economic miracle based upon 'Asian values' and was having to fight off excessively large capital flows into the country. On 21 May he was a deposed crony capitalist as credit lines to Indonesia had been pulled and the country's financial system destroyed, its economy collapsing and its people killing each other. This business of capital inflow and capital outflow was not just about the dance of figures across a Bloomberg screen.

The Investors' Forum was an exhausting affair consisting of about eight one-hour meetings in a day and client entertainment in the evenings, and it lasted for four days. When it ended we retreated across the Pearl River Delta to the still fairly sleepy Macau and the old Bella Vista hotel. With Macau to be handed back to the PRC in December 1999, the hotel was to close and become the residence of the Portuguese consul general.

Macau was not to stay fairly sleepy. It now takes in more at the gambling tables than Las Vegas. Gambling has been illegal in China since the CCP came to power in 1949. Make of that what you will.

Beware the Montana free dollar

26 May 1998, Hong Kong

To recover from the excesses of seven days in May (CLSA China Forum and IF98), I spent the weekend in Macau. With the assistance of the odd pint of Guinness and some wishful thinking, the combination of low-rise buildings, the occasional firebomb and the firecrackers of bullets can remind one of home. However, the one thing that Macau cannot remind you of is Hong Kong.

It is still today the colonial backwater that Hong Kong remained well into the 1960s. The fact that the Portuguese began the development of Macau 288 years before the annexation of Hong Kong by the British has not guaranteed the colony's success. Although the last ten years have brought significant reclamation, the ensuing property boom is just an edifice of modernity that augurs no sudden success.

Over the ups and downs of Hong Kong, from political crisis to political crisis, property price bust to property price boom, the colony of Macau has never posed a competitive threat to Hong Kong. This failure to undermine Hong Kong, either structurally or during its cyclical weaknesses over 157 years of history, needs explaining in light of the mounting consensus that Hong Kong is now facing a massive loss of competitiveness.

So if Hong Kong is losing market share, who is taking it? Is Java the new Manhattan for Asia? Are the management consultants of Kuala Lumpur about to flood Asia with their innovative ideas on balance sheet management and corporate governance? Why aren't the stockbrokers of Bangkok doing the bulk of the trade in the shares of Cheung Kong instead of selling sandwiches?

As far as I am aware, the commercial bankers of Manila are not about to challenge the growing dominance of HSBC in the region. So let's say this is not Asia but the United States. After a prolonged battle, the Montana Free

Men are seceding from the United States. The first act by the new country is to devalue the Montana Free Dollar – a wonderful and inevitably accurate nomenclature for the new currency.

Instantaneously the property prices of Manhattan must begin to correct. It is clear that the corporate lawyers of Manhattan are about to be replaced by farmers, and the cowboys will start rounding up the share certificates. How can anybody believe that Manhattan can remain competitive against the Montana Free State? Needless to say the arrival of this happy band of malcontents now steering the Montana economy will not result in a loss of sleep by Mayor Giuliani. Nobody would predict the demise of Manhattan if a nearby agrarian or industrial state with limited financial services expertise devalued its currency.

However, just such an analogy is used every day to suggest that Hong Kong is losing 'market share'. The question remains: to whom? If Macau with its almost identical geographical location and its glut of cheap property hasn't succeeded in taking that market share over 157 years, then should we really expect Jakarta, Kuala Lumpur, Manila, Seoul, Taipei or Bangkok to suddenly do what Macau has failed to do?

It is worthwhile listing some of the creatures on the capitalist food chain who have been largely absent from financial services due to the rude health of the Asian economies, the overvaluation of equities and protectionism: currency investors, bond investors, vulture funds, private equity funds, high-quality corporate management, MNCs. So the strong economic growth has gone and the massive overvaluation of equities is no longer.

It should thus come as no surprise that in the first portion of the Asian crisis, numerous brokers of that overvalued equity lost their jobs. Now to believe in the services recession in Hong Kong, you must believe that the financial services industry is locked in its own version of the Jurassic layer and is incapable of change. You must believe that the evolutionary nature of the industry has been abolished and there is no incentive for the rest of the capitalist food chain to arrive in Asia. If you believe in stasis or even atrophy, then clearly you can foresee the services recession in Hong Kong. If you believe in anything else, then you have to believe that when the icing and marzipan layer of stockbrokers are removed, there is still a huge cake of assets which has to be restructured, managed, repackaged and sold.

So in the short term Asia's financial services capital has fewer equity brokers than it had before. As yet, I am not aware of the setting up of a welfare fund or a soup kitchen – it's difficult to get the staff to do a good range of bisques and consommés these days.

Well, it's been ten months of crisis and the bulk of the shedding of labour in that business is behind us. That business is not financial services but merely one sub-genus of it. Sitting in Hong Kong it is possible to see the new growth path of the financial services industry as lawyers, MNC managers and M&A experts descend on the SAR. When Brian Parker (CLSA ex head of Hong Kong research) arranged his furniture removal to the UK he was told that, for the first time in over a year, the flow of furniture into Hong Kong was now offsetting the outflow. At an educated guess, ten months of crisis is a sufficient time frame to allow the new players in the financial services business to get into gear and get moving to Asia. The worst may be past and the best yet to come.

The best is the boom in financial services which will occur as Southeast Asia and China move to the free market system. Like the United States in the early 1980s, the future for many Southeast Asian companies is dire as they suffer a similar fate to many of the corporations of the rust belt. From the ashes, a stronger industrial base will develop, but if you invest there you take the risk that you end up as fodder for the creative destruction process.

Of course, had you invested in Manhattan in the early 1980s, you would have seen a boom on the island as the victory of markets over regulation created a boom in the financial services industry. The same analysis could be made between London and Leeds, Newcastle, Liverpool, Glasgow, etc. When a country or region adopts a free market system, the real money to be made is in the financial capitals.

Of course, it was always possible to sell into the immediate recession associated with that structural change. Selling equities at 1,000 on the Dow Jones Index (DJI) seemed pretty smart in 1981 when the Dow crashed to 776 in August 1982. With the DJI at 9114, providing a 14% CAGR in capital since 1981, such a strategy does not appear to be so clever. The Hang Seng Index has fallen 43% during the period in which the Asian currency crisis has instigated a major victory for the forces of the free market! Time to buy or time to sell?

With the benefit of hindsight it seems silly, but there was indeed a lot of commentary that Hong Kong had become uncompetitive and many of its services jobs would be destroyed or move to cheaper bases in Asia. It turned out that not only did that not happen, but that China's rapidly growing industrial base was much more competitive than was then understood. Hong Kong was partly Asia's Manhattan, but it was to be primarily China's Manhattan. Hong Kong of course retained its position as the services centre for Asia, closely pursued by Singapore.

The redundancies that were now sweeping through the stockbroking and fund management industries in Asia dampened the animal spirits of those who survived. There was an availability bias that led to those who controlled portfolios believing that a massive shrinkage in the financial services industry was underway in Hong Kong. This myopia led many to miss the fact that a whole new food chain of financial service professionals was developing.

The negative outflow of jobs was all too painful and visible, but the inflow of new forms of capital and capitalists was virtually invisible to the portfolio manager. Institutional investors were just too close to the destruction in the financial services sector to realise that it was a form of creative destruction that would, on a net basis, not be that negative for Hong Kong's service industries. When it's the investment professionals themselves who are in the eye of the storm of creative destruction, it becomes almost impossible to remain objective.

While the stockbroking community contracted and deflated, the people of Hong Kong went to the polls to elect representatives to the Legislative Council in May 1998. This was not democracy as most people would understand it, with only 20 of the 60-member council appointed by direct election. These were dark days for Hong Kong and I well remember smiling every time I walked past an election poster for Christine Loh's Citizens Party that read, "Optimism is a Strategy". Those are sage words and ones that would have held investors in good stead given the Hang Seng Index was approaching its lows of August 1998.

Perhaps people power was spreading in Hong Kong now that there were direct elections to the Legislative Council. Passengers on some of the intra-island ferries in Hong Kong were so outraged by the rise in fares that they seized control of the ships. Shortly after these events, I was having dinner with one of the senior executives of the company that owned these particular ferries. We dined at Petrus, a fine French restaurant at the top of the Island Shangri-La hotel with views across Hong Kong harbour looking north.

My dining companion was outraged about what had happened to his ferries and knew exactly where the blame should lie. "I tell you it's all because you get one vote and I get one vote and they," he said, pointing out across the harbour to the bright lights of the city beyond, "they all get one vote." It was clear to him that I had not fully understood the enormity of the situation, so he repeated, "They all get one vote!" That democracy, even in this highly constrained form, could come as such a shock to the business interests of Hong Kong said much about the past, but also the future for Hong Kong.

Do the right thing

28 May 1998, Thailand

First the bullish case. Those investors attending CLSA's IF98 presentation of the government of Thailand will have heard a very dramatic statement by Dr Pisit Leatham, the deputy finance minister. According to Dr Pisit, capital inflows into Thailand in April were so strong that the authorities were able to see significant reserve accumulation. This accounts for the fall in interest rates and the stability in the currency since around 16 March. There has been strong upward pressure on the baht since that date and the authorities have refused to permit a rise in the currency and instead have been buying US dollars and selling baht and thus easing domestic liquidity and reducing interest rates.

With no sign of a slump to a current account deficit and every sign of steady continued capital inflow into the country, this state of affairs is likely to continue. The bulls would argue that the ingredients for a bull market in Thailand have thus been in place since around 16 March and the weakness of the equity market is due to external events, particularly the weak yen, which has discouraged investment in the emerging markets. Assuming external stability, the bulls would argue that the steady fall in interest rates in Thailand will lift equity valuations.

I usually have few problems in being dogmatic, but on this occasion the balance between the bull and bear camps is close. In three years of writing strategy on Thailand I have never found myself so optimistic, but on balance I remain a bear. I still believe that the forces of structural change in Thailand are so extensive and negative for the profitability of indigenous companies that they will overpower the positive cyclical forces in Thailand which are now clearly building a head of steam. Our team on the ground is still concerned from a micro basis that equities in Thailand are overvalued. Thus this macro investor remains a bear.

However, for micro investors who can see companies which can adjust to the structural change and are fairly priced, there is safety in entering the Thai equity market. For the first time in three years the macro risks to valuation on good companies at good prices are to the upside. In the great Thai bear market, investors lost money on good companies at good prices due to the macro conflagration. Those days are past now. Due to a lack of good companies at good prices, the SET Index is likely to continue to fall. However, the good micro investors can now ignore the macro conditions and get back to their knitting. Happy hunting.

It was getting close to a 50/50 call now as to whether one should buy or sell Asian equities. This was a good time not to have to write anything and be forced to call buy or sell, and so I went on holiday. While I was away in June, the crisis in Asia spread to Russia as the country's foreign exchange reserves dwindled and it struggled to push through the reforms to the tax regime that would secure IMF support. The potential for an economic crisis in Russia, a nuclear power, focused minds among developed world policy makers. The fact that something more than further bailout packages was brewing was evident when the United States intervened in the foreign exchange markets to support the yen on 17 June.

This intervention was both a great surprise and very successful. The oft-repeated mantra of the US secretary to the Treasury had long been that the United States favoured a strong US dollar policy. Now this same secretary to the Treasury was intervening in the market by selling US$2bn to buy yen in an attempt to depress the US dollar exchange rate:

> I felt that the conditions that can make a currency intervention effective might well be present. The first was that the yen-dollar exchange rate, now at 147 yen to the dollar, seemed to have gone to a real extreme – the yen was approaching free fall. American manufacturers, who were always worried about the level of the dollar, were becoming truly alarmed. The second condition was that the intervention would be supported by policy changes. Japanese officials were prepared to make a series of statements supporting economic reforms we were encouraging such as closing insolvent banks ... The final condition was the psychological element of surprise.

Robert Rubin, *In an Uncertain World: Tough Choices from Wall Street to Washington*, 2003

That surprise exchange rate intervention came the week before President Clinton's visit to China. Larry Summers flew to Japan on 18 June and then on to Beijing to join President Clinton. Once again, we had to read between the lines, but the flight path of Summers in particular suggested that the United States and Japan together had committed to do what they could to prevent the decline of the yen in return for a pledge from China not to devalue the renminbi.

China had been more vociferous about the decline of the yen than about the decline of the other Asian currencies and was concerned that the yen's decline was undermining their competitiveness. That an agreement between the three powers was made to weaken the US dollar and strengthen the yen remains the best interpretation of what happened in Asia in June 1998. It was another one of those key policy decisions that really improved the outlook for Asia and the yen did not rise further; by September it was in steady decline. I missed the big news of that intervention on 17 June as I was still in Bordeaux celebrating Scotland's draw with Norway in the football World Cup. I caught up with that news when I returned to Hong Kong on 12 July and changed my mind. It was time to buy Asian equities.

PART FOUR
The bottom

Whizzbangs, warfare and those cyclical things

14 July 1998, Hong Kong

Consumers with bonuses,
Credit cards flinging,

New cars leaving showrooms,
And tills that are ringing,

"Cheap loans for property" all bankers sing,
These are a few of those cyclical things!

When the banks bust,
When machines rust,
When I'm feeling bad,
I picture a few of these cyclical things,
And then I don't feel so bad.

'Those Cyclical Things' (with apologies to Rodgers & Hammerstein)

It has been six weeks since the last *Solid Ground Daily*. Over that period, with all the certainty of an approaching freight train, the powers of global deflation have savaged the South African rand and intensified the pressure on the Russian ruble. To me the growing impact of the Asian crisis was actually visible as we witnessed the accumulation of Indonesian furniture in the following far-flung corners of the developed world: Brossac in Aquitaine, France; Bangor in County

Down, Northern Ireland; Edinburgh in Scotland; Cobham in Surrey, England; Alexandria in Virginia, USA.

Even with the Asian economies struggling through with almost non-existent financial systems, the repercussions from events in the region are becoming increasingly visible in the developed world. To add to these global woes, the yen has slipped from 138.8 to 141.3 to the US dollar and would have gone further without the good offices of the US Treasury. It is thus not surprising that, with the forces of deflation still rampant, the Asian equity and currency markets took further significant 'hits' during the period (see Table 4.1).

Table 4.1: Performance of Asian markets from 29 May 1998

	Rel. to MSCI FE	Absolute
Hong Kong	+4.0%	−8.2%
Singapore	+2.1%	−9.9%
Malaysia	−18.7%	−28.2%
Thailand	−8.1%	−18.9%
Indonesia	−7.8%	−18.6%
Philippines	−5.7%	−16.7%
Taiwan	+13.0%	flat
South Korea	+11.6%	−1.5%
India	+2.4%	−9.6%
Pakistan	−18.9%	−28.5%
China	−11.2%	−21.6%

Remarking on the sickly inevitable progress of this freight train to one of CLSA's excellent sales/traders ("the best in the business", according to the recent *Euromoney/Global Investor* poll), he sagely remarked that the good news was that we had already been hit and were thus lying injured at the side of the tracks. While the rest of the world remains on the tracks facing the freight train, Asia has already been smashed and flung from the tracks.

While not immune to repercussions from damage further down the line, the region has suffered the most serious blow from the deflationary freight train. So, as our sales trader remarked, would you rather be alive but bruised on the side of the tracks, or standing in front of an oncoming freight train? In one situation your health is guaranteed to deteriorate, but in the other there is a significant probability that your health will improve, having survived the impact.

The scale of the damage already inflicted is indicated by the percentage fall in US dollar terms of Asian markets from their peaks: Thailand –90%, Indonesia –90%, Malaysia –80%, South Korea –85%, the Philippines –67% and Hong Kong –51%. Proof, if it were ever needed, that the sales/traders in the trenches have a lot to tell Haig-like strategists about whizzbangs, warfare and investment survival.

Not every country in Asia has suffered similar injuries from the collision with deflation. In some economies where banking systems were overextended in foreign currencies and/or property, the internal organs have been irreparably damaged and donors are now actively sought. Until these nations have replaced such internal organs with foreign transplants, it would be dangerous to back them to be winning any races.

For the following nations, the recapitalisation of the banking system will be a *sine qua non* for recovery: Thailand, Malaysia, Indonesia, South Korea, the Philippines (perhaps). However, other jurisdictions appear to have suffered no life-threatening damages to the key internal organ that is the financial system: India, China, Hong Kong, Singapore. In these jurisdictions the impacts have been restricted due to the limited importance of foreign trade (China and India) or the prudence of the banking system (Hong Kong and Singapore).

In these jurisdictions there is thus a much higher probability that the seeds of creation sown in the destruction of asset prices, productive capacity and wages will blossom into an economic recovery. In dealing with the new global environment, these markets are fortunate in having such isolation (China and India) or are already significantly progressed in adapting to the new environment (Hong Kong and Singapore).

As *The Solid Ground Daily* has argued for over a year, some jurisdictions in Asia face severe cyclical problems (India, China, Hong Kong and Singapore) while others must undergo major structural changes (Thailand, Indonesia, Malaysia, the Philippines and South Korea). For those jurisdictions where the banking system is intact and functioning, one does not have to be a starry-eyed visionary to see a cyclical recovery. Such a recovery is being created in the normal fashion by alterations in asset prices, capacity and wage levels. These equity markets, where cyclical recovery is highly probable, now represent excellent relative investments for any global investor and barring a global equity market collapse, significant price appreciation is likely.

It is the easiest analysis in the world to tar Asia with the same brush of structural collapse and ignore the simple and highly profitable rules associated with cyclical investment. Most Asian investors are discouraged in attempting cyclical analysis by disastrous commitments of capital to markets which then witnessed a structural collapse: Thailand, Indonesia, Malaysia and South Korea.

However, the difficulty in timing does not invalidate this cyclical approach to investment when the economic structure remains sound and significant pain has already been endured. So it's time to attempt to stand up, move some limbs and convince ourselves that the internal damage is limited. If convinced in the soundness of the body, it is time to think of a few of those cyclical things.

Of course, there is no tangible evidence of any cyclical improvement – there never is when equity markets are reaching their bottom. Although not with as much certainty as one would expect in the science of physics or chemistry, there are clear historical relationships which suggest that an economic improvement will indeed materialise. Perhaps this time these laws have been suspended. The depressed price of equities is certainly suggesting this. History suggests that this is just such a time when one should step up to the plate and be a buyer of sound economies and sound companies.

It was time to buy. There were few signs of any improvement in the real economy and when the economic data became available it was very clear that none was underway in July 1998. The optimism was based more on a recognition that Asia was now the source of the deflation shock that was rolling across the world and there was a rising possibility that the collapse in equity prices was discounting some or perhaps all of that shock. Other global equity markets were only just beginning to register the global impacts from the Asian crisis, helped by the realisation that Russia was on the edge of collapse.

Most of my colleagues believed that this sudden optimism was just the natural reaction of a man who had had too long a holiday. If so, I recommend long holidays in bear markets because the MSCI Asia ex Japan Index was to bottom just six weeks after I published this piece of research. It may have been correct that my long holiday played a role, as I returned to the office somewhat unanchored from the consensus view that had witnessed more weeks of share price meltdowns. Having stepped away from the carnage in financial markets perhaps I did get a better view of when value was reasserting itself in the Asian stock markets.

It was quite a holiday, the highlight of which came in Kitty O'Shea's bar in Paris after the Brazil v Scotland World Cup football game. I bumped into Norman Whiteside, former Manchester United and Northern Ireland footballer, and we stood on the bar together and entertained the people of Paris with a rendition of *Danny Boy*. My animal spirits were definitely lifted, whatever the impact this may have had on those that were there to listen.

Follow the money

15 July 1998, Regional

In the past there have been fortunes to be made in Asia by following the flow of direct investment streams. In the old days such flows produced a double whammy, indicating that domestic assets were potentially cheap/competitive and also, through the fixed exchange rate regimes, such flows boosted money supply growth.

Things have changed today, but by mapping the new flows of funds into Asia it may be possible at least to indicate areas of value. The following is a list of foreign M&A activity in Asia since 1 January of this year compiled by Bloomberg. It does not include in-market mergers but focuses on transactions where foreign companies have purchased assets from or stakes in Asian companies (for this purpose, Hong Kong and Chinese companies are treated as in-market transactions).

The list includes any reports of greenfield investments, although on the whole these investments proceed unreported and thus are significantly understated. Although the list is not necessarily complete, as it is a survey of one news service, the 95 reported transactions provide a reasonable sample from which some general conclusions can be drawn:

- Heidelberger Zement, Holderbank Financiere Glarus, Lafarge Asia Pacific, Cemex are all bidders for Semen Gresik.
- Tenggara Cement was bought by Holderbank.
- Walmart acquired four stores from Korea Makro and six sites in South Korea. Opens six stores in China.
- Abitibi-Consolidated and Norske Consolidated bought assets of Hansol Paper and formed a new three-way joint venture.
- Blue Circle bought 20% of Fortune Cement.
- La Moderna bought Hungong Seed and ChoongAng Seed for US$117m.
- Enso of Finland paid US$80m for 19.9% of Advanced Agro of Thailand.
- Interbrew bought a 50% stake for US$250m in a JV with Oriental Brewery.
- International Lottery & Totalizator Systems Inc bought 52.5% of Prime Gaming Philippines from Berjaya Group.
- GE Capital bought US$517m in Thai car loans.
- Kemira Oji of Finland agreed to buy Hanwha Chemicals' hydrogen peroxide plant in Ulsan for US$39m.
- Dow Chemical bought its partner's 20% stake in its South Korean joint venture.
- Novartis bought the crop-protection products unit of Oriental Chemical Industries of South Korea.

- DBS bought Sri Dhana Securities for US$5.8m.
- Kim Eng Holdings bought Nithipat Capital & Securities for US$2.96m.
- Seagram's invested US$90m to take a majority stake in its South Korean whisky joint venture.
- Volkswagen agreed to buy a 60% stake for US$111m in Lamborghini owned by ex-President Suharto's son.
- Metropolitan Life Insurance bought a US$1bn convertible bond in Korea Life, which could amount to 60% of the company.
- Metropolitan Life Insurance invested US$1bn in Daehan Life Insurance.
- Clark Material Handling Company paid US$30m for Samsung Heavy Industries' forklift business.
- Taiwan China Development Corporation bought a 6.8% stake in Malaysian Pacific Industries, a semiconductor maker, for US$39m.
- Merrill Lynch said it will buy 51% of Phatra Securities for around US$61m to US$68m.
- Novus Petroleum Ltd said it bought energy assets in Egypt from a South Korean group headed by Samsung Corp.
- Commerzbank said it will buy 30% of Korea Exchange Bank for US$250m.
- AES of Arlington, Virginia, plans to buy the power business of Hanwha energy for US$644m and invest US$230m more to complete one of the South Korean company's plants.
- Hewlett-Packard agreed to buy Samsung Electronics' 45% stake in Hewlett-Packard Korea.
- SBC Warburg told the Thai government that it wants to buy the remaining 51% stake in domestic brokerage SBC Premier Warburg.
- Malaysia's Sime Darby said it had agreed to sell its Sandestin Resorts unit to Intrawest Corporation of Canada for US$131.5m.
- GE Capital said it will enter the Philippine insurance industry by purchasing Philippines Asia Life Assurance from the Knights of Columbus of the USA.
- Kohap has signed a letter of intent to sell Emtec Magnetics of Germany.
- SC Johnson & Son of the USA will pay about US$27m to acquire the pesticide business of Samsung Pharmaceutical.
- Tesco PLC agreed to buy a 75% stake in Thai retailer Lotus from the Charoen Pokphand Group for US$181m.
- Shingo Paper Co said Norske Skogindustrier agreed to buy its South Korean newsprint plant for US$175m.
- Samsung Group said it will raise US$1.2bn from GE, Corning Inc and other US companies.

- Samsung agreed to sell 90% of Samsung Heavy Industries' construction arm to Volvo for US$572m.
- Daewoo Corp agreed to an offer from IRI to buy a stake in, and ally with, its Ansaldo transportation and engineering company.
- Korea Tungsten said Iscar Ltd of Israel agreed to buy its tungsten carbide tools division for US$150m.
- Soros Quantum agreed to buy 23% of Thai broker Adkinson Securities.
- Royal Ahold said its JV in Malaysia agreed to buy seven supermarkets there. The stores were purchased from Yahona Corp.
- Malayan United Industries said its associate unit Regent Group agreed to sell Radisson Hotel Atlanta for about US$54.4m.
- P&G bought a 91.6% stake in Sangyong Paper for US$158m.
- Aboitiz Equity Ventures Inc said it sold its 30% share in Pilipinas Kao Inc to the chemical company's Japanese parent.
- Usinor SA said it will raise its stake in Thainox Steel from 28% to 61%.
- Hanil Group said it sold its 50% stake in JV synthetic fibre company to partner Asahi Chemical Industry.
- Sanwa Bank paid US$50 for an additional 5.8% of Siam Commercial Bank.
- Hyundai Electronics said it sold Odeum Microsystems to Oak Technology.
- First Pacific of Hong Kong and Indonesia's Salim group said they will sell California's United Commercial Bank for US$120m.
- Blue Circle Cement said it is looking at one or two other opportunities in the Philippines after having announced plans to buy US$22m in debt convertible into shares of Republic Cement.
- Malaysian Resources Corp plans to sell up to 20% of its Malakoff unit to the UK's National Power.
- Taiwan's Yuanta said it bought 108m shares at 10 baht apiece in Nava Finance & Securities for a 24% stake.
- Hotel Properties is negotiating to sell part of its stake in Canary Riverside development in London.
- ICI said it is considering up to a US$100m investment in South Korea and is looking at Dongsung Chemical.
- BASF agreed to pay US$600m last month to buy Daesang Groups lysine business in South Korea.
- Bowater Inc bought Halla Pulp & Paper for US$175m.
- Metropolitan Life said it bought the remaining 49% of its South Korean JV from Seoul-based Kolon Group for US$15.6m.
- Norske Skog said it plans to buy 90% of South Korean newsprint plant Chong Won from Shinho Paper.

- Norske Skog acquired 70% of Shinho Paper's Thai newsprint plant for US$35m.
- CMS Energy said it paid US$60m for a 50% interest in a 300-megawatt power plant under construction in Thailand from Soon Hua Seng Group.
- First Pacific said it would raise US$1.8bn by selling Hagemeyer NV.
- Prince Alwaleed Bin Talal said he plans to invest US$150m in Daewoo Corp and Hyundai Motor Co.
- ABN AMRO is buying 75% of Bank of Asia, paying an initial US$183m.
- Thai Danu Bank completed the sale of a majority stake to a group led by DBS.
- China Development Corporation will pay US$15m for a controlling interest in Bangkok Bank's Bangkok First Investment and Trust.
- Sithe Energies announced a definitive agreement to acquire a 33.6% interest in COCO of Thailand for US$100m.
- George Soros and three other investors will pay US$15m for a 15% stake in Thai steel producer Nakornthai Strip Mill.
- CP Pokphand sold Shanghai Motorcycle JV for US$13m.
- HKCB, wholly owned by Lippo Group, sold half of its insurance division for US$8.4m to Reliance National of the USA.
- Lai Sun sold its stake in Delta Hotels & Resorts. Canadian Pacific paid as much as US$66m for Delta.
- HS Group of South Korea said it sold its interest in two JVs to Parker-Hannifin for US$12m.
- Berjaya Group sold its shares in Parkway Holdings and Alpha Healthcare, raising US$21m.
- GE Capital said it bought a majority stake in the credit card unit of the Central Group of Cos, Thailand's largest retailer.
- Royal Garden Resort of Thailand said a fund managed by Schroder Capital Partners (Asia) will pay US$8.7m for a 22% stake in the company.
- Michael Jackson agreed to invest at least US$100m to build a theme park for children at a ski resort owned by Ssang Bang Wool Group. He plans to build a resort called Neverland Asia.
- Regent Pacific agreed to purchase a 22% stake in Daeyu Securities for US$10m.
- Dairy Farm International said it has taken a 31% stake in Indonesian supermarket chain PT Hero Supermarket for US$36.4m.
- GE Capital said it bought 49% of Asia Finance for US$6.7m.
- GE Capital bought the 20% it didn't already own in Bangkok-based GS Capital Corp.
- Lectra Systems bought Hong Kong's Pan Union International.
- Accor SA said it now owns 95.9% of Accor Asia Pacific after it offered to pay US$193m for the stake it didn't already own.

- Banque Bruxelles Lambert (BBL) increased its stake in Indonesia's Bank Mashill to 18.1% from 16.9%. BBL bought 750,000 shares at a price of 425 rupiah in the open market on 15 January.
- Sumitomo Chemical said it acquired 50% of Dong Woo Pure Chemicals for US$33m from Oriental Chemical Industries.
- United Technologies Corporation, which makes Otis elevators, amassed a 9.62% stake in Dong Yang Elevator.
- Kolon International sold equity worth US$20m in a subsidiary – a 36.4% stake – to Fanuc, its Japanese partner.
- LTCB will pay US$7m for 1% of Siam Commercial Bank.
- Indosuex WI Carr will buy 49% in Union Securities of Thailand, supplanting Saha-Union as majority shareholder.
- Kohap sold its chemical operation to European Multimedia for US$130m and its 13.6% stake in KNC to a US company for US$2m.
- Prudential Securities said it agreed to buy the HK and Singapore operations of Nava Finance & Securities.
- An investment company of Prince Alwaleed bin Talal said it bought 3% of hotel properties.
- Singapore Power said it would pay US$175m for control of certain power production assets of Indonesia's APP.

And a few from late 1997:

- An investment company of Prince Alwaleed bin Talal said it bought 3% of the Malaysian carmaker Proton.
- Laem Thong Bank sold 400 million new shares to a group of three investors, Sheikh Ahmad Al-Sabah, Soafer Capital and affiliates of Thailand's UCOM.
- Goldman Sachs bought a 29% stake in Dusit Thani Pcl.

One country notable by its absence from the list is Indonesia. So far the foreign foray into that country seems to consist of a scramble for Semen Gresik and another attempt at overseas diversification by Dairy Farm in buying Hero Supermarkets and an ill-timed small increase by BBL in its stake in Bank Mashill.

While there are numerous deals in both Thailand and the Philippines, foreigners have been slow to commit funds to Malaysia. The outstanding deals to date have been: Prudential of the UK increasing its stake in the local JV, CDC investing US$30m in Malaysian Pacific Industries, Royal Ahold buying supermarkets from a Japanese seller, National Power of the UK buying 20% of Malakoff and Prince Alwaleed bin Talal buying 3% of Proton.

It was happening: deals were flowing and capital was finding a clearing price. The Asian equity markets were not to reach their lows until 1 September despite the very clear evidence that foreign capital was arriving in some size in the region. The problem by July was that global financial markets were beginning to price in the impact of the deflation flowing from Asia and their decline was echoing around the world and forcing a decline in equity prices globally.

There was a particular focus on Russia, but the mantra I heard repeated every day was that no nation with nuclear weapons would ever be allowed to fail by the international community. It was an opinion almost universally shared by investors that Russia was 'too nuclear to fail'. The few people I met who had invested in Russia were particularly adamant on this point and it was clear that this was a key reason why they had invested in the country, particularly in its high-yielding local currency denominated government debt.

The ruble was linked to the US dollar and there was a huge yield pick-up, particularly if you borrowed US dollars, and your risk, it was argued, was underwritten by the international community – so what could possibly go wrong? If the IMF and global governments could find funds to 'bail out' Indonesia, Thailand and South Korea it was obvious that funds would be found to prevent a devaluation of the ruble or any default by this major nuclear power. I never heard the faith in this belief diminish until the day Russia devalued and defaulted on its debt.

Not all of the investments that made press headlines in the summer of 1998 were to actually materialise. Michael Jackson, who had openly supported Kim Dae-jung's election campaign and attended the president's inauguration in Seoul in February 1998, was never to build Neverland Asia.

Jim Fisk, Jay Gould, Chartres Cathedral and the body of Mr Bentham

22 July 1998, Regional

The gold crash devastated the US economy for months and even years. In one week, from September to October 1st 1869, the total mass of gold and stock on Wall Street dropped in value by an estimated $100 million, an amount comparable to several billions today … EL Godkin's The Nation regarded Fisk and Gould's antics as symptoms of a public moral crisis. Why should such men "whose one passion is money-making" and to whom speculation "is a delightful game" quit … "when few people thought worse of a man for having been engaged in a successful corner".

Aside from the tongue-lashings by Garfield's Committee, the press, and other respectable citizens, the law never laid a finger on the gold bandits.

Kenneth D Ackerman, *The Gold Ring*, 1988

On the floor of the great Cathedral of Chartres an intricate, convoluted design is carved. It looks like a great emblem, Celtic in appearance, adding decoration and elaboration to an otherwise austere setting. It is no such thing. It is in fact a maze pattern, around which sinners were forced to crawl on their knees in an act of penance. In cultures around the world, the concept of penance is still vibrant and anybody who feels the need can journey to Westport in Mayo, where you can crawl up the mountain Croagh Patrick on your knees.

Whether ingrained by the church or other cultural forces, our desire to see penance done remains intact to the present day. This cultural inheritance is now impeding rationality with regard to the Asian equity markets. At this stage in the Asian business cycle, it is important to remember that the dynamics of the cycle are amoral. Market forces are not schooled in philosophy or morality.

I sense an air of growing discontent among the Western financial community. There is a feeling that the flagellation of Asia is not complete. Indeed, where conditions permit, certain Asian authorities have had the audacity to reduce their self-flagellation. Shame. Penance has not been done. How can salvation result?

In Indonesia, South Korea and Thailand, the banks are just not being whipped as vigorously as we had all been promised. Indeed, like it were Maundy money, some governments of the region are handing out low interest rates with apparently wild abandon. The response from the Western financial community is to insist that we cannot be witnessing salvation unless the promised gross flagellation has indeed been inflicted. Any indication that relief is upon us is thus to be ignored.

To repeat, market forces have neither passed through a seminary nor studied the speeches of Mother Theresa. Market forces are akin to those same natural unwilled and undisciplined forces which result in rivers reaching the sea, pigs eating spuds and tigers eating pigs. Capital flows towards profitable opportunities, capital feasts on labour and strong capital feasts on weak capital. Capital is amoral in its rush to profitable opportunities as a river is amoral in its rush to the sea. We can debate the justness of the impact of this movement of market forces, but such studies are best left to philosophers and priests rather than players in capital markets.

It is market forces which have collapsed demand and propelled most of Asia into current account surpluses. It is those market forces which have created that net buying of the currency. It is capital's search for good returns which is resulting in capital inflows into the region beginning to accelerate. It is the net buying of Asian currencies which is permitting currencies to stabilise, while at the same time interest rates are falling.

It is unwilled and undisciplined market forces that are thus alleviating foreign debt burdens, reducing the cost of domestic debt and opening access to foreign capital for distressed local companies. Following a period of gross capital destruction and liquidation of labour, a new equilibrium is developing. Against the background of those operations of market forces, it should not surprise anyone that the authorities in Asia may back down from commitments to flagellate their banking systems. It may not simply be as necessary as it was when there were deficits, capital was fleeing, interest rates were rising and there was no hope in sight for foreign buyers.

Now we may feel that this will let many people off too lightly. The owners of these banks would probably not agree, as following any recapitalisation the dilution of family wealth since June 1997 will have been truly immense. Judging the justness of the allocation of pain is a wasteful and unprofitable activity. (Those interested in so recalibrating the calculus of pleasure and pain can journey to University College, London, and commune with the stuffed corpse of Mr Jeremy Bentham.)

Bad commercial bankers are not serial killers. We should not see their survival, liberty or improved prosperity as a moral affront. There are hundreds of ex-bad bankers walking around the United States today, bailed out of paying for their economic 'crimes' by the policy of the Federal Reserve in 1990–91. It should not come as a shock to anyone to know that there are hundreds of new bad bankers in the United States whose 'crimes' will only be revealed in the next economic downturn.

Indeed, according to John G Medlin Jr, chairman emeritus of Wachovia Corporation and arguably the United States' greatest banker, credit standards in the United States are at their weakest point in 40 years. Know any bad bankers in the United States? Of course not. At this stage in the business cycle they're heroes and John G's ruining the party.

It would be nice if market forces could purge with moral precision only the guys in the black hats. They don't. Often they kill the guys in the white hats, and everybody must know at least one family friend and a good business person who was dragged under by a bad creditor. Readers of The Solid Ground of March last year might even remember the catalogue of Malaysian 'entrepreneurs' who apparently self-destructed in the mid-1980s crash. By the early 1990s they were back in charge, making the same bets all over again. Not very just, but that's the way it is. Donald Trump is still at the table and still playing. Jim Slater is an investment guru. Philosophers may crave the allocation of guilt, but investors should accept the operation of market forces.

So why the sudden belief that the promised government/IMF programmes are the only legitimacy? If there is any lesson from the events of the past year in Asia, it is that the will of government is of secondary importance to the power of market forces. For a prolonged period we have all criticised the attempt by governments to corral market forces to achieve their own ends.

Currently market forces are acting to alleviate the worst conditions of the Asian crisis, bypassing some government-mandated programmes. In a bizarre twist we are now criticising market forces for producing stable currencies and falling interest rates and insisting that governments attempt to force through their own agendas. If the market looks like it can cope with the problem, then let it. Should the government of South Korea be telling Commerzbank that they cannot recapitalise Korea Exchange Bank? The markets and not governments will be the driving force out of the current morass. We can ignore the market dynamics and await the purging of the evil ones by government mandate, but such a purge will simply not come if there is a stable currency, falling interest rates and fresh equity injections.

So it may be that Asia is not completely remade in the West's image. It may be that not all the structural flaws in the system are eradicated in this great flood of capital destruction. We may regard the parts of the old Asia that survive as dusty anachronisms that detract from the efficiency of the systems. Does this mean that corporate cash flows cannot improve? Does this mean that earnings growth cannot resume? Does this mean that equity prices will continue to languish? No.

Throughout history, investors have shown a wonderful ability to ignore even the severest structural problems during a cyclical upswing. Those investors who run scared of China's structural problems today paid 16× historic earnings for H shares at the top of the business cycle. Many investors convinced themselves that Japan's structural weaknesses were actually structural strengths, and they bid up Japanese equities to 82× earnings!

It may be that portfolio flows will shun any market-driven stabilisation in Asia and improving cash flows. It may be that portfolio flows will only watch recapitalisation occur via FDI inflows. It may be that un-eradicated structural flaws will mean that portfolio investors will refuse to buy Asian equities ever again. History would suggest that such puritanical pursuit of the 'clean' structure gets rapidly abandoned during the cyclical party.

Jim Fisk and Jay Gould attempted a great gold corner and when it failed they walked away from all their buy tickets. The whole US economy was brought to a halt. The courts, with some persuasion from Boss Tweed, found that their gold purchases were not binding contracts. In the great gold price collapse, it was the sellers who went bust.

Jim Fisk survived all criminal prosecution and held onto his directorships only to be gunned down by his ex-girlfriend's lover two years later. Jay Gould died a natural death in 1892 leaving a fortune of US$70m, which would be worth close to US$2bn today. In what may be a unique case, where two individuals actually caused a business downturn by themselves, they remained unpunished. Following 1869 there was an 1870, and an 1871, etc. ... Without any punishment of Jay and Jim, the business cycle turned and investors started making money again. Sometimes life is just like that.

There was to be no purge of the bad guys and though some faded into history, few faded into incarceration. The usual suspects were never rounded up. The market was clearly ignorant of any need for retribution that institutional investors had decreed to be essential in the purge of the system. This piece was a recognition that there would not be a complete victory for the new form of capitalism that foreign investors insisted had to occur to make Asian equities investible.

As early as 1998, a new global financial architecture was being formed from the stability that capital inflows and current account surpluses were now bringing to Asia. This was not to be the last crisis when the demands for the punishment of the guilty continued to ring, sometimes for years, after the price of equities had bottomed. That markets are amoral is often forgotten and, as we have discovered since the Asian financial crisis, a fact that has major political ramifications.

One hundred years after Fashoda

28 July 1998, Regional

> The scramble for Africa bewildered everyone, from the humblest African peasant to the master statesmen of the age, Lord Salisbury and Prince Bismarck ... Africa was sliced up like a cake, the pieces swallowed by the five rival nations – Germany, Italy, Portugal, France and Britain (with Spain taking some scraps) – and Britain and France were at each other's throats ... Why this undignified rush by the leaders of Europe to build empires in Africa? Anglo-French rivalry explains a great deal – but not enough. Historians are as puzzled now as the politicians were then.
>
> **Thomas Pakenham, *The Scramble for Africa*, 1991**

A memorable peace conference, as it was a memorable conflict, no
longer of individuals engaged in a race for accumulation, but of
grouped monopolistic interests; an oligarchy of oil, steel, and railroad
overlords in conflict with the power of another railroad monopoly. Here
were profound symptoms of a new phase of the industrial or capitalist
revolution: the great monopoly or Trust can make unlimited profits when
confronted with unorganised, divided sections of consumers and vassals;
on such grounds it is irresistible.

Matthew Josephson, *The Robber Barons*, 1934

In February, I attended a shindig known as the Presidents' Forum where a meeting
of the great and the good from East and West took place to discuss the way forward
for Asia. As mentioned in *The Solid Ground Daily* of 25 February, there was
unanimity from the Western management consultants as to the road forward for
corporate Asia. The call went out for downsizing, re-engineering, concentration
on core competencies and – most importantly – co-operation with MNCs.

At the time, *The Solid Ground* suggested that history proposed another route
which may also be possible. During a similar period of deflationary collapse
on returns in the United States, the 'robber barons' began to form the great
monopolies which could reduce excess capacity, fix prices, improve returns and
increase their wealth. This was as natural a response in the 1890s as it is in the
1990s when, in most global industries, supply significantly outstrips demand.

As the quote from Josephson above shows, it was incredible how quickly
the warring powers of capital came to see that the only way out of their turmoil
was through co-operation. In February, *The Solid Ground* suggested that we
could see similar patterns developing in Asia, with local companies banding
together to fix prices, reduce costs and survive the current turmoil. This analysis
was wrong. It was too parochial.

What we are witnessing in Asia is global capital rushing to buy Asian capacity
in its need to at least create concentrated oligopolies in the current deflationary
(too much supply/not enough demand) environment. In that environment, the
capitalists' scramble for Asian capacity can be seen as perhaps as inexplicable
as the politicians' scramble for Africa at the turn of the last century.

At its most mystifying peak (17 September to 4 December 1898), the French
and English armies stood facing each other ready to do battle over a sandy
island called Fashoda, 700 miles up the Nile from Khartoum. Nobody knew
exactly why they were there and it was very difficult to argue for any economic
abundance which would flow from the upper Nile even if the Mahdist forces
could be subdued. The point was the British had to be there because the French

were there, and vice versa. That was the dynamic which drove the political scramble for Africa, and it is a similar logic among capitalists which is driving the scramble for Asia.

You may not think that it's rational, and there is no function on a calculator which can explain it, but it has happened before and it is happening again. Not until the French got involved in the Congo did the British feel the need to get involved in Nigeria. Not until the British got involved in Egypt did the French feel the need to get involved in Morocco. Not until the British and the French started carving up Africa did Bismarck start staking his claim for Germany. Whether one scorns that reasoning or not, one should not argue with the consequences. One deal begets another, which begets another, etc.

My error in February was similar to that of the analyst who attempted to predict the political future of Africa by studying indigenous political developments. Anyone who conducted such analysis in 19th-century Africa badly misjudged the role which Africa would play as a sub-plot in the great play for domination in Europe. Similarly, Asia, now that it needs capital and is open to offers, is caught up in a great play for oligopoly by global capital. It may be that the managers of such capital are adjusting to the forthcoming deflation and are thus much more proactive than their late 19th-century brethren.

More cynically, it may be that the only quick fix for profits is to buy in capacity and slash costs. If top-line growth is sluggish, how else is a manager to get profits up, share prices up and stock option values up? Perhaps it is better to label the push for global mega-mergers as 'a scramble for revenue'. Whatever the motivation behind the scramble for size, it has been evident in the global arena for the past couple of years without – until now – impacting Asia. The dire need for fresh capital in Asia is now bringing it to centre stage, as was, briefly, that sandy island Fashoda on the upper Nile.

There are some very simple dynamics behind the developing scramble. For the producers of commodities the dynamics are simple – they must own the low-cost producer. If the South Koreans have to dump their pulp and paper capacity at distressed prices, then I will have to be involved in the bidding process. If my competitor gets capacity cheap in a commodity business, then my profitability will, in due course, be challenged.

Of course because all the key players are forced to turn up and bid, the selling price probably will not get ridiculously cheap. Still, just by being there to keep the price 'honest', the player in the global commodity business is ensuring their future profitability. In such a way, commodity-producing capacity is clearing at a dramatic pace across Asia, from cement companies in the Philippines, Malaysia and Indonesia, pulp and paper companies in Thailand and South Korea, and chemical companies in South Korea.

So while we all ponder over the latest discounted cash-flow analysis or premium-to-book value analysis for Asian companies, we may be pursuing a form of analysis which is as useful a predictor of the future as a study of African tribal politics in the late 19th century. We are just beginning to see part of a great global game played out in Asia which may owe more to late 20th-century capitalist dialectics than the use of a pocket calculator with future value functions. One cannot now look at Asia in isolation from global events in the realm of capital.

The world was facing the prospect of considerable deflation, a force that had been largely absent since the 1930s. I thought this would be bad news for global equities, but I was wrong. One of the reasons I was wrong was that strong corporations reacted to the threat by increasing their oligopoly power. I could see that happening as early as July 1998, but I did not fully appreciate its impact, how long it could last, nor how much leverage could be employed to push it to extremes.

In theory there were legal limits to prevent the formation of oligopolies, but changes in such legislation, particularly during the Reagan administration, had watered down these protections. On the ground in Asia, we could see the loss of purchasing power, the gross excess capacity and the very cheap exchange rates that augured a profound deflation for the world. Business responded to this combination by seeking to agglomerate capacity and the Herfindahl-Hirschman Index, a commonly accepted measure of market concentration, would now enter a prolonged rise.

For every action there is a reaction, and capital reacted to the threat of deflation by seeking market concentration much as the robber barons had reacted more than 100 years before. With that greater concentration came greater political power and another shift in the socio-political balance that flowed from events in Asia triggered by the flow, ebb and then flow again of global capital.

Long-term investment and the fate of poor PEGI

31 July 1998, Malaysia

The deals of the mid-1990s had a terrifying similarity to the deals of the early 1980s. Of course, investing in emerging markets one has to take a long-term perspective. Had one spotted the renaissance of Malaysia from commodities producer to industrialised nation, then surely over that period one would have reaped significant gains. Well, the best way to find out is to look at the history of a real company called Malayan Colleries.

Stage 1, Colonial to Independence: In 1918 Malayan Colleries Limited was founded. However, by the 1960s, the company's deposits had been exploited and all that remained was basically a shell company.

Stage 2, Independence to Pan-El: In 1965 the management of Malayan Colleries acquired Pan-Electric Industries and the company then changed its own name to Pan-Electric & General Industries. In 1973, the company changed its name again to PEGI. In 1978, PEGI spun off its Singapore business (this spin-off became the now infamous Pan-Electric Industries, which defaulted on US$400m when a series of share buybacks collapsed in 1985). Following the spin-off, PEGI's remaining assets were fixed deposits and once again it became a shell company.

Stage 3, the Great Commodities Boom and Bust: In 1979 Ghafar Baba bought a controlling stake in the PEGI shell. In early 1980 the company bought Dunlop Holdings of the UK. Within months, the recession in the UK resulted in a collapse at Dunlop Holdings. The company's other investment, the Golf Course Inn in the Cameron Highlands, lost money from the time it was acquired. In 1980 PEGI bought a 25% stake in what is now known as FACB. The value of the investment in FACB collapsed due to the company's badly timed and highly leveraged diversification into property. At the worst stage of the recession, PEGI lost the skills of Ghafar Baba when he was appointed deputy prime minister of Malaysia!

Stage 4, Malaysia Industrialises: By 1990, under the new management of Mah Siew Chin, the decision was taken to turn PEGI into a strong information technology company to benefit from the rapid industrialisation of Malaysia. Management acquired computer-related companies. What happened next is well described in *Changes of Ownership of KLSE Companies*: "Somehow things did not quite work out and Mah resigned as MD in 1993. In July 1994, shareholders of PEGI were advised that the company was selling off all the IT companies for RM4.25m cash in an MBO exercise."

Stage 5, the Great Property and Equity Boom: In 1994, following the failed venture into IT, the board decided to concentrate on property and particularly its development in Kepong Town Centre called Kepong Entrepreneurs' Park. In 1995, in a further move to reposition the business for the new era, the directors disposed of the remaining manufacturing assets to partly finance the acquisition of the Ipoh stockbroking company Kin Khoo & Co.

Stage 6, Imperial Ambitions: At the February 1996 AGM, the company's name was changed to Asia Pacific Holdings to reflect the fact that its new business strategy was to pursue infrastructure projects in China and India.

So, how is Asia Pacific Holdings faring as a property and broking company in these difficult days? For shareholders, there is good news and bad news. The good news is that the Kuala Lumpur Stock Exchange recently lifted the trading ban it placed on Kin Khoo due to issues concerning capital adequacy. The bad news is that losses in the year to 31 March 1998 were US$18.2m and the share price has fallen 90% from its 1997 levels. In fact the share price is now 21% below the level reached in 1987 following the resignation of Ghafar Baba and the great crash.

So will Malayan Colleries/Pan Electric & General Industries/PEGI/Asian Pacific Holdings disappear after 70 years of adventures in capitalism? Well, the company still has a market cap of US$18m and history suggests that only a fool would predict that it can't rise again. Such is the long-term nature of investment in emerging markets.

As we heard from Bagehot earlier, when there is 'blind capital' it will be devoured. There is never any shortage of local entrepreneurs who are enfranchised by the abundance of 'blind capital' to play whatever the game is in this particular boom. Malaysia just happened to provide some of the best examples of where some very old companies can be constantly reinvented to meet the demands of investors at any given time.

Throughout my time in Asia, the prevailing view among foreign investors was that they were bringing new and more sophisticated means of capital management to the region. My experience was that the locals were much more efficient in extracting capital at a good price to use it in whatever was likely to make money at that time. With most having shorter-term time horizons, often companies that sounded like industrial companies and showed investors their industrial capacity had actually bet the balance sheet on property speculation or whatever the other hot game in town might have been.

Locals are always better at working out the only game in town and leveraging someone else's capital to play it. Sometimes they are smart enough to hear the chimes at midnight, but often they are not. The foreign investor then often expresses outrage that gambling has been going on with the company's capital! This cycle seems to have been repeating since portfolio investors first plunged into emerging market portfolio assets with the liberation of Latin America from colonial rule in the 1820s.

Revulsion, pursuit cycling and passionate intensity

3 August 1998, Regional

On numerous previous occasions, *The Solid Ground* has quoted from Professor Kindelberger's work, which was based on the model created by Hyman Minsky. That model proved useful in indicating that the conditions for a crisis were present. During the crisis it proved useful in indicating that we had not yet reached the conditions which augured the end of the revulsion stage. However, the model now indicates that we are witnessing the end of the revulsion stage and thus the end of the downward swoop in Asian asset prices.

The evidence of revulsion is abundant. The trading volumes of the Asian equity markets are clear enough indicators that very few investors wish to play the Asian equity game. There is a growing list of cheap investments in Asia which are becoming cheaper on a daily basis and nobody wants to buy:

- Despite the equity recapitalisation of COCO, its convertible bond still yields 19% in US dollars to put/maturity.
- There are a host of listed companies which have been recapitalised by strategic partners at premium prices, but their share prices have not reacted positively.
- The valuations of US dollar-earning companies in Indonesia are only justifiable if the correct US dollar discount factor is three times the current US 30-year Treasury yield.
- The market capitalisation of Hong Kong, the financial capital of China, is less than that of GE.
- Many Asian insurance companies continue to report earnings growth but are trading on a fraction of embedded value.
- Currencies witnessing significant net buying still yield close to 20%.
- Small companies in Hong Kong are trading on 3× earnings.
- Some China stocks have market capitalisations which are just in excess of their cash balances.
- H shares are trading on 0.4× book at a time when the CCP is concentrating all its considerable firepower on the task of reflation.
- The market capitalisation of Indonesia's dominant cigarette company is ten days' worth of Philip Morris's cash flow.

Portfolio investors who were overweight these investments at much higher prices are now frightened to buy into the same investments at significantly lower prices. There are good reasons for fear. Fortune has not favoured the brave and in particular many investors have been badly impacted by their involvement in the Thai banks' rights issues of 1Q 1998. While many recognise the cheapness of such situations, there is a clear unwillingness to buy while share prices are going down. This is revulsion.

Kindelberger's model indicated that a lender of last resort would have to appear before the revulsion process would end. In Southeast Asia and South Korea it had proved, after a few failed attempts, to be the IMF that fulfilled that role. In August 1998 investors could not see a lender of last resort for China and Hong Kong. I had argued that China was quite capable of reflating its own economy without need for a lender of last resort, but there was still no evidence that it was doing so.

With the benefit of hindsight we can now see that the US Federal Reserve acted as the lender of last resort, not just for Asia in general, but for Hong Kong and China in particular. This was not yet evident by early August, but on 4 September Alan Greenspan spoke in California and stated that "it is just not credible that the United Sates can remain an oasis of prosperity" given what was happening in the rest of the world. He was not to cut US interest rates until later that month, but his willingness to do so had been flagged up by his speech of 4 September. Relief in the form of easier monetary policy from the central bank running the world's reserve currency was now just a few weeks away. Investors in Asian equities still had to weather the storms of August.

The great inflexion?

5 August 1998, Regional

So what happens if one company gains competitiveness through a falling currency while the other loses it? Well, if the Asian equity markets continue their slump, the answer to that question is that the share prices of both companies fall. This is intuitively incorrect. With the ports of Long Beach and San Francisco reporting Asian imports growing at 17% and 19% by volume, respectively, there is every reason to believe that Asia's competitiveness has increased dramatically at the expense of the United States. Surely that swing in competitiveness should depress the value of US capital and boost the value of Asian capital? Impacts on the real economies suggest that just such a movement should be underway.

Last week I counted over 60,000 redundancies by US companies in the preceding two months attributable to the impact of the Asian crisis. Analysts focus on the demand shock from lower Asian consumption and the growing supply coming from the region. However, they miss the key bear factor for the United States – the great capital expenditure boom is over.

There are already too many goods chasing too little demand. Increasingly, US companies are responding by buying the cheap capacity of Asia rather than by adding plant, machinery and equipment for their US facilities. Now an end to the capex boom within the United States itself would really put the brakes on the US economy and DJI earnings. Many who see the grinding halt to the capex boom believe that the ensuing manufacturing slowdown can be offset by the rise and rise of the services sector. If so, then things have changed dramatically in the United States.

It was too early to be talking about a decline in capital expenditure in the United States. US capital expenditure as a percentage of GDP rose from an already high 8.6% of GDP in 1998 to a post-world war two high of 9.3% of GDP in 2Q 2000. It then began a steady decline and, by the end of 2019, had reached just 5.5% of GDP, the lowest level recorded since 1963. A prolonged period of low investment did come to the United States, but not before a last surge from 1998 to 2000 that kept economic growth, spurred by lower inflation and interest rates, high and the stock market soaring.

The slowdown in capital expenditure in the United States came against a background of a rise in the country's non-financial corporate debt-to-GDP ratio from 189% in 1998 to 229% by the peak of the US business cycle in December 2007. This rapid rise in corporate debt occurred as the rate of capital investment declined, illustrating that something had changed and that aggressive financial engineering was underway. The market system adapted to the deflationary forces emanating from Asia in ways I had not foreseen in 1998.

Why is US$250bn not a large sum of money?

6 August 1998, Regional

A billion here, a billion there and sooner or later you're talking real money.

CEO of Ford following the recapitalisation of Jaguar Cars

I read in the newspapers that some very erudite investment bankers have calculated that US$250bn will be necessary to 'recapitalise Asia'. Even in the modern world of finance this is rather a large sum of money and clearly any investor can work out that if a US$250bn hole has to be filled, then the supply of corporate paper may significantly outstrip demand. It would thus clearly be dangerous to buy Asian equities before we have significantly eaten into that US$250bn pie. Or would it? No.

Before doing those sums we must begin by separating our financial world from the real world. While the real world consists of physical assets, the financial world consists of the capital structure which we choose to erect around such physical assets. The good news is that we have destroyed financial capital and not physical capital. Well, according to the best sources accreted around Asia's physical assets (and to which in our world we give a financial value), there is US$250bn more of financial liabilities than financial assets. Now let's see how in the modern world of finance you don't have to write a cheque for US$250bn to fill a US$250bn hole.

As with a corporate balance sheet, the US$250bn deficit is the gap between assets and liabilities. With the exception of the banks, where depositors are involved, those liabilities are basically shareholders' equity and loans. Immediately there is a clear difference here between an accounting item and writing that big cheque. What happens if I simply don't pay back all the liabilities?

Let's just start with stiffing the foreigners. According to the BIS data, foreign bankers have lent US$389bn to Asia and that does not include any sums accessed through the offshore banking sectors of Singapore and Hong Kong. Well, even if we pay back the local bankers in full, but get the foreigners to take 60¢ on the US dollar, the size of the financial hole has just shrunk by US$155bn to US$94bn.

Anybody who thinks that the foreign bankers are getting out of Asia with 100¢ on the dollar following an 80% fall in collateral values in US dollar terms should seek investment guidance from Enid Blyton. Thus more than half of this Asian problem is not Asian at all, but is a problem for the shareholders of the financial institutions of Belgium, Holland, France, Germany, the UK and the United States.

Cynics would say that such a hit to foreign commercial bankers would be the death-knell for Asia's future, as access to loans would dry up. Such cynics ignore the fact that the BIS banks increased their lending to Latin America by US$8bn from 1995 to 1996 and by US$22bn the next year, despite the losses associated with the tequila crisis. Such cynics ignore the fact that bankers are practised at lending to newly capitalised physical assets.

Donald Trump still has bankers and some of the physical assets of Adsteam are now recapitalised and considered blue-chip clients by Aussie bankers. Anyway, next time around, bankers will not be lending to AYZ Co of Thailand or even to the Thai government, but to a subsidiary or associate of ABC Multinational Corporation. That will be different.

It is just plain wrong to say that if foreign bankers take a 40¢ in the US dollar hit on their loan books, they will never lend to Asia again. In the write-down exercise there is no flow of cash, merely the recognition by foreign bankers that they have made a mistake, and suddenly the US$250bn problem has halved. Suddenly there is a US$94bn problem.

The existence of that US$94bn hole assumes that local bankers are repaid in full and, as we all know, that is very unlikely. Corporate liabilities are likely to shrink again as local banks get into the same write-down and rescheduling business as the foreign banks. The consensus seems to think that this time we'll be lucky to get away with 30% non-performing loans in the domestic commercial banks.

So the commercial banking sector will see a further reduction in its liabilities as the local banks do not get 100¢ on the dollar for their loans. Of course the cynic will proclaim that in this instance we are only moving the liability within the system from companies to commercial banks. They would suggest that this is an accounting legerdemain which will not shrink the US$94bn number any further. The cynic is wrong.

It is clearer by the day that a significant portion of the non-performing loans of the domestic sector will end up in government hands. This should not surprise anybody as it is exactly what happened in the United States during the savings and loan crisis and in Sweden where they nationalised the banks. It is standard operating procedure.

The governments are already in the business of raising funds to provide banks with cash in return for their non-performing loans. Full nationalisation may be necessary. The cynic will argue that this still has no effect on the US$94bn hole as we have only moved the problem from companies to commercial banks to government. Of course what the cynic fails to notice is that the hole in the balance sheet has passed from the private sector to the public sector.

We invest in the private sector. So when the bankers' equity has been written off, the government will end up with the remaining net liability of the commercial banking system. Clearly the legacy from the crisis is that public debts become much larger and debt-to-GDP ratios rise from their current negligible levels. However, the good news is that they would not rise so high as to preclude any future involvement in the EMU under the Maastricht criteria!

When the governments end up shouldering significant portions of private sector debt, the US$94bn hole begins to shrink very rapidly. Now it's time to get to the real money – foreign recapitalisation. Well, according to the Securities

Data Company, we have already seen US$8.2bn of MNC buying in Asia ex Japan in 1998, and the CLSA Recapitalisation Watch shows a rapid acceleration in deals since then. Now suddenly Asia's assets are being wrapped around a sustainable capital structure. The liabilities are shrinking as foreign banks take write-downs and the government shoulders some private sector liabilities and foreign equity is injected to do the rest.

Of course we are not recommending that you buy into any situation where the bankers get into the business of loan write-downs. They may require some equity participation to save face and the degree of dilution is unpredictable. It is possible to make money even when that occurs if the equity is priced cheaply enough and one correctly guesses the demeanour of the bankers. Profitable but risky.

At CLSA we are recommending companies that have passed our CLSA Stress Test™. They are companies with positive cash flows even today and where we foresee such positive cash flows being sustained throughout the economic downturn. Thus they are companies where the equity will not have to be partitioned.

In many cases these are companies which have already seen significant capital injections from strategic foreign investors. These investors can also see the positive cash flow situations and have provided the capital boost necessary to repair any damage caused by the rise in foreign currency liabilities. It is these cash-flow positive companies (which in some cases are already recapitalised) which will be the market leaders of tomorrow.

So US$250bn is a big number, but it is not a real number to the extent that it involves somebody writing a cheque for that sum. Once the bankers have suffered their now regular flagellation and the Asian governments have assumed their burden, the recapitalisation of Asia's private sector can be done for a fraction of the US$250bn number. As the flow of capital into Asia accelerates, it is clear that very rapidly a new capital structure is accreting around Asia's physical assets. Already we've had at least US$8.5bn in foreign capital inflows in six months. Remember, as the man said, "A billion here, a billion there and sooner or later you are talking real money."

Probably the most important factor in ending the crisis was that foreign bankers were persuaded to roll over their foreign currency loans to Asia. It was still a surprise just how much forbearance there was by foreign banks. From its peak in 1997, Thailand's external debt declined from US$93.4bn to just US$76bn by 1999. For South Korea, external debt in 1999 was the same as it had been in 1997, and for Indonesia, external debt fell more dramatically from US$163bn in 1997 to US$91bn in 1999.

The situation stabilised within a year and then, slowly at first, foreign currency debt began to rise again. The rush for the exits by foreign bankers stopped in most places even before the end of 1998. Often through persuasion from their central bankers, the commercial bankers stopped pulling credit from Asia and the capital hole stopped getting deeper. The headline number for the size of the recapitalisation caught the eye and dissuaded some from investing, but it ignored the realities of how bankers have to operate when faced with such huge potential losses.

Portfolio investors were very much outsiders looking into the crisis facing developed world bankers in Asia. We should have been making more effort to understand the dynamics at play and realise that at some stage the bankers would choose to extend and pretend with their Asian credit exposures, rather than pursue a prolonged retreat equivalent to a burnt earth strategy. This profound shift by bankers was not just crucial for the stability and recovery in Asia. It allowed developed world bank management to keep their loans to Asia at higher values on their balance sheets than would otherwise have been possible.

The fear I expressed that their losses in Asia would result in losses, diminution in capital and a constriction in their global lending was ill-founded. Had I realised just how powerful this force was in August 1998, I would not have been so focused on what seemed an inevitable deflationary crisis for the rest of the world flowing from Asia. The international banking cycle had turned and that was enough to stabilise the global financial system.

I was not the only one to miss that the extend and pretend approach by foreign commercial bankers would work. Global policy makers, fearing a global financial collapse, would now act aggressively to reflate the global economy as the ramifications from the Asian financial crisis were increasingly threatening the stability of their own financial systems.

Mr Schmidt goes to Singapore

7 August 1998, Global

In spite of their high rhetoric, threats, and claims that "cooperative" countries like Mexico and Venezuela would receive better terms than the prodigals, the banks finally caved into Argentina and gave it an even more lenient package than they had given Mexico the summer before. All of which proved to the world that the banks had never had any bargaining position in the first place. They never had a choice: if they refused to allow Argentina more time to pay off and more money in the meantime, they would have to declare default and take an excruciating blow to their earnings.

S C Gwynne, *Selling Money*, 1986

A visit to any financial bookshop will reveal a selection of wordy tomes on the workings of 'the credit cycle'. Jim Grant has made a profession out of analysing and interpreting that cycle in a series of books and in his newsletter. To the bystander, any analysis of the credit cycle is like some form of deranged Esperanto where enthusiasts attempt to rival each other in their knowledge of the obscure.

I plead guilty to joining in what has become a satisfyingly unfashionable – but by no means redundant – pursuit. There should be an onus on all those who engage in the demonic Esperanto to give it a human face and make it understandable to all. It is thus time to write the history, not of the credit cycle, but of the credit officer cycle. It is time to prepare the groundwork for such a study and simultaneously show how Asia is just reaching a very bullish stage of the credit officer cycle.

Following are two purely fictional accounts of the credit officer cycle in two purely fictitious commercial banks. The first is an attempt by me – who has never worked in commercial banking – to construct the typical credit officer cycle. The second analysis has been submitted by an ex-commercial banker who does not wish to be named. It is expressed in terms of memos which were or were not actually written, depending upon how many beers the author has had at the time.

The Credit Officer Cycle I

One day in 1992, the CEO of Big European Bank was reading his copy of *Newsweek*. *Newsweek* carried an article about the huge sums of capital which were needed in Asia to finance the high levels of growth in general and more specifically to upgrade the infrastructure. Now business was not good in Europe as economic growth was sluggish. Everybody knew that Asia was undergoing an economic miracle and what could be safer than lending for infrastructure development?

The CEO thus suggested to the board that they get into the business of lending money in Asia, where demand was clearly so large and risks low. Sometime in early 1993, Big European Bank set up an office in Singapore. They hired some credit officers with local experience and a chief credit officer, Mr Wong, who was known to have the necessary good local 'contacts'. Big European Bank then got into the business of using its high credit ratings to access US dollar funds in the euro markets and pass these funds onto the Asian borrower while taking a nice mark-up.

With no domestic Asian currency bond markets, demand was very strong. The beauty of the whole situation was that the Asian borrowers were generating de facto US dollars, their exchange rates were fixed, to service the US dollar loans and the economic miracle underpinned cash flows and asset prices. With business so good, Big European bank kept pushing more and more funds towards the Singapore office as it was still difficult to lend in Europe.

The credit officers were strained to lend the funds, particularly as all the other European banks had now caught onto this neat low-risk business opportunity. Mr Wong had to pump his contacts harder and harder to be at the top of the list of those from whom borrowers would accept money. Of course, one day in 1997 the borrowers were not generating de facto US dollars and there was no Asian economic miracle.

After several months, when interest payments from Asian borrowers to Big European Bank were non-existent, Mr Wong was summoned to head office. He explained how bad things had got and expressed an opinion that not only would they not receive interest, but that an 80% collapse in collateral values would mean that they should not expect much return of principal. He believed with judicious rescheduling they could get back 60¢ on the US dollar in due course.

The board was furious. How could their chief credit officer have lent so badly? How could they trust him to extricate them from this terrible relationship with his 'contacts'? Did Mr Wong really believe that they could take a provision that was 40% of the billions of US dollars they had lent?

To sort out the mess, Big European Bank selected one of their young thrusters from head office. They would see whether he had the mettle to turn things around and was cut out for senior management. Sadly, Mr Schmidt sent back a report featuring the complete incompetence of the previous credit team, the lax administrative procedures and the optimistic recovery forecasts of Mr Wong. He was convinced that much bigger write-downs would be necessary. He convinced the board that it was best to forget this exotic foray, take provisions equivalent to 60% of loans and let him get on with the business of salvaging what he could.

The board could see no other option. Over the next two years, the high-flyer cut deals across Asia against the cushion of the big provisions on the balance sheet and he actually managed to salvage about 50¢ on the US dollar. Big European Bank got a write-back, and high-flyer got a promotion to head of global credit with a big corner office.

Following the write-down, the much smaller Singapore office then sees no bad loans for a prolonged period of time and it makes good profits. Indeed, as the economy starts to pick up it is increasingly able to lend to good credits at good prices … etc.

The good news for Asia is that we have reached the stage when Mr Schmidt's report has hit the CEO's desk in Europe and Big European Bank is now committed to write-downs in Asia. The shifting of a significant portion of the Asian debt burden to Europe can now begin.

The Credit Officer Cycle II

Memo 1: For weeks, the line has been complaining about the role of head office in restricting marketing officers from getting on with the job, and waking up to the opportunities out here in Asia. Competitors are jumping ahead; just today we lost three more transactions which could have generated US$4m in income, and we have these expensive overheads to pay for.

Memo 2 (sometime later): We know the conditions back in head office are slow and that unless revenue increases our ranking at home will slip. We are delighted the Chairman was able to recently tour Asia (he got to walk on the Great Wall of China, ride a sampan down the Li River, play golf in Bali and even visit Ho Chi Minh City). His announcement about the bank support for Asia has been splashed all over the local papers.

Memo 3 (sometime later): The decentralised credit process is a great success. Decisions are being made locally, where there is good understanding of local conditions. We have been able to catch up to our competitors (but we shouldn't become complacent as they are hitting us hard on pricing and have relaxed most of their documentation criteria). Our prime minister is visiting next month and our best corporate clients will be invited to the reception which we are sponsoring at the new hotel (we helped finance this) in the new business district (we also helped finance most of this). Our clients love us, and more and more opportunities are opening up.

Memo 4 (sometime later): Yes, we know one or two clients have had some teething problems with their new plants, but by extending terms and conditions we will be sure to keep their good patronage. We have now fully investigated documentation and our legal rights, through local lawyers, but as most of our facilities are on position (unsecured), it isn't that relevant. In many cases, it would be embarrassing to ask our clients to now provide security, after such a long relationship.

Memo 5 (sometime later): We are distressed to hear that the credit department is being closed down and credit officers are being called back to head office. We don't believe this is the right move, as the current problems we are experiencing are certainly just teething ones and related to a hiccup in the business cycle.

Memo 6 (sometime later): The massive provisions made by the bank for its Asian exposure have been blamed on macroeconomic developments that were unforeseeable. Contagion has exacerbated problems, with the region contaminated by bad debts. Credit controls have been tightened and we are confident no future reoccurrences are likely.

Memo 7 (quite sometime later): For weeks the line has been complaining about the role of head office in restricting marketing officers from getting on with the job and waking up to the opportunities out here in Asia. Competitors are jumping ahead; just today we lost three more transactions which could have generated US$4m in income, and we have these expensive overheads to pay for.

The good news for investors in Asia is that memo 6 has just been written and sometime later you can expect memo 7.

I had written the first of these scenarios and my friend Richard Pyvis, a former banker from Australia then running CLSA's direct investment business, had written the second. I failed to understand the full global ramifications of the fact that we had got as far as memo 6, where developed world bank capital had been preserved and very soon falling interest rates would spur another credit cycle. I had left Asia by the time memo 7 arrived, but of course it did arrive and once again credit flowed freely throughout Asia.

Credit officers received some very potent signals during the Asian financial crisis that they were not to forget. That the IMF, supported by developed world governments, could help to reduce their losses in offshore foreign currency lending was something they already knew, but it was nice to have it confirmed. The real revelation was that central banks, particularly the US Federal Reserve, would alter monetary policy in reaction to problems in the credit system. In early August we still did not understand that the tail could wag the dog. The revelation that changed the world of credit forever would come only in late September from a building in Greenwich, Connecticut. Before we understood that and got to bask in the power of lower US dollar interest rates, Hong Kong had to endure another attack on its exchange rate.

As my time in Asia was coming to an end I thought it might be a good idea to do some research for a book. The Taiwanese stock market was increasingly open to foreigners, but it was very clear that this was another Asian market that was idiosyncratic. Of course, every market had its experts so I decided to write a book called *Investing with the Taiwan Masters* and so I journeyed to Taipei to interview the five fund managers with the best risk-adjusted returns.

I was delighted that they were all prepared to meet me and some of them spoke English. I always began with the preamble by explaining why I had come to see them and congratulating them on their excellent performance. The first question was always the same: "To what do you attribute your ability to produce high risk-adjusted returns through your investment in the Taiwan stock market?" The answer was the same in each case whether in English or Mandarin: "Special informations."

No doubt one would have received a very similar answer from investors in the City of London many decades before. That was until trading on "special informations" was made illegal. It would have been too short a book to have found favour with a publisher. While I was in Taipei the financial ground shook in Hong Kong and the Asian financial crisis was ending with a bang and not a whimper.

From the end of August 1998 interest rates had been ticking up again in Hong Kong. It was widely understood that this was the result of what was known as the 'double play'. In September 1997 the capital exodus had spiked Hong Kong dollar interest rates higher and the result had been a 40% decline in the Hang Seng Index. Some investors now reasoned that they could engineer a capital exodus and profit if they had short sold the Hang Seng Index. They reasoned that they would make much more money shorting the equity market than they might lose by borrowing Hong Kong dollars and selling those dollars to create a capital exodus and a spike higher in interest rates.

I had argued from September 1997 that such a play would not be attempted because it would fail. The shock of September 1997 and the slowdown in Asia was clearly impacting GDP growth in Hong Kong and it seemed likely that there had been a major improvement in the SAR's current account situation. The more that deficit disappeared the more difficult it would be for an engineered capital outflow to force the HKMA to intervene in the foreign exchange markets, thus forcing local interest rates up and most likely the Hang Seng Index down.

I also reasoned that foreign portfolio investors had already sold large positions in Hong Kong equities and even if they were panicked into selling, as I had witnessed in September 1997, their selling would be much more limited than it had been. The attack on the currency board system in September 1997 therefore seemed to me to have acted to significantly strengthen the system and made any attack on the Hong Kong dollar even less likely to be successful.

A second episode occurred in January 1998, associated with the collapse of Peregrine Securities, and this was only likely to have further improved Hong Kong's external accounts. It was clear that some investors disagreed with my prognosis that the improvement in Hong Kong's external accounts made further attacks on the currency board system futile and by August 1998 the 'double play' was back on. It is not clear just how much money was borrowed to achieve the aim of pushing interest rates higher by selling Hong Kong dollars, but it was enough to push interest rates higher and by 13 August they were 300bp higher than US rates. The tactic was working because in the first nine trading days of August the Hang Seng Index had fallen by 16%.

Sometime in that period Gary Coull came to see me and said that someone connected with the government had asked if we might have any ideas about what could be done to counteract the so-called 'double play'. I only had one idea and that was that China could announce it was diversifying some of its US dollar foreign exchange reserves into Hong Kong dollars. The prospect of such inflow into the Hong Kong dollar would, I argued, more than deter capital outflow, keep interest rates low and prevent any profits being made in shorting the Hang Seng Index.

That was an action that would have horrified many in terms of interfering with the market mechanism through which the price and quantity of money were allowed to adjust through market forces. I didn't much like it myself, but neither did I like what seemed to be clear manipulation of the price and quantity of money by investors for their gain, but at a huge cost to the local economy and people.

It was possible that the mere threat to diversify China's reserves in such a fashion would have been enough to turn the tide of capital flows. This was a diversification that could always be reversed again once it was proven to be effective in preventing profits from the 'double play'. It was not difficult to argue that there were sound fundamental reasons why China should hold a large portion of its reserves in Hong Kong dollars given its significant trading relationship with the SAR.

I wrote a brief paper on that idea which went to Gary and that was the last I heard of that. Somebody, though, did have an idea that was to be actioned, and that action really horrified many people in the financial markets in Hong Kong and well beyond.

On the morning of Friday, 14 August, representatives of the SAR's three largest stockbrokers were called to a breakfast meeting at the China Club in Hong Kong. They were invited by the local government's Finance Bureau, but were surprised when they arrived to meet Norman Chan of the HKMA, the body that operated the currency board system. The HKMA placed large buy orders for Hong Kong equities that morning. Those purchases were to be carried out in secret that day and the buying was to last for ten days. The plan was to deprive the speculators of the prospect of profiting from their short position on the Hang Seng Index and thus nullify their prospects of profits from the double play – their cost of borrowing Hong Kong dollars had already risen to make one part of the trade less attractive.

If the plan worked, the speculators would be forced to close down their shorts on both the Hong Kong dollar and the Hang Seng Index and interest rates would return to normal. It worked, and the Hang Seng Index rose that day and so far it has never returned to the levels witnessed at the height of the 'double play'.

The Hang Seng Index rose 8.5% that Friday, and after the close the Hong Kong government announced the plan. There was instant outrage, particularly from the financial community. It was seen as the end of Hong Kong by many. This was clearly the end of the 'positive non-interventionism' that Sir John Cowperthwaite and others had bequeathed to Hong Kong. It was a sign that the state would be allocating resources and not the private sector.

Alan Greenspan criticised the action and Milton Friedman called the action "insane". Capital outflow from Hong Kong accelerated as this fear of what the apparent end of *laissez-faire* policies meant for the future of the SAR. So while the Hang Seng Index continued to rise, Hong Kong interest rates went even higher and closed at a peak of 19% on 28 August.

There were many in financial markets who thought that this intervention would mean the end of the currency board system. One day in that period someone came to see me in the glass koala to tell me that there were queues at the banks, bank runs had begun and the markets had concluded that it was the end for the Hong Kong dollar's link to the US dollar.

Well, if the end had come, I thought I had better go and see it. I went downstairs and walked through Admiralty and stopped at every bank I could find. What I saw were indeed the large queues of people that I had been told about. However, it was not a bank run. Yes, there were people withdrawing their Hong Kong dollar deposits and switching to US dollar deposits. However, there were also plenty of local people who were switching from US dollars to Hong Kong dollars given the very attractive interest rates then on offer. I could see the financial community panicking, but I did not see the people of Hong Kong panicking and the currency board held firm; and as of 2020 the Hong Kong dollar remains pegged to the US dollar at its 1998 level.

I was not in Hong Kong on 14 August or for most of the following week and did not then put anything on paper regarding my own reaction. A few weeks later though, I wrote the following:

> With so much nonsense currently talked about in reference to Hong Kong's structure, it is worthwhile returning again to the role which net buying or selling of the Hong Kong dollar plays in determining all the other key factors which set Hong Kong's asset prices. Recently I read an article on Bloomberg by David De Rosa, stating that Hong Kong had joined Malaysia in choosing the road of the isolationist as the way forward. When people start describing Hong Kong as isolationist, yet presumably laud the free market approach of European nations such as France, it is time to get back to the very basics. For almost all of its history, Hong Kong has operated a currency board system. It continues to do so. Thus, asset prices will be determined for the net demand for the Hong Kong dollar. It really couldn't be simpler. Now in France, things are very different and one had better beware the government and its heavy hand when attempting to determine the direction of asset prices. So again, back to basics. Why is it that supply and demand of Hong Kong dollars is basically all that matters as one seeks to forecast the direction of equity prices in Hong Kong? ... This analyst believes that the destructive market forces in Hong Kong have run their course.

On 17 August Russia devalued the ruble and on 19 August it defaulted on its foreign currency debt. Investors had bet against the exchange rate value of the Hong Kong dollar, but had bet big on the stability of the ruble because Russia was 'too nuclear to fail'. It was a bad month to be in the currency speculation business. When shocks of this magnitude occur and gearing is high there is likely to be a casualty. It was the scale and provenance of the casualty that was to shock financial markets.

Lament for the Durian

2 September 1998, Malaysia

Here's the story of the Durian
The fruit the authorities came to blame
For what it never did
Put it in a prison cell
But one time it could have been
The champion of the world.

'After Hurricane' (with apologies to Mr Dylan)

So farewell then, Malaysian equity market. From emerging market supernova to black hole of capital in five years. Mr Warhol would be agog at how you 18 million people stretched your 15 minutes to almost ten years – Spice Girls take note. Congratulations on your achievement. Your market capitalisation-to-GDP ratio ascended to the world's highest as the world's unrealistic expectations accumulated on your shoulders.

Mr McWhirter, from the *Guinness Book of Records*, racked up Malaysia Airlines platinum card status with the need for frequent visits to your country. You raised the capital to build the world's two largest buildings. You set your sights high on Putrajaya, the Multi-Media Super Corridor, the longest building in the world, the city on stilts and an artificial island the size of the Isle of Man (this last, surely, just an act of folly).

Through an accident of history, the MSCI bequeathed upon you a lower cost of capital than most nations could dream of. With such a bequest it was easy to challenge the alleged efficiency of markets. Like Sydney, Dallas, Tokyo and London's Docklands, you took the opportunity to think big when the cost of capital was small. In *The Malay Dilemma* you gave us the blueprint for the creative and then destructive dynamics of wealth redistribution through an equity market.

On the way up it worked with all the deadly precision of a Swiss watch. Predictable and beautiful and so easy to understand. Now fashion has changed. Now to foreigners you are like your much misunderstood Durian – prickly on the outside and stinking in the middle. So when does *guanxi* become crony capitalism? When share prices fall.

So farewell then, Malaysian equity market, may we meet again – when the current generation of global investors has retired or is bullish on Bangladesh; when *The Sun* and *The Daily Inquirer* extol the virtues of emerging market equity diversification; when the word 'Renong' is condemned to the dustbin of history like Pan-Electric; when having the world's two tallest buildings will once again be considered an asset and not a liability; when, like Myanmar, no international investor can find you on the map in the boardroom; when your share certificates line the walls of august investment houses in the City of London, 18 months before you are restored to the MSCI indices; and when the Durian is once again considered to be a uniquely Asian fruit with uniquely 'Asian values'.

Farewell. Travel safely. Keep your head above the waters and your eyes fixed on the other side of the river. For we will see you again but in another distant cycle. It may be a long wait but always remember the words of Virgil:

Forsan et hoec olim meminisse iuvabit
(One day, perhaps, it will be a delight to remember even these things)

Selamat Jalan

It was not until 1 September 1998 that the Malaysian prime minister had had enough and imposed capital controls. That it had taken this long, given his long-professed views regarding the iniquity of 'foreign speculators', should have been the only surprise. Sadly, for many investors it did come as a surprise and some dreadful conversations were then to be had with both their boss and the end client. I had surmised in December 1997 that equity investors would be trapped in Malaysia by capital controls, but most investors refused to believe it was possible and now here it was.

In this eulogy for Malaysia I got a bit carried away. Most foreign observers at this time were strongly supporting the reformer Anwar Ibrahim, who promised to bring not just economic change but more democracy to Malaysia. Anwar was sacked from his government posts on the day this report was written and expelled from the ruling party. By 20 September he was in jail. That a country following such a path could continue as a member of the international community seemed unlikely.

Malaysian GDP rebounded strongly in 1999 and life went on. Renong, the poster child for conglomerate expansion in the boom, was seized by the government in 2001 on the basis that it posed a threat to the stability of the country's financial system. The country's return to the MSCI indices happened much more quickly than I would ever have dared forecast – in February 2000. The *FT* has composed an index that tracks the return on Malaysian equities before and through the crisis to the current day. In US dollar terms, the Malaysian Stock Index in 2020 was 26% below the level it reached at its peak on 5 January 1994.

Most of the pieces reproduced in this book were written in the early hours of the morning in Hong Kong and usually published by 9 am Hong Kong time. They were written in haste and of course one often forgot that their circulation was wider than just the investment community. I was subsequently told that this comment calling Malaysia "the Durian republic" was read out by an opposition MP in the country's parliament and I would be wise to avoid travelling to Malaysia for the foreseeable future. I have travelled to Malaysia many times but only once tried the Durian. That is not an uncommon occurrence.

Need the world sleep easier?

8 September 1998, Global

Oh Lord, won't you short me
Some Daimler-Benz
My friends are long treasuries
I must make amends
Worked hard all my lifetime
No help from my friends,
Oh Lord, won't you short me
Some Daimler-Benz.

(Apologies to Janis)

The rally in European equities yesterday was truly amazing. It suggests an act of mass delusion in these markets if the rally in Asian equities was really a catalyst for that movement. So events in Asia resulted in a 1.2% rise in the price of Daimler-Benz, but the global deflationary dynamic has not been reversed … There are three key forces driving the upward movement in Asian equities and all three are inherently bearish for European and US equities.

The first short-term phenomenon is that the upward surge in Asian markets is an act of short covering by highly leveraged distressed investors. That need to cover and realise what liquid assets they can indicates growing distress in the global financial system. Combined with the bankers' existing growing distressed loans in the emerging markets, it is probably the tip of the iceberg in relation to a contraction in credit in the global system.

In particular, that credit contraction is likely to begin in the financial markets where risks to lenders have appeared low in bull markets but are rapidly showing their true colours as highly risky. If the surge in Asian markets is partly driven by this contraction in credit and short covering, then it is clearly a bear indicator for the European and US stock markets and not a bullish indicator.

At least as importantly, the movement in the Asian equity markets represents the fact that the Asian markets are the most adapted to the new deflationary dynamics. The devaluations of last year and the ensuing economic chaos have resulted in unskilled wages in Asia plummeting in US dollar terms. As part of this dislocation, domestic demand has ground to a halt. Asia is now selling more than it is buying. Across the rest of the world, all the other emerging markets are trying to adjust to these new Asian surpluses.

Simply put, events in Asia and Japan have forced everybody else to sell less and thus to begin to adjust internal demand accordingly so that fixed exchange rates can be defended. In Asia this has already happened, particularly in South Korea, Thailand, Hong Kong and China, where such adjustments have been made and large surpluses are being racked up.

In a deflationary environment, the safest place to invest is in those markets which are racking up large current account surpluses. This is only true should those surpluses be matched by a stability in the movement of capital and that is the stage which Asia is now reaching, with MNC capital being a very positive force when combined with the current account surpluses. Clearly this dynamic is not good news for European and US markets. Asia has only reached this new equilibrium by buying less from the rest of the world and selling more. Neither of those swings in supply and demand could be characterised as a positive for Europe or the United States. They are clearly negatives, which will in turn force an adaptation in the United States and Europe to the deflationary dynamic.

The size of that adjustment will be on a much smaller scale than that which occurred in Europe. However, the adjustment has yet to begin and it is either a currency adjustment or an adjustment to the price of domestic unskilled wages which may only be achievable through a recession. Asian equity markets are recovering as the world realises that they are well progressed through the adjustment phase and thus perhaps risk premiums should be falling and not rising. However, they have only got to this stage by pushing the problem across the globe. That is clearly not good news for US and European equity markets.

So the world should not be sleeping easier. The recovery of Asia's asset prices is at the expense of spreading instability in the rest of the world. The bad news is that equity markets in the rest of the world will continue to suffer negative impacts. The good news is that Asia will continue to outperform against both emerging market and developed market equities.

This piece was very wrong. The cuts in US interest rates and the decline in the US dollar exchange rate worked almost magically not just to stabilise demand, but to accelerate it. Look at any chart of developed world economic growth in 1998 and 1999 and there is little sign that anything perturbed the economic expansion of that period.

With the benefit of hindsight, we know that the impact on some forms of labour was to be dreadful and many skilled and unskilled jobs were to be wiped out, but that happened over a long period and at a pace that did not interrupt consumption-led growth in the developed world. I was not the only one who then expected a dreadful deflationary bust to spread from Asia to the rest of the world:

> The annual meetings of the IMF and World Bank were renowned for glittery social gatherings, and the conclave held the first week of October 1998 was no different, notwithstanding the dismal state of global economic affairs ... Yet as the liquor flowed, the tuxedo-clad waiters hovered, and the string quartets serenaded, the mood among the partygoers was bleak, sometimes shockingly so. Vernon Jordan, the high-powered attorney and Clinton golfing buddy, held a dinner party in his northwest Washington home, and asked five or six of his most prominent guests, including Larry Summers and Jim Wolfensohn, to say something after dinner about where the global economy was going. Their assessments "all had the same world-is-coming-to-an-end theme", recalled James Harmon, then President of the U.S. Export-Import Bank, whose wife remarked to him as they were leaving the party: "My God, we're all going to be buying canned goods!"

Paul Blustein, *The Chastening: Inside the Crisis that Rocked the Global Financial System and Humbled the IMF*, 2001

It was at this same annual meeting that world policy makers discussed establishing a new financial architecture for the world. They failed to agree. We continue to live with the dangerous consequences of that failure.

Oops, there goes another rubber tree plant

11 September 1998, Global

The only perfect hedge is in a Japanese garden.

Gene Rotberg, former World Bank treasurer

Well, that slow-motion car crash continues, with very predictable shards of glass and crumpling of metal. Three highly predictable events occurred yesterday – the deflationary pressure continued to batter Latin American equity markets, the Bank of Austria doubled its provisions for losses in Russia and the United States reported its biggest ever trade deficit.

Day after day it's the same. Last night Latin America entered the end game as interest rates rose and capital's rush for the door accelerated. Equity markets were impacted: Mexico −9.8%, Argentina −13.3%, Brazil −15.8%. Brazil lost at least US$1.8bn in capital flight according to central bank estimates. That brings the total since August to US$16bn. The yield spread on its US dollar debt increased a further 274bp to 1,710 basis points over US Treasuries.

Still the great debate goes on as to whether they will or won't devalue the currency. This debate is truly a waste of time for the equity investor. It's either devaluation or deflation, in response to the surge in the number of very cheap people in Asia. Now why would you want to be long equities during either deflation or devaluation? In October last year you could have chosen to be long Hong Kong or long South Korea. Now one devalued and you lost a lot of money and the other deflated and you lost quite a lot less. However, even where the currency held you lost money.

Asian stock markets had bottomed on 1 September and a recovery was underway in global stock markets. However, the crisis did roll onto Latin America and the IMF was soon to create a package of support. The Brazilian real was devalued, falling from 1.2 to the US dollar to 2.1 between January and March 1999. Perhaps it was that devaluation that marked the end of the crisis, or was it the appointment of a new central bank governor in Brazil – a former adviser to George Soros?

Asia rising?

18 September 1998, Global

Well it's been a long time, but in the past month or so Asia has finally begun to outperform global markets.

As suggested yesterday, at this stage the BOJ is doing its turn centre stage and attempting to produce a consumption boom which would move Japan rapidly into a current account deficit. I believe the chances of that being successful are at best one in ten, but most investors seem to think that one in a 100 would be a fairer price to quote on this one.

Anyway, at some stage it seems highly likely that the steward of the world's reserve currency will have to get into the business of providing liquidity relief to prevent the global commercial banking system producing a huge global credit contraction. So the US dollar is likely to face a larger trade deficit, a rapid slowdown in capital inflows and the prospect of lower domestic interest rates. Now how dangerous is it to have a global investment portfolio so aggressively betting on a weak yen and a strong US dollar?

The biggest beneficiaries of all of these dynamics are Asian equities. If Japan takes up the easy money running, and problems with the US dollar mean no collapse in the yen, then Asia benefits. Should Japan's efforts fail, the United States kicks in, adding even greater liquidity globally and even further increasing the prospects of a weak US dollar. If these efforts to prevent a major global credit contraction fail, would you rather be in a major deficit country with the prospect of collapsing capital inflows or in a surplus region where the capital exodus is over (if only in some cases because capital extraction is not possible)?

The blip since early August that has produced an outperformance in Asia relative to other global equities is sustainable. It represents the major inflexion point for currencies and markets which *The Solid Ground* suggested was occurring in early August ('The Great Inflexion' – 5 August 1998). It is still not too late to overweight Asian equities.

It was the move by Alan Greenspan to reduce interest rates that finally stopped the long rise of the US dollar and the long decline of the yen. The Asian authorities were getting into the business of managing their exchange rates relative to the US dollar again and now they were linking to a weak currency. From its low on 1 September 1998, the MSCI Asia ex Japan Index rose 133% to a peak in early February 2000. That was quite a recovery, but it was still a sideshow to the main capital market party, as over the same period the S&P500 rose by more than 50%.

That rise in the US stock market took equity valuations in the world's largest stock market to new record highs and ended the careers of many equity investors who had used the historic range of equity valuations as a guide to future returns. Far from setting the scene for a deflationary bust, the Asian financial crisis had set the scene to accelerate one of the greatest US equity bull markets in history. New record high valuations were to be justified by a conclusion that new record low risks were on offer. There was a problem in Greenwich, Connecticut, and a solution brewing to that problem at the headquarters of the Federal Reserve Bank of New York that would transform investors' perception of risk and kick-start the age of debt.

The decomposing composers

24 September 1998, Global

There appear to have been some problems at Mr Meriwether's Long-Term Capital Management (LTCM). According to the newswires, emergency credit lines have had to be extended. LTCM is no ordinary fund management company. Let Bloomberg explain:

> Many of Meriwether's partners, including Lawrence Hilibrand and Eric Rosenfield, helped Salomon earn billions of dollars trading bonds. Hilibrand, for example, collected a US$23m pay check in 1991 for the profits he generated. Together the partners accounted for more than a third of the firm's capital. They were among Wall Street's stars. Robert Merton is a Harvard Business School economist who won the Nobel Prize for economics last year with Myron Scholes for work in valuing options.

Well there are three potential scenarios which would explain this little local difficulty. Each has radically different consequences for global markets.

1) The fund is suffering the natural consequences from too much gearing in a bad market. The consequences for the markets from this are bad but not terrible. The LTCM experience may change other commercial bankers' perspective on the risk characteristics of credit extended to hedge funds. If that occurs then there will be a further contraction in the credit in the financial markets. It is very difficult to estimate how large the credit outstanding to the hedge funds still is. Anyway, this is just another straw in the wind of the contraction in credit which is inevitable anyway given the apparent major diminution in developed world bank capital. The pace of contraction would accelerate. Of course it may be good news for the assets which the hedge funds are short as they scramble to cover and pay back their creditors. Good news for Hong Kong equities?

2) Mr Meriwether and the ex-Salomon's team got their equations wrong. This is very bearish for global markets. Among the binarist cognoscenti (definition: those who believe that 0 and 1 have all the answers for forecasting), LTCM are the star players. If they can get it wrong then there must be a prospect that the lesser binarists might be having problems with their equations. This is terrible

news. According to the BIS there is US$30trn outstanding in interest rate swaps alone. If the big binary guns could get the equations wrong then how big could the mispricing in the global derivatives business be? Of course the reply will be that such mispricing will come out in the wash in our new hedged world and thus there is not a problem. However, the wealth swings away from one bank and to another due to mispricing could threaten the stability of that bank. Then who is hedged? If even the boys at LTCM have got a problem with their equations, then the world has got a potentially massive problem.

3) There's a problem with Mr Merton's and/or Mr Scholes' equations. This does not even bear thinking about. If any of those equations are wrong, it is difficult to see how we have a global financial system.

The good news is that scenario 1 is probably the most likely of these three scenarios. This means that the LTCM simply speeds up the already highly likely contraction in credit in the financial markets. It means that things start to happen very fast from here and the safest positions in the world are those which are the reverse of the global hedge funds. Great news for Asian equity investors, particularly those in Hong Kong.

Anyway, another era in global investment appears to be fading away. In days of yore, Mr Morgan moved the markets and investors hung on every word of Jesse Livermore. Then it was the turn of Bernie Baruch to stride the stage. Latterly, Gerry Tsai and the other gunslingers had all the answers. As the decades pass new composers arrive and new tunes are played. The pantheon fills up but the music goes on forever and as the Monty Python team once reminded us, "you can still hear Beethoven, but Beethoven cannot hear you" (The Decomposing Composers: Jones, Palin, Tomlinson).

On the night of 21 September 1998, a cross-section of US commercial banks had been called into the offices of the New York Federal Reserve and told that they need to work out a rescue plan for a company called Long-Term Capital Management. The tale of the collapse of this investment company has been well told elsewhere, but it had become simply too big to fail given the likely consequences had it been forced to unwind its highly leveraged positions in financial markets quickly.

The bailout allowed an orderly unwinding of the company's positions, but even more importantly there followed, in quick succession, three cuts in US interest rates. To most financial market participants it had become clear, rightly or wrongly, that the monetary policy of the world's reserve currency would react to bail out those investors who had made bad bets – if they had made them in sufficient scale to threaten the stability of the financial system.

Where once the so-called 'happy Puritan', former US Federal Reserve Chairman William McChesney Martin, had declared that the job of the Federal Reserve was "to take away the punchbowl just as the party got going", here was a central banker determined to permit parties but keen to prevent hangovers. Investors are very good at working out what the new game is in town, and it was now clear that it was more leverage and not the less leverage that I had expected to be the consequence of the deflationary bust emanating from Asia. That much of this leverage was to be concentrated on financial markets and not in the addition of productive capacity was to define the age of debt that followed.

The willingness and alacrity with which the US Federal Reserve altered interest rates surprised almost everyone, and it worked. Global economies shrugged off the deflationary shock emanating from Asia. By 1999 the Asian economies were growing again and South Korea's real growth rate that year was an astonishing 10.7%.

Investors learned a very powerful lesson as to the power of the US Federal Reserve and how, if changes in financial markets imperilled its economic targets, they could expect the US Federal Reserve to respond with lower interest rates. There was an enticing prospect that the tail, in the form of financial markets, could wag the dog that was the monetary policy of the central bank running the world's reserve currency.

It was an enticing prospect because if the central banks, and particularly the US Federal Reserve, could be relied upon to clean up after bubbles, rather than seek to prick them, the use of much more leverage was a very likely road to riches. It proved to be so and in the United States and elsewhere, debt-to-GDP levels spiralled ever higher. There were more composers of financial engineering than ever.

In 2002 I met Paul Volcker for the first time at a conference in the Bahamas. He was complimentary about my forecast concerning growing structural weaknesses in the US banking system, though of course it was another five years before those weaknesses were exposed. Volcker never, in my experience, criticised his successor, but certain comments on what was going on in the world made it clear that he did not fully approve of the course of US monetary policy.

Later, over drinks, I asked him one on one when he thought that US monetary policy had begun to go wrong. He answered with just four letters: "LTCM." The US Federal Reserve's intervention to organise the bailout of LTCM, but more importantly the interest rate cuts that followed soon after, changed the world. The new financial architecture, which was the legacy of the Asian financial crisis, meant that cheap credit would be abundant as Asia's booming foreign exchange reserves and lower export prices depressed developed world inflation and interest rates.

It was also clear, following Greenspan's adjustment in monetary policy to save an over-leveraged hedge fund, that operating with ever higher amounts of debt was safer than previously thought. The policy choices in Asia and the United States in response to the first major deflationary crisis of the post-world war two period had built the foundations for the age of debt.

I also later met Myron Scholes when we both spoke at an investment conference in Frankfurt. I spoke on financial history and he listened and we discussed the presentation. We both stayed for the gala dinner afterwards, not knowing that the main entertainment was 45 minutes of stand-up comedy – in German. A few days later he asked me by email why I thought financial history was a science and I replied that it wasn't. That was the end of the conversation. The binarist and the historian should be friends, but as with the cowboy and the farmer, this is easier said than done.

The future in black and pink

23 September 1998, Global

Well another day and another truly incredible copy of the *FT*. Under normal circumstances there can be little value in simply regurgitating quotations from a newspaper you will have read yesterday. However, on this occasion, tomorrow's fish and chip wrapping contains information which should be right at the top of the agenda for the global investment community, but which seems to play second fiddle to the playful pedantics of the US president. So apologies to those of you who have read yesterday's *FT*, but here are some excerpts which should be cause for emergency meetings of global asset allocation committees:

> The International Monetary Fund said yesterday that controls on inward movement of capital could be a useful tool for some countries, and admitted that opening economies prematurely to free flows of capital constituted "an accident waiting to happen".
>
> Given that there are limits to the pace at which financial sectors can be strengthened, policymakers need to undertake an orderly opening of their financial systems and may need to consider imposing temporary measures to restrain certain types of inflow. (Quoted from the IMF report on international capital markets)
>
> The report also emphasised problems arising from the use of cross-border loans between banks, which can be quickly withdrawn. Excessive use of such funding could be prevented by placing requirements on recipient bank liabilities as well as their assets, or by changing capital requirements on lending banks.
>
> The report said that the slowness of bank regulators in many emerging markets meant that the non-traditional measures might be warranted, such as limiting the safety net to a narrow group of banks, increasing international involvement in banking systems and placing limits on foreign borrowing by banks, companies and individuals.

So much for the prescriptions for our current ailments from the IMF. Now, are those prescriptions the intellectual musings of a glorified think-tank, or do they in any way represent the views of the banks' political masters – its controlling shareholders? Well it is difficult to get any take on that, but the current chairman of the G7, Tony Blair, had some comments to make on the issue in New York yesterday. Once again from yesterday's *FT*:

In a speech to the New York Stock Exchange, Mr Blair said the international financial community needed to respond effectively to acute short-term liquidity crises, particularly those caused by loss of market confidence rather than by economic policy failures … Mr Blair said reform was not a matter of a few technical changes and urged other countries to commit themselves to "build a new Bretton Woods for the next millennium".

Now the use of the phrase "Bretton Woods" conjures up all sorts of terrible creatures for global capital. Of course the new structure need have no similarities, but it is only similar in that it is a new financial infrastructure. However, the problem with this new infrastructure is that last week the president of the United States told us that its aim would be to "tame and limit the swings of boom and bust" in the global economy.

Would the IMF's stop-gap measures restricting capital movements be out of place in achieving that immense goal? So it would be scaremongering to say that capital movement restrictions of Bretton Woods proportions are being proposed. However, the wheel is still in spin and if the politicians' aim is to tame the global business cycle then that huge political goal must have serious implications for the owners of capital.

So far we've covered just two stories on page 9 of the international *FT*. But before we leave page 9, some sobering thoughts on the condition of the global banking system:

John Mingo, a senior adviser to the Fed's Board of Governors, said:

> "We should begin yesterday to construct the accord [Basle Accord on bank capital ratios] because today the accord is very much a lose/lose proposition". It was "useless for regulators and costly for banks, because more and more banks were engaging in regulatory capital arbitrage", he said. This involved the use of securitisation and other financial innovations to allow banks to "assume greater risk, while showing no change or even an increase in capital ratios", according to David Jones, an assistant director at the Fed.
>
> Banks achieved this through a variety of methods, including "cherry picking". Since the Basle Accord did not differentiate in its treatments of loans based on risk, banks were tempted to securitise their highest quality credits while leaving lower quality loans on their balance sheet. Banks also used "special purpose vehicles" to originate the assets being securitised. This remote origination also enabled banks to reduce the amount of capital needed for regulatory purposes. By March of this year,

for example, the ten largest bank holding companies had more than US$200bn of such securitisation programmes outstanding or more than a quarter of their total risk weighted assets, according to Mr. Jones.

Financial Times, **22 September 1998**

In simple English that means that capital adequacy ratios are an accountancy myth. Indeed in attempting to subvert the standards and increase gearing, bankers have been deliberately worsening their credit quality as they securitise good credits and hold bad credits. So how alarming are those sums? Well the US$200bn in those "special purpose vehicles" of the top ten US bank holding companies is larger than their core capital of US$170bn!

Remember that the key way of bypassing such Basle Accord rules is via off-balance sheet derivatives. The BIS estimated that at the end of last year there was US$30,000bn in credit market exposure outstanding in interest rate swap agreements. That's 24× the core capital of the developed world banking system, and that's assuming that Japanese banks have all the core capital which they are reporting.

Of course interest rate swaps are only one form of off balance sheet derivative. We had all better hope that the rocket scientists put the right equations into those laptops and that that practice represents a genuine improvement in our understanding of risk rather than just another mystified form of extrapolation. If the gearing in the banking system is really much larger than the BIS data reveals, then the damage to bank capital from any 'accidents', global or local, will be so much worse.

Just one final word from page 9:

Tony Blair, the British Prime Minister, yesterday set a 12-month deadline for reform of the International Monetary Fund and World Bank and called on fellow heads of government to show "the leadership the world so desperately needs".

Great. So if the world can find such unified leadership we may have a solution in 12 months. When was the last time that a politician promised a lasting solution to any problem and hit their initial deadline? In the meantime, we are going to have to deal with those acute short-term liquidity crises which Mr Blair discussed and realise that the actual credit expansion by the global banking system has been truly immense – regardless of what BIS data shows.

Now all we need to do is find that leadership (any suggestions?) and wait at least 12 months. In the meantime, we hope that governments do not get so desperate during that period to pursue the 'stop-gap' measures which the IMF recommends or pursue mistaken unilateral measures. On that note, it is time to leave page 9 and journey to page 7:

> Brazil yesterday stepped up its call for leading industrial countries to put together a convincing plan of action to abate the turmoil in international financial markets, including a cut in US interest rates. "Without a co-ordinated plan, the crisis will not be conquered," said Pedro Malan, Brazil's finance minister, speaking at a conference in Rio De Janeiro.

So without a co-ordinated plan from the World Bank meeting in early January the crisis will not be conquered. Now exactly what is plan B for Brazil? I think we should be told. Of course there are other interest groups who may be seeking relief before the 12-month deadline set by Mr Blair – page 20 of the *FT*:

> "The Japanese, the Koreans and the Russians are dumping [steel] in record tonnages," says John Correnti, chief executive of Nucor, now the second largest US producer. "They can't possibly sell it at these prices and make money" … Faced with such a gloomy outlook, US steel makers are likely to respond in familiar fashion – by reaching for their lawyers. The inexorable machinery of the trade courts seems likely to grind into gear in the coming months with the biggest anti-dumping campaign mounted by Big Steel since 1983.

Big Steel does not seem to be of a mind to wait 12 months and there may be problems in Europe within that 12-month period. While we are all waiting for the establishment of the 'financial architecture of the 21st century' around 12 months from today, hoping that no 'stop-gap' measures are necessary, the IMF has warned us of potential banking problems in Europe. Turn to page 3 of the *FT*:

> In its annual report on international capital markets, the IMF said that in the early years of monetary union, "there might be several tendencies for systemic risks to increase temporarily". It said the lender of last resort had not been assigned to any single institution under monetary union. "Consequently, there is no central provider or co-ordinator of emergency liquidity in the event of a crisis."

So as we wait for the new financial architecture and as European banks have bet well in excess of their core capital on foreign currency loans to the emerging markets, the world's second largest economy – Euroland – is operating without a lender of last resort. So to paraphrase Princess Leia in *Star Wars*, "Help us Alan Greenspan, you're our only hope. Help us Alan Greenspan, you're our only hope. Help us Alan Greenspan, you're our only hope .... "

The point of this regurgitation from a newspaper you will have all read yesterday is to point out that governments could be forced into certain 'stop-gap' measures as they plan the financial architecture for the 21st century. While those measures, which partially restrict capital flows, seem unpalatable today, they will seem a lot less unpalatable to politicians if short-term liquidity problems are not addressed, the leverage in the global banking system begins to unwind and nobody in Europe assumes the role of the lender of last resort.

Already such 'stop-gap' measures are openly recommended by the IMF and the political necessity for such actions is more likely to grow than abate. Now if that's not worth an emergency asset allocation meeting, perhaps the editorial from the world's leading financial newspaper should be. Time to turn to the editorial on page 17 of the *FT*:

> Countries with less sound banking systems and looser macroeconomic policies would be well advised to adopt temporary limits on debt-creating capital-inflows. It would be better for the IMF not to pretend it can bail out countries that do so inadequately.

> Lex on page 18 suggests more specific restrictions on capital movement: A quiet life behind a wall of capital controls is, of course, an option. But the price-access to international capital markets only on penal terms is a heavy one. Penalising only short-term flows through reserve requirements would be a possible halfway house. But what governments really should be watching is not speculative flows but short-term lending.

So even the mouthpiece of capital agrees that short-term capital movement is the 'fall guy' for the forthcoming crisis. For the first time in 20 years the wheel is spinning with a view to perhaps resetting the balance between governments and markets. Analysing politicians is much more difficult than analysing markets. However, we are all going to have to try. It's all there in black and pink.

In September 1998, it was already obvious that regulatory arbitrage was rife in the global banking system, and that the securitisation underway was acting to permit greater leverage and also weaken bank balance sheets. Mr Mingo and Mr Jones had told everyone in 1998 what the consequences would be if nothing was done and nothing was done.

The securitisation business continued to grow and the bank balance sheets continued to weaken. Financial liberalisation continued and the Glass-Steagall Act, which had split retail banking from more risky financial activities, was partially repealed in 1999. Those in the Clinton administration who wished to extend greater regulation to the derivatives markets were defeated by those who believed that markets were quite capable of regulating themselves. The world was to pay a heavy price for ignoring the warnings from Mr Mingo and Mr Jones available in the *FT* many years before the so-called Great Financial Crisis erupted in 2007.

That some major change in the global financial architecture was coming seemed more likely when Tony Blair's comments of late September were followed by similar comments from President Clinton in October. Speaking at the annual meeting of the World Bank and the IMF in Washington DC in October 1998, President Clinton backed Tony Blair's call for reform and spelled out the danger to democracy itself if nothing was done:

Creating a global, financial architecture for the 21st century; promoting national economic reform; making certain that social protections are in place; encouraging democracy and democratic participation in international institutions – these are ambitious goals. But as the links among our nations grow ever tighter we must act together to address problems that will otherwise set back all our aspirations. If we're going to have a truly global marketplace, with global flows of capital, we have no choice but to find ways to build a truly international financial architecture to support it – a system that is open, stable and prosperous.

To meet these challenges I have asked the finance ministers and central bankers of the world's leading economies and the world's most important emerging economies to recommend the next steps. There is no task more urgent for the future of our people. For at stake is more than the spread of free markets, more than the integration of the global economy. The forces behind the global economy are also those that deepen liberty, the free flow of ideas and information, open borders and easy travel, the rule of law, fair and even-handed enforcement, protection for consumers, a skilled and educated work force. Each of these things matters not only to the wealth of nations, but to the health of nations.

If citizens tire of waiting for democracy and free markets to deliver a better life for themselves and their children, there is a risk that democracy and free markets, instead of continuing to thrive together, will shrivel together.

Nothing was done. Greenspan's reduction in interest rates sparked a much more rapid economic improvement than the policy makers at the IMF in their 'the world is coming to an end' mode could have expected. The hard bargaining to "build a new Bretton Woods for the next millennium" never took place. As stability returned, the need to make difficult political decisions could be delayed. What remained was a new global financial architecture based upon exchange rate policy decisions taken in Asia that for two decades produced surpluses that moved jobs from West to East, depressed inflation and interest rates, and directly led to the biggest increase in leverage the world had ever seen.

The Asian crisis had ended in September 1998. The stock markets boomed and then the economies recovered – some of them, like South Korea, in spectacular fashion. I packed my bags and left Hong Kong on 30 September. As part of my departure as a full-time employee of CLSA, I had committed to a three-week round-the-world trip to visit the company's clients and a fourth week in Latin America visiting the company's newly acquired operations there. My last client meeting took place over lunch in the Bahamas in late October. When the meeting was over, I walked onto the beach, removed my socks and shoes, and went for a paddle.

As a postscript to the end of my full-time career on the front line of finance, I spent the final week of October in Mexico, Brazil and Argentina. This was my first visit and I knew almost nothing about the region, but that did not seem to matter. All the focus was on whether their exchange rate management regimes would survive the deflationary storms blowing from the east and I was now supposed to be an expert on such issues. It turned out that my main role was to discuss the durability of the exchange rate policies with the company's customers and the customers of our joint venture partners.

On a Wednesday, having arrived in Sao Paulo in the early morning, I found myself that afternoon boarding a helicopter from the top of a skyscraper. The pilot seemed to enjoy weaving his way between the buildings of the city – I did not. We landed on the roof of a bank towards the edge of the city and walked into a large meeting room. It was dominated by a very large painting of Napoleon on a rearing white steed. I remember thinking at the time that this was a peculiar image to choose as inspiration for bank management seeking to balance risk and reward in its credit book.

I presented on what I thought was the probability of a devaluation of the Brazilian real. Although there was quite a lot of pushback during the meeting, I got the impression that most people in the room were resigned to the fact that the Brazilian real would have to devalue and it did so in January 1999. The reception I received in Argentina was very different indeed.

Argentinians, I was told, did not think much of Brazilians and they explained, in meeting after meeting, that they were made of much sterner stuff. Not only had they learned their lesson from previous currency devaluations, but they had a very special weapon because they too, like Hong Kong, operated a currency board system.

Following these meetings with policy makers and commercial bankers, I prepared for a larger presentation with clients in which I would argue that the Argentinian currency board system would break. This was not what they expected. After all, I had been expounding on the strength of the Hong Kong currency board system through the Asian financial crisis and a series of speculative attacks. I was there, it turned out, to provide reassurance on the strength of this mechanism, not to suggest that it could not work in Argentina. My reasons for suggesting that the currency board would break caused even more outrage.

It was my opinion then, as it is today, that very few democracies could operate a currency board system. That system works by enforcing a particularly vicious business cycle that often includes deflation. Deflation usually includes a decline in wages that is usually a result of high unemployment and can force people to default on their debt and lose their homes and other possessions. Such an adjustment in a democracy produces forces that can endorse the political change that offers to lift the yoke of deflation enforced by a currency board system.

Hong Kong was not and is not a democracy. No such political change was possible in Hong Kong, but in Argentina it was very possible indeed. I also argued that the currency board system creates a vicious credit cycle that few commercial bankers can cope with and can lead to liquidity and solvency issues for commercial banks. The audience in Buenos Aires took these arguments, particularly the argument relating to possible socio-political change, as a great affront to the character of their nation. It didn't help that when asked if a currency board system had ever broken, I replied that it had – in Argentina.

Unlike Brazil, Argentina did not devalue its exchange rate in 1999. The period from 1998 to 2002 is known in Argentina as *The Great Depression* as the inevitable deflationary adjustment took hold, and it culminated in 2002 with the devaluation of the currency. Instead of costing one peso to buy one dollar, as it had when I visited in 1998, by the middle of 2002 it cost 3.6 pesos. By 2020 it cost 136 pesos on the black market to buy one US dollar.

The Hong Kong dollar remains at its 1998 exchange rate. Both countries were running a currency board system in 1998, but both were not equally equipped to cope with the economic, financial, social and political consequences of that system.

In Buenos Aires I came across a shop selling old bank notes. I bought a one million peso note issued in the early 1980s and a five centavo note issued in 1890 when Argentina was one of the richest countries in the world. I flew from Buenos Aires and arrived at our new home in the Scottish countryside just a few days after my 34th birthday and almost exactly three-and-a-half years since I had left the UK for a life in Hong Kong. Things did also change here; but compared to the pace of change, destruction and chaos I had witnessed in Asia, it seemed like no change had happened at all.

To decompress, I decided to double trench dig our new vegetable plot. A week later it was finished, and I felt that I had begun a return to a normal pace of life and in the spring I would be able to sow in well-prepared ground. Meanwhile, in the world of finance, the Asian financial crisis had prepared the ground and the seeds were being sown for the biggest credit boom in world history. That growth and the terrible harvest that followed are the story of *The Age of Debt*.

PART FIVE
The beginning not the end

That the Asian financial crisis was followed soon afterwards by what we have come to know as the Great Financial Crisis is something that we could not have known in 1998. We could not know because world debt levels, as measured relative to the size of economic output, were not at particularly high levels in 1998. The very high levels of debt that were to take the world to the brink of financial disaster had not yet been created.

In the United States, where the best long-run data is available, the country's total non-financial debt-to-GDP ratio had risen from 121% in 1952 to 187% by 1998. In just the ten years from 1998 to 2008, it was to rise to 248% of GDP. Relative to the size of its GDP, the country added almost as much debt in ten years as it had added in the entire post-world war two period.

The rapid addition of this excessive level of debt, in the United States and elsewhere in the developed world, is the key reason why a recession in 2008 almost became a depression in 2009. That debt boom was a direct consequence of choices made by politicians in response to, and in the aftermath of, the Asian financial crisis.

Asia's massive accumulation of foreign currency reserves

The Asian financial crisis built the foundations for the age of debt in myriad ways. Most importantly, it convinced emerging market policy makers, particularly those in Asia, that they needed to hold very high levels of foreign exchange reserves as a buffer to protect them from very volatile short-term capital flows.

This book has analysed the capital exodus from Asia that brought many Asian countries to near bankruptcy and forced them to accept policies, as part of their IMF bailout packages, that were anathema to many local politicians and peoples. The lesson many Asian policy makers took from this humiliation is that they needed ever larger foreign exchange reserves to offset any future capital outflows that might lead them to once again have economic and social policies imposed upon them. It was a message that resonated even in those countries that had seen stable exchange rates and growth through the crisis period and, in particular, in the PRC.

Despite constant concern among the investment community and in policy circles, China was an island of stability in Asia throughout the crisis. However, Chinese policy makers witnessed the collapse of what they too had considered an Asian economic miracle and altered their policies in such a way as to lead to the greatest accumulation of foreign reserves in history. China had already been forced to devalue its exchange rate in 1994, when its foreign exchange reserves had reached a perilously low level of US$21bn.

Reserves had grown strongly since the devaluation and, much to many people's surprise, had continued to rise through the Asian financial crisis; but evidently the buffer to protect China from a collapse that could subject the country to external diktat was considered too low. From the end of 1998 to their peak in June 2014, China's foreign reserves were to grow from US$145bn to US$3,993bn! While that was by far the largest increase in foreign exchange reserve levels in Asia, China was not the only Asian country to pursue a policy of massive foreign exchange reserve accumulation. Table 5.1 shows the growth in other Asian countries' reserves from 1998 to 2019.

Table 5.1: Growth in Asian reserves ex China

	US$bn 1998	US$bn 2019
Japan	203	1,256
Hong Kong	89	441
India	27	427
South Korea	52	398
Taiwan	64	345
Singapore	75	278
Thailand	28	215
Indonesia	22	122
Malaysia	25	99
Philippines	9	78
Vietnam	2	78
Bangladesh	2	31
Cambodia	1	19
Pakistan	1	13
Sri Lanka	2	7

The growth in the foreign reserves of Asia ex China from the end of the Asian financial crisis to the end of 2019 has been US$3,205bn. While Japan has led that rise in reserves, the emerging markets of Asia have also seen immense rises in their foreign exchange reserves. While some of this accumulation is the result of capital gains and income on the initial investment, the vast bulk of it relates to the exchange rate intervention that has been the cornerstone of Asian economic policy after the Asian financial crisis. It was those policy choices, made unilaterally and without the agreement of any of those countries' trading and business partners, that fuelled the age of debt.

This accumulation of foreign assets was focused on the purchase of US Treasury securities and had the impact of structurally depressing yields on what is still considered the global risk-free rate. The forced purchasing of US government debt by Asian central banks funding their purchases by expanding their balance sheets freed up savers to fund other ventures. Those ventures were funded with equity, but increasingly with the particularly cheap debt that resulted from the depression of the risk-free rate caused by Asian central banks' excessive reserve accumulation.

That no 'new Bretton Woods' was created by agreement after the crisis allowed the creation of an ad hoc system that was to fuel the rise in debt and the social and political dislocation that has, for at least the past decade, threatened the developed world with economic, financial and social collapse. The avoidance of what would have been incredibly difficult negotiations to establish an agreed 'new financial architecture' has left a dreadful legacy.

Reflating and recapitalising Asian economies

The political choices made in Asia were easy choices with powerful positive economic consequences – initially on a global basis. Building large foreign reserves after the crisis was easy, as all it involved was simple foreign exchange intervention to prevent the appreciation of the Asian exchange rates from the incredibly cheap levels that most had reached during the crisis. The act of intervention to prevent appreciation not only led to the accumulation of foreign reserves, but created domestic liquidity as the foreign currency was purchased with money created by the Asian central banks in exchange for the foreign currency.

This was a quick route to reflate and recapitalise the Asian economies, but it persisted well beyond the period when such reflation and recapitalisation were necessary to rebuild after the crisis. Those who pursued such policies gained greater competitiveness and, through the creation of more domestic liquidity, also achieved higher domestic-led growth.

When positive net capital inflows returned to Asia, this added to the consequent rise in foreign exchange reserves as further intervention was necessary to prevent exchange rate appreciation. For Asian policy makers this was a simple policy to pursue and it brought rapid economic recovery and a prolonged period of growth. The only risk was that their trading partners would object to such manipulation of exchange rates that provided such a subsidy to their exporters at the cost of their foreign competition.

For the leaders of the developed world, terrified in 1998 that a new great depression was on its way, this seemingly cheap and largely surreptitious path to recapitalisation and higher growth in Asia was not unwelcome. It was a quick way to fill what had looked like Asia's huge capital black hole and avoid the need for further loans from the IMF and developed world governments. That it was also producing ever-cheaper imports to boost consumption, while depressing inflation in the developed world, was also welcome.

The non-system

That what was often mistakenly referred to as the 'savings glut' from Asia forced developed world interest rates lower, making credit cheaper and more available, also did not hinder the electoral chances of politicians. This was no 'savings glut', but the clear consequence of massive exchange rate manipulation. That those artificially undervalued Asian exchange rates were stripping some forms of blue-collar jobs from the developed world was something largely ignored as booming economies saw new, though usually less rewarding, jobs created.

In what rapidly became benign economic conditions post-1998, there was simply not enough political capital to be expended by developed world politicians to stop the formation of this new financial architecture by the individual political choices of Asian countries. The system that has prevailed since then – referred to by Paul Volcker in his book, *Keeping At It*, as the *non-system* – is still a system even if it was one that was never agreed among all the parties in the way that the Bretton Woods *system* was agreed.

The lack of a founding agreement for the new financial architecture established in the wake of the Asian financial crisis does not mean that it was not a monetary system; it is just that it was not an agreed system. That this *non-system* system prevailed indicated that it delivered outcomes that benefited most parties, regardless of their lack of agreement to its foundation.

However, it was a system all but guaranteed to funnel the benefits to the developed world, mainly through the availability of cheap debt, to those engaged in asset price speculation. That it could fuel this debt-driven dangerously unstable and inequitable form of growth was evident to all. That developed world policy makers took no action to stop it, by negotiating for the establishment of a new financial architecture not prone to creating such instability and dangerous financial engineering, says much about the incentives and time frames of those who determine policy.

Indeed, not only did that move to create a more stable financial architecture not occur, but through China's entry to the WTO in December 2001, Volcker's so-called *non-system* became dramatically more unstable. The rise in foreign reserve accumulation accelerated further, driven by ever larger Chinese current account surpluses, and the pace of the growth of debt in the developed world leapt even higher.

The explosion in debt levels across the world

Just how this rapid rise in world foreign reserves fuelled a debt boom in the developed world is hardly a secret. A country engaged in the accumulation of foreign exchange reserves is in the business of buying the government debt of other countries. The mandate for the central banks that mainly conduct such intervention limits them to holding safe and very liquid assets as part of their reserves. As government debt is one of the few assets deemed to meet both criteria, the consequence is that the decision to intervene to prevent an appreciation of the exchange rate leads the intervening authorities to buy the government debt of other countries. Most countries focus their foreign reserve accumulation on the US dollar.

While the role of the US economy within the global economy has been shrinking steadily for many decades, the role of the US dollar in the international payments and financial system remains dominant. If your reserves are to act as a buffer to allow you to pay for the things you need to import or to allow you to meet foreign financed liabilities, then you will need to hold primarily US dollars in your reserves.

As of 2020, about 62% of such reserves are held in the form of US dollars and this percentage has not altered materially in the past few decades. Thus any government that has seen the rise in foreign exchange reserves over the past few decades has seen a rise in their holdings of US dollars and also in the debt of the US government – Treasury securities.

With foreign central bankers providing such a large proportion of the funding for the US government and other developed world governments, the savers of the world were free to fund more debt for the private sector. With the flood of forced central bank buying the yields on government debt, yields were kept lower than they would otherwise have been in relation to domestic growth and inflation.

The flow of cheap goods to the developed world from Asia – a product of their artificially depressed exchange rates – also depressed inflation, adding to the downward pressure on interest rates. The social capital system of north Asia continued to target full capacity and full employment above profits also acting to cap global inflation.

Developed world interest rates trended lower, reacting to the decline in global inflation. In the developed world, there were fortunes to be made by availing oneself of the ever cheaper debt to finance purchases of assets, whether property, equities or bonds, that rose ever higher fuelled by the combination of low interest rates and high economic growth. Those who benefited from these impacts of the *non-system* owned the assets that rose as a result of this process and those that utilised debt to buy those assets became very rich indeed.

While the asset owners, the leveraged players and their agents benefited from the boom, those whose jobs were negatively impacted by competition from Asia saw their standard of living decline. The rise and rise of foreign exchange reserves thus did much to exacerbate the inequality of both income and wealth in the developed world, while increasing the fragility of the economic system through the addition of ever higher levels of debt.

From the end of 1998 when the Asian financial crisis ended, the level of world foreign exchange reserves increased by US$7.5trn to peak in the middle of 2014. Over that period, total credit to the US non-financial sector rose by US$25.3trn. The data for the rest of the world is only available from December 2001, but from that date until world foreign reserves peaked in June 2014, non-financial debt rose from US$38.7trn to US$119.2trn.

Thus the direct contribution to debt availability from the purchase of government debt for reserve accumulation was large, but still a small part of the explosion in world debt levels. Whatever the direct impact of government debt purchasing by Asian central banks, the indirect impacts were of a much greater magnitude. These indirect impacts were largely the result of how developed world central bankers sought to adjust monetary policy as a consequence of the *non-system* that brought a long-forgotten problem back onto their agenda – deflation.

The fear of deflation

The fear of deflation among central bankers is a direct legacy from a great mistake they made around 90 years ago. As the economic crisis that began in 1929 got worse, the central bankers did nothing to offset the destruction of money that resulted from the distress in their commercial banking systems. The initial economic contraction created a contraction in commercial bank lending which, due to the nature of the fractional reserve banking system, destroyed money.

Even worse, many banks were forced to close and with bank deposit guarantee schemes not then in operation, even more money was destroyed. That the major contraction in the amount of money in the economy turned a recession into a depression is not widely contested.

The scale of the error was a particular feature of an influential study of US monetary history by Milton Friedman and Anna Schwartz called *A Monetary History of the United States 1867–1960*. The extent to which the monetary policy mistake of that period is seared into the memory of central bankers is best illustrated by a speech made by Ben Bernanke, then a governor of the US Federal Reserve Bank, on the occasion of Milton Friedman's 90th birthday:

> Let me end my talk by abusing slightly my status as an official representative of the Federal Reserve. I would like to say to Milton and Anna: Regarding the Great Depression. You're right, we did it. We're very sorry. But thanks to you, we won't do it again.

The mental scarring among central bankers runs deep and it manifests itself as a fear of deflation from whatever source it comes. From the Asian financial crisis onwards, the world's central banks, led by the US Federal Reserve, fought a battle to prevent deflation. That much of that deflation came from cheap exports from Asia is evident from the links between US import price inflation and the headline US inflation rate.

It is debatable as to whether that form of imported deflation really threatened to ever create a recession and depression, but central bankers were not prepared to accept the risk of finding out. Thus they kept interest rates at remarkably low levels to ward off deflation even in periods when economic expansion was robust. A key indirect impact from the undervaluation of Asian exchange rates was thus to force developed world central bankers to hold interest rates far too low to ward off the deflation that populated their nightmares.

Ben Bernanke, also speaking in 2002, explained just how important it was for a central bank to generate inflation to protect the economy from the impact of any deflationary shock:

> The basic prescription for preventing deflation is therefore straightforward, at least in principle: Use monetary and fiscal policy as needed to support aggregate spending, in a manner as nearly consistent as possible with full utilization of economic resources and low and stable inflation. In other words, the best way to get out of trouble is not to get into it in the first place. Beyond this common-sense injunction, however, there are several measures that the Fed (or any central bank) can take to reduce the risk of falling into deflation.
>
> First, the Fed should try to preserve a buffer zone for the inflation rate, that is, during normal times it should not try to push inflation down all the way to zero. Most central banks seem to understand the need for a buffer zone. For example, central banks with explicit inflation targets almost invariably set their target for inflation above zero, generally between 1 and 3 percent per year. Maintaining an

inflation buffer zone reduces the risk that a large, unanticipated drop in aggregate demand will drive the economy far enough into deflationary territory to lower the nominal interest rate to zero.

Remarks by Governor Ben S Bernanke before the National Economists Club, Washington DC, 'Deflation: Making Sure "It" Doesn't Happen Here', 21 November 2002

The more imported deflation pushed domestic inflation below the 'buffer zone', the more accommodative developed world monetary policy had to be to generate the domestic inflation to offset that imported deflation. US import prices, excluding petroleum, did not exceed their level of end 1995 until August 2007. By 2020 US import prices were just 4% higher than they were at the end of 1995.

Ever more debt

The creation of ever more money, created by central banks in exchange for their foreign currency assets, did produce more economic growth and consumption in Asia, but it also produced higher supply. In China, the state-owned banking system was particularly adept at funding ever greater capacity, rather than the ever greater consumption that had characterised the growth in developed world bank credit for the last 30 years. The state-directed flow of capital played a key role in adding ever more capacity, dampening Chinese inflation and thus the price of Chinese exports.

While cheap imports from Asia were not the only force acting to depress inflation in the developed world, technological breakthroughs also played an important role. They were a key factor that forced developed world central bankers to run particularly low interest rates in an attempt to maintain the inflation buffer. Trying to create inflation in the face of such deflationary forces proved ultimately fruitless and deflation erupted in 2009 and also in 2015 in the United States and in some countries in 2020.

With each deflationary bust, market-determined interest rates fell further and the central bankers reacted with ever more aggressive monetary policy settings. For some the ever easier monetary policy, combined with the belief that governments and central bankers would always act to bail out financial markets, encouraged the addition of ever more debt.

Using debt for the purchase of assets is a dangerous business as declines in asset prices can result in negative equity. That so many people were prepared to take that risk was also a consequence of the Asian financial crisis. The crisis in Asia triggered a wave of volatility in asset prices that forced a large financial institution in the United States to appeal to the US Federal Reserve for help.

In September 1998 such help was forthcoming as the US central bank orchestrated a bailout of LTCM through a consortium of commercial banks. At the same time, the US Federal Reserve was cutting interest rates with the aim of warding off the dangerous impact of falling asset prices for those who had borrowed to buy them. That the monetary policy of the central bank that ran the world's reserve currency could change to ward off the damage from such financial speculation changed everything.

Where once the motto of central bankers was to take the punchbowl away just as the party got going, it was now to provide plenty more punch as a palliative for the hangover. Those borrowing to purchase assets saw a shift in the risk/reward ratio that favoured using even more gearing. That perceived reduction in risk came as the *non-system* forced interest rates to stay low, credit availability to remain high and asset prices to rise. There could be no more favourable conditions to promote financial engineering and to establish the age of debt.

That the new financial architecture created from the fires of the Asian financial crisis led to the age of debt is clear if we look at the counterfactual. What would have happened had Asia, including China, moved to flexible exchange rate regimes following the crisis? In that situation, their exchange rates would have risen rapidly and then stabilised to create a balance of payments that balanced without any rise or decline in Asia's foreign exchange reserves.

Had they not intervened in the foreign currency markets, they would not have locked in their competitiveness and not have run permanently large current account surpluses. In a rising exchange rate regime, they would not have been able to keep export prices down, exporting deflation and forcing developed world central bankers to keep interest rates low.

They would not have been large buyers of developed world debt, acting to depress interest rates and free up private savings to fund ever more private sector borrowing. Developed world central bankers would have been more in control of their own monetary policy and also less frightened by the ghost of deflation emanating from Asia.

The higher interest rates necessary to control inflation through mitigating growth would have created a double negative for the net present value of cash flows and thus asset prices. Leverage would have been more expensive and less available, and its use more dangerous given the lack of levitation of asset prices. With less leverage in the system, there would have been a prospect that the failure of large financial institutions could have been permitted without fear of systemic risk.

It would have been a world where credit was more expensive and more dangerous to deploy. No doubt, debt levels would have risen and perhaps then fallen, but we would not have seen the structural rise in the world's non-financial debt-to-GDP ratio from 191% at the end of 2001 to 243% by the end of 2019.

One person's liability is another person's asset

Monetary history at its highest level is a history of how countries have struggled to establish financial architectures that they thought would benefit their own nations. Until the 18th century, it was thought that the pursuit of policies to maximise external surpluses was the best route to national prosperity – a policy called mercantilism. By the 18th century, through the work of David Hume, Adam Smith and others, it was recognised that such a financial architecture was not conducive to a greater wealth of nations. Thereafter there was growing agreement that greater co-operation among states to establish stable exchange rates and to open their economies to free trade was a benefit to all.

Progress was not in a straight line and not overnight, but gradually fewer states pursued mercantilist policies. The key legacy of the Asian financial crisis is that Asian nations did consider that the wealth of their nations could only be secured by the mercantilist policy perhaps still best summed up by the title of Thomas Mun's 1664 mercantilist classic, *Treasure by Foreign Trade*. It is a treasure supposed to defend Asian nations from a crisis and the external imposition of a form of capitalism local policymakers regard as inimical to their own values. It has been a pursuit of treasure that has created a deeply unstable global financial architecture prone to collapse, and has led to wealth inequality and deep political divides.

The current *non-system* would never have happened by the design and agreement of those who now suffer from it. Those who gathered at the Mount Washington Hotel at Bretton Woods, New Hampshire in the summer of 1944 – schooled in the work of David Hume and Adam Smith, and still burnt from the protectionism of the 1930s – built a system designed to redistribute foreign reserves within the new financial architecture. The reserves amassed by one state triggered as their counterparty growth in domestic commercial bank reserves.

Growth in such reserves usually triggered faster bank credit growth, faster money supply growth, faster economic growth, inflation and a deterioration in the external accounts. That deterioration in the external accounts in the managed exchange rate regime acted to reduce foreign reserves and tighten domestic monetary policy, and thus the credit and business cycle continued. The circulation of foreign reserves within the system was the basis for stability.

No member of such a system could ever permanently amass Mun's foreign treasure and it flowed between the members of the system as the key driver of their credit cycles. The mechanism through which it was redistributed was one of credit cycles, but one where the outflow of reserves, when economic booms were great and external deficits large, limited just how great credit booms could become.

The Bretton Woods system also restricted the free movement of capital to ensure that the economic adjustments associated with the shift in those reserves was at a pace that the financial system and society could likely adjust to. With reserves circulating within such a system and acting to regulate the scope and duration of the credit cycle, there was no prospect that reserves could rise to the astronomical levels we have seen post the Asian financial crisis.

The creation of a sealed system where reserves were redistributed would have put some form of break on credit cycles, but there was no such break in our *non-system*. As we have seen, the accumulation of reserves of this magnitude, due to the operation of the *non-system*, has fuelled the biggest debt boom in history. The only way it stops, and it has been perilously close to stopping in recent years, is when debt is so high that it simply cannot be serviced.

That we are now near that point is clear and it leaves policy makers with stark choices as to the nature of the default now inevitable on the excessive debt burden. The most likely weapon of choice to reduce the debt burdens created by the *non-system* will be the creation of inflation to destroy the real value of debt. As one person's liability is another person's asset, this is a destruction that will fall heavily upon the savers that are the owners of such obligations.

The Asian financial crisis created a scramble for foreign reserves in the region that was permitted because it was much easier to permit it than oppose it. That it brought near-term benefits to both Asia and the developed world helped politicians to accept that it was an acceptable policy. However, the consequences of those easy political decisions, made in the aftermath of the crisis, have created the unstable *non-system* that will continue to deliver the economic, financial, social and political instability that has already plagued the 21st century.

The age of debt was birthed in the crisis described in this book. How it developed, how it will end and what you can do about it will be the subject of the next book.

INDEX

www.ingramcontent.com/pod-product-compliance
Ingram Content Group UK Ltd.
Pitfield, Milton Keynes, MK11 3LW, UK
UKHW021926080125
453225UK00004B/234